Just Universities

CATHOLIC PRACTICE IN NORTH AMERICA

Just Universities

CATHOLIC SOCIAL TEACHING CONFRONTS CORPORATIZED HIGHER EDUCATION

Gerald J. Beyer

FORDHAM UNIVERSITY PRESS
New York 2021

Fordham University Press has no responsibility for the persistence
or accuracy of URLs for external or third-party Internet websites
referred to in this publication and does not guarantee that any
content on such websites is, or will remain, accurate or appropriate.

Fordham University Press also publishes its books in a variety of
electronic formats. Some content that appears in print may not be
available in electronic books.

Visit us online at www.fordhampress.com.

Library of Congress Cataloging-in-Publication Data available online
at https://catalog.loc.gov.

Printed in the United States of America

23 22 21   5 4 3 2 1

First edition

To my former teachers, especially Otto Hentz, SJ and David Hollenbach, SJ:
You are the reason that I became a Christian educator,

and to my parents:
You enabled me to pursue my dream

Contents

Preface

I finished writing this book a few months before two events of seismic proportions occurred. These events will dramatically shape the landscape of higher education in the near future and perhaps beyond. In some respects, they may challenge the arguments in this book. In many ways, however, they create a new urgency to the issues treated in *Just Universities*.

In the early spring of 2020, the COVID-19 pandemic forced colleges and universities across the United States and around the world to close their campuses and to rapidly implement online learning. Online learning has been expanding for almost two decades, with some proponents identifying it as a way to reduce the exorbitant cost of higher education. Detractors have decried it as a shell of what higher education should be. Because of the pandemic, hordes of professors and students were simultaneously thrust into virtual teaching and learning, with many of them having no experience with it. Some have heralded this shift as a harbinger of the future: higher education completely (or almost completely) taking place online as a way of making it more widely accessible. On the other hand, preliminary data shows that a majority of students were not satisfied with "attending" classes while in their bedroom, basement, or in a parking lot if they did not have access to high-speed internet at home.

The financial costs to higher education thus far during the pandemic have been massive. Some experts contend that as many as two hundred colleges and universities in the United States risk closure in the near future. While not all observers agree with such dire predictions, one thing is clear: The vast majority of institutions of higher learning are facing unexpected and in many cases major financial challenges as a result of the COVID-19 pandemic. At the same time, students and parents are questioning more forcefully whether the historically high tuition rates and fees are justified, especially if learning is happening remotely. Professors are wondering (in the pages of *Inside Higher Ed* and *The Chronicle of Higher*

Education, for example) about whether university decision makers are being fully transparent when they enact faculty and staff layoffs, salary and benefit reductions, and other cost-cutting measures. The current crisis is fomenting even more faculty mistrust of administrators, who they contend (whether rightly or wrongly) will use the situation to further accelerate the corporatization of higher education. Who decides what sacrifices need to be undertaken and according to what criteria? Are institutions doing their best to protect the most vulnerable students, contingent faculty, and staff from financial ruin? Can increased endowment spending soften the blows, or do intractable market forces prevent paying out a few more percentage points in the coming year? Moreover, if campuses reopen in the midst of an ongoing pandemic, is it safe to learn together in crowded classrooms, dine in large cafeterias, and reside in dormitories that some epidemiologists liken to cruise ships in terms of viral transmissibility? These are just some of the complicated questions that the COVID-19 pandemic has generated among faculty, students, staff, and administrators. The situation has exacerbated longstanding problems in higher education, while also creating new ones.[1]

Roughly three months into the COVID-19 outbreak in the United States, the murder of George Floyd, a forty-six-year-old Black man, by a Minneapolis police officer sparked massive protests across the country. The problem of police brutality and the killing of Black men and women, as well as Native American and Latina/o people, has plagued this country throughout its history. But the particular brutality of Mr. Floyd's murder, which followed shortly after the horrific slayings of Ahmaud Arbery and Breonna Taylor, broke the dam of anger, frustration, and anguish in a way that the United States has never seen. The intensity and scope of the protests are historically unparalleled.[2] While some White supremacists remain intransigent, the vast majority of Americans finally are committing to saying "Black Lives Matter." Catholic colleges and universities must move beyond platitudes and vacuous statements regarding diversity and commit to radical, systemic change. As I discuss in this book, the history of Catholic higher education on this score is mixed, with some tangible, laudable improvements and persistent shortcomings. If Catholic colleges and universities fail to undergo wide-ranging transformations to promote diversity, racial equity, and inclusion on their campuses, they now risk falling out of step with the overwhelming majority of young people in the United

States, for whom these are crucial issues. The time for lethargy in the face of White supremacy—whether in making curricular decisions, in hiring and admissions policies, or in other areas of campus life—is palpably over.

The turmoil of the present moment, marked by the twin pandemics of COVID-19 and systemic racism, may hamper achieving in the foreseeable future some of the loftiest goals and aspirations that I argue for in these pages, especially at institutions facing bona fide financial crises. On the other hand, I believe the issues that I raise about Catholic higher education's inadequacies and its achievements, and the moral framework that I develop for evaluating them, will become even more relevant. The road ahead will be difficult. Vexing choices and compromises will need to be made at times. Nonetheless, Catholic institutions of higher learning cannot abandon the principles, values, and virtues of the Catholic social tradition if they wish to remain faithful to their mission. In these turbulent times, even more vigilance and determination are demanded now than was true prior to this book's completion. The temptation to jettison Catholic social teaching in favor of corporatized higher education will be even greater. The argument in this book holds that this would constitute a betrayal of the mission of Catholic higher education, and that the richness of the Catholic social tradition points to practical ways forward.

Just Universities

Introduction

I do not relish writing this book. Undertaking it is risky for several reasons. First, I run the risk of appearing to be an ingrate who "bites the hand that feeds him." I have benefited tremendously from Catholic educational institutions. In eighth grade I was awarded a scholarship to a prestigious Jesuit prep school. A kid from a working-class background scoring so highly on the entrance exam attests to the dedication of the teachers at my Catholic grade school. I recall with gratitude how Sr. Joanne spent countless hours after school tutoring a small group of us in preparation for such exams.

God's providential hand had much more in store for me. On a particularly memorable summer day, my parents received a phone call from Fr. Royden B. Davis, SJ, dean of the College of Arts and Sciences at Georgetown University. Fr. Davis announced that I had been awarded a need-based, full-tuition scholarship endowed by the McShain family.[1] This news came on the heels of a somewhat unlikely acceptance to the university, which occurred in part thanks to the support of the rowing coach who recruited me. The script could not have been written any better: A first-generation college student was accepted to one of the nation's finest universities, and he did not have to take on massive student debt to matriculate.

Years later I was awarded a generous fellowship to undertake doctoral studies in theological ethics at another excellent Catholic university, Boston College. I was blessed to have the opportunity to study there with world-class scholars and students from across the globe. Uncannily, my luck did not run out there. While completing my dissertation, I successfully landed a tenure-track job at Saint Joseph's University, the Jesuit university in my hometown. Like most native Philadelphians, I feel ineluctably drawn to my hometown—in spite of its warts. Therefore, I was elated when Villanova University gave me my second tenure-track job after ten years at Saint Joseph's.

With this kind of windfall, which we Catholics often call grace or divine providence, I will always remain indebted to Catholic educational institutions and to the many extraordinary teachers, staff, and administrators who run them. Several of my university professors patiently mentored me as I went through significant growing pains. Writing this book, which often takes a critical stance, arises out of a debt of gratitude to them and to my passion for Catholic higher education. Like James L. Marsh, who spent three decades teaching at Catholic universities, "I love these institutions as much or more for what they can be as for what they are."[2] Marsh contends that Jesuit, Catholic universities have largely failed to adopt a radical critique of the American neoliberal empire. For my part, I shall argue that US Catholic colleges and universities have not escaped neoliberalism's deleterious effects on higher education more generally.[3] Neoliberalism transforms the market into the "means, the method, and the end of all rational and intelligent behavior," as the Jesuit provincials of Latin America maintained some years ago.[4] The corporatization of higher education, one of neoliberalism's nefarious consequences, has created significant obstacles to Catholic institutions fulfilling their mission, as I shall discuss.

To be clear, I acknowledge and appreciate that Catholic colleges and universities in the United States serve students and society in laudable ways. They have grown from substandard schools in their early years to become fine institutions of higher learning that serve the common good, overcoming myriad impediments along the way.[5] However, I argue in this book that many of these institutions have failed to embody the values of the Gospel and the principles of Catholic social teaching (CST) in some important institutional policies and practices. As a result, they have perpetuated injustices on their campuses. Moreover, the stakeholders on these campuses bear responsibility for the choices that created these injustices. They have to decide whether they want to attempt to remedy those injustices, even if the economic, legal, and political context of US higher education places some constraints on them. While difficult circumstances can hinder our freedom to choose, Victor Frankl's words nonetheless ring true: "Everything can be taken away from a man [sic] but one thing: the last of all human freedoms—to choose one's own attitude in any circumstances, to choose one's own way."[6] What the Catholic tradition calls "internal" and "personalist" freedom can never be usurped or abdicated.[7]

Contrary to a common misperception, Catholic colleges and universities are neither owned by the Catholic Church nor under the control of the Vatican, the United States Conference of Catholic Bishops, or their founding religious orders. Since the separate incorporation of most institutions in the 1960s, Catholic colleges and universities have been run by mostly lay boards of trustees and have achieved institutional autonomy.[8] The church therefore can neither force Catholic colleges and universities to teach the Catholic social tradition nor mandate that their daily operations be guided by it.[9] Over the last fifty years there has been much disagreement about what makes a college or university Catholic. Because these institutions are largely self-governing, boards of trustees, administrators, faculty, and staff decide how to express their Catholic identity and which teachings, if any, will be embodied in their institutional policies and practices.[10]

The eminent historian of Catholic higher education Alice Gallin OSU has written that the "'culture' of Catholicism has undoubtedly been weakened or, in some cases, lost" on Catholic campuses.[11] Philip Gleason has described an "identity crisis" in Catholic higher education.[12] David O'Brien has lamented the "'chronic contentiousness' that so often surrounds the 'Catholic university.'"[13] Attempting to remain faithful to the Catholic tradition has not been easy while seeking to achieve academic "excellence" understood in secular terms, navigating the complex legal landscape required for state funding, demonstrating commitment to "American values" such as freedom, and being beholden to various ranking systems.[14] The confusion surrounding Catholic mission and identity in higher education, chronicled by scholars such as Gallin, Gleason, and O'Brien, concerns this book insofar as this confusion has enabled injustices to occur unchecked on our campuses. Put another way, this book is a constructive work in Christian social ethics, not a historian's account. I write as a Catholic ethicist and a participant engaged in the subject matter, hoping to make a contribution toward a better future for Catholic higher education.

As a White male who has overcome class barriers by obtaining the right educational pedigree, I have benefited from many of the inequities that pervade the academy in the United States. No one has ever asked me, for example, if I plan on getting pregnant before applying for tenure. Nor has anyone ever likely pondered whether I obtained my job or attained tenure because of my race. I have also not been burdened with endless requests to serve on committees because I represent an underrepresented group on campus. As a member of the shrinking tenured professoriate, I enjoy what can be called "tenure-track privilege." I am blessed with a salary, benefits, and professional development opportunities that a growing majority of part-time faculty at colleges and universities deserves but will likely never attain, through no fault of their own.[15]

I am aware that it is perilous in the academy to speak from one's experience, as I have chosen to do in this book. Many academics have a strong bias against incorporating personal reflection since it allegedly undermines "serious" intellectual work.[16] Nonetheless, I hope to demonstrate throughout this book that personal experience and other ways of knowing mutually enhance each other to produce the best kind of scholarship.[17] I also undertake this project with the knowledge that it may not be well received among some of my peers in the world of Catholic higher education. Let me state the issue frankly: While I herald many "promising practices" of Catholic universities as examples for others to emulate, this book encourages those of us who inhabit this milieu to confront a number of uncomfortable truths. Just as a penitent reluctantly confronts his or her failings during an examination of conscience—as I know personally—institutions and their stakeholders often gaze at their shortcomings begrudgingly.

However, the "structures of sin" (an important concept of Catholic moral theology) of many Catholic colleges and universities are undeniable: educating a vastly disproportionate number of affluent students, thereby calcifying class barriers; maintaining a "country club" atmosphere rather than one of an institution that challenges the status quo; unjust compensation structures that provide some with exorbitant salaries and others with poverty level wages; precluding women and other minoritized persons from being full stakeholders in the university; pumping millions of dollars into athletics while slashing academic budgets; investing funds in unethical corporations and accepting donations from them to build endowments, etc.[18]

This book will demonstrate that some Catholic institutions have addressed these issues in a way that coheres with CST more effectively than others. Indeed, there are success stories to tell. Nonetheless, much work needs to be done, and the Gospel and Catholic social teaching demand it. In pointing out the failures of Catholic universities, I do not intend to demonize anyone or to moralize. I recognize that many, if not most trustees, administrators, and department chairs are good people struggling to succeed in the tightly competitive market of higher education during challenging fiscal times. These colleagues diligently attempt to balance the books while preserving the Catholic mission and identity of their institutions. Nonetheless, I firmly believe that we at Catholic institutions must collectively undertake an examination of conscience. I believe that we can do better, even if it will not be easy.

This book will arouse the emotions and perhaps the ire of some readers, as it confronts the unjust racial, gender, and class-based structures that stifle the full flourishing of many colleagues and students. Discussing racism, White privilege, classism, homophobia, and economic injustices within our hallowed halls, not just "out there" in American society and the world more broadly, remains largely unwelcomed.[19] I have already been falsely dubbed a "union surrogate" by one Catholic university administrator. Some tenured colleagues have expressed distaste for the work I am doing. Others have warned me about backlash that could jeopardize future career advances in the academy. Nonetheless, for reasons that will become apparent, I feel called to write this book at this time. I simply cannot brush it aside any longer. I also contend that those who care about Catholic higher education should confront the subject matter of this book. In my judgment, these issues will continue to be largely ignored unless Catholic scholars devote more serious attention to them, both in their academic work and in their daily lives on their campuses. I argue that all stakeholders at Catholic institutions (students, faculty, staff, administrators, and board members) must promote what the Nigerian Jesuit theologian Agbonkhianmeghe E. Orobator calls "domestic justice," or justice "at home." Orobator exhorts the church to practice "domestic justice" within its own structures in order to be a credible proponent of integral human development.[20] As educators, students, staff, and administrators at Catholic institutions, we must heed the call of the 1971 World Synod Bishops in *Justitia in Mundo*: "Anyone who ventures to speak to people about justice must first be just in their eyes."[21] While defenders of the status quo in Catholic higher education resist change, others are already confronting the problems raised in this project. I hope this book aids them in their efforts to build solidarity and to promote the common good in higher education.

My own background and intellectual and spiritual journey inclines me to write this book. Having been blessed with so many opportunities at Catholic universities, I have a good deal of insider's knowledge of them. As an undergraduate student and recruited varsity athlete, I caught a glimpse of the best and the worst that Catholic universities offer. My position as a faculty member for fifteen years at two Catholic universities has entailed committee work, advocacy, and dialogue dealing with justice issues on my own campuses, as well as gaining insight from colleagues in a number of other settings. For example, I served for three years on the Committee for Socially Responsible Investment of the Maryland Province of the Society of Jesus. I am an Executive Committee member of Catholic Scholars Worker Justice, which has urged the trustees and administrators of Catholic universities to support the right to unionize, just wages, health benefits, and job security.[22] I also served on the Advisory Committee of the Just Employment Project, which is spearheaded by the Kalmanovitz Initiative for Labor and the Working Poor at Georgetown University.[23] I sit on Villanova University's Committee on Socially Responsible Proxy Voting and serve as vice president of our AAUP (American Association of University Professors) chapter. I am also the chair of the Pennsylvania AAUP Catholic Colleges Caucus. I have spoken on numerous Catholic campuses about the subject matter of this book. Many of my interlocutors on these visits have helped to shape my thinking.

In short, these myriad experiences have afforded me the opportunity to listen to and learn from administrators who devise the policies; from faculty and staff who implement the policies; from adjuncts who cannot pay for necessary medical treatment despite working at multiple institutions; from students who rack up massive debt because they can't afford to attend college otherwise; and from custodial or food service employees who feel unappreciated, and sometimes abused, by the university. I have also heard the pain of students, faculty, and staff who face challenges because of their race, gender, or sexual orientation. These encounters give rise to a duty to collaborate with others to ensure that Catholic colleges and universities remain faithful to their institutional mission, which I argue must include creating policies and structures imbued with the ideals of Catholic social teaching.

My vocation as a Christian ethicist also requires me to undertake this project. I cannot in good conscience teach at a Catholic institution without attempting to promote greater fidelity to the Catholic tradition's social teaching. My own credibility as a Christian educator and scholar is at stake. My courses seek to equip students with analytic tools to reflect on how Christians can and should live out their faith in society by striving for justice and the common good. I therefore feel compelled to demonstrate how rigorous intellectual inquiry can promote this end in our own university communities. Pursuing this project helps me to harmonize my scholarship with my desire to live as a disciple of Jesus Christ. Having written about solidarity for more than fifteen years, I want to build solidarity with others in the struggle for justice and human rights for all at Catholic institutions of higher learning.

The initial chapter problematizes the contemporary context in which Catholic colleges and universities operate in the United States—namely, that of corporatized higher education. I argue that the corporatization of the university has infected higher education with hyperindividualistic practices and models imported from the business world. This phenomenon hinders the ability of Catholic institutions to fulfil their mission, which includes creating an environment imbued with values and principles of CST such as respect for human rights, solidarity, and justice. At the same time, my book demonstrates how Catholic social teaching can provide a bulwark against the further erosion of important aspects of the mission of Catholic universities. In other words, my book illustrates how Catholic social teaching can undergird a just model of higher education in the age of the neoliberal, corporatized university. The final section of this chapter introduces the reader to the values and principles of CST, which should inform the policies and practices of Catholic institutions and counteract the values of corporatized education.

Successive chapters analyze worker justice on Catholic campuses; the degree to which Catholic universities open their doors to economically disadvantaged students; socially responsible investment of university resources and environmental stewardship; racial inclusion and justice; and justice issues related to gender and sexual orientation on campuses. Each chapter will contain a theoretical exposition of Catholic social teaching on the pertinent issues. These chapters will also apply the teaching by evaluating practices and policies at Catholic institutions of higher learning in the light of CST's normative ideals. In addition, I will highlight "promising practices" and recommend ways in which Catholic universities can better foster commitment to CST in a given area.[24]

Taking account of the myriad ways that more than 250 Catholic colleges and universities in the United States do or do not embody the principles of CST would be a massive undertaking that exceeds the scope of one book. This book cannot possibly exhaust the issues pertinent to any evaluation of a Catholic university's operations. Therefore, I have selected issues that I believe are among the most pressing concerns. Each of them should be of major concern to Catholic universities given the clear positions of CST in these areas.[25] However, this does not imply that other salient issues do not exist. This book highlights individual institutions that exemplify colleges and universities that are doing well in the areas of concern, those that are making strides, and those that are failing to do so. The book also tries to delineate trends across Catholic institutions of higher learning. Many other institutions could be held up as models or critiqued in the light of CST. The cases and examples I have chosen are meant to be illustrative, and to reflect the diversity that exists among Catholic colleges and universities.

Much of the data necessary for my analysis is publicly accessible. I originally set out to obtain information and personal perspectives via interviews of employees at Catholic universities. In truth, however, after just a few interviews I decided to eschew reporting what I learned because of the perceived fear of repercussions among some interviewees.[26] In Chapters 5 and 6, I rely heavily on the voices of minoritized members of academe by engaging their scholarly work extensively. I understand that academic prose often "assimilates" the work of other scholars, citing them in footnotes but not in the narrative. I include the names of those whom I cite in Chapters 5 and 6 in my narrative intentionally, as minoritized scholars have far too long been coopted or ignored without being properly credited. Given my social location as a White, straight, cisgender, and tenure-privileged male, I do not wish to speak for them, but to learn from them and draw conclusions in the light of Catholic social teaching.

To reiterate, this book does not intend to be a full-blown sociological analysis.[27] As a constructive work in Catholic social ethics, it utilizes data in order to examine the situation on Catholic campuses, to advance normative arguments about the need to pursue aspects of Catholic universities' mission with greater zeal, and to propose ways to do so. In other words, it utilizes the method of CST referred to as "see, judge, act." Pope John XXIII explained this method lucidly: "The teachings in regard to social matters for the most part are put into effect in the following three stages: First, the actual situation is examined; then, the situation is evaluated carefully in relation to these teachings, then only is it decided what can and should be done in order that the traditional norms may be adapted to circumstances of time and place. These three steps are at times expressed by the three words: *observe, judge, act*."[28]

To my knowledge, no scholarly book has considered Catholic universities' policies and practices in the light of Catholic social teaching in a systematic way. Thus, I hope to add an important, overlooked dimension to the conversation about the identity and mission of Catholic universities today. I do not claim that this book represents the final word on this subject, however. It is far from perfect, but at a certain point I needed to put it forward in spite of its imperfections. I intend for it to be an initial step, a "conversation starter" for a much-needed discussion. I understand that my viewpoint is biased and incomplete, just as any human being's "horizon" is limited by her or his biases.[29] If this book helps to generate more serious and sustained consideration of the ways that CST should shape the life of Catholic institutions of higher learning, it will have served its purpose as a constructive work in Christian ethics. Hopefully those who disagree with my arguments will recognize that they can only ascertain the fullness of truth by listening to perspectives different than their own, just as I may reach it only by listening to them. As the great philosopher and spiritual leader of Solidarność Fr. Józef Tischner argued, this recognition is "the first condition" of genuine dialogue.[30]

1 The Mission of Catholic Higher Education in the Age of the Corporatized University

My students and I were having an excellent semester in my course on economic ethics, or so I thought. The students seemed engaged, coming to each class eagerly prepared to partake in discussion. On one particular afternoon, I had a memorable conversation with a student from the class, who remains one of the most brilliant students I have ever taught (he later obtained a fellowship in a doctoral program in one of the hard sciences at an elite university). He told me that he was enjoying learning about Catholic social teaching on economic life, but he was doubtful of its relevance to "real-world" issues. Ever the candid conversation partner in addition to his intellectual acumen, Peter bluntly stated that he failed to see institutions actually trying to embody the principles of Catholic social teaching, including our own Catholic university.[1] In his view, if it is impossible or impractical for a Catholic university to implement CST, how can we think that secular institutions will do any better? Peter grew up a devout Catholic, but he had clearly grown tired of what he perceived as hypocrisy in church-related institutions. "Do as I say, not what I do" was no longer working for this bright and inquisitive young man.

Catholic institutions of higher learning must demonstrate their own willingness to implement the church's social teaching, such as its insistence on the human dignity and rights of all, in order to preserve its credibility. Over the years, numerous students have candidly stated that learning about Catholic social teaching is pointless when they fail to see Catholic institutions living up to the tradition's own ideals. Others have sat in my office and expressed their dissatisfaction, and sometimes despair, over what they perceive to be the university's reduction of the ideals of Catholic social teaching to mere rhetoric. Students often recognize when food service and janitorial staff are not paid living wages. Many are deeply disturbed by this fact, as well as by the shockingly low wages of adjuncts and the resistance to unions on Catholic campuses, despite the church's full support of the right to just wages and unions.[2] Such violations of the church's own social teachings often challenge the faith of Catholic students. As theologian Johannes Baptist Metz has argued, many young Christians yearn for a church that adopts more "radicalism" in the struggle for social justice and less "doctrinal rigorism."[3] In recent decades, one out of three baptized Catholics has left the church, often citing "hypocrisy" and "other moral failures" as reasons.[4] While many young Catholics either remain disillusioned with the church or have abandoned it altogether, research also shows that young Catholics want to know that their faith makes a difference in the world.[5] Dean Hoge concludes in his study of young adult Catholics that "if the relationship between social justice and a specifically Catholic identity were more immediate to young adult Catholics, their perspective might be more concerned with structural approaches, aggregate effects, power and institutional systems—in keeping with contemporary church teaching regarding social justice."[6] Thus, confronting injustices on our campuses and illuminating how CST positively influences our institutions is vital to the faith formation of our students. Although this book focuses on Catholic colleges and universities, it also has implications for Christian universities of all types, as young Christians from many denominations often leave their churches in search of more socially progressive communities.[7]

By virtue of their identity and mission, Catholic universities are urged to promote Catholic social teaching and to consider its prescriptions for a more just and peaceful world.[8] As the United States Conference of Catholic Bishops (USCCB) has stated, "if Catholic education and formation fail to communicate our social tradition, they are not fully Catholic."[9] The aim is not simply to transmit knowledge, but to help shape the minds and hearts of our students so they can transform the world for the better.[10] In other words, we should seek to aid them in conscience formation. If teaching CST is to have this kind of transformative effect on our students, Catholic educators and institutions must move from talk to action. Modeling the ideals of the Catholic social tradition is even more important than teaching these ideals in the classroom. The late Catholic ethicist William Spohn trenchantly discussed the formation of students' consciences, maintaining that "we learn that a wise, compassionate, and committed life is possible from the living witnesses whom we know. The ideals that guide conscience do not reside in the starry heavens but in actual people we admire."[11] Rick Malloy, SJ, the university chaplain and former vice president of Mission and Ministry at the University of Scranton, puts the matter this way: "The moral praxis of our Jesuit institutions creates the context within which the practicality of the practice of moral norms and values by our students does, or does not, make sense. One concrete means to form the moral conscience of our students is clear: struggle to make Jesuit schools truly moral institutions."[12] The same can be said, of course, about all Catholic institutions. If we practice what we preach (and I believe our students are *hearing* about the values of the Gospel and Catholic social teaching on our campuses), our "students will be more likely to develop as moral persons." If, on the other hand, we fail to model those values, "we will be subtly communicating to our students that it makes more sense to 'Look out for Number One,' 'Grab All the Gusto You Can' and forget the poor and oppressed of our world."[13] The commodification of higher education has created an environment increasingly dominated by both the "power and the ethic of the marketplace."[14] If we leave this trend unchecked, we implicitly tell our students that they are engaged in a market transaction, meant for their pleasure and prosperity. In this scenario, it makes good sense to cheat or to plagiarize, as those routes may be the most "efficient" road to "success."[15]

In his 2008 address at the Catholic University of America, Pope Benedict XVI stated that above all, Catholic universities must be a place where young people "encounter the living God who in Jesus Christ reveals his transforming love and truth (cf. *Spe Salvi*, no. 4)."[16] This encounter, he argued, must have both "informative" and "performative" dimensions. Fostering this encounter should entail more than just "communicating data." The life of the campus community must manifest commitment to truth and love.[17] In other words, if we want our Christian students to grow in their faith and in their relationship with Jesus Christ and to become citizens responsible for the common good, we need to show them what the truth, beauty, and justice of the Catholic tradition looks like when incarnated.[18] They will not likely be attracted to the values of the Gospel if they do not see them in reality, or at least perceive that we are trying to embody them to the best of our ability. The individualistic, hedonistic, consumerist, promiscuous, and relativistic culture that characterizes much of college life today will remain embedded unless we show our students another way.[19] As Malloy argues, "students . . . deeply desire to free themselves and form communities in light of Jesus's call to serve and love others. They just aren't being shown how."[20] Malloy adds that every year 1,400 deaths and 70,000 sexual assaults and rapes happen as a result of drinking on college campuses. According to a White House Council on Women and Girls report, our nation's campuses—where one in five women report being sexually assaulted—put women at risk more than in other environments in our society.[21]

Catholic institutions are generally no better than secular universities at eschewing the "beer and circus" culture that Murray Sperber described almost two decades ago.[22] Of course, many of our students admirably exemplify the love and discipleship of Christ in myriad ways, and I have had the privilege of meeting some of them. But there are many more (like me during my earliest student days) who fall into destructive patterns of behavior such as binge drinking or other addictions while struggling to discern their true nature and calling. To add to these problems, many students at our universities see college as a gateway to the world of high-class living. In deciding a course of study and a future career, making a commitment to the common good takes a back seat to individual success, very often conceived in terms of earning a salary in the highest income bracket. Giving in to the desires of the "I want it now" consumer, many colleges and universities create a country club atmosphere, replete with state-of-the-art fitness centers, stadiums, restaurants, and retail shops, rather than a place of learning.[23] As I will discuss throughout this book, Catholic institutions often fall prey to this trap, failing to challenge the status quo in this and in many other ways.

The Corporatized University and the Neoliberal Project

The corporatization of the modern university partly explains why Catholic universities fail to fully impress upon our students that the good life, the life God intends for us, entails loving one another and creating communities where the dignity and rights of all are respected. This point will become more obvious throughout this book. At this juncture, I want to describe the paradigm that informs many decisions at our Catholic colleges and universities today, a paradigm that conflicts with CST.

By corporatization of the university, I mean "an institution that is characterized by processes, decisional criteria, expectations, organizational culture, and operating practices that are taken from, and have their origins in, the modern business corporation." Corporatized universities are "characterized by the entry of the university into marketplace relationships and by the use of market strategies in university decision-making."[24] These strategies include, among others: responsibility-centered management (forcing individual colleges and departments to be fiscally independent); viewing students as customers and emphasizing "customer satisfaction"; heavy reliance on quantitative metrics to measure performance; hierarchical organizational structures; downsizing or elimination of departments (especially in the humanities) because they fail to generate revenue; the marketing and "branding" of the institution; the increasing number of managers and administrators; and accepting funds from corporations in exchange for influence over research and academic programming.[25] According to Marc Bousquet, the corporatized university engages in a bevy of business endeavors (from apparel sales and selecting vendors for books, food services, etc., to copywriting intellectual property) in order to enhance revenues and contain costs. In this way institutions of higher education are "commercialized: they're inextricably implicated in profoundly capitalist objectives, however 'nonprofit' their missions."[26]

The corporatization of the university goes hand-in-hand with the commodification of higher education. Though not true of all students, many view higher education as simply another good to be purchased in the marketplace.[27] Faculty members are often seen as "cashiers" who should above all strive for the "consumer satisfaction" of their high-paying customers, i.e., students and their parents.[28] Students and their parents now frequently choose majors based on potential earnings data.[29] A widespread perception exists that studying a field to follow a passion or to become an educated citizen—hallmarks of liberal education—is passé. Too many higher education leaders and professors have recoiled from teaching students ethics, civility, and that "good fortune confers a responsibility to live generously toward the less fortunate."[30] Universities must brand and market themselves to compete for customers, driving a facilities "arms race" that uses noneducational amenities to lure students.[31] Institutions commodify students "to the extent they become simply objects that keep the university afloat with cash," as James Keenan states.[32] This capitalistic vision of education views education as an entitlement of those who can pay for it, and leaves students who cannot as fodder for the lending industry.[33] Some evidence suggests that university presidents and boards do not always use endowments to buoy essential academic programs or to provide more financial aid when possible. Instead they engage in "endowment hoarding" to maintain their own reputation as fundraisers.[34] None of this is entirely new, as money and capitalistic values have always influenced US higher education. However, the "raw power" of money in shaping the entire landscape of higher education in recent decades is unprecedented.[35]

A veteran of several different academic institutions, Bousquet has also described the "corporate welfare university."[36] He points to the various ways in which "corporate shareholders" benefit from high-priced higher education and the simultaneous "faculty proletarianization." He maintains that the coffers of for-profit educational institutions have bloated over the last several decades, largely as a result of the ability to pay "casual faculty" low wages and no benefits (more on this in Chapter 2) while simultaneously charging exorbitant tuition and obtaining federal tax dollars. It is important to note that although nonprofit institutions of higher learning do not channel these savings to shareholders in the form of dividends, they do provide benefits to corporate beneficiaries. Among these are "shouldering the cost of job training, generation of patentable intellectual property, provision of sports spectacle, vending goods and services to student markets, and conversion of student aid into a cheap or even free labor pool."[37] David Kirp points out that academics and their institutions increasingly acquiesce to demands from "students, donors, corporations, politicians" to control the "priorities in higher education."[38] Some critics argue that the business world wants education to be shaped in a way that produces workers who will serve their interests.[39]

In the last thirty years of "managed higher education," the corporate class has also benefited from a growing number of well-paying managerial posts. Administrators have hired more administrators, increasingly from outside academe. They have simultaneously reduced the number of tenure-track faculty positions and decreased the pay of the majority of campus workers.[40] The American Association of University Professors (AAUP) has noted that from 1976–2011 nonfaculty professional positions grew by 369 percent. Full-time executive positions increased by 141 percent. Tenure-track positions only grew by 23 percent, while part-time faculty swelled by 286 percent.[41] According to Bousquet, "the university under managerial domination is an accumulation machine. If in non-profits it accumulates in some form other than dividends, there's all the more surplus for administrators, trustees, local politicians, and a handful of influential faculty to spend on a discretionary basis."[42] Furthermore, university management wants to "remake competing campus cultures in its own image."

Toward that end, university administrators have developed a deep sense of "solidarity" among themselves in opposition to faculty, according to Bousquet. They have been extraordinarily successful at eradicating "faculty culture" (e.g., academic freedom in teaching and research) and implanting "cultural materialism" in its place.[43] Eliminating tenure-track posts and hiring more adjuncts (an issue discussed in more detail in the next chapter) and professional staff solidifies managerial control over university matters that were once in the domain of tenured faculty, in addition to providing a cost-cutting mechanism. In the corporatized university, the shared governance that promotes faculty and administrator collaboration in decision-making disappears in favor of top-down managerial control.[44]

This account does not intend to depict administrators as villains and faculty as paragons of virtue. As I shall discuss, many faculty members themselves have embraced the corporatization of the university. Moreover, some administrators understand the value of shared governance (fortunately I have worked with some of them). The AAUP rightly recognizes administrators and trustees who demonstrate outstanding commitment to shared governance. In fact, the board of trustees and the former president of Santa Clara University, Paul Locatelli, SJ, received the inaugural award in 1999.[45] However, the 2015 debacle at Mount St. Mary's University in Maryland illustrates what can happen when the management style of the corporatized university runs amok. *The Chronicle of Higher Education* aptly called this fiasco a "corporate test case" that "failed miserably."[46] The university's then-president fired two professors, and a provost was compelled to resign, for criticizing both the policies that hurt students and the president's harsh rhetoric about struggling students.

The corporatization of the university reflects the larger neoliberal agenda to destroy solidarity among workers.[47] The "neoliberal assault on universities" subjects faculty (and staff) to a constant barrage of "crises," austerity measures, and so-called reforms in order to "soften the resistance of faculty to change."[48] Neoliberalism also promotes the retreat of the public sector in favor of the private sphere, which explains the major cuts in public funding of higher education even as tuition becomes prohibitive for many students.[49] In short, the seismic changes that have occurred over the last several decades at universities must be seen in a larger political and economic context—the ascendancy of neoliberalism.

St. John Paul II aptly characterized neoliberalism in 1999:

> More and more, in many countries of America, a system known as 'neoliberalism' prevails; based on a purely economic conception of man, this system considers profit and the law of the market as its only parameters, to the detriment of the dignity of and the respect due to individuals and peoples. At times this system has become the ideological justification for certain attitudes and behavior in the social and political spheres leading to the neglect of the weaker members of society. Indeed, the poor are becoming ever more numerous, victims of specific policies and structures which are often unjust.[50]

Neoliberalism, the dominant ideology of our time, entails economic policies such as privatization, deregulation, and tax cuts for the wealthy and corporations.[51] However, as Keri Day contends, it also represents a worldview and "cultural project" that seeks to "create a different community of persons" in which "persons are nothing more than material means toward the ends of another person's goals."[52] Neoliberalism has ordained self-interest as the primary feature of human personhood and has fostered the human tendency to competition in all spheres of life.[53] It has attempted to eradicate "all forms of solidarity capable of challenging market-driven values."[54]

Given the pervasive influence of the ethos of neoliberalism on contemporary life, we should not be surprised that it has changed higher education for the worse (though many of us are unaware of this).[55] Scholars have documented the explicit ways the business community and international institutions such as the IMF and World Bank have brought the neoliberal paradigm to the hallowed halls of our universities.[56] I will discuss this further in Chapter 4. For now, I want to stress that the corporatization of the modern university and the commodification of education both emanate from and promote larger, monumental shifts in values and practices found in advanced capitalist societies, quintessentially in the

United States.[57] Michael Sandel, one of the preeminent philosophers of our era, encapsulates this transformation as the movement from having a market economy to "being a market society."[58] As Sandel puts it, "the expansion of markets, and of market values, into spheres of life where they don't belong . . . is one of the most significant developments of our time." His book *What Money Can Buy: The Moral Limits of Markets* discusses myriad examples of how the market's values and mechanisms have infiltrated just about every aspect of modern life. From the mundane ability of individuals to drive in carpool lanes for a fee, to absurdities like being paid to advertise on one's forehead, to practices like wealthy couples paying women halfway around the world to carry surrogate pregnancies, Sandel laments that just about everything can be bought and sold. Among the consumer "products" that can be bought in our market society are seats at prestigious American universities (an issue I shall discuss in a subsequent chapter). Against the dominant modus operandi, Sandel rightly contends that the very nature of some goods, relationships, and values dictates that they not be demeaned by putting a price tag on them.[59]

Those familiar with Catholic social teaching know that Sandel is in good company. A few decades ago Pope John Paul II called attention to an "idolatry of the market" that "ignores the existence of goods which by their nature are not and cannot be mere commodities."[60] The Pope also maintained that excessive focus on "false and superficial gratifications" through consumption and on maximizing profit has generated "alienation" in Western societies. Alienation takes place when the "value and grandeur of the human person," along with her capacity for self-giving, is supplanted by the view that other persons are instruments of profit and/or self-gratification. John Paul argued that alienation occurs when human beings are used as a means rather than recognized as ends in themselves. In a capitalist society, this happens when human beings are treated like commodities. Succinctly stated, socialism produced alienation, but John Paul also recognized alienation in the dangerous tendency of market economies to commodify everything.[61] In more recent years Pope Benedict XVI and Pope Francis have repeated this concern.[62] The current pontiff forcefully stated:

The worship of the ancient golden calf (see Ex 32:1–35) has returned in a new and ruthless guise in the idolatry of money and the dictatorship of an impersonal economy lacking a truly human purpose. The world-wide crisis affecting finance and the economy lays bare their imbalances and, above all, their lack of real concern for human beings; man is reduced to one of his needs alone: consumption.[63]

Succinctly stated, Catholic colleges and universities operate within the context of corporatized higher education and the larger neoliberal project, which challenges their ability to fulfill their mission. Let me now turn specifically to Catholic institutions of higher learning in the age of the corporatized university.

The Corporatized University and the Mission of Catholic Universities

Like their US secular counterparts, Catholic universities vary in the degree to which they have succumbed to corporatization and the "market fundamentalism" critiqued by Sandel, the recent popes, and other thinkers.[64] Nonetheless, Catholic colleges and universities have certainly not remained immune to the corporatization of the university.[65] Renowned Catholic theologian David Hollenbach, SJ, questions whether or not US Catholic universities can remain faithful to their mission and identity today if they operate like corporations. He fears that the "pursuit of institutional advancement at the best Catholic universities can be a tool serving the self-interest and privilege of the powerful." He cautions that seeking elite status by many Catholic universities has caused even their leaders to have "amnesia about their poor, immigrant roots."[66] Catholic universities are run by board members and increasingly by administrators with vast experience in the worlds of business, finance, and industry. However, like the majority of Roman Catholics, they often possess little more than a superficial understanding of Catholic social teaching.[67] The Association of Jesuit Colleges and Universities (AJCU) has explicitly acknowledged this leadership problem: "The majority of our lay people come without adequate formation or interest in learning about and implementing the mission beyond humanistic concerns, like 'care of the person' or a 'commitment to service.' In the absence of a 'thick' understanding of the tradition, these good and well-intentioned leaders will be uncertain about how to hire faculty and administrators who explicitly engage the university's mission and establish and promote programming that links directly to our Jesuit, Catholic identity."[68]

William Byron, SJ, who served as president of three universities and on ten boards, commends lay leaders for bringing valuable skills from the business world. He concedes that board members should provide needed oversight on "brand building" and "product differentiation." However, board members also need to be educated about the "Catholic identity of the institution." They must remember that the "institution is grounded in the person and teachings of Jesus Christ" and that the "bottomline" cannot justify policies "that deplete in a qualitative way the institution's human assets: its students, employees, and others."[69] Former Association of Catholic Colleges and Universities president Alice Gallin, OSU, also believes that the expertise and fundraising ability of lay trustees has been essential to the success of Catholic education. In her view, as lay people became trustees in the 1960s and 1970s, they wanted to preserve the "Catholic character" of their institutions. Nonetheless, she also contends that not enough was done to help them understand the mission of the institutions they served.[70]

The majority of board members at US colleges and universities hail from the business world or from professional services such as accounting, law, or medicine.[71] Although still a minority, university presidents also increasingly come from the corporate world. This makes some sense, given the growing need to fundraise because of waning state financial support.[72] In my judgment, however, if board members, administrators, and faculty members with power are primarily trained in US business schools or economics departments, there is reason to believe that they may not embrace the social anthropology that undergirds CST.[73] CST sees the human person as a member of an interdependent family; the person's nature and destiny is fulfilled in solidarity with others and through sustained commitment to the common good (see the section of this chapter below on the principles and themes of CST).[74] On the contrary, US business education has largely abandoned its original commitments to "service and calling" in favor of "neoliberal utopianism" that prizes self-interest and profit maximization, according to Rakesh Khurana of Harvard Business School.[75] Both modern economics and the curricula of US business schools tend to emphasize a contrasting understanding of the human person as *homo economicus*. This reductionistic anthropology holds that humans always act "rationally," construed as acting in order to maximize self-interest.[76] "This economic man (*homo economicus*) is utterly self-serving and only interested in maximizing his immediate utility. Economic man is therefore only engaging in transactional, short-term oriented encounters with others."[77] This view of the human person undergirds neoliberalism and informs much of current management theory and practice.[78] The anthropology of *homo economicus* leads to a leadership and organizational culture that is adversarial, competitive, "efficiency oriented" and "centered on hierarchies and top-down decision-making."[79] In this regard, Keenan and others have argued that universities resemble "fiefdoms," in which "administrators function like feudal lords."[80]

Research demonstrates that students who are predominantly exposed to this individualistic anthropology in economics and business courses tend to behave as self-interest maximizers and see human beings as fundamentally in competition with one another.[81] Michael Pirson of Fordham University's Graduate School of Business has therefore argued for eschewing the "economism paradigm" of business education, leadership, management theory, and corporate governance structures in favor of a "humanistic paradigm." The latter adopts an anthropology based on a "renewed Darwinian theory" in the light of contemporary neuroscience and behavioral economics, while evolutionary psychology posits that human beings are not simply self-interest maximizers. Rather, humans have four basic drives: to acquire, to bond, to comprehend, and to defend. According to the humanistic paradigm, human beings are "intrinsically motivated to self-actualize and serve humanity through what they do."[82] As Pirson and Lawrence point out, this understanding of the human person has much in common with Aristotle's notion of *zōon politikon*, which sees human beings as social by nature (like Catholic social teaching). This humanistic model must displace *homo economicus* in order to prevent financial crises like that of 2008 from happening again and to promote "the sustainable development of business in the future."[83]

To be clear, faculty members in all fields, not just business or economics, bear responsibility for the persistence of flawed understandings of the human person, community, and the mission of Catholic universities. As Gallin maintains, at a certain point in the history of Catholic higher education, lay and religious faculty alike began to prioritize "academic excellence" and "competitive achievement in the various disciplines of study" over "character formation and moral development of young people."[84] As employees in the corporatized university and denizens of the larger neoliberal world order, many faculty have consciously or subconsciously embraced *homo economicus*. Many academics have put their heads in the sand while "neoliberalism's war on higher education" has been occurring.[85] With some exceptions, they have often remained in their silos churning out work in their disciplines rather than striving against corporatization and for the common good. As Keenan maintains, this problem predates the corporatization of the university. The long and lonely process of writing a dissertation initiates academics into the "isolationist culture" of the academy, which rewards individual toil and achievement much more than teamwork and contribution to the community.[86] However, corporatization has exacerbated the problem. Faculty members have largely "adapted to the conditions of our profession by developing a culture as steeped in the ethos of productivity and salesmanship as one might encounter in the business world."[87] Anyone who has ever attended an academic conference will recognize the truth in this statement!

Even worse, some academics function as "gated intellectuals," who legitimize the neoliberal global order by giving it intellectual "cover," as Giroux states. These shills eschew any responsibility for the hordes of marginalized people afflicted by neoliberalism.[88] This includes, as I will discuss in the following chapters, ignoring the plight of colleagues who work as contingent faculty members and students who struggle to afford their education. Some academics reject the status quo of corporatized higher education and its deleterious consequences, but many acquiesce due to fear and/or fatigue. Research indicates that the extreme emphasis on productivity at the corporatized university has led many academics to feel overworked, stressed out, and hopeless.[89]

To summarize, if decision-makers at Catholic colleges and universities hold a view of the human person that is antithetical to the anthropology of the Catholic tradition, they may make governance decisions that are at odds with CST. A distorted understanding of human nature that depicts human beings as fundamentally in competition with one another and not capable of making compromises for the good of the community will not lead to a management style and policy decisions rooted in CST.[90] This does not mean that all university leaders consciously embrace *homo economicus* and have conspired to advance the neoliberal agenda described here. In addition, Catholic colleges and universities certainly sometimes adopt practices and policies that contradict the spirit of *homo economicus*, as the positive examples in this book will demonstrate. There are numerous forces at work on Catholic campuses, many of them good. Nonetheless, well-intended board members, administrators and faculty members may import or tacitly accept corporate models of financial and personnel management into Catholic higher education, while not seriously contemplating how solidarity, justice, human rights, the common good, and the option for the poor should shape the university's internal policies and structures. As I have seen firsthand, those university leaders who conscientiously introduce concepts from CST into conversations about university operations may meet strong resistance.[91]

Catholic social teaching, however, insists that these ideals serve as guiding principles for our institutions. Saint John Paul II's Apostolic Constitution on Higher Education *Ex Corde Ecclesiae* makes this clear:

> A Catholic University pursues its objectives through its *formation of an authentic human community animated by the spirit of Christ.* The source of its unity springs from a common dedication to the truth, a common vision of the dignity of the human person and, ultimately, the person and message of Christ which gives the Institution its distinctive character. As a result of this inspiration, the community is animated by a spirit of freedom and charity; it is characterized by *mutual respect, sincere dialogue, and protection of the rights of individuals.* It assists each of its members to achieve wholeness as human persons; in turn, everyone in the community helps in promoting unity, and each one, according to his or her role and capacity, contributes towards decisions which affect the community, and also towards maintaining and strengthening the distinctive Catholic character of the Institution.[92]

CST enumerates a substantial list of human rights that the university community should protect, such as the right to a just wage, freedom of association, education, affordable health care, rest (at least one day per week and a yearly vacation), retirement pensions, unemployment insurance, workers compensation, parental leave, and participation in decision-making.[93] The affirmation of these rights has obvious policy implications for Catholic universities, as this book will demonstrate. In fact, canon law mandates that church institutions embody CST in their policies, reflected in requirements to pay just wages and to recognize employees' right to unionize.[94] As the United States Conference of Catholic Bishops' document *Economic Justice for All* states:

> All the moral principles that govern the just operation of any economic endeavor apply to the Church and its agencies and institutions; indeed the Church should be exemplary. The Synod of Bishops in 1971 worded this challenge most aptly: "While the Church is bound to give witness to justice, she recognizes that anyone who ventures to speak to people about justice must first be just in their eyes. Hence, we must undertake an examination of the modes of acting and of the possessions and lifestyle found within the Church herself."[95]

Ex Corde Ecclesiae brings into further relief the conflict between the ideals that should govern Catholic universities and the capitalistic values of the corporatized university. Successive chapters in this book will elucidate the nature of this conflict in greater detail. For now, I aim to establish that Catholic teaching dictates that Catholic universities cannot ignore CST in their institutional policies and commitment. In order to dispel any doubt on the matter, let me list what *Ex Corde* considers "*essential characteristics*" that "every Catholic University, as *Catholic*" should display:

1. a Christian inspiration not only of individuals but of the university community as such;
2. a continuing reflection in the light of the Catholic faith upon the growing treasury of human knowledge, to which it seeks to contribute by its own research;
3. fidelity to the Christian message as it comes to us through the church;
4. an institutional commitment to the service of the people of God and of the human family in their pilgrimage to the transcendent goal which gives meaning to life.[96]

Furthermore, CST holds that education, like other public goods, cannot and should not be commodified. To assume that the market alone can assure all human goods is tantamount to "idolatry of the market," according to John Paul II.[97] Like health care and other goods, CST maintains that education is a human right owed to all people, not something to be sold like cigarettes or candy.[98] Thus, the logic of the market should not dominate Catholic higher education.[99] If we demonstrate by our policy decisions and institutional arrangements that our values can be forsaken in the name of "efficiency," "fiscal responsibility," "innovation," "market competition," etc., we convey to our students that living out the Gospel and Catholic social teaching costs too much, thereby affirming the nihilism and relativism already in the air.[100] In the words of the late Fr. Dean Brackley, nurturing the faith of our students requires "orthopraxis, including conspicuous respect for the rights of workers and all vulnerable members of the learning community."[101] In short, Catholic universities must both expose their students to Catholic social teaching across the curriculum (not only in theology classes), advance justice and solidarity in the world, and embody CST *intramurally* in order to fulfill their role in the church's mission of evangelization.[102] I argue in this book that the latter of these areas has been the most neglected.

Expanding the Conversation about Mission and Identity

Ex Corde Ecclesiae discusses evangelization as an important element of the mission of Catholic universities. It defines evangelization as "bringing the Good News into all the strata of humanity, and through its influence transforming humanity from within and making it new."[103] John Paul II argues that in addition to communicating the truth of the Gospel, universities must evangelize by "upsetting, through the power of the Gospel, humanity's criteria of judgment, determining values, points of interest, lines of thought, sources of inspiration and models of life, which are in contrast with the Word of God and the plan of salvation."[104] The university's task in evangelization is thus to be "a living *institutional* witness to Christ and his message, so vitally important in cultures marked by secularism, or where Christ and his message are still virtually unknown."[105] In his apostolic exhortation *Evangelii Gaudium*, Pope Francis has recalled this dimension of the mission of Catholic universities, which are "outstanding environments for articulating and developing this evangelizing commitment in an interdisciplinary and integrated way." According to Francis, Catholic universities must serve as a "valuable resource for the evangelization of culture" and search for appropriate ways of undertaking this endeavor in situations where cultural currents and dominant trends oppose the values of the Gospel.[106] Thus, an essential element of the mission of every Catholic university requires challenging the dominant paradigm of the corporatized university in order to render the Gospel credible in a pervasive, institutionalized culture that rejects it. In order to achieve this goal, the university must demonstrate the possibility of creating structures and policies imbued with the values and principles of CST. "Today more than ever, the Church is aware that her social message will gain credibility more immediately from the *witness of actions* than as a result of its internal logic and consistency," as John Paul II put it.[107] More than two thousand years earlier, Jesus of Nazareth thus admonished his disciples, "You will know them by their fruits. Are grapes gathered from thorns, or figs from thistles? In the same way, every good tree bears good fruit, but the bad tree bears bad fruit" (Matt 7:16–18).[108] Succinctly stated, Catholic universities must build solidarity with the oppressed and promote "justice and liberation from every kind of oppression," both beyond and on their campuses, in order to evangelize.[109]

In recent decades, a spate of books has considered how Catholic universities should fulfill their mission and sustain their ecclesial identity in the contemporary pluralistic American context.[110] These books tend to focus on how the university should transmit the content of the Catholic faith through theology courses, Catholic studies programs, and in the broader curriculum. Some discuss issues of academic freedom, hiring for mission, and the place of the Catholic university in the broader academy. Fewer deal with the universities' responsibility to promote justice, solidarity, and the option for the poor in more than a passing way.[111] There are some noteworthy exceptions. David O'Brien's book *From the Heart of the American Church: Catholic Higher Education in American Culture*, which was published in 1994, argued that "the goal of Catholic education" should be the formation of students dedicated to justice and peace. O'Brien maintained that "education for justice and peace" cannot occur without scholars committed to it. Yet, he contended at the time that "the notion of intellectual life lived in terms of justice remains controversial and threatening to many in the academy and in the church."[112] More recently Thomas Rausch's *Educating for Faith and Justice: Catholic Higher Education Today* and Suzanne Toton's *Justice Education: From Service to Solidarity* rank among the best articulations of the theological and ethical foundations for every Catholic university's Gospel-based mandate to act for justice in the world.[113] Readers looking for a robust theological justification for a Catholic university's responsibility to promote justice should engage these works. Both Rausch and Toton find inspiration and the theoretical bases for this aspect of mission from the prophetic musings and living witness to the Gospel of the Jesuit martyrs of the UCA (Universidad Centroamericana José Simeón Cañas). They especially value Ignacio Ellacuría and other important figures such as Oscar Romero and Pedro Arrupe.[114] In moving to concrete means of fulfilling this role, Rausch and his fellow contributors see community-based learning, service immersion trips, and other educational programs as fruitful means of cultivating solidarity with the poor and the marginalized.[115] Toton (my former colleague at Villanova University) moves beyond curricular endeavors to concrete examples of action for justice in broader society. Having taught service learning courses for ten years myself, I concur with her that such experiential learning encounters with the poor only represent important "first steps" toward the solidarity with the poor called for by the university's mission.[116] I have witnessed numerous students undergo the beginnings of a *metanoia*, or conversion of the heart, which can be the wellspring of solidarity. Research attests to this transformative dimension of service-learning.[117] Yet, solidarity as understood in CST must move beyond awareness and crisis intervention to contemplating the causes of the suffering of the marginalized and oppressed and to acting with them in order to promote structural and systemic change.[118] Toton rightly warns that Catholic universities can be lulled into thinking they have fulfilled their mandate to promote justice in the world by maintaining strong service-learning programs, which at best help succor the needs of the poor but do little to bend the broken world toward the Reign of God by dismantling unjust social structures. In my judgment, university officials eagerly tout the plethora of students engaged in service activities in soup kitchens, underfunded schools, hospices, and other community organizations as evidence of fulfillment of the mandate to work for justice and the common good. However, service learning, while meaningful and well-intentioned, "cannot substitute for the kind of action required to affect structural and systemic change," and it can distract from "the time-consuming organizing, strategizing, mobilizing, confronting, reconstituting and negotiating that is part and parcel of action for justice."[119]

The gospel call to "action on behalf of justice" (a phrase from the 1971 Synod of Bishops' document *Justice in the World*) and creating solidarity with the poor requires greater risk-taking by the university in order to help transform the world, as Toton contends.[120]

The recent volume *A Vision of Justice: Engaging Catholic Social Teaching on the College Campus* focuses on theoretical discussions of CST and its concepts but also provides some inspiring examples of students, faculty, and staff at Catholic universities going beyond charity to do the work of justice, engaging in solidarity with marginalized immigrants, the poor, victims of human trafficking, and promoting sustainability and care of God's creation.[121] Undoubtedly, many more members of Catholic campuses put CST in action in their local and distant communities. However, the encouraging stories in *A Vision of Justice* and those akin to them most often involve doing justice *ad extra*, or beyond the walls of the university. Such efforts to transform broader society constitute important elements of a Catholic university's mission.[122] However, doing justice in the world does not exonerate Catholic institutions from promoting justice and human rights within their walls. I therefore argue that Catholic universities must also risk being prophetic by showing the academic industry in the United States that there is a more humane and just way of maintaining institutions of higher learning. As John Paul II stated, "If need be, a Catholic university must have the courage to speak uncomfortable truths which do not please public opinion, but which are necessary to safeguard the authentic good of society."[123] They must also critically interrogate the individualistic conception of the human person so dominant in the American psyche in order to a promote a "true Christian anthropology, founded on the person of Christ, which will bring the dynamism of the creation and redemption to bear on reality and on the correct solution to the problems of life."[124]

In the American context, where many demonize the poor and blame them for their plight, this task requires universities to adopt the option for the poor, one of CST's bedrock principles, in their institutional practices.[125] Catholic leaders such as the former superior general of the Jesuits Peter-Hans Kolvenbach, SJ, have urged creating institutions of higher education that keep principles such as the option for the poor at the forefront of their research, teaching, and admissions policies.[126] The Association of Catholic Colleges and Universities has also issued a vision statement that calls upon Catholic institutions to "continue to strive to incorporate CST into all aspects of their institutional life."[127] Trustees, administrators, faculty, staff, and students are thus tasked with finding another way, of being a "sign of contradiction" (see Lk. 2:34; Acts 28:22) in the corporatized higher education industry.[128] Academics in the areas of finance, management, economics, and other fields can and should use their expertise to discern how to make Catholic institutions better conform to the norms of CST while remaining financially viable.

In order for this to occur, faculty, administrators, board members, and students must gain a deeper appreciation for the Catholic institution's mission and for Catholic social teaching. Attaining this outcome can only be the product of sustained formation and community-building, not perfunctory nods in the direction of mission.[129] We need what Parker Palmer calls "transformative conversations on campus" to occur more regularly.[130] This requires all members of the university community to exit their silos. The corporatized university and neoliberal ethos militate against this by pitting us against one another and creating "time poverty."[131] As bell hooks laments, educational communities in the US have lost the "feeling of community." Nonetheless, we must therefore confront our "feelings of loss and restore our sense of connection" if we are to change the status quo and pursue our mission more earnestly.[132] I would add that the rank and tenure standards for professors should valorize commitment to this work, rather than paying lip service to it and lionizing "star" researchers much more heavily.[133]

Some promising work is already being done in this vein at Catholic institutions. For example, Regis University instituted a three-year program that introduces new faculty, administrators, and professional staff to the "spiritual and intellectual ethos" of the university.[134] The length of this program implies that it has a better chance of achieving its goals than the often-encountered cursory orientation to mission. The program's guiding document "Traditions" contains a robust discussion of what it means to be a Catholic, Jesuit university. Most notable for this analysis is the document's mention of "institutional practices faithful to the Christian message," the formation of "authentic human community" on campus, and "maintaining the highest ethical relationships within the Regis community as well as with partners, suppliers and other business entities, the Catholic Church, other religious traditions and educational institutions."[135]

Given Byron and Gallin's concerns cited above regarding boards, colleges should provide a similar program for board members. As Bishop Robert McElroy stated at a conference for trustees held at the University of San Francisco, the duty to advance the mission of a Catholic institution belongs to all board members, not just full-time employees.[136] At Villanova University, Dr. Barbara Wall implemented a rich seminar on Catholic social teaching for faculty and staff.[137] Administrators and board members could also benefit from this type of seminar given their shared responsibility for mission. Furthermore, mandatory units in courses across the curriculum could ensure that all students gain a better grasp of Catholic social teaching in order to understand how their institutions should embody CST and reject the "playground of unregulated freedom" style of much US higher education.[138]

The subsequent chapters in this book consider concrete ways to shape various aspects of the life of the Catholic university "within its own walls" in accordance with CST, which as John Paul II and the USCCB maintained, spells out the demands of the Gospel with greater specificity.[139] Catholic social teaching permits moving from more general biblical values and norms to actions, policies, and institutional priorities. A brief examination of CST will clarify this issue and articulate the normative framework used throughout the rest of the book.

A Brief Overview of Catholic Social Teaching

Catholic scholars have produced a number of excellent summaries and commentaries on Catholic social teaching over the last few decades.[140] Those who wish to take the institutional mission of the Catholic university seriously ought to study these kinds of works. For those readers unfamiliar with the values and principles of CST, I can only provide here a broad-brush overview of them. Subsequent chapters will expand on these concepts as they relate to the issues at hand.

The Dignity of the Human Person

This idea, rooted in the Genesis creation story, tells us that the image of God (*imago Dei*) exists in all persons (Gen. 1:27), which connotes the equal dignity of all members of the human family.[141] Vatican II's *Gaudium et Spes* argues that the incarnation of Jesus Christ restored the fullness of human dignity, which was marred by original sin.[142] Thus, Christ enables human beings to participate in his salvific activity in the world and the building of the kingdom of God by embodying solidarity.

Many people both within and beyond Christian churches posit human dignity as the philosophical foundation of human rights.[143] As Catholic legal scholar Mary Ann Glendon observes, human dignity is the ultimate value enshrined in the UN Universal Declaration of Human Rights.[144] The Catholic tradition holds that the social ministry of the church exists to safeguard human dignity. According to David Hollenbach, "Human dignity is not an abstract or ethereal reality but is realized in concrete conditions of personal, social, economic and political life. The history of papal teaching has been a process of discovering and identifying these conditions of humanity. These conditions are called human rights."[145] In other words, the charge to protect human dignity requires promoting human rights in all areas of human life. For example, CST holds that the dignity of the worker demands that she or he "cannot be treated simply as a commodity" and has certain inalienable rights.[146] Recent papal social teaching emphasizes not only the unique dignity of the human person, but the dignity of all God's creation as well. Human beings therefore have the duty to respect and to safeguard all living creatures and the natural environment.[147]

Human Rights and Duties

Catholicism has long endorsed human rights, which are indispensable for protecting human dignity.[148] The church, which is made up of imperfect human beings, has at times failed to protect the human rights of all.[149] However, observers such as noted political scientist Samuel Huntingdon have regarded the Catholic Church as one of the primary defenders of human rights in the twentieth century.[150] Catholic teaching first embraced so-called social and economic rights, while later coming to acknowledge political and civil rights.[151] Saint John XXIII's encyclical *Pacem in Terris*, often deemed Catholicism's Magna Carta, represents the most systematic and extensive presentation of rights and duties in the Catholic social tradition. It contains the first listing of the full panoply of rights endorsed by Catholicism. David Hollenbach has usefully categorized the rights affirmed in *Pacem in Terris* as "bodily rights, political rights, rights of movement, associational rights, economic rights, sexual and familial rights, religious rights and communication rights."[152]

The fulfillment of human rights is the linchpin of peace.[153] Catholicism also holds that human rights demarcate "the minimum conditions for life in the community."[154] Human dignity is threatened when people cannot participate in society as a result of debilitating social, political, and economic conditions. In other words, the chief responsibility of a society is to ensure that individual rights are respected and "coordinated with other rights" so that each individual can fulfill her or his duties in society and promote the common good.[155] According to Catholic teaching, both rights and duties are dictates of natural law, which means they arise from the very nature of the human person. As John XXIII put it, "rights as well as duties find their inviolability in the natural law which grants or enjoins them."[156] Appealing to Romans 2:15, he contends that God has "has stamped man's [sic] inmost being with an order revealed to man [sic] by his conscience; and his conscience insists on preserving it."[157] The order found in the universe is embedded in human personhood and forms the basis of the human person's inviolable dignity. Thus, human nature itself, imbued with dignity by the Creator, is the basis of all human rights.[158]

Catholic social teaching also grounds human rights in the theology of the Christian tradition. Jesus Christ is ultimately the foundation and source of all rights.[159] God unites God's very self to every human person through the incarnation of Jesus Christ. The doctrine of the incarnation holds that God became human in Jesus Christ and remains present in all humanity. Although human dignity was tarnished by original sin, Jesus Christ fully restored it by becoming one of us. Catholic teaching insists on respecting this sacred dignity, which requires safeguarding human rights.[160]

The Social Nature of the Human Person

Catholic theologians Michael and Kenneth Himes acknowledge the Catholic natural law perspective on human nature and human rights, but they also stress that the Trinitarian nature of God reveals to us what it means to be human and provides a robust theological foundation for human rights. To love and to be loved is the essence of being human.[161] Unlike philosophical liberalism, social contract theory, rational choice theory, and similar approaches, Catholicism posits that the human person is inherently social.

Human beings are naturally members of multiple communities (family, civic, religious, national, racial, ethnic, the human community, etc.). This social anthropology of Catholicism undergirds the contention that all human beings are obligated to recognize the dignity of others and to work together for the common good.[162] Although a communitarian spirit has existed in certain eras of US history and imbues some segments of society today, radical or excessive individualism pervades our contemporary culture and political discourse.[163] The social understanding of the person in CST challenges radical individualism. Margaret Thatcher famously said that "there is no such thing as society," only individuals. Catholicism flatly rejects this claim. Catholicism requires that we mirror the loving relationships of mutuality present in the Trinity in our interpersonal relationships and that we construct societies that do so as well.[164]

The Common Good and the Public Order

The notion of the common good and public order is also derived from the social nature of human beings.[165] CST defines the common good as the "sum total" of material, spiritual, political, and cultural conditions that make it possible for women and men to fully flourish as human beings. The common good is not analogous to a pie to be divided up; rather it is indivisible and remains common. Thus understood, pursuit of the common good is an essential task of societies and the global human family.[166] *Gaudium et Spes* states: "Every social group must take account of the needs and legitimate aspirations of other groups, and even of the general welfare of the entire human family."[167] In other words, all human beings have a right to share in the common good and a duty to foster it. As Hollenbach contends, fostering the common good requires more than tolerance toward one's neighbors and fellow citizens; it requires active solidarity with them.[168] More privileged members of the community may need to relinquish some of their privileges for the sake of the common good.[169] Yet, unlike libertarianism and extreme forms of communitarianism (such as communism), CST seeks to preserve both the rights of individuals and the common good, seeking a balance between the two. Furthermore, like the Pauline notion of the Body of Christ (see I Cor. 12:12–26; Eph. 4), CST holds that the well-being of the individual depends on the welfare of the entire human community; the suffering or deprivation of one member diminishes the good of all.[170] This conception of the common good directly contrasts with the "sink-or-swim" outlook of neoliberal capitalism and the "NIMBY" ("not in my back yard") mentality in American society. This idea also starkly departs from the vision of the "good life" that many Americans hold, which cherishes individualistic success and prosperity above all.

All members of society must contribute to the common good in accordance with their own gifts and abilities. All organizations, including local authorities and the state, hold responsibility for the common good.[171] John Courtney Murray, SJ, argued that the whole of society is responsible for the common good, while the state always maintains direct responsibility for that part of the common good called the public order.[172] According to Vatican II's *Declaration on Religious Freedom*, in order for the state to maintain the public order, it must provide for: (1) the protection of the rights due to all citizens in accordance with justice; (2) "public peace"; and (3) "public morality."[173] Sometimes the state will need to play a coordinating role, while various civil actors take responsibility for directing various aspects of the common good. Yet, the state may need to undertake a more direct role in some areas, such as public education and overcoming poverty, given their scope and complexity.[174] Catholicism has long valued the voluntary, independent organizations that make up civil society such as labor unions, neighborhood associations, cooperatives, professional organizations, political parties, etc. The state should not usurp their roles, but rather work in tandem with them. Thus the Catholic understanding of the common good envisions fruitful cooperation between the state and voluntary organizations. The following concept elaborates on this claim.

Subsidiarity and Socialization

Both controversial and often misunderstood, the principle of subsidiarity was developed to ensure that governments work in tandem with individuals and local groups to promote the common good.[175] In other words, subsidiarity protects the right and duty of participation of all in the shaping of and benefiting from the commonweal.[176] It also points to the obligation of larger entities, such as the state, to help individuals and smaller groups play their part. Persons cannot fulfill their right and duty to participation in the good of society if they suffer from poverty, discrimination, unemployment, untreated illnesses, etc. Both civil society and the state have the responsibility to create the conditions for the full participation of all in the common good. In the words of Pope John XXIII, "intervention of public authorities that encourages, stimulates, regulates, supplements, and complements, is based on *the principle of subsidiarity*." When possible, it is better for smaller, local groups to solve their own problems.

However, Catholic social teaching posits that larger entities, including governments, have a responsibility to assist individuals and communities when they cannot effectively solve their own problems. Moreover, for more than fifty years CST has acknowledged an increasing role for the state in socioeconomic affairs as a result of growing complexity and interdependence, a process that CST calls socialization, commonly known today as globalization.[177] Individuals and local communities can hardly be expected to effectively promote their well-being when globalization has stifled the sovereignty of entire nations.[178] In the context of this book, it is worth pointing out that the idea of subsidiarity not only applies to the relationship between society and governments, but also to the relationship between employees and employers.[179]

Solidarity

Solidarity militates against a distorted notion of subsidiarity, which mistakenly purports that charity alone suffices to assuage the suffering of the poor.[180] Solidarity in CST is grounded in natural law, numerous biblical passages, and Christian theological doctrines.[181] Succinctly stated, the Catholic social tradition postulates three key elements of solidarity: (1) the recognition of human interdependence and corresponding obligations to others that flow from it, especially obligations to the marginalized; (2) a firm commitment to the common good, which requires creating social structures that promote the participation and rights of all; and (3) willingness to work with others across boundaries of class, gender, race, sexual orientation, ethnicity, religion, and nationality to foster an inclusive common good. The first aspect of solidarity entails the recognition that human beings are by nature interdependent. As Franciszek Kampka writes, solidarity involves "the attitude of mutual empathy among members of a community, becoming aware of their deep similarities and interdependence, and deepening them by experiencing the needs of others just as we experience our own needs."[182] This recognition of a shared humanity and common fate with all people disposes us to attend to "the wounded one and the cry of pain" among us.[183]

The fact of interdependence gives rise to ethical obligations toward others in the personal, social, economic, cultural, political, and religious spheres of social life.[184] Direct, immediate aid is necessary when a situation gravely threatens a person's or group's health, bodily integrity, or psychological well-being. However, solidarity requires moving beyond temporary assistance to "a *firm and persevering determination* to commit oneself to the common good," as Pope John Paul II maintained. Solidarity is much more than "a feeling of vague compassion or shallow distress."[185] It must go beyond short-term aid to be embodied in policies, institutions, and social structures that eliminate the causes of the suffering of the wounded, the poor, and the oppressed.[186] Solidarity seeks to restore to the poor what is rightfully theirs, as those who embody it "recognize that the social function of property and the universal destination of all goods are realities that come before private property."[187] In other words, solidarity must be "institutionalized" so that all people, including the marginalized, can participate in and benefit from the common good.[188] Genuine participation entails using one's abilities and resources to promote both one's own rights and flourishing, and those of the community.[189] In this regard, solidarity differs from compassion and almsgiving, which assist passive recipients. Solidarity empowers the marginalized to become active members of the community in order to be able to "bear another's burdens."[190]

Unlike Weberian, Marxist, and other exclusivist conceptions of solidarity, the Catholic tradition posits the possibility of highly inclusive solidarity across classes, genders, races, religions, and nations.[191] Catholic thought envisions such communities of solidarity existing on the local, national, and global levels.[192] In short, the Catholic tradition sees solidarity as both a virtue that individuals should possess and a characteristic of institutions and social relations. Solidarity should shape various aspects of economic, political, and social life both within and among nations. While not denying the possible necessity of conflict for the sake of justice, Catholicism holds that solidarity is possible across the full spectrum of social relations.[193] In other words, the Catholic ethic of solidarity requires creating and sustaining the common good and the rights of all people on the local, national, and global levels. As *Gaudium et Spes* states, "solidarity must be continually increased until it is brought to perfection."[194]

Preferential Option for the Poor

Although the scope of solidarity is universal, CST urges a particular solidarity with the poor, oppressed, marginalized, and infirm. CST has adopted the phrase the "preferential option for the poor" to encapsulate this obligation.

The notion of a preferential option for the poor, which John Paul II incorporated into official CST in his 1987 encyclical *Sollicitudo Rei Socialis*, originated in Latin America.[195] The CELAM (Latin American Episcopal Conference) documents from Medellin (1968) and Puebla (1979) used the term, while liberation theologians Gustavo Gutierrez, Jon Sobrino, Juan Hernández Pico and Archbishop Oscar Romero popularized it in their writings and speeches.[196] The church's reading of "the signs of the times," particularly the widespread poverty in Latin America and throughout the Global South, led to embracing the option for the poor.[197]

While the phrase originated in the latter part of the twentieth century, the idea itself has roots in the Bible and throughout the history of the Christian tradition. As Gustavo Gutierrez wrote in his seminal article on the topic, the biblical texts pointing to the option for the poor are plentiful.[198] In fact, according to Evangelical theologian Ronald Sider literally hundreds of biblical verses attesting to God's special attention to the poor fill about two hundred pages.[199] Powerful writings of the Patristic era, such as those by St. Basil, St. John Chrysostom and Clement of Alexandria, strongly condemn both living a luxurious life and being indifferent to the plight of the poor, who have a right to those goods necessary to survive.[200] Pope Francis has spoken in a similar vein on numerous occasions.[201]

As John Paul II stated, the church, like the Creator, must adopt "a 'preferential,' not exclusive option" for the poor.[202] God loves all people, but just as a parent cares for an ailing child in a special way, God shows particular love for the poor, who have urgent needs. The same can be said of the church's solicitude. Looking beyond its own ecclesial boundaries, the Catholic tradition goes a step further to maintain that "the poor have the single most urgent economic claim on the conscience of the nation."[203]

Adopting a preferential option for the poor requires us to direct our consumer choices, investment of wealth, talent, and human energy toward this end. It forbids those of us who belong to the upper and middle classes from being blinded by our comfortable lifestyles to the plight of the world's poor.[204] Like solidarity, the option for the poor must also be embodied in our institutional policies and structures. Making donations or volunteering our time, while meaningful, does not fulfill the Gospel mandate to adopt the option for the poor.

Justice

The origins of modern Catholic social teaching on justice can be traced back to Aristotle, Aquinas, and later Pius XI, who added the term "social justice" to official CST. The "Social Catholics" in nineteenth-century Europe reacted against the abuses of the workers during the Industrial Revolution by urging that "it is not enough to alleviate the misery of the poor with your gifts. You must go beyond charity to justice."[205] More recently Pope Benedict XVI argued that charity and justice, which are integrally related, are equally requirements of Christian discipleship. According to the Pope,

> *Charity goes beyond justice*, because to love is to give, to offer what is "mine" to the other; but it never lacks justice, which prompts us to give the other what is "his," what is due to him by reason of his being or his acting. I cannot "give" what is mine to the other, without first giving him what pertains to him in justice. If we love others with charity, then first of all we are just towards them. Not only is justice not extraneous to charity, not only is it not an alternative or parallel path to charity: justice is inseparable from charity and intrinsic to it.[206]

Thus, in order to fulfill the command to love the neighbor, the Christian disciple must first help him or her obtain that which all human beings rightfully deserve.[207] CST elucidates this by pointing to human rights as the minimum demands of justice.[208] CST also distinguishes between commutative, distributive, and social justice. Commutative justice pertains to justice in exchanges. For example, the worker owes to his or her employer an honest day's labor, while the employer owes to his or her worker a fair wage for that labor. In Catholic thought, distributive justice requires that the resources of the society are distributed equitably, which means that although differences in wealth and income can be acceptable, at a minimum the basic needs of all persons must first be met. In addition, in accordance with the Patristic notion of the universal destination of all goods, distributive justice implies that all people have a right to those goods necessary for their own and their family's flourishing. Social justice implies that "persons have an obligation to be active participants in the life of society and that society has a duty to enable them to do so."[209] Behaviors, laws, policies, and social structures that cause the marginalization of individuals or groups violate the norm of social justice.

Participation

The right and duty of participation pervades all of the themes of Catholic social teaching.[210] Solidarity, justice, subsidiarity, and the common good aim at procuring the right to participation for all, a right that has been explicitly stressed in Catholic social teaching since the 1971 World Synod of Bishops' document *Justitia in Mundo*.[211] According to CST, the right to participation functions as the precondition of all other rights. When this right is breached, the realization of all other rights remains in jeopardy.[212] Empirical evidence shows people must be able to participate substantively in the conversations about their welfare in order to secure their rights and promote the common good.[213]

In *Justitia in Mundo* and elsewhere, Catholic social teaching has maintained that all persons have the right and duty to become "principle architects of their own economic and social development."[214] Participation in this sense entails both the right and duty of every member and numerous groups of a given society to contribute to and benefit from the common good.[215] Authentic participation contributes to true human flourishing, "the fulfillment of the self," as Karol Wojtyła put it. Human beings are meant to contribute concretely to the flourishing of the community.[216] Theologically speaking, authentic participation contributes to the building of the Kingdom of God.[217] As members of a community, exercising this right and duty requires the willingness to cooperate with others, to make compromises when necessary, and to take seriously the expertise and wisdom of others.[218] Nonetheless, the very nature and dignity of the human person mandates that those with power or "expertise" should not preclude the meaningful participation of all in the decisions that affect their lives and the good of the community.[219] The right to participation checks "top-down" decision-making.

CST specifically emphasizes that all workers have the right to participate in the operations of their workplace in a "fully human way" and to participate in wage and benefit negotiations. Economic processes, including wage and price determinations, must not take place over the heads of workers, especially the poor, whose livelihood depends on them to the largest degree. In short, the right to participation calls for decisions to be made as often as possible by the persons most directly affected by these decisions in the workplace, while also providing them the resources needed to implement these decisions.[220] Later sections of this book will spell out the implications of this teaching for Catholic higher education.[221]

A Place at the Table for All?

Thus far I have emphasized the need to embody the principles and values of CST in institutional policies of Catholic universities. I have discussed this need as a matter of the faith and moral formation of students, coherence with Catholic teaching, and an intrinsic element of evangelization and Christian discipleship. However, what I propose is also a way to promote the rights of all and the common good in higher education. It has been my experience, and continues to be my hope, that all stakeholders at Catholic universities, regardless of their religious affiliation, can find shared values that promote a vision of higher education contrary to the problematic corporatized version. CST can serve as a resource for all who wish to partake in this endeavor, and as a bulwark against the further corporatization of the university.

By its very nature, CST lends itself to building bridges with people and traditions beyond the Roman Catholic Church. In 1963 Saint John XXIII signaled a major shift in CST with his encyclical *Pacem in Terris* (Peace on Earth). Never before had a pope addressed an encyclical to "all men [sic] of goodwill." However, John XXIII used this formulation to convey his desire for cooperation among Catholics and non-Catholics alike in the urgent endeavor of peace building.[222]

Catholic social teaching shares much in common with other traditions and universal values. The UN Universal Declaration of Human Rights (UNDHR), which John Paul II deemed "one of the highest expressions of the human conscience of our time," promotes many of the same rights as CST.[223] He also affirmed "wide areas of cooperation" between the UN and the church in protecting human rights.[224] In addition, many of the world's great religions endorse these same rights, as evidenced by the 1998 Universal

Declaration of Human Rights by the World Religions.[225] Workers' rights, which the next chapter will treat, find support in Islam, Judaism, Buddhism, most major branches of Christianity, and other religions.[226] Despite differences in motivation and interpretations of particular human rights, this convergence has enabled people from many faiths and secular humanists to find common cause in the promotion of human rights throughout the world.

There is no reason why it should be any different within the confines of a Catholic college or university, where people from various backgrounds share the concern for human rights and the common good. I have witnessed Protestants, Jews, Muslims, Hindus, atheists, and agnostics support the values of CST at Catholic institutions. Given the potency and deep roots of the corporatization of the university, moving to a model of higher education oriented toward human rights and the common good will require support from a broad coalition of people. Catholic colleges and universities need a critical mass of people well versed in the Catholic tradition in order to be able to articulate, explain, and actively promote the Catholic mission and identity of the institutions.[227] However, as Christian Smith explains, a diverse faculty enables "exchange and engagement" and leads to a "fuller understanding of the truth."[228]

All faculty, staff, administrators, students, and trustees can broadly support the mission as I have conceived it here if they share core values such as transparency, respect for human dignity and rights, commitment to the common good, and a view of education that rejects corporatization and commodification and promotes human and ecological well-being. There are many allies today in the struggle for justice, solidarity, human rights, and environmental sustainability in higher education. Numerous groups, such as the American Association of University Professors (AAUP), The New Faculty Majority, The Coalition of Contingent Academic Labor (CO-CAL), the Association of American Colleges and Universities, and The Association for Sustainability in Higher Education (ASHE) espouse many of the priorities for higher education advocated in this book on the basis of Catholic social teaching. Although I cannot systematically explore their continuity with CST, later chapters will feature some of these groups.[229] Building diverse alliances around shared goals and values is crucial to the task this book advocates.

Many, if not most mission statements of Catholic universities, advert to key themes of CST, such as social justice, solidarity, and the common good. Therefore, undertaking the task I am advocating in this book is also a matter of truthfulness (or to put it in terms of the lingua franca of the corporatized university, "truth in advertising"). When these mission statements function as little more than slogans, students, faculty, and staff become jaded toward the institution. Already the 1967 Land O'Lakes statement, signed by representatives of several of the nation's most influential Catholic universities, recognized the need "to practice what we preach":

> The total organization should reflect this same Christian spirit. The social organization should be such as to emphasize the university's concern for persons as individuals and for appropriate participation by all members of the community of learners in university decisions. University decisions and administrative actions should be appropriately guided by Christian ideas and ideals and should eminently display the respect and concern for persons.[230]

If what I have argued is correct, living up to this idea of the Catholic university is a matter of institutional fidelity. It is a matter of what heroic dissidents like Václav Havel, the agnostic writer and eventual president of Czechoslovakia, and Adam Michnik, a Polish Jew and historian, called "life in truth."[231] The Polish labor priest and martyr Blessed Jerzy Popiełuszko maintained that living a life in truth meant living in accordance with one's conscience.[232] The solidarity of consciences, the deepest kind of solidarity, calls everyone to be a person of conscience.[233] For the heroes of the Velvet Revolution and Solidarność, being a person of conscience did not necessarily require explicit belief in God. However, life in truth required defending a view of the human person as one imbued with inviolable dignity and the capacity and obligation to realize freedom in solidarity with others for the common good. This shared anthropology allowed for Christians, Jews, atheists, and agnostics to unite in a common cause that respected but transcended their differences.[234]

Havel and Michnik, like many other dissidents, were tortured and jailed for years. Havel nonetheless insisted: "I am not on the side of any establishment. . . . I merely take the side of truth against lies, the side of sense against nonsense, the side of justice against injustice."[235] Michnik regretted that many Poles supported the Communist regime out of fear. However, with the rise of Solidarity, Poles began to "spit out the gag" by expressing their opposition. No longer would they live a lie, which, according to Michnik, "establish[es] all of one's relations with other people as relations based on pretence."[236] Popiełuszko paid for his commitment to truth with his life. He had insisted that preserving one's own human dignity required standing by "the truth in all situations in life . . . even if this is going to cost us dearly."[237] Lying causes the human person to become "a slave" and "debases" human dignity. Popiełuszko, like John Paul II, believed that human freedom is attained above all by living in accordance with the truth.[238] In the US context, Black freedom fighters like Dr. Martin Luther King Jr. and Malcolm X held similar views. King, for example, stated that a person "dies when he [sic] refuses to take a stand for that which is true."[239] Like King, Malcolm X's unwavering pursuit of truth led to his death. Shortly before his demise, he penned words worthy of pondering today: "I've had enough of someone else's propaganda. . . . I'm for truth, no matter who tells it. I'm for justice, no matter who it is for or against."[240] Elizabeth Cady Stanton also affirmed the relationship between truth, dignity, and life itself. In her words, "The moment we begin to fear the opinions of others and hesitate to tell the truth that is in us, and from motives of policy are silent when we should speak, the divine floods of light and life no longer flow into our souls."[241]

Put another way, living a lie constitutes living an inauthentic life. Charles Taylor notes that the notion of authenticity resonates today because of the emphasis on self-fulfillment and being true to oneself in our time. However, Taylor contends that authenticity requires transcending the self and fostering solidarity with others. His point echoes CST's call to solidarity as a means of self-fulfillment, as well as Havel's insistence on commitment to something greater than—transcendent to—ourselves:

> The agent seeking significance in life, trying to define him or herself meaningfully, has to exist in a horizon of important questions. . . . Only if I exist in a world in which history, or the demands of nature, or the needs of my fellow human beings, or the duties of citizenship, or the call of God, or something else of this order matters crucially, can I define an identity for myself that is not trivial. Authenticity is not the enemy of demands that emanate from beyond the self; it supposes such demands.[242]

The context of the corporatized university may not be as menacing as what Havel, Michnik, Popiełuszko faced in Communist Eastern Europe or what King, Malcolm X, or Cady Stanton confronted in their racist, misogynistic society. Nonetheless, their words and witness serve as a lodestar. Living in truth at Catholic colleges and universities requires all to commit themselves to the basic values of the institution's mission. It is a matter of authenticity. As I have stressed, many members of Catholic higher educational communities willingly and admirably promote the values of CST. On the other hand, many have chosen to attend or to work at Catholic colleges and universities for reasons that have nothing to do with the university's task to promote solidarity, human rights, and the common good.[243] However, when we at Catholic institutions fail to try to support the basic values of the university's mission, we resemble the shopkeeper in Havel's famous work, *The Power of the Powerless*, who displays a sign from the Communist Party in his window solely because he wants to maintain his relatively comfortable life.[244] All members of a Catholic higher educational community—regardless of their religious affiliation—should search their consciences and stand up for the values of the university's mission that they can in good faith promote, rather than remain in their silos or become "gated intellectuals." They should "spit out the gag" by denouncing the corporatized university as anathema and by calling for a university that actualizes the vision of social life proffered by CST. They should defend the notion that the raison d'être of higher education is to promote the "whole development of the person" and the common good.[245] While this may require sacrifice, it will ultimately be rewarding. As Michnik maintained, "you score a victory not when you win power but when you remain faithful to yourself."[246] Those who believe that higher education should be marked by cutthroat competition, bottom-line thinking harmful to people or the planet, elitism, conspicuous consumption, and market-driven rewards and punishments ought to consider whether their conscience allows them to work at a Catholic college or university.[247] We must also be aware, as Keri Day warns, that to be a "witness to truth" in the present moment challenges us because "neoliberal forces breed a sense of apathy and inefficacy in us that we can transform broader society."[248]

Christians working in the academy must not "check their discipleship" at the entrance gate to the university. In this connection, it is worth recalling Vatican II's exhortation to overcome the "split between the faith which many profess and their daily lives," which is "among the more serious errors of our age."[249] Popiełuszko put the matter starkly: "You will not preserve your full dignity by carrying around the rosary in one pocket and a little book of totally contrary ideology in the other. You cannot, at one and the same time, serve God and Mammon . . . you have to make a choice."[250] Christians are thus always obliged to ask, in accordance with Jesus's command to love the neighbor, who are the people "lying on the road" in our midst (see Lk. 10:25–38)? They must contemplate how to act analogously to the Samaritan in the context of corporatized higher education.[251] Discipleship, which may entail personal cost to those who challenge the entrenched bureaucracy of corporatized universities, requires overturning "power structures in . . . our communities, as well as an equitable distribution of resources and fuller participation in communal life."[252] Discipleship demands "faithfulness" to the Gospel, not focusing on "success."[253] In other words, Christian disciples must be ready to fail in the face of resistance to the Gospel, while striving to embody "Jesus' way as concrete and specific guidance to be followed" rather than a "vague ideal or principle . . . or teaching ideals too high to actually put into practice."[254]

Traversing the trail from the modern corporatized university will be steep and treacherous at times, but CST provides clear guidance along this path. Implementing CST in their policies and practices might also make Catholic colleges and universities more competitive. For example, they might be in a better position to appeal to potential students and donors who wish to support egalitarianism and social justice. Institutions such as Berea College have been able to connect with benefactors who want to support its mission to provide high quality education for the economically disadvantaged. Catholic universities, on the other hand, have done a relatively poor job of soliciting gifts exclusively for the purpose of promoting the values and principles of Catholic social teaching on our campuses. Embodying the vision of Catholic social teaching is challenging and costly, particularly at this time of financial uncertainty for many institutions. Yet, there is greater potential for Catholic universities to focus on their mission, and real risks to failing to try. As the Carnegie Council study "Three Thousand Futures" augured, only "those universities that have a well-defined and well implemented sense of identity will survive and thrive."[255]

Having elaborated the context and rationale for my analysis, I will now turn to issues that require sustained efforts in order to pursue our mission as Catholic institutions in good faith.

2 Embodying Solidarity on Catholic Campuses: The Case of Worker Justice

Years ago I had a conversation with a colleague that changed the direction of my research and writing. At some point this colleague and I started to confide in each other about our successes, failures, hopes, and struggles in our work. He shared with me the incredibly painful story of his family life and career over the last decade. He and his family had come to the United States in order for him to pursue a doctorate in religious studies. He taught for ten years at a Catholic university as an adjunct, and later as a one-year nontenure-track appointee while completing his doctoral dissertation. During this time, his child became very ill. The child needed to be hospitalized for an extensive period of time and required lengthy follow-up care. As a doctoral candidate and adjunct faculty member he could not afford to buy health insurance for his family. Because they could not afford to pay for the expensive care without insurance, he and his family made a very difficult decision. My friend would remain in the United States to pursue his dream of a doctorate and subsequent tenure-track position, while his wife and child would return to their native land to obtain the long-term care that they needed.

As if this situation were not already horrendous, my colleague was told the university could no longer offer him employment. After toiling for so many years, and becoming an excellent teacher in the process, he was replaced by a freshly minted PhD candidate who had already published more than he had. Unlike this candidate (and me), my friend did not have the luxury of publishing articles as a fully funded graduate student without major teaching responsibilities. All of his time was consumed by teaching four or five courses per semester, writing his dissertation, and being a father and husband. Thus, in spite of his dedication to his students, success in the classroom, and imminent dissertation defense, he was essentially told he was expendable. This situation transpired at a *Catholic* university, a place where the rights of the worker should be respected and his or her family should be treated as the "first and vital cell of society."[1]

During my fifteen years in the academy I have befriended a number of adjunct faculty members. One colleague talked of his health problems and the fact that he desperately needed dental work that he could not afford to have done. Others described the harried and chaotic lifestyle dictated by their situation, moving constantly between one university and another, trying to find enough courses to teach in order to survive financially. Cognizant of their stories, I would move to and from my own Christian ethics classes, discussing with my students solidarity, human rights, and the option for the poor in Catholic social teaching. I was, and continue to be, acutely aware of the contradiction. Some of my students understood this as well. The majority, however, had no idea that many adjuncts make poverty wages (as I shall discuss below). Many students have done excellent work promoting justice for workers in their university's supply chains by demanding that their university apparel come from suppliers who respect workers' rights. Often at the urging of students, Catholic universities have affiliated with the Worker Rights Consortium toward this end.[2] But what about those who serve students their food, maintain their dormitories, and teach their classes as adjuncts? Many students, parents, and alumni do not know that US higher education employs a two-class system of educators. Even if many people in Catholic institutions of higher learning turn a blind eye to the plight of contingent faculty, the dire situation of these employees has become harder to ignore. Individual cases of destitution and suffering have increasingly caught the attention of the media. For example, the story of a twenty-five-year teaching veteran at Duquesne University, who lost her battle with cancer and died in poverty after being terminated by her employer, made headlines.[3] The personal narratives of adjuncts who must rely on food stamps and Medicaid to support themselves and their families in spite of their hard-earned PhDs have also found their way into *The Chronicle of Higher Education*, NPR, *PBS Newshour*, and other popular outlets.[4] News of adjuncts in the US living in cars or being homeless has even reached other countries.[5] Groups such as New Faculty Majority, The Coalition of Contingent Academic Labor, and the Coalition on the Academic Workforce have shined a light on the situation by providing access to personal stories, pertinent data, and organizing and advocacy strategies.[6] Some students on Catholic campuses and elsewhere have begun to take notice, to issue protest letters, and to participate in National Adjunct Walkout Day.[7]

What may perhaps be described as a new university subculture has even arisen. As Marc Bousquet writes in *How the University Works: Higher Education and the Low-Wage Nation*, "the plays, films, testimony, and propaganda of contingent faculty are components of a faculty culture in transition."[8] Contingent faculty have produced creative protest works of art such as Linda Jankos's film *Teachers on Wheels*, John Kloss's pointed cartoons, anthologies such as Michael Dubson's *Ghosts in the Classroom*, and the blog *Invisible Adjunct*.[9] Even the United States House of Representatives has taken notice, issuing a report in January 2014 called "The Just-In-Time Professor."[10] As executive director of New Faculty Majority Maria Maisto states, "the steep costs of contingency are now in full view."[11]

This chapter examines the situation of contingent faculty in the light of Catholic social teaching. Contingent faculty include part-time adjuncts, full-time, nontenure-track faculty, postdoctoral teaching fellows, and graduate assistants. While there are certainly differences in the situations of these types of faculty members, they all face many of the same struggles associated with the casualization of the academic workforce. In this chapter, I focus mainly on adjunct faculty, as they are the largest group of contingent faculty and face the direst circumstances. I use the terms "adjunct" and "part-time" interchangeably because they widely operate this way in the academy. However, I agree with the AAUP and others that these terms are problematic. The work of this group of university professors is anything but peripheral to higher education today.[12] Many who are considered part-time by the universities spend as many if not more hours on teaching than professors considered full-time, who often do more research than teaching.

I will appeal to the notions of solidarity, justice, the option for the poor, the common good, and the workers' rights tradition of CST to evaluate the adjunct situation. After describing the situation on the ground, I argue that complicity in the unjust treatment of adjuncts at Catholic universities glaringly violates CST. Moreover, perpetuating this situation by appealing to its purported inevitability, budgetary constraints, or the excuse that "everybody else is doing it" seriously undercuts the mission of Catholic institutions of higher learning.[13]

While this chapter focuses mainly on contingent faculty, highlighting the situation of adjuncts in particular, many of the arguments apply to

other groups of workers on Catholic campuses. Many custodians, food service workers, security personnel, groundskeepers, and others face low
wages, outsourcing, union busting, and cuts to benefits.[14] I do not wish to
imply here that their situation is any less important or dire. I emphasize
the plight of adjuncts for several reasons. First, academicians at Catholic
colleges, like me, have a particular obligation to fight for justice alongside
adjuncts because we directly benefit from their unjust situation. As Jan
Clausen and Eva-Maria Swidler correctly put it, "Unfortunately, it is not
simply that you, tenured person, enjoy a degree of freedom that I do not
(but which might theoretically be extended to me); instead, your low
teaching load and routine participation in the ritual remnants of shared
governance are afforded through my exploitation and exclusion from the
'normal' process. The structural constraints that may be, at best, theoretically visible to you are engraved on my psyche, my scholarship, and my
daily teaching schedule."[15] Unfortunately, "isolationism and a lack of solidarity" has led most full-time faculty to turn a blind eye to the situation
of adjunct faculty, who labor "almost as indentured servants," according
to Catholic ethicist James F. Keenan, SJ.[16]

In addition, Catholic institutions of higher education have more stal-
wartly resisted the unionization of adjuncts than other types of employees. Many of the Catholic universities currently engaging in union busting
against adjuncts trying to organize have accepted unionized workers in
other sectors on their campuses. In my estimation, administrators believe
that paying adjuncts what they rightly deserve vis-à-vis their tenure-track
faculty counterparts will cost universities much more than paying other
employees a living wage.[17] Some administrators view unions as hostile
"outsiders," as I will discuss. Furthermore, a persistent culture of disbe-
lief at universities regarding the adjunct situation may also have stalled
movement on the issue. Although the treatment of adjuncts is clearly the
"elephant in the room," as I shall demonstrate, tenure-track faculty and
administrators often cannot fathom that those who hold master's or doctoral degrees could possibly be poor or marginalized. Eager to believe in
the meritocracy of the academy, they consciously or subconsciously fault
adjuncts for not excelling enough to earn a tenure-track post.[18] After all,
for academics the doctoral degree confers status and a certain kind of
power in the academy, or so some faculty still imagine. However, as Bousquet and others have written, that power has been eviscerated in the

modern corporatized university (see Chapter 1 and below), especially among contingent faculty. Finally, many tenure-track faculty, now a minority on many of our campuses, who are aware of the adjuncts' plight do not want to cede whatever power and financial security that remains to them. Rather than fight alongside adjuncts for their cause, they prefer to protect their own welfare.[19]

The Situation on the Ground on Our Campuses

In an open letter to Catholic colleges and universities, 135 Catholic scholars, including eight past presidents of the Catholic Theological Society of America, declared that many adjunct professors today rank among the poor and vulnerable in our society.[20] Unfortunately, empirical data and myriad personal anecdotes verify this claim, even if some adjuncts do not suffer from an exploitative situation. The treatment of adjunct faculty at Catholic universities often violates the *preferential option for the poor*. These principles demand that university budgetary decisions must place the rights of the poor first.[21]

Although some adjuncts have additional salaried jobs outside academe, approximately 75 percent do not.[22] Most contingent faculty members view teaching as their profession. They work years and sometimes decades plying their trade.[23] Former AAUP president Cary Nelson and his coauthor Stephen Watt deem the casualization of the academic workforce the single "most serious problem in higher education."[24] Furthermore, "adjunctification" did not arise by happenstance.[25] Rather, it has been the cornerstone of the strategic corporatization of the university.[26] In 1969 more than three quarters of all college professors held tenure-track positions.[27] As of 2015, only 14 percent of professors hold tenure.[28] According to AAUP data, 71 percent of all college instructors are contingent faculty: 40 percent part-time or adjunct faculty members; 17 percent full-time nontenure-track faculty members; and 14 percent graduate student employees. From 1976–2011 part-time and full-time, nontenure-track faculty jobs ballooned by 286 percent and 259 percent respectively.[29] As I will discuss in more detail in Chapters 5 and 6, minoritized faculty and women are disproportionately affected by adjunctification.

The national median adjunct pay for a three credit course in 2010 was $2,700.[30] A more recent estimate is $2,923.[31] Nonunionized adjuncts generally earn less than their unionized counterparts. In 2010 the union wage premium was about $600 per course.[32] In some recent cases the union wage premium was much more substantial.[33] Disparities in pay also depend on discipline, geography, and race. For example, engineering instructors' median pay per course was almost $2,000 more than instructors of developmental education courses. According to the Coalition on the Academic Workforce, a negligible gender-based pay disparity exists among adjuncts, but "part-time faculty respondents who identified themselves as Black (not of Hispanic origin) earn significantly less than other racial and ethnic groups at a median per-course pay of $2,083 (table 31). By comparison, median pay ranged from $2,500 per course for Hispanic or Latino/a or multiracial respondents to $2,925 for Asian or Pacific Islander respondents."[34]

The annual pay of adjunct faculty puts them in or "on the edge of poverty" according to the House Committee on Education and Labor study. Respondents typically reported earnings from $15–$20,000.[35] The AAUP observed that in 2016–17 the average total pay from a single institution for part-time faculty teaching on a per-section basis is $7,066. This pay is "well below the federal poverty line for a family of two" of $16,240. A part-time professor working on a per-section basis teaching six courses at two different institutions would garner earnings "near the poverty line" according to the AAUP. In the same year, the average pay for full-time professors across all ranks was $80,895, with full-time assistant professors earning on average $69,206.[36] Other data indicate that 31 percent of part-time faculty live near or below the federal poverty line.[37] A recent study from the UC Berkeley Center for Labor Research reports that 25 percent of all part-time professors receive Medicaid and/or food stamps.[38] From 2007–10 alone, the number of PhD holders receiving food stamps and/or other kinds of federal aid more than tripled.[39] Compounding the problem, most adjuncts do not receive health care and retirement benefits from their employer, and the cost of purchasing is too prohibitive on an adjunct's salary.[40] Clearly many adjuncts are among the "hyper-educated poor."[41]

Reliance on adjuncts varies at Catholic colleges and universities, but these institutions generally reflect the larger national trends. Many Catholic institutions now have more part-time than full-time faculty members.[42] Adjuncts at numerous Catholic institutions have publicly denounced their working conditions. Among others, part-time faculty members at Duquesne University, Loyola Marymount University, Manhattan College, Loyola University Chicago, Gonzaga University, Seattle University, Saint Joseph's University, Georgetown University, Notre Dame de Namur University, and Fordham University have expressed their desire for just pay, health benefits, access to resources such as office space, and real representation in shared governance.[43] As I will discuss below, some institutions have reached agreements relatively amicably with their adjunct faculty members, while others have engaged in protracted and sometimes acrimonious disputes with them. Some Catholic universities have attempted to thwart the efforts of adjuncts to unionize. These adjuncts have turned to unions because they feel that their universities' administrators have not addressed their concerns. They also lament that their treatment, which often includes lack of resources such as office space to meet students, lack of adequate notice to prepare for a course, and time deficits due to the need to teach at multiple institutions negatively impacts student learning.[44] Information concerning the pay of part-time faculty at Catholic institutions is hard to obtain. According to AAUP data, religiously-affiliated institutions pay adjuncts teaching on a per section basis almost $2000 less on average than the annual pay for private independent institutions.[45] This data does not tell us anything about Catholic institutions specifically. The only data publicly available for Catholic institutions is self-reported to *The Chronicle of Higher Education* database. While this data does not yield definitive conclusions, it does create the impression that Catholic institutions pay adjuncts similarly to other types of institutions and exhibit large variations among themselves. Table 1 notes the lowest self-reported pay per course and the highest at the sample institutions. I have excluded entries from adjuncts at law schools at these institutions.

To reiterate, this data is limited. More transparency and discussion are needed about adjunct pay at Catholic institutions. In addition to being a small sample, most of the entries come from between 2013 and 2015. Even though this data set is incomplete, it can still be useful. In particular, underlining the lowest part-time professor pay per course reveals how the worst compensated adjuncts are faring. In addition to the pay scale, some adjuncts at these sample institutions also provided comments about their situation. Although some are positive, others bespeak a pattern of

Table 1. Self-Reported Adjunct Pay per Course at Selected Catholic Institutions

U. of San Diego	$5,000–5,250	Duquesne U.	$2,600–4,200
Santa Clara U.	$4,725–7,000	St. John's U. (Minn.)	$1,500–4,000
Georgetown U.	$4000–8,500	Marquette U.	$3,000–$4,500
Fairfield U.	$3,840–4,595	U. of St. Thomas (Minn.)	$3,000–5,500
Fordham U.	$3,700–5,067	Seattle University	$2,580–4,000
Villanova U.	$3,175–5,010	Regis U. (Colo.)	$2,200–3,225
DePaul U.	$3,000–$6,000	Marymount U. (Va.)	$2,400–2,900
Saint Joseph's U. (Pa.)	$3,000–$4,440	Benedictine U. (Ill.)	$2,252
Boston College	$3,500–7,000	Ursuline College (Ohio)	$2,000–2,050
Merrimack College	$2,650–3,500	U. of Dallas	$2,000–2,500

Source: *The Chronicle of Higher Education* database at https://data.chronicle.com/

exclusion, exploitation, and a feeling of being a second-class citizen. While there are some exceptions, Catholic institutions generally have relied on adjuncts to carry a heavy burden and have treated them much like their counterparts at secular institutions.

Exploitation and Injustice Have Many Faces on Campus

Abysmal, unjust salaries and lack of access to affordable health care are not the only kinds of injustice that adjuncts face. They encounter various other kinds of marginalization. Adjunct faculty often do not even have shared office space, a telephone, photocopying privileges, and access to teaching materials at the university, all of which are needed to fulfill the job.[46] They must wander transiently from university to university to make ends meet, often spending hours commuting. Like temp workers, they are often hired "just in time," leaving little or no time to prepare syllabi and to gather course materials.[47] In addition, adjunct faculty have little to no say in curriculum development or university governance. They are often not permitted to attend departmental meetings where important decisions are made that affect them.[48] Their pictures, bios, and credentials seldom adorn university web pages, as only tenure-track faculty make the cut. In other words, they often have no voice and their presence in the community is limited. Furthermore, contingent faculty usually do not enjoy the protection of academic freedom, which traditionally has empowered tenure-track professors to present uncomfortable truths to their students, the University community, and broader society. They therefore report feeling more vulnerable to resentment and retaliation.[49]

I have repeatedly learned from my students that most of them assume that all faculty members are treated and paid equally. Although some tenure-track faculty and administrators try to form relationships of solidarity with adjuncts, some in those privileged positions refuse to refer to them as faculty.[50] I witnessed an administrator publicly excoriate a contingent faculty member for using the title professor, stating "You are just an adjunct." More often I have observed subtle ways of not acknowledging the worth and dignity of adjunct colleagues.

It is no wonder that some contingent faculty have sensed that they are either "homeless," invisible, disposable, or subhuman in the eyes of others around the university.[51]

This excerpt from Michael Dubson's essay "I am an Adjunct" in *Ghosts in the Classroom* expresses this sentiment poignantly:

> I am an adjunct. . . . I bought the bag of lies we called the American dream. I was intoxicated on the Nitrous Oxide idealism forced upon me in graduate school. I believed caring, working hard, doing a good job mattered, and would add up to something concrete. Instead, I find myself on a wheel that turns but goes nowhere. I don't expect this situation to change. I know I have joined the huge group of teachers who become permanent adjuncts, who do a good job only to get one more chance to do it again. . . . I have watched my self-esteem drop, drop, drop from doing good work that is, theoretically, enhancing the self-esteem of my students. I have seen the tired eyes, the worn clothes, the ancient eyes of long-term adjuncts. I have looked into their eyes as they have failed to look back into mine. . . . I've watched people fall into obsessive relationships with their idealism in their pedagogy because it is the one defense against despair. . . . I am a dreamer. I am an idealist. I am a victim. I am a whore. I am a fool. I am an adjunct.[52]

One recent study concludes that the higher levels of "workplace stressors" and "anxiety, depression and stress" experienced by dedicated nontenure-track faculty harm not only the faculty themselves but the institution as well.[53] The detrimental effect on learning outcomes, retention rates, and student graduation has been documented.[54] Some observers of the situation have highlighted the negative images that contingent faculty have absorbed, mainly from administrators and full-time faculty. However, others point to the "refusal to succumb to inferiority complexes" and successful empowerment and "self-advocacy" of contingent faculty. In other words, while many adjuncts experience the despair that Dubson describes, others have been standing tall and fighting back.[55] Regardless of these divergent responses by the faculty to their plight, their situation is properly called exploitation.

Exploitation occurs when human beings cause "needless suffering" to other human beings, as the philosopher of Poland's Solidarność movement, Fr. Józef Tischner maintained. What Tischner calls the "moral exploitation of work" takes place when workers find themselves in "a situation of some sort of untruth." The natural "dialogue" between workers and employers breaks down, which means "the work contract has not borne reciprocity."[56] Tischner's concept of exploitation reminds us of the ancient notion of commutative justice, adopted by modern CST, which holds that each participant in an exchange should be given their due.[57] When this does not occur, exploitation "causes a pain similar to that inflicted by a lie or by treachery. Exploitation is a form of betrayal to humankind. The exploited person feels like a betrayed person – and has every right to feel this way."[58] Tischner explicitly refers to unjust compensation as this type of exploitation and a form of betrayal.

Adjunct colleagues undertook graduate studies with the hope and expectation that they would be able to follow their passion, fulfill their vocation, and earn a decent living. However, corporatized colleges and universities have created a mirage that masks gross injustice by constructing shiny new academic buildings, luxury student apartments, and expensive athletic and recreation facilities while operating like sweatshops.[59] The situation resembles what John Paul II deemed the "proletarianization" of the professoriate in 1981. Although the pontiff may have penned these words primarily to describe the situation of labor in Communist countries like his native Poland, he also presciently described the situation that many aspiring higher education professionals face today:

Movements of solidarity in the sphere of work-a solidarity that must never mean being closed to dialogue and collaboration with others-can be necessary also with reference to the condition of social groups that were not previously included in such movements but which, in changing social systems and conditions of living, are undergoing *what is in effect "proletarianization"* or which actually already find themselves in a "proletariat" situation, one which, even if not yet given that name, in fact deserves it. This can be true of certain categories or groups of the working "intelligentsia," especially when ever wider access to education and an ever increasing number of people with degrees or diplomas in the fields of their cultural preparation are accompanied by a drop in demand for their labour . . . or when it is less well paid.[60]

Many higher education "insiders" and observers have argued that this form of proletarianization, i.e., adjunctification, is inevitable given the exorbitant cost of tuition. However, that argument may not bear scrutiny.

A Matter of Priorities

Since the 1970s, the rise of the "lumpen professoriate," a "super exploited core of disposable workers" that carries out most undergraduate teaching, did not occur because of decreasing demand for higher education.[61] Apart from the few years after the 2008 financial crisis, demand for higher education has not waned.[62] Steve Shulman, professor of economics and research director for the Center for the Study of Academic Labor at Colorado State University, argues that higher education, unlike most sectors, has inelastic demand. He points out that from 2007 to 2014 total enrollments grew by 15.3 percent. Shulman also contends that "colleges and universities often claim that they are unable to afford certain expenditures when they simply are choosing other expenditures instead. The problem is not their overall financial capacity so much as it is their priorities."[63] In other words, the massive rise in part-time positions and the concurrent decline in full-time posts—the primary reason for the impoverishment of university faculty—did not happen due to financial exigency or an oversupply of academics. As Marc Bousquet has pointed out, the putative "surplus" of doctoral degree holders could be completely eliminated by returning to the 1972 proportion of tenure-track to nontenure-track faculty in just one large state such as New York or California.[64] However, it is much cheaper to pay contingent faculty to teach students than full-time faculty. Bousquet notes that some administrators have willingly embraced exploiting contingent faculty as a cost cutting mechanism.[65] Budget models such as Responsibility Centered Management, or RCM, "create powerful incentives" to employ much cheaper labor as academic units (colleges and departments) can generate more revenue from tuition.[66] In short, employment as a university professor once provided a path to financial stability in the US. Today it often leads to a treacherous path toward poverty. There are certainly colleges and universities that face economic hardship, and a few may have to close each year.[67] However, it is hard to argue that higher education as a whole cannot afford to compensate part-time faculty better, as Shulman demonstrates.[68]

As they have struggled to survive, many part-time faculty have simultaneously watched athletics budgets at their universities skyrocket. According to a report by the Delta Cost Project, spending on athletics has increased twice as fast as spending on academics at NCAA Division I public universities. Large coaching salaries, state-of-the-art facilities, and scholarship aid for student-athletes constitute the bulk of these costs. Institutions spend three to six times more per student-athlete than on the average student's instructional costs.[69] Even Division III schools without football increased spending by 112 percent from 2003–2004 to 2011–12.[70] Meanwhile universities decreased their spending on libraries from 3.7 percent to 1.8 percent of their operating budgets between 1982 and 2012.[71]

Coaches are often the highest paid employees at the university, sometimes in the entire state in the case of public universities.[72] From 2005–2006 to 2011–12 the median Division I-A basketball coach's salary increased by more than 100 percent, while full professors at doctoral institutions saw a 4 percent increase over the same period. Coaches in many other sports earned much higher percentage increases than full professors.[73] The average pay of men's basketball coaches in the NCAA tournament surpasses $1.7 million, while the average pay of all NCAA sports coaches is $800,000.[74] Average salaries for assistant coaches often surpass those of adjunct faculty and sometimes those of assistant professors' starting salaries.[75] Travel expenses and athletics scholarships each cost in the millions, adding to the high cost of sports.[76]

According to research done by the Center for College Affordability and Productivity, the benefits to universities for their massive outlays on athletics appear to be limited at best. Only a handful of elite athletics programs, all in the Division I Football Subdivision, actually bring in more revenue than they spend. Most universities have a net loss of millions of dollars each year on athletics.[77] For example, in 2012 only twenty-three athletics programs out of more than 1,000 member institutions of the NCAA generated surplus revenue. All twenty-three institutions were division 1A. Even after including revenue from individual donors and corporate sponsors, television and radio broadcasting contracts, ticket sales and all other sources, "the institutional subsidy in 2012 accounted for 27.5 percent of the athletics program budget in D1-A, 73.0 percent in D1-AA, and 81.7 percent in D1-AAA."[78] All students, not just athletes, often pay athletics fees in order to fund these subsidies. These fees sometimes exceed $1,500.[79] The *Chronicle of Higher Education*'s investigation of the "athletics arms race" concluded that from 2010 to 2015 "public universities pumped more than $10.3 billion in mandatory student fees and other subsidies into their sports programs."[80]

Furthermore, there is no conclusive evidence that the majority of prospective students greatly value an institution's athletics program when deciding whether or not to attend. In fact, a New America Foundation 2015 study revealed that only 4 percent of prospective students listed "athletics or sports teams" as the most important factor for choosing a college. Cost (63 percent), majors and minors offered (56 percent), and availability of financial aid (49 percent) were the three most frequently cited reasons. Only 23 percent stated that athletics or sports programs were very important (8 percent) or important (15 percent), ranking last among fourteen possible factors.[81] Research also shows that bumps in applications following successful seasons are minimal and ephemeral at best. It is also not clear that more applications translate to more or "higher quality" enrollments.[82] In addition, the "free advertising" that intercollegiate athletics garner is an inefficient way to spend money. Universities could directly buy advertising more cheaply.[83] Moreover, while sports can certainly have a salubrious effect on its participants, an overemphasis on athletics may exacerbate the "beer and circus" culture on many campuses to the detriment of deep learning.[84] Elka Peterson-Horner and Rick Eckstein contend that the evidence that intercollegiate sports benefits its participants is perhaps exaggerated and that diverting resources from academic spending "reflect[s] a commercialized and corporatized 'neoliberal' university, where branding, marketing, and profit maximization trump educational substance."[85] Eckstein has also written about how "commercialized and commodified" intercollegiate sports are harming young people by "driving the problematic youth sports pay-to-play pipelines." These "pipelines" pressure parents and their children to pay tremendous financial, physical, and psychological costs in their quest for the elusive athletics scholarship, which only one third of collegiate athletes obtain, with a majority of those receiving partial scholarships. In this vein, Eckstein describes "a higher-education led betrayal of childhood fun" in sports.[86] For all of these reasons, trimming athletics budgets should be considered as a source of revenue for nontenure-track faculty compensation and a mission-driven imperative.[87]

To be clear, this is not a jeremiad against college athletes, who many people feel are commodified and exploited by universities seeking notoriety and lucrative television contracts.[88] As I mentioned in the introduction, I was a recruited athlete who participated in a varsity sport for four years, as was my brother. My brother and I grew as human beings, formed transformative relationships, and learned tremendous life lessons thanks to high school and intercollegiate rowing (which we did despite our working-class background).[89] I understand the value of sports, and do not call for their abolishment from universities. I am merely arguing that expenditures on athletics facilities and coaches' salaries, for example, must be considered in the context of CST and the impoverishment of many campus workers, including adjuncts.

I also lament that intercollegiate sports are now much more thoroughly commercialized and commodified than when I participated in the 1990s, as I will discuss later in this book. Sports should be a form of enjoyment, camaraderie, and one means among others to promote physical and mental well-being, not a high-stakes industry.[90] The "athletics arms race" that prods universities to build ever bigger and more expensive facilities saps resources that could be spent on ensuring all campus workers are paid a living wage. In this vein, Fr. Bill Miscamble decries the $400 million Campus Crossroads project at Notre Dame, which includes academic buildings but actually demonstrates "the subjection of the academic mission of the university to the needs of the all-powerful axis of athletics and development." In his view, the main purpose is "to gain 4,000 luxury or premium seats in the stadium."[91] Georgetown's new John R. Thompson Jr. Intercollegiate Athletics Center cost $60 million and has been described by a former Georgetown basketball player as "better than some pro facilities."[92] Villanova recently spent $65 million to upgrade its basketball arena, which was paid for by donations.[93] More and more Catholic institutions are heavily spending on athletics facilities, not just the powerhouses like Notre Dame, Georgetown, and Villanova. For example, Duquesne University announced a $45 million renovation to its basketball arena in 2018.[94] At Loyola University Chicago, students protested against the use of $2 million in tuition revenue toward a new $18.5 million athletics facility.[95]

Although in some cases funding for such state-of-the-art facilities might come from private donors, money is often siphoned away from academic and mission-related priorities at many institutions.[96] Furthermore, Catholic universities that spend tens of millions on athletics facilities while not paying a living wage convey a message inconsistent with CST to students, faculty, staff, alumni, and the world. The message is that the university community prioritizes sports entertainment over the basic rights and dignity of all human beings. I am not suggesting that all donations toward athletics are immoral (though some may be, depending on the source, as I discuss elsewhere in this book). However, from the standpoint of CST, it would be worth asking donors to contribute to a fund to enable paying a living wage to all employees of the university. To reiterate, CST requires that everyone's basic needs are met prior to devoting resources to nonessential goods. As St. John Paul II once stated, just as Jesus told Zaccheus (Lk 19:1–10) to come down and follow him "today," the basic rights of the poor cannot be put on hold until tomorrow.[97]

Moreover, principles such as the preferential option for the poor and solidarity require examining all areas of university budgets, not just athletics, to find potential sources of revenue needed to meet the basic needs of all employees on campus. For example, if an institution truly cannot afford to pay its adjunct faculty better, it is reasonable to ask if tenure-track faculty must attend conferences every year, which can cost well over $1,000 annually per faculty member. Attending conferences is an important form of continuing education for faculty, enabling them to keep abreast of the latest developments in their field and bring them back to the classroom. However, CST holds that basic rights, such as the right to healthcare, adequate nutrition, and a living wage, trump other kinds of desired goods. All members of the community must be willing to make sacrifices so that the basic needs of everyone can be met.[98] Nonbasic expenditures can be gradually reintroduced after basic needs have been addressed.

In this connection, the rapid growth in administrative costs must also be examined. As I mentioned in Chapter 1, growth in administrative posts exponentially outpaced the growth in full-time faculty positions. A massive shift in financial expenditures at universities occurred, moving salary dollars away from full-time faculty toward nonfaculty employees. From 1978–79 to 2013–14 median salaries of presidents at private universities grew by 171 percent above the rate of inflation. The average salary of chief business officers and chief academic officers increased by more than 125 percent and 100 percent respectively. During the same period the salaries of professors at all ranks grew by 50 percent or less.[99] As of 2016–17, the average salary for presidents at religiously affiliated institutions was three times more than that of full professors.[100] In 2015 fifty-eight college presidents earned over 1 million dollars, including deferred compensation and bonuses.[101] Some universities pay top administrators 20 to 30 times the pay of an adjunct, and sometimes pay coaches as much as 100 times more than adjuncts.[102]

Athletics coaches and high-ranking administrators at Catholic institutions often make salaries well beyond the highest paid full-professor, to say nothing of adjunct professors (Tables 2 and 3).

The salaries of Boston College personnel are not listed in the tables because the president's reported income is zero, as his salary is remitted to his religious order. However, the football coach made $2,514,859, and the basketball coach made $1,463,235 in 2018, according to USA Today's NCAA Coaches' Salaries database.[103] Villanova University paid its basketball coach $2,585,041 in 2018.[104] Notre Dame paid its football and basketball coaches $2,129,638 and $1,227,910 respectively in 2018.[105] Many of the top earners at Boston College and Notre Dame in the most recently reported years in The Chronicle of Higher Education database are athletics personnel.[106] Even schools that are not athletics powerhouses dream of success in sport, and pay for its pursuit. For example, in 2011 Marquette's three highest earners were athletics personnel.[107] Saint John's University paid its basketball coach almost $2 million in 2011.[108] In the same year, head coaches at Seton Hall, Gonzaga, and Creighton earned about 1 million dollars.[109] Many other Catholic institutions paid coaches almost

Table 2. Compensation of Catholic University Presidents and Next-Highest-Paid Employee in 2011

Institution	Total Annual President's Compensation	Next-Highest-Paid Employee	Total Annual Compensation
Georgetown U.	$851,317	Men's Basketball Coach	$2,656,796
DePaul U.	$833,306	Men's Basketball Coach	$2,274,592
U. of St. Thomas (Minn.)	$762,100	Dean, Law School	$393,135
U. of Notre Dame	$746,401	Vice President/CIO	$2,667,713
U. of the Incarnate Word	$691,514	VP for Finance and Tech	$273,301
Saint Leo University	$627,344	Vice President	$252,930
Bellarmine U.	$611,539	Provost	$217,030
Duquesne U.	$609,293	Men's Basketball Coach	$448,844
Sacred Heart University	$601,910	Former Pres./ Professor	$530,356
Univ. of Dayton	$566,608	Dean, Law	$516,586
University of San Diego	$528,764	Men's Basketball Coach	$579,334
Catholic U. of A.	$522,685	Professor of Physics	$415,456
St. Edward's U.	$511,480	Vice Pres. for Fin. Affairs	$272,800
Notre Dame of Maryland U.	$493,289	Dean, School of Pharmacy	$270,409
Total	$8,957,550		$11,769,282
Avg. Annual Compensation	$639,825		$840,663

Source: Dan Bauman, Tyler Davis, and Brian O'Leary, *The Chronicle of Higher Education*, "Executive Compensation at Public and Private Colleges" (2011); https://www.chronicle.com /interactives/executive-compensation#id=table_private_2011

Table 3. Compensation of Catholic University Presidents and Next-Highest-Paid Employee in 2016

Institution	Total Annual President's Compensation	Next-Highest-Paid Employee	Total Annual Compensation
Georgetown U.	$1,406,230	CIO	$1,344,372
		Men's Basketball Coach	$3,967,988
Duquesne Univ.	$1,354,464	Men's Basketball Coach	$1,027,688
U. of the Incarnate Word	$1,065,355	VP for Business and Tech	$360,642
U. of Notre Dame	$1,056,872	Vice President/CIO	$4,491,381
Sacred Heart U.	$886,700	Sr. Vice President	$407,050
Univ. of Dayton	$874,632	Men's Basketball Coach	$2,033,832
Marquette U.	$873,718	Men's Basketball Coach	$1,826,575
DePaul U.	$870,428	Men's Basketball Coach	$1,386,041
Seton Hall U.	$868,579	Men's Basketball Coach	$1,789,740
St. Leo University	$791,998	Vice President	$297,849
U. of San Diego	$774,194	Men's Basketball Coach	$503,160
Iona College	$744,646	Men's Basketball Coach	$552,011
St. Edwards U.	$693,949	V.P. Admin. & Academics	$425,579
Saint Louis Univ.	$693,192	Men's Basketball Coach	$1,890,731
Total	$12,954,957.00		$22,304,639.00
Avg. Annual Compensation	$925,354.07		$1,394,039.94

Source: Dan Bauman, Tyler Davis, and Brian O'Leary, *The Chronicle of Higher Education*, "Executive Compensation at Private Colleges" (2016); https://www.chronicle.com/interactives/executive-compensation#id=table_private_2016

Table 4. Fifteen Highest-Paid Employees at Saint Joseph's University in 2011

Employee	Total Annual Compensation
Men's Basketball Coach	$902,651
Interim president	$413,901
Dean, School of Business	$357,932
Women's Basketball Coach	$332,014
Assistant VP Athletic Development	$287,388
VP for Administrative Services	$285,064
VP for Finance and Treasurer	$252,990
University General Counsel	$250,478
VP Mission and Identity	$235,452
VP for Planning	$233,979
VP External Affairs	$227,365
VP Student Life/Associate Provost	$216,532
Provost	$271,764
Associate Dean, School of Business	$252,941
Chief Technology Officer	$235,174
Total	$4,483,861
Average Annual Compensation	$320,276

Source: 2011 IRS 990 Form taken from the *Economic Research Institute* website

half a million dollars or more.[110] At Saint Joseph's University, for example, three of the top five earners in 2011 were athletics personnel (Table 4).

Undoubtedly, coaches contribute much to the success of athletics teams. Many also help foster the character development of athletes. Likewise, many administrators work assiduously and effectively to keep Catholic universities financially solvent. Coaches and administrators deserve to be compensated fairly for their hard work and the pressures they face.[111] Donors increasingly endow coaches' salaries, in which case they do not deplete university resources that could be used elsewhere.[112] Nonetheless, Catholic institutions must examine their employees' pay scales, from top to bottom, in the light of Catholic social teaching, even if this is a sensitive and difficult conversation. Fans, alumni, and "market rates" may largely drive the rising salaries of coaches and administrators, but CST requires evaluating wages from different perspectives.[113] The pay scales of Catholic colleges and universities cannot simply reflect those of corporate America.

Catholic Social Teaching on Just Wages

Concern for a just wage has roots in the Bible (see Deut 24:14; Lev 19:13; Jer 22:12–14; Jas 5: 4).[114] Medieval thought on fairness in exchanges also adumbrated modern Catholic social teaching on the just wage.[115] Pope Leo XIII's encyclical *Rerum Novarum*, which built on Bishop von Ketteler's defense of a just wage, underscored the right to a just wage explicitly and emphatically.[116] Pope Leo's cognizance of the "misery and wretchedness" of the poor and the "callousness of employers and the greed of unrestrained competition" prompted him to promote the right "to procure what is required to live."[117] Leo argued that the right to receive a wage that is enough to "support the wage earner in reasonable and frugal comfort" is grounded in a "dictate of human nature."[118] According to natural law, human persons must preserve their lives and those of their family members. For the poor, who do not own capital, this can only be achieved by earning just wages.[119]

Pope John Paul II correctly ascertained just remuneration as the "key problem of social ethics" in the context of worker justice because without just compensation for work, human beings cannot afford the essential goods needed to flourish, such as food, shelter, health care, education, and access to culture. The degree to which all workers are compensated justly also determines "the justice of the whole socioeconomic system" because for most people only wages can ensure access to the goods God "intended for common use."[120] Promoting the right to a just wage thus represents one of the most important ways of embodying CST's principles of solidarity and the option for the poor, which are not optional aspirations, but rather necessary "proof" of "fidelity to Christ."[121]

In other words, CST holds that a just wage must *at least* be a living wage. All workers are owed a living wage out of justice.[122] According to CST, a living wage must enable workers to adequately attend to their own and their dependents' "material, social, cultural, and spiritual life."[123] In other words, a just wage fosters "integral human development."[124] It must also allow for savings and security in the event of unemployment, sickness, and old age. Wages below a "living" wage will lead to *marginalization*.[125] Therefore, failure to pay a living wage violates the principle of justice as understood in CST because it does not respect the worker's right to *participation* and his or her dignity. Moreover, in accordance with the principle of participation and the principle of *subsidiarity*, wages should enable all workers to provide basic goods for themselves and their families (low wages necessitate government or charitable organizations' provision of them). If all workers were to receive at the very least a "living" wage they would be able to attain the most basic and essential goods for human flourishing.[126] Catholic social thought has thus traditionally promulgated a just wage as the key method of empowering the poor.[127] In this way, the dignity of all workers and their right to participation is more greatly respected than in a system that heavily requires government subsidies for food, housing, etc. due to the prevalence of insufficient remuneration for work. Succinctly stated, the procurement of the right to participation requires a living wage. The Catholic ethic of solidarity requires defending the living wage because it represents the best way to ensure the basic human rights necessary for participation in the community.

In addition to being a living wage, a just wage must also be "equitable" and "sustainable."[128] In order for a wage to be equitable, it must fairly reflect the employee's contribution to the individual enterprise and to the common good. In this regard, Catholic social teaching decries the payment of unjustly low wages and excessive wages. Pope John XXIII maintained in his encyclical *Mater et Magistra* that "disproportionately high" wages are unjust, particularly when many workers are not paid a living wage.[129] Business ethicist Robert G. Kennedy specifies that according to CST "no one has a just claim on an income more than sufficient to meet the requirements of decent human life until every member of the community has received a minimum income" at least equivalent to a living wage.[130] Finally, a just wage should also be sustainable, meaning it must be determined so as to ensure a company's reasonable financial success and stability while attempting as much as possible to pay living wages to all employees.[131]

CST also stresses the right to a "family wage," which would enable one wage earner to support a family. In a two-parent household, the income of one parent should enable the other to undertake the work of raising children.[132] The wage amount needed to support these ends will vary according to time and geography, even within a given country, but the underlying principle remains intact regardless of era and place.[133] Furthermore, as John Paul II contended, states must enact "careful controls and adequate legislative measures to block shameful forms of exploitation, especially to the disadvantage of the most vulnerable workers, of immigrants and of those on the margins of society."[134]

CST rejects the market fundamentalist approach to wages. As St. John XXIII contended, "the remuneration of work is not something that can be left to the laws of the marketplace; nor should it be a decision left to the will of the more powerful. It must be determined in accordance with justice and equity."[135] As Chapter 1 recalled, the magisterium has declared that the church must abide by the church's teachings on worker justice, including the payment of just wages.[136] In fact, canon law mandates that church institutions embody CST in their policies, reflected in requirements to pay just wages and to recognize employees' freedom of association.[137] Even though Catholic universities are not canonically ecclesial institutions, their Catholic status should compel them to attempt to incorporate these principles into their policies and structures. Thus, the often-heard argument that professors in areas such as business are paid more than, say, philosophy or education, because "that is what the market bears" is dubious at Catholic institutions.[138] More importantly, paying adjuncts below a living wage while paying some administrative or athletics personnel 30 to 100 times more conflicts with CST.[139] The large gap between adjunct pay and tenure-stream salary is also unjustifiable. Determining what would constitute equal pay for equal work at universities among all professors will be complex, as some positions require scholarly publication and administrative work, while other positions do not.[140] Nonetheless, CST demands approximating equal pay for equal work, one of the primary goals of the New Faculty Majority, more closely than the status quo.

In fact, many of the goals of the New Faculty Majority, such as access to health care and participation in faculty governance, should be supported in the light of CST.[141] The right to participation demands that all faculty have a real stake in shared governance.[142] In addition to the right to a just wage, CST advocates rights to benefits necessary "to ensure the life and health of workers," as John Paul II stated in *Laborem Exercens*. All workers therefore have a right to affordable healthcare, rest (at least one day per week and a yearly vacation), retirement pensions, unemployment insurance, workers compensation, and maternity leave, according to CST.[143] The realization of these rights forms the "minimum conditions" necessary for the protection of the dignity of the worker, solidarity, and justice.[144]

The dignity of human labor and the rights attached to it do not depend on the kind of work done. In other words, according to CST the "market value" of work does not ascribe the level of remuneration and benefits for it. Rather, Jesus Christ himself toiled as a manual laborer, thereby revealing that the dignity of work and the rights flowing from it come from the fact that a human being does it, not the work itself.[145] Therefore, in the context of the university, the president, CFO, provost, faculty member, custodian, food service worker, security officer, and faculty member—full or part time—have equal rights as workers. Violating Catholic social teaching on the rights of workers on campus runs the risk of causing scandal.

Adjuncts and the Struggle for Unions

Contingent faculty realize that unions are not a panacea.[146] Nonetheless many adjuncts, including those at Catholic institutions, have increasingly determined that joining a union represents the best means toward a better future for themselves and for higher education.[147] Several faculties at Catholic colleges and universities have held successful unionization drives in the last several years. However, some Catholic universities have waged expensive legal battles to forestall union elections. Although they have publicly offered numerous arguments against unionization, their legal gambit has hinged on their putative right to religious freedom. The Association of Catholic Colleges and Universities, the Association of Jesuit Colleges and Universities, and the Lasallian Association of College and University Presidents offered this argument in their amicus brief supporting these universities.[148]

On the positive side, "more than 600 Catholic institutions" embody CST by respecting the rights of their employees to form unions and to engage in collective bargaining, according to the Catholic Labor Network's Catholic Employer Project.[149] Numerous unionized faculties appear on the list. "Nontenured" or adjunct unionized faculties include St. Mary's of California, Notre Dame de Namur University, Georgetown University, Trinity University of Washington, Loyola University Chicago, St. Louis University, Fordham University, St. Francis College (New York), Le Moyne College, and St. Michael's College (Vermont). Full-time faculty members are unionized at The University of Scranton, Fairfield University, University of San Francisco, Saint Leo University (Florida), St. Xavier University

(Illinois), Laboure College, University of Detroit Mercy, St. John's University, and D'Youville College (New York).[150]

Faculty unions at places such as at the University of San Francisco, the University of Scranton, and Le Moyne College have existed for decades.[151] In some recent cases university administrators have worked harmoniously with faculties holding unionization drives. For example, in accordance with its just employment policy, Georgetown University recognized the right of its adjunct faculty to unionize. The administration maintains good relations with unions on campus.[152] According to presidential advisor Lisa Krim, "taking a neutral position has actually served Georgetown very well. In subsequent dealings with the newly formed union, we brought a whole lot of good faith to the table, which really helps a lot."[153] A spokesperson for the union stated that the University's administration was "not just neutral but very cooperative throughout the entire process. . . . They really upheld their social values."[154] The adjuncts, represented by Service Employees International Union (SEIU), have negotiated their first contract with the administration in a spirit of collaboration. The contract provides pay increases, greater job stability, a faculty development fund for adjuncts, and a course cancellation fee.[155] The Georgetown experience belies the claim used by some administrators that the presence of a "third-party" union precludes collaboration between employer and employee.[156]

In a public letter, President James Donahue of Saint Mary's College of California, a Catholic ethicist, affirmed the right of the contingent faculty to unionize. He justified his position by stating that "a Catholic College in the Lasallian tradition of the Christian Brothers" must respect the "principles of social justice and the dignity of all persons." He went on to say, "for this reason, it is my firm belief that the decision to unionize or not rests entirely with our contingent faculty and is theirs alone to make as they consider what is best for themselves and their families."[157] The union-negotiated contract covering May 2016 through June 2019 includes academic freedom protections, antiharassment and discrimination clauses, a graduated salary scale with a range from $4,800 per course to $9,023 at the highest step, and a course cancellation fee.[158] In a "continuing effort to partner and dialogue with the contingent faculty union" the administration agreed to language safeguarding unemployment insurance, which many adjuncts cannot access due to vague contracts.[159] The university also promotes transparency by providing salary scales for staff, full-time, and part-time faculty on its website.[160] At another institution in California, Notre Dame de Namur University, full-time and part-time faculty worked together toward unionization. The university did not file legal objections to unionization, as the university's "social justice mission" guided deliberations on campus. Eventually both the part-time and full-time faculty elected to unionize. Rather than seeing each other as competitors for scarce resources, they recognized their shared interests and engaged in collective bargaining together with the administration. The administration agreed to pay increases, job security measures, and other benefits.[161] Unfortunately tensions between the administration and faculty appear to have risen again. Several full-time faculty have been laid off.[162] Time will tell if the breach can be repaired. Nonetheless, the full-time and part-time faculty's uniting in solidarity itself represents a positive outcome given the solipsism that often characterizes tenure-track faculty in the corporatized university.

Some institutions have expressed reluctance to recognize a faculty union but did so after a period of disagreement or conflict. At Loyola University Chicago, the administration initially argued that a National Labor Relations Board (NLRB) union election among adjunct faculty would violate the University's right to "be free from government entanglement."[163] After unsuccessful attempts to gain legal exemption from NLRB jurisdiction, the university recognized the union. Adjuncts then urged the administration to engage in collective bargaining over a two-year period. Following a one-day strike, the administration and union ratified a three-year contract. This contract has made significant improvements to working conditions of adjuncts, including better compensation, greater job security, and course cancellation fees.[164] Fordham University also reportedly resisted faculty unionization initially, citing that the institution's religious freedom would be "abridged" by coming under NLRB jurisdiction.[165] Faculty and students submitted a petition to the administration seeking better treatment of adjuncts and a Just Employment Policy akin to Georgetown's (which will be discussed below).[166] One demonstration on campus allegedly became heated, with students later sanctioned.[167] Among others, New York's mayor Bill De Blasio urged Fordham to respect the right of the adjunct faculty to unionize.[168] In May 2017 the university president announced his decision to recognize the union after "conversations with my fellow Jesuits" and acknowledging that "organized labor has deep roots in Catholic social justice teachings."[169]

Although there have been positive developments on Catholic campuses, some colleges and universities continue to resist unionization campaigns. According to the Catholic Employer Project, Manhattan College, St. Xavier University (Illinois), Duquesne University, Carroll College in Helena (Montana), and Seattle University have contested union elections by adjunct faculty.[170] Accounts of union busting on these and other Catholic campuses have been publicized.[171] Union busting tactics can include hiring "union avoidance" firms, subjecting workers to antiunion propaganda at "captive audience" meetings, impeding efforts to unionize through litigation, and retaliation toward workers attempting to organize.[172] Catholic college and universities have stalled unionization drives when they have sought an exemption from NLRB jurisdiction. Like the cases above, these institutions have maintained that if a government agency such as the NRLB asserts its authority over them it is a violation of their religious freedom.[173] They are also concerned that NLRB involvement "requires government functionaries to judge the manner in which we implement our faith in a university context."[174] They believe it is intrusive for a governmental institution such as the NLRB to "troll through the university's practices" to determine if it has a substantially "religious mission."[175] The legal appeals process involved in religious exemption cases prevents adjuncts from unionizing because the results of a union election must be impounded until the process is over. In other words, because this process will likely take years, it has a union busting effect.[176]

As I have argued elsewhere, the religious freedom argument ultimately lacks merit.[177] A government agency like the NLRB may not have the competence to determine whether or not a Catholic university advances a religious mission, as "religious mission" can and has been variously interpreted by Catholic institutions themselves. However, NLRB oversight has no tangible, adverse *effect* on a Catholic institution's ability to pursue its mission. Being deemed a "non-religious institution" according to the NLRB's legal definition does not prevent Catholic institutions from carrying on their religious mission in this case. For starters, as University of St. Thomas law professor Susan Stabile points out, almost all Catholic colleges and institutions already subject themselves willingly to governmental oversight via "regional agencies regarding terms and conditions of the employment of their faculty and of faculty/university relations. That they do so suggests that being subject to NLRB oversight would not impose a unique burden on their institutions. Accreditors already impose requirements on them as to faculty governance, academic freedom and other matters that relate to terms and conditions of employment."[178]

Moreover, if the NLRB asserts jurisdiction, it does not require Catholic universities to do something that violates their tradition's teaching. The NLRB has not interfered in mission matters by, for example, seeking to end the long-standing exemption from religious antidiscrimination laws in order to give preference to Catholics in hiring.[179] In terms of the basic rights of the worker, Catholic teaching itself largely aligns with, and even surpasses, American labor law.[180] When a Catholic institution refuses to recognize the right of its adjunct faculty to unionize, it violates its own tradition's teaching, not a heteronomous legal injunction imposed upon it by a governmental authority. Rather, the right to unionize is something that official Catholic teaching itself has continually endorsed at least since Leo XIII's 1891 encyclical *Rerum Novarum*.[181] The right to form and participate in unions without "risk of reprisal" constitutes one of the "basic rights of the human person" and serves the common good, according to the Pastoral Constitution on the Church in the Modern World, *Gaudium et Spes* (one of the most authoritative church documents).[182] St. John Paul II deemed unions "an indispensable element of social life."[183] Pope Francis recently echoed him, declaring that "there is no good society without a good union."[184] The USCCB has explicitly stated that "All church institutions must also fully recognize the rights of employees to organize and bargain collectively with those institutions through whatever association or organization they freely choose."[185] Canon law itself recognizes the right of church employees to the freedom of association, which includes the right to unionize.[186] In addition, a nation's civil laws, such as labor laws, essentially become canon law as long as they "are not contrary to divine law and unless canon law provides otherwise" according to canon lawyer Fr. Sinclair Oubre.[187] Thus, being a Catholic institution of higher learning does not entitle a university to circumvent labor laws that protect the basic rights of workers.

In 1993 Saint John Paul II directed Vatican officials to recognize the long-stated desire to form a union of the Association of Vatican Lay Employees (ADLV). John Paul II's experience as a manual laborer in Poland greatly influenced his decision to formally recognize the union of Vatican employees.[188] In the pope's words, "through his own experience of labor, I dare to say, this Pope learned the Gospel anew. He noticed and became convinced that the problems being raised today about human labor are deeply engraved in the Gospel, that they cannot be fully solved without the Gospel."[189] If Saint John Paul II supported the union of Vatican employees, on what basis do Catholic universities refuse to recognize a union freely elected by a group of its employees such as adjuncts?

Catholic universities can avoid the putative problem of "government entanglement" that NLRB jurisdiction over a union election allegedly creates. They can simply allow a free and fair union election to take place without NLRB involvement.[190] Unions and workers often prefer such "card check" elections, which a mutually agreed upon arbitrator or respected community leader oversees. As Catholic labor law professor David Gregory points out, workers have been repeatedly harassed or even fired by the employer, who can use the protracted process of an NLRB union election as a stall tactic.[191] Thousands of unionized Catholic parochial school teachers have a long history of collective bargaining outside of the NLRB process. Catholic universities opposed to NLRB interference yet not proposing the option of a card check election render their "religious freedom" argument a red herring.[192]

Catholic Social Teaching on Human Labor, Solidarity, and Conflict

Some legal scholars and administrators have offered a different argument, which seems peculiar given the church's long and ongoing history of supporting Catholics working in and for labor unions.[193] For example, Kathleen Brady has contended that the antagonistic model of collective bargaining in the National Labor Relations Act (NLRA) "presumes and perpetuates" a more conflictual relationship between employers and employees than Catholic social teaching envisions. This model impinges upon the ability of Catholic institutions to practice the spirit of "brotherhood and cooperation" envisioned in management-labor relations by CST. Thus, NLRB jurisdiction would violate the religious freedom of Catholic colleges and universities.[194] For their part, administrators in Catholic hospitals and universities have sometimes claimed that unions prevent the congenial relationships between managers and workers envisioned by Catholic teaching.[195]

Other labor law experts disagree that the NRLA necessarily engenders conflict in the workplace. According to James Gross of Cornell University's Industrial and Labor Relations School, the NLRA does not compel anything beyond "requiring employers and unions to bargain with each other in good faith."[196] However, even if the NLRA did "presume and perpetuate" conflictual management-employee relations as Brady contends, it is a fallacy to say that Catholic institutions cannot possibly strive for the collaborative ideal of CST. "Presume and perpetuate" does not mean "require." Analogously, laws requiring Catholics to accept the right of people to hoard private property excessively (a violation of Catholic teaching) do not prevent them from sacrificing their own material goods to promote the welfare of others and the common good.[197] Living the gospel does not require being free from the jurisdiction of civil law, unless it unequivocally requires violating natural law. Catholic teaching, as proposed for example by John Paul II in *Veritatis Splendor*, holds that civil laws such as the prohibition against murder are the "precondition" to living the more virtuous path of charity and solidarity.[198]

Concrete examples have shown that the NLRA leaves space within which a form of labor-management relations imbued with the spirit of *caritas* can be cultivated. I have already mentioned the recent Georgetown experience.[199] While it has not always been easy, Catholic teachers' unions and their diocesan employers have learned to have "very positive and collaborative relationships" in many cases.[200] According to Adam Reich's participant-observer account, relations *improved* after a union was finally recognized after many years of mistrust between workers and management and union avoidance at Santa Rosa Memorial Hospital in California.[201] Susan Stabile has noted that the Catholic Hospital Association (CHA) has accepted the application of the NLRA to Catholic hospitals rather than seek a religious exemption. However, the CHA has also pursued the more cooperative model of CST, as discussed in the 2009 USCCB document *Respecting the Just Rights of Workers: Guidance and Options for Catholic Health Care and Unions*. This landmark document calls for cooperation between management and labor while underscoring the rights of workers in Catholic healthcare institutions, including the right to unionize.[202] Collaborative labor-management partnerships that reflect

CST's emphasis on worker participation in decisions that affect them and the overall work process have been implemented outside of the Catholic context as well. In this vein, MIT management professor Thomas Kochan argues that "the best employers and worker organizations could do is what Kaiser Permanente and its union coalition are doing—build partnerships that nurture employee engagement. Workers respond well to these partnerships."[203] This labor management partnership, "the largest and most ambitious labor management partnership in the history of US labor relations," might serve as an example for others.[204] Thus, lived experience defies the claim that NLRA forces workers to remain at "arm's length" from management.[205]

In addition to experiential counterevidence, this line of argument suffers from a flawed theoretical understanding of CST. In particular, it denies the role of conflict in promoting solidarity. Indeed, CST has consistently advocated a "collaborative relationship" between workers and management, as Brady and others contend.[206] CST certainly eschews the notion of intractable class struggle.[207] However, CST does not naively assume that employers are always benevolent. CST's continuous insistence on the right to unionize and collective bargaining is rooted in the recognition of an imbalance of power that gives owners an unfair advantage over workers.[208] In addition to being a "natural" form of association among workers, CST also sees unions as a necessary "reaction" to their precarious situation, which has perdured since the Industrial Revolution.[209] While unions are not a "mouthpiece for class struggle," they function as a "mouthpiece in the struggle for social justice" in a world that systematically denies the rights of workers, according to St. John Paul II.[210]

In a similar way, the *Compendium of the Social Doctrine of the Church* affirms myriad rights of workers, including the right to just wages and to form unions, but correctly maintains that "these rights are often infringed, as is confirmed by the sad fact of workers who are underpaid and without protection or adequate representation. It often happens that work conditions for men, women and children, especially in developing countries, are so inhumane that they are an offence to their dignity and compromise their health."[211] Citing John Paul II, the *Compendium* further states that "unions grew up from the struggle of workers . . . to protect their just rights vis-à-vis the entrepreneurs and the owners of the means of production." Furthermore, "the practice of authentic solidarity among workers" remains more important than ever because their rights continue to be violated by employers.[212] Pope Benedict XVI reiterated the urgency of workers' forming associations "that can defend their rights" in his 2009 encyclical *Caritas in Veritate*. According to the pontiff, "grave danger to the rights of workers" exists in underdeveloped, emerging, and advanced capitalist societies in part due to efforts to hamper unions.[213] In other words, CST recognizes that the present context, which I described above as neoliberalism's war against workers, evinces some of the pernicious consequences of the imbalance of power between owners and workers, which often leaves workers at the mercy of their employers.[214] Thus, Pope Francis recently stated that trade unions must be "prophetic" by keeping watch over both workers within unions and those who "do not yet have rights." A trade union fulfills its role when it, like the great prophet Amos, "denounces those who would 'sell the needy for a pair of sandals' (see Amos 2:6)."[215]

The church's teaching eschews "cheap solidarity," which categorically rejects conflict for the sake of superficial harmony, for example between an employer and employees.[216] CST explicitly acknowledges that solidarity may require conflict in the name of justice. In oppressive situations such as exploitative work, solidarity aims to "hold up a mirror for the oppressor" so that he or she may recognize their violations of justice and rectify them. In practicing solidarity in this situation, one should attempt dialogue first, but when these methods fail, then shaming, civil protest, nonviolent resistance, and strikes may be undertaken.[217] Thus, John Paul II advised Solidarność that "solidarity must come before conflict . . . yet it also triggers conflict . . . but not conflict that treats another person as an enemy and seeks his or her destruction."[218] Solidarity "presupposes taking sides with the most needy [sic] people . . . to defend their rights and attend to their just claims," according to the pontiff.[219] In short, CST acknowledges "the positive role of conflict" when it is "takes the form of a struggle for social justice."[220] Of course, the goal of the struggle for justice cannot be the annihilation or forceful suppression of the oppressor. Rather, "peacemakers" ultimately seek their oppressors' conversion, the overturning of unjust social structures, and building just communities without concealing disagreement.[221]

While CST prefers cohesion in the workplace, workers may engage in strikes "as a kind of ultimatum to the competent bodies, especially the employers."[222] *Gaudium et Spes* maintains that "although recourse must always be had first to a sincere dialogue between the parties, a strike, nevertheless, can remain even in present-day circumstances a necessary, though ultimate, aid for the defense of the workers' own rights and the fulfillment of their just desires."[223] Thus, it makes little sense to argue that Catholicism cannot accept and comply with a system of collective bargaining that falls short of its ideal vision for labor management relations. CST itself realistically acknowledges that the ideal will not always be possible in particular circumstances. While collaborative relationships between labor and management should always be pursued, cheap solidarity in the workplace must be rejected, as it "can lead workers to acquiesce to unjust conditions or be forced to accept them by the 'benevolent' *paterfamilias*, who purports to know better than the workers themselves what is best for them."[224] Succinctly stated, an accurate reading of CST demonstrates that appeals to cheap solidarity cannot justify rejecting unions in Catholic workplaces.

Unfortunately, the evidence also reveals that Catholic employers themselves too often fail to model "brotherhood and cooperation," thereby necessitating unions, in the eyes of their workers. In other words, many Catholic institutions of higher learning seeking exemption from the NLRA do not live up to the idealized vision of management-labor relations that Brady or these employers themselves tout. As Stabile rightly contends, "The problem is that Catholic colleges and universities have not modeled the vision Brady offers. The employee groups seeking unionization have done so because Catholic colleges and universities have not offered a cooperative model of collective bargaining and appear to treat their employees no more lovingly than secular institutions of higher learning do."[225] As I argued above, Catholic colleges and universities have not remained immune to the corporatization of the university.[226] Like many Catholics generally, university decision-makers may be ignorant of or reject CST's vision of labor management relations.[227] Some may reflect the antiunion bias in neoliberal culture, which almost half of US Catholics have imbibed.[228] When administrators import models from the corporate world (exclusively market-based pay schemes, cutting costs on the backs of workers, viewing students as customers and professors as service providers, etc.) they flout Catholic social teaching on workers' rights. In this situation, workers' rights cannot be suspended in the air waiting for an "eschatological" vision of workplace harmony. As Saint John Paul II said on

numerous occasions, the rights of the poor, the marginalized, and the oppressed cannot be put on hold.[229]

This is not to say that workers and unions always pursue their claims
in the appropriate ways. I have repeatedly defended in public the right of
all campus workers to unionize, including contingent faculty. In accordance with CST, I have argued that the workers themselves have the
right to choose their union representation. At the same time, I have ascertained that some union organizers and leadership may need to contemplate how the Catholic higher education context differs from other
sectors. For example, compromises must be found on thorny issues such
as what kinds of healthcare coverage can be directly provided by plans offered in a Catholic institutional context. University administrators and
union leadership alike must embrace CST's emphasis on the right to participation of all "rank-and-file" employees in decision-making. In addition,
union organizers sometimes hasten escalation tactics prematurely, as dialogue in academic settings often moves slowly. Of course, there are times
when escalating to protest and even a strike may be appropriate, as CST
supports such measures when dialogue fails, or management demonstrates
its unwillingness to bargain in good faith.

Despite any shortcomings, unions cannot legitimately be "kept off" our
campuses, as some administrators wish.[230] The USCCB understands that
neither unions nor management always strive for the hospitable relationship proposed by Catholic social teaching as the ideal. The bishops nevertheless maintained in their 2012 Labor Day statement: "When labor
institutions fall short, it does not negate Catholic teaching in support of
unions and the protection of working people, but calls out for a renewed
focus and candid dialogue on how to best defend workers. Indeed, economic renewal that places working people and their families at the center of economic life cannot take place without effective unions."[231] Both
management and labor must avoid caricaturing and demonizing, which
stifle genuine dialogue and collaboration.

The Scandal of Union Busting and Unjust Wages

I have argued that Catholic universities should not use legal recourse to
forestall unionization efforts.[232] This is the case even if the courts might
plausibly uphold the religious exemption that Catholic universities seek

from the jurisdiction of the NLRB. Catholic universities availing themselves of the courts will likely create a hostile environment, the environment that Brady precisely wants to avoid. The expensive legal battles that
some institutions are fighting surely will lead to a more rancorous situation between adjunct faculty and the administration.[233] In this connection, St. Paul's rebuke of wealthy Corinthians using the courts to take
advantage of poorer citizens is instructive:[234]

> I say this to shame you. Is it possible that there is nobody among you
> wise enough to judge a dispute between believers? [6] But instead, one
> brother takes another to court—and this in front of unbelievers! The
> very fact that you have lawsuits among you means you have been com-
> pletely defeated already. Why not rather be wronged? Why not rather
> be cheated? [8] Instead, you yourselves cheat and do wrong, and you do
> this to your brothers and sisters. (I Cor. 6:5–11 NIV)

In the present situation, Catholic university administrations are behaving
analogously toward adjunct faculty members who wish to unionize by en-
snaring their unionization drives in protracted and expensive legal
battles.[235] Many adjuncts clearly represent the marginalized in current
universities. Catholic universities and their leaders function as the elite,
as evidenced by their use of some of the most powerful law firms in the
country to defeat their adversaries in court. They should instead follow
the guidelines developed in the USCCB document *Respecting the Just
Rights of Workers*. These guidelines commit both sides to a mutually acceptable "fair and expeditious process" that avoids protracted legal and
jurisdictional battles that delay unionization efforts.[236] Catholic institutions of higher learning that pay enormous sums of money to high-
powered law firms to assert their exemption from NLRB jurisdiction,
while at the same time fighting the efforts of adjuncts to unionize, flout
Catholic social teaching. The question must be asked, what message are
these institutions sending to their students and to the larger society about
the applicability of Catholic social teaching to real-world problems? In fact,
union busting universities tacitly support the neoliberal global order in
which workers' efforts to form unions are met with threats, violence, and
even death, rather than challenge it.[237] Given the church's clear insistence
on the rights of all workers to unionize, including at Catholic workplaces,
the actions of these institutions run the risk of causing scandal.[238]

According to Boston College law and theology professor M. Cathleen Kaveny, "causing scandal in the theological sense connotes performing an action that increases the possibility that other persons who witness the action will engage in morally objectionable activity themselves."[239] Moreover, scandal arises when the action taken cannot reasonably be explained to those in the Catholic community as being consistent with the values of the tradition.[240] Apart from antiunion bias among some Catholics, it hardly seems plausible that Catholics could fathom Catholic universities, already expensive, using large sums of money to fight the efforts of grossly underpaid adjuncts to unionize, especially given CST's steadfast affirmation of the right to unionize.

In her study of the Catholic concept of scandal, Angela Senander rightly contends that "the scandal of sin within the Church obscures the proclamation of the Good News."[241] In my judgment, union busting on Catholic campuses has a deleterious effect on the faith formation of the students and impedes the evangelizing mission of the university.

Standing in solidarity with workers on our campuses by promoting their rights is a component of the evangelizing mission of Catholic universities. As I argued in Chapter 1, Catholic doctrine holds that evangelization must entail promulgating CST and must include promoting solidarity and the rights of all human beings.[242] Succinctly stated, serious consideration of Catholic teaching on the subjects of unions, higher education, and evangelization leads to the conclusion that the unionization of adjuncts does not constitute a threat to the mission of Catholic universities. Rather, union busting by administrators seriously undermines the evangelizing mission and identity of Catholic universities. In order to be the countercultural "sign of contradiction" (Lk. 2:34) that recent popes have challenged Catholic universities to be, they should do everything possible to militate against the nefarious war against workers ongoing today, not partake in it.

Forbidding unions on Catholic campuses will not bring about a more loving and harmonious employer-employee relationship. When administrators, trustees, or university lawyers raise this contention, the option for the poor of CST requires giving precedence to the voices of the marginalized, which in this situation are the adjunct faculty, not the administrators who fight their efforts to unionize. Catholic teaching holds that the marginalized and oppressed have an epistemological advantage in ascertaining the truth about situations of injustice because they are not blinded by the lure of power and assets.[243] Thus, if the majority of adjuncts maintain that unionizing will better foster the recognition of their rights as workers on Catholic campuses, they should be heard and acknowledged. Catholic teaching insists that workers themselves have the right to unionize or not. Administrators, bishops, managers, or trustees at Catholic institutions may not usurp that right for any reason.[244]

Catholic teaching holds that when certain basic human rights, such as the right to unionize, are not protected by law, they remain in jeopardy. In order to truly protect a human right, its realization must not be determined by the predilection of those who hold power over other human beings. According to CST, the state and other institutional structures must defend such basic rights today, just as the state needed to defend the rights of workers during earlier phases of "primitive capitalism."[245] Therefore, the church and church-related institutions such as Catholic universities should work with the state to strengthen the right to unionize. If necessary, Catholic institutions should encourage changes to parts of the NLRA that do not reflect the current reality of worker/management partnerships and employee participation. They should not try to hide behind a religious exemption from the legal protection of workers' right to unionize enshrined in the NLRA. Engaging in such tactics, especially when many adjunct faculty are already denied the right to a just wage and health care, undermines their credibility as Catholic institutions of higher education and signifies the uncritical embrace of the neoliberal, corporatized university. Moreover, union busting constitutes formal cooperation in evil (which is never permissible) and can be a mortal sin if undertaken while conscious of Catholic teaching on the right to unionize.[246]

The failure of faculty who enjoy tenure-track privilege to stand in solidarity with their adjunct colleagues, while benefiting from their exploitation, amounts to what Kaveny calls "appropriation of evil."[247] The benefits tenure-track faculty enjoy due to the exploitation of adjuncts may desensitize them to the injustices occurring around them. However, Catholic moral theology holds that one of the conditions for permissible (material) cooperation in evil is that there is a reasonable chance of remedying the evil and that one must do what is possible to mitigate it.[248] Thus, I argue that tenure-track faculty must work together with adjunct faculty to improve the situation of adjuncts. This does not absolve tenure-track professors from confronting the unjust treatment of all workers on campus when it occurs. As Pope Francis has recently said, "In the spirit of the Jubilee of Mercy, all of us are called to realize how indifference can manifest itself in our lives and to work concretely to improve the world around us, beginning with our families, neighbours and places of employment."[249] In the concluding section of this chapter, I will briefly discuss some recent efforts to improve the working conditions of other types of workers at Catholic colleges and universities.

Promising Practices and Proposals for Promoting Worker Justice on Campus

While I have largely focused on the case of injustices toward adjunct faculty members, examples of Catholic colleges and universities embodying CST in the treatment of their workers do exist. Students, faculty, administrators, and staff have advocated the vision of CST on worker justice on some Catholic campuses, with success, resistance, or mixed results.

In 2011 Georgetown University community members took a stand for worker justice that paved the way for later positive developments such as the adjunct unionization campaign. Students from the Georgetown Solidarity Committee, cafeteria workers, and faculty jointly supported the unionization effort of campus food service staff, who were directly employed by Aramark. The undergraduates played a key role in helping to unionize the workers, who felt they were being mistreated and deserved better wages. One worker told students and faculty his harrowing story about being forced to come to work during a blizzard shortly after his appendix was removed. The weather conditions deteriorated so badly that he had to stay overnight at a nearby hotel without his post-op medications, rather than going home. Other employees spoke of verbal harassment and abuse on the job.[250] In addition to the pressure and solidarity among these community members, the University administration stepped up by issuing a letter to Aramark's CEO, reminding him that the University's just employment policy guaranteed, among other things, the right to "freedom of association without intimidation." Moreover, the letter stressed that "Georgetown University's mission as a Catholic and Jesuit institution includes principles and values that support human dignity in work, and respect for workers' rights."[251] In April 2011 Aramark recognized the union chosen by the workers. Since then, the workers' situation has substantially improved.

The worker's success would not have been possible without the unwavering solidarity of the students. In addition, the university had already adopted a just employment policy in 2005, which it requires all subcontractors to uphold. The policy mandates that all workers be paid a living wage, whether subcontracted or directly employed by the university. It also identifies a number of other workers' rights, including the right to unionize and the right to a workplace free of safety hazards or harassment. In addition, the policy confers benefits such as library privileges, access to English as a second language classes, and shuttle services.[252] Georgetown's Just Employment Policy (JEP) and subsequent efforts on campus to enforce it are highly commendable.[253] For example, in 2013 students and staff confronted the owner of a restaurant on campus who had been accused of wage theft by some of his employees. As a result of its attention to workers' rights, the Catholic Labor Network honored Georgetown University in 2014 for modeling how Catholic institutions can implement employment policies rooted in Catholic social teaching.[254] As was mentioned above, the JEP served its purpose by protecting the right of adjuncts to unionize at Georgetown in 2012. Georgetown took yet another progressive stance in 2018 by recognizing the graduate student employees union, while many other institutions, including Boston College and Loyola University Chicago, chose not to acknowledge graduate student employees' right to unionize.[255]

For all its merits, however, the JEP does have a major flaw. The compensation policy (of a required living wage) has not yet been fully applied to adjuncts thus far. Even though the adjunct union's first contract contained real gains, as I noted above, it is hard to argue that the $4,700 minimum per course in 2016 constitutes a living wage, even if it is a significant improvement from the previous level of between $2,300 and $3,000.[256] According to the MIT living wage calculator, the "minimum subsistence wage" for the DC area for a family of one adult and one child is about $63,000 before taxes.[257] Fortunately, the newest collective bargaining agreement moves in the right direction by mandating a minimum of $7,000 per three credit course by fall of 2019, but still falls short even for adjunct professors teaching as many as eight courses per year.[258]

The positive outcomes of the JEP at Georgetown should not overshadow the fact that the JEP did not originate in a completely harmonious fashion. Students, staff, and faculty engaged in actions of various sorts for several years prior to the JEP's adoption in 2005 to urge the university to uphold its Jesuit, Catholic traditions in the treatment of its workers. Some of these actions were collegial, such as dialogue and personal testimonies of workers. Some were more confrontational, such as a hunger strike undertaken by twenty-six students for eight days.[259] During the protest notable leaders such as Richard Trumka, head of the AFL-CIO, District Congressional Delegate Eleanor Holmes-Norton, and Jos Williams, president of the DC Central Labor Council, came to campus to express their support.[260] It is hard to know exactly which undertakings and pressures most directly spawned the JEP. Nonetheless, the lesson to be learned from the Georgetown experience is that when enough people from various groups in the community support a cause, it encourages institutions to move in the right direction. In this situation, decision makers can confidently move forward knowing that not all members of the university community see it simply as a corporation governed solely by the laws of the market. In the future, it will be crucial for members of Catholic campuses to engage in sustained, thoughtful, and strategic campaigns to win the rights of all workers, including adjuncts. To recall John Paul II's words, solidarity sometimes requires standing firmly in opposition to the status quo.

Other Catholic institutions of higher education have adopted policies promoting the rights of workers, though none appear as comprehensive and robust as Georgetown's JEP. For example, Loyola University New Orleans students performed a "social justice audit" in 2005. Eventually this led to a University vendor policy requiring all companies that do business with the University to pay a wage at least equivalent to the federal poverty line for a family of four (still well below a living wage), recognize their employees' right to unionize, provide "access to an affordable, high-quality health care plan," and other benefits.[261] The preamble to the policy states that it was born of the University's "commitment to social justice, the common good and the value of finding God in all things."[262] Students, faculty, and staff on other campuses have advocated for just employment and/or living wage policies, though they have sometimes been met with resistance. This was the case at the nation's wealthiest Catholic university, Notre Dame, where students appropriately insisted that CST calls for living wages.[263]

In some ways, Le Moyne College has instituted policies affecting their adjuncts that reflect CST. Adjuncts at Le Moyne unionized in 2007. For example, adjuncts are eligible for a partial reimbursement of healthcare costs. The university sets aside a pool of $12,500 annually for this purpose. This is laudable, even if it must be divided among the pool of adjuncts. Other Catholic institutions allow adjuncts to buy into the university's health care plan at 100 percent cost, which is often not feasible given their low salaries. Adjuncts are also eligible for professional development grants.[264] In my judgment, it is not a coincidence that Le Moyne's adjuncts are unionized and that they have such benefits, even if unions cannot always guarantee better employment terms and conditions. The unionized adjunct faculty at the University of San Francisco also have some benefits. For example, adjuncts who have taught for at least one year with at least twelve credits are eligible to enroll in the university's health plan, with the university subsidizing a portion of the cost. Adjuncts are also eligible for teaching development funds.[265]

Even in situations where one segment of the workforce on campuses has won some rights, advocates of worker justice must remain vigilant. For example, janitorial workers, who are outsourced, do not fare as well at Le Moyne. The Occupational Safety and Health Administration (OSHA) has filed multiple lawsuits for workplace safety violations against Le Moyne. Students and faculty have also protested against the janitorial staff's low wages (an average of about $16,000 per year) and unsafe working conditions.[266] Many workers on our campuses are subcontracted, and their employers do not always live up to the values of CST even if our institutions aspire to do so. Georgetown's JEP sought to address this problem. The relatively good situation of adjuncts at Le Moyne, with a concurring bad situation for janitors, underscores the precariousness of workers even at institutions where some jobs come with dignity and justice. In other words, we cannot assume that because a university does the right thing for one group of workers, it will necessarily respect the rights of other groups on campus. For example, Duquesne University recently announced that it will raise the minimum pay of about one hundred of its full-time workers to $15.00 per hour. This is a welcomed step. However, the university's exclusion of part-time faculty and about 390 contract food service and bookstore workers, while contesting the right of adjuncts to unionize, highlights this problem.[267]

The reflections in this chapter suggest a number of steps that can be taken to better promote worker justice in accordance with the Catholic social tradition on our campuses. First, other members of university communities must stand in solidarity with adjuncts. As I argued above, tenure-track faculty especially bear this obligation, as they directly benefit from the exploitation of adjunct faculty. In 2009, the members of the Theology Department at Marquette University passed a resolution demanding healthcare benefits for the University's adjuncts, citing Catholic social teaching's understanding of healthcare as a human right.[268] This kind of action moves in the right direction, but solidarity in CST calls for more. For starters, tenure-track faculty should form relationships with our contingent faculty colleagues: Talk with them, listen to their stories, and hear their concerns, hopes, and aspirations. Solidarity and the preferential option for the poor of CST require giving precedence to the voices of the marginalized. On many campuses, those are the voices of adjunct faculty, not those who fight their efforts to unionize. To reiterate, Catholic teaching holds that the marginalized and oppressed have an epistemological advantage in ascertaining the truth about situations of injustice. Thus, if the majority of adjuncts maintain that unionizing will better foster the recognition of their rights as workers on Catholic campuses, they should be heard and acknowledged. As Catholic social teaching makes clear, workers alone get to decide whether they unionize, not their bosses. All members of the university community should advocate with adjuncts for better pay, health benefits, and unions if they have decided to unionize. Students have an important role to play, as they have successfully advocated for justice and the rights of janitorial and food service workers on Catholic campuses, as well as workers in their universities' supply chains.[269] More recently, students at Fordham and Loyola University Chicago took up the cause for justice for adjuncts.[270] Even if some students would remain indifferent and entranced by their idyllic surroundings, at least some students on our campuses would be willing to support justice for contingent faculty. Thus, Catholic educators must raise awareness of worker justice issues, including the crisis of contingency, on campus among their students.

Solidarity also requires shared sacrifice. Recognizing the controversial nature of this proposal, I advocate that tenured faculty (like myself) and well-paid administrators should be willing to make reasonable sacrifices and forsake some of our administrative class and/or tenure-track privilege. Thus, colleges and universities could consider voluntary solidarity pay cuts if no other funds can be found in the budget to pay adjunct faculty justly. CST's insistence that those with greater resources should pay higher taxes, which is rooted in the Lukan injunction "from everyone to whom much has been entrusted, even more will be demanded" (Lk 12:48), analogously applies to shared sacrifice in an academic community setting.[271] For example, those earning more than $200,000 at Catholic universities could take a 10 percent pay cut. This can be scaled so that higher earners contribute even more, while those making below this amount may give up an equitable portion of their salary. All tenured faculty might take a 2 percent pay cut, again using a sliding scale in both directions depending on the salary. Pretenure faculty should not be asked to make a financial sacrifice, as their earnings are substantially lower than faculty with tenure and seniority. The university in turn must guarantee that the resultant savings will go directly toward adjunct pay and benefits, not toward building projects, athletics, or any other expenditure. A policy like solidarity pay cuts can only be decided upon after sustained reflection and conversation among all community members.

In the course of such conversation, other types of sacrifices might be considered in order to assuage the plight of contingent faculty. For example, at St. Catherine's University in Minnesota, full-time members of the Theology Department embodied solidarity by relinquishing administrative course releases and accepted more students into their courses so that faculty on one-year contracts would not be laid off.[272] In all cases of shared sacrifice, transparency about the institution's budget for such conversations is a prerequisite. Universities must engage in serious conversation about whether or not their current expenditures on athletics and nonessential building projects are justifiable in the light of Catholic social teaching given the deplorable situation of adjuncts and other campus low-wage employees (and prohibitive tuition costs, which I will discuss in the following chapter).[273] The percentages I have used above for solidarity salary cuts are somewhat arbitrary, and determining whether expenditures are truly essential or not entails myriad factors and complex decision-making. Moreover, shared sacrifice via salary reductions will not eradicate the adjunct problem. Nonetheless, such action is a step in the right direction consistent with solidarity in CST. An example will demonstrate the difference it might make for those earning low wages. A reduction of the salaries of the highest-paid earners at Saint Joseph's University (Table 4) by 10 percent would save approximately $450,000. Given that Saint Joseph's has roughly four hundred adjuncts, each one's yearly income could be increased by about $1,125. Another 2 percent of salary transferred from tenured faculty to adjuncts might generate about another thousand dollars per capita.[274] This may not seem like much to some, but when the average pay per course is approximately $3,000 with a $12,000 maximum per semester, an extra $2000 annually is a start.[275] This kind of increase moves the scale, albeit too slowly, toward the minimum of $5,000 per course for all adjuncts called for in a Mayday Resolution endorsed by the New Faculty Majority and other adjunct advocacy groups.[276]

Finally, Catholic colleges and universities should consider adopting a just employment policy akin to Georgetown's JEP. Spearheaded by the Kalmanovitz Initiative for Labor and the Working Poor at Georgetown, scholars, staff, and students from several Catholic colleges and universities have promoted the Just Employment Project, which encourages all Jesuit and Catholic institutions to adopt a policy akin to the draft policy they created. Administrators, faculty, and staff at Catholic colleges provided feedback on the draft policy, which was initially presented at the Justice in Jesuit Higher Education conference at Creighton University in August, 2013. Students on several Jesuit campuses have discussed the draft policy and engaged in conversation with their universities' leaders about adopting it. The Harrison Institute for Public Law at Georgetown later collaborated with the Kalmanovitz Initiative to produce a model policy.[277] Committees have formed to explore the possibility of implementing a just employment policy on campuses such as Loyola University Chicago, Saint Joseph's University, and John Carroll University.[278] As of this writing, Loyola's committee has produced a robust report with detailed recommendations. The president has responded favorably to many of them, while not approving others.[279] One can only hope that all Catholic colleges and universities will someday endorse a JEP—one that unequivocally recognizes the rights to a living wage, to forming unions, and to health care. Doing so will help them to embody the tenants of Catholic social teaching more faithfully and to fulfill their mission more effectively. Catholic institutions should reject the neoliberal economy and its corporate model, which exploits workers to maximize shareholder value, through actions that are not just perfunctory mission statements.

3 Catholic Universities, the Right to Education, and the Option for the Poor

Recruiting, Admitting, and Retaining Economically Disadvantaged Students

Early in my career I had the privilege of learning with a remarkable young man who overcame incredible odds to come to Saint Joseph's University.[1] Growing up in a slum in Nairobi, Kenya, he often went to bed hungry in a home with no running water. A bright and intellectually curious child, he attended one of Nairobi's best high schools, until he was forced to drop out to support himself. At this point he became a "Chokoraa"—a "homeless scavenger"—in his native Swahili. Life for him on the streets was unimaginable. He escaped multiple brushes with death, while some of his friends perished violently.[2]

Not knowing if and how he would survive, this young man's fortune took a dramatic turn. A missionary from the United States provided him with the financial assistance to complete high school. Moved by her faith and generosity, he decided to devote his life to assisting children like himself by helping to establish a boarding school. While assisting these children, life presented him with an opportunity that he would never have imagined: a chance to attend a university in the United States. A graduate of Saint Joseph's University who was volunteering in Nairobi put him in contact with several Jesuits there. They recommended him for admission to Saint Joseph's. Thanks to the support of the university community, he was able to attend. The efforts of the Saint Joseph's alumnus and the university serve as wonderful embodiments of the ideals of Catholic social teaching, which obligates all people to stand in solidarity with the poor.

Many Catholic colleges and universities tout uplifting stories about reaching out to promising students from disadvantaged backgrounds, but these stories are relatively rare on our campuses.[3] Most of the poor, both in the US and globally, remain excluded from the halls of our institutions. At many institutions the majority of students come from affluent backgrounds. Although we can and should celebrate stories like this one, many Catholic universities fail to sufficiently embody Catholic social teaching's option for the poor in their recruiting, admissions, and retention policies.

Catholic social teaching has long championed the right to education of all people, including the poor. In the American context, the Roman Catholic bishops have argued that all of society must "make a much stronger commitment to education for the poor."[4] Recent trends in American higher education reveal this is not the case at the university level. In fact, many American universities have adopted a "preferential option for the rich." Some elite colleges and universities even have more students from families with income in the top 1 percent than from the lowest 60 percent of earners taken as a whole. About one in four of the wealthiest students attend elite institutions. Conversely, "less than one-half of 1 percent of children from the bottom fifth of American families attend an elite college; less than half attend any college at all."[5]

Because Catholic thought strongly affirms the right to education for the poor, it is important to ask whether Catholic colleges and universities mirror these national trends, or have they more successfully provided opportunities for advanced learning to those from economically disadvantaged backgrounds? If they have not been able to open their doors more widely to those from the lower economic echelons of society, have they at least done as much as possible to move in that direction? In other words, have they exercised solidarity with the marginalized and the preferential option for the poor, two of the key principles of Catholic social thought? This chapter is an initial attempt to answer these questions. Toward that end, it uses information pertaining to a sample of Catholic colleges and universities. The data does not account for situations at every Catholic institution of higher learning. However, it brings to the fore empirical demographic realities and normative evaluations that pertain to many of them.

The argument of this chapter unfolds in several stages. First, the chapter provides a brief overview of empirical trends concerning the access of students from economically disadvantaged backgrounds to higher education in the United States. Next, it discusses the right to education in Catholic social thought. This section of the chapter highlights Catholic social teaching's emphasis on the importance of education in overcoming poverty and fostering the right to participation in the life of society. Relying on interdisciplinary perspectives, it also argues that in the US knowledge-based society the right to education must include access to higher education, particularly for the economically marginalized. A subsequent chapter will examine the distinct, but sometimes related disadvantages in access faced by racially minoritized students.

The second part of the chapter will present empirical data concerning the socioeconomic background of students from selected Catholic colleges and universities. The data will include information such as the percentage of students from economically disadvantaged backgrounds, the percentage that receive financial aid, the percentage that do not apply for financial aid, etc. It will present comparable data from secular institutions in order to show that Catholic institutions of higher learning generally do not fare better than their secular counterparts in granting access to low-income students. In fact, it will reveal that they often have fewer economically disadvantaged students.

Finally, I will draw some normative conclusions about the degree to which these Roman Catholic universities promote the right to education of the poor and suggest how they might be able to realize this goal to an ever greater degree. Acknowledging that these Catholic institutions face budgetary constraints, the normative conclusions will point to ways in which the right to education of the poor can and should be realized progressively. This part of the chapter does not intend to be exhaustive, rather it aims to begin an "examination of conscience" that all Catholic colleges and universities should undertake.

Higher Education in the United States: A Preferential Option for the Rich?

A good deal of evidence suggests that US higher education is a privilege enjoyed disproportionately by the wealthy, while the poor are largely excluded from it. As many as 95 percent of US colleges are reportedly beyond the reach of low and moderate income students.[6] *The Chronicle of Higher Education* thus entitled a series dedicated to the topic, "The Growing Divide." It concludes that "By almost every statistical measure, the divide between the haves and the have-nots in higher education—among students as well as institutions—is growing."[7] In recent years nonprofit organizations like the Education Trust, New America Foundation, and leading researchers like Harvard economist Raj Chetty and his research team at Opportunity Insights have shined a light on the problem.[8] As the New America Foundation put it in a 2016 report, "the news is that things are mostly getting worse" for low-income students.[9] Only one out of nine young adults from the lowest income quartile will attain a bachelor's degree or higher by the time they reach twenty-four. Eight of ten from the top income quartile will do so.[10] Such statistics challenge the common misperception that if you are smart enough and work hard, you will have an equal chance of earning a degree from a high-quality American university.

The most glaring inequalities exist at America's most prestigious institutions of higher learning, which should be more capable of affording a place to the poor given their large endowments. Scholars estimate that at the 468 most selective colleges, high-income students are overrepresented by 45 percent (relative to their share of the population), while low-income students are underrepresented by 20 percent.[11] The Education Trust deems those US higher educational institutions (generally private, selective, and wealthy institutions) where less than 17 percent of the student body receives Pell grants (i.e., come from families with income levels below about $50,000) "engines of inequality."[12] The Pell Grant indicator is imperfect because it does not "catch" students slightly above the income ceiling. However, many experts maintain that it remains the best estimate of how many low-income students attend a given institution of higher learning.[13] Nearly half of all US students are Pell-eligible today.[14] Yet, on average private institutions with over $1 billion in their endowments have student bodies with only 16 percent Pell grant recipients, while private institutions with less than $100 million endowments have 41 percent on average.[15]

Some of the nation's wealthiest institutions have begun to enroll more Pell-eligible students in recent years. For example, in 2004–2005 Princeton and Harvard had 7.8 percent and 8 percent Pell-eligible students respectively.[16] Today each institution enrolls almost 17 percent.[17] However, much of the growth in Pell Grant recipients at many institutions in the last decade can conceivably be accounted for by the expansion of the Pell program itself, not a greater effort of the institutions to diversify their student body economically.[18] Moreover, other studies confirm that economic diversity among students remains elusive at many of the nation's most selective universities. Children of the wealthiest 1 percent of Americans are 77 times more likely to attend an "Ivy+ College" (the Ivys plus University of Chicago, MIT, Stanford, and Duke) according to a recent landmark study.[19] The New American Foundation attributes the persistent lack of low-income students at many of our nation's wealthiest universities to "stingy" need-based aid policies and "a powerful enrollment management industry [that] has emerged to show colleges how they can use their institutional aid dollars strategically in order to increase both their prestige and revenue."[20] In other words, financial aid has increasingly been used to attract high test-scoring students to boost institutions' rankings and perceptions, rather than assisting the neediest students. Colleges and universities reportedly spend $11 billion on non-need-based financial aid. Nonprofit institutions of higher learning, both public and private, dole out nearly *twice* as much in "aid" dollars to students in the *highest* income quintile as they do to students in the lowest income quintile. In the 1990s that ratio was the inverse.[21]

As the New America Foundation points out, "a college's commitment to helping low-income students can't be measured along a single dimension."[22] In addition to the prevalence of Pell grant recipients as a proxy for low-income students, another important factor is what the neediest students pay on average after grant and scholarship aid, i.e., net price. Admitting large numbers of Pell-eligible students while not meeting their financial need and/or requiring them to take large student loans does not truly demonstrate a commitment to educational equity and economic diversity.[23] The New America Foundation's research reports entitled "Undermining Pell" have found that that "hundreds of colleges expect the neediest students to pay an amount that equals at least half of their families' yearly earnings." Their most recent report dealing with both public and private institutions also states that the number of colleges and universities asking students from families earning less than $30,000 to pay $10,000, $15,000, $20,000 or more increased, with 94 percent of private colleges asking for $10,000 or more.[24] While some institutions struggle to meet the financial need of the most deserving students due to lack of resources, other wealthy institutions spend their aid dollars on attracting "the top students, as well as the most affluent." Thus, paradoxically "only a small number of private colleges" are using financial aid dollars in ways that help the neediest students; others often provide aid packages to students from much higher income brackets.[25] The New America Foundation concludes that "some private nonprofit colleges are making extraordinary efforts to recruit, enroll, and financially assist low-income students. Unfortunately, they are few and far between."[26] As I will discuss in more detail below, some Catholic colleges and universities are among those charging the highest net price to low-income families, while many largely fail to enroll such students at all.[27]

Public institutions generally surpass private institutions in providing access for low-income students. Almost half of the 591 public four-year colleges and universities considered by the New America Foundation "enroll at least 25 percent low-income students" and have a net price of under $10,000 for these students. However, in recent decades many public institutions have followed the trend to use aid dollars to chase after "star" students, simultaneously making it harder for financially needy students to afford a college education even though such institutions were historically founded to equalize access to education.[28] At UVA, for example, only 11.7 percent of students who enrolled in 2016 received Pell grants.[29] Among full-time students, more than 65 percent of students come from families in the top income quintile (roughly $110,000 or higher), while only 2.8 percent come from families in the bottom quartile (about $20,000 or less).[30] Although UVA ranks among the least economically diverse institutions, it does keep the net price for low-income students just under $10,000. Nonetheless, the New America Foundation calls UVA and other public institutions such as William and Mary and the University of Michigan "Country Club Public Institutions." Such institutions are characterized by low Pell enrollments and relatively low average net cost for their few low-income students. They "tend to overwhelmingly serve the well-to-do."[31] According to a report on flagship public universities published by The Education Trust, forty-four out of fifty schools had fewer low-income students by 2006 than they did in 1992.[32] Institutions like UVA, University of Colorado-Boulder, University of Delaware, University of Pittsburgh, James Madison University, and University of Wisconsin-Madison, have found themselves on The Education Trust's "engines of inequality" list.[33]

Friends and family, including my brother, attended Temple University, which the Baptist minister Russell Conwell founded in 1884 to provide access to higher education for poorer, working-class denizens of inner-city Philadelphia. However, the university has increasingly enrolled students from affluent suburbs. The number of students matriculating from the city's public schools has dramatically waned in the last twenty years. In addition, the average income of students receiving financial aid has significantly increased.[34] Temple enrolls substantially more Pell-eligible students (32 percent) than many private institutions in the area. However, these students pay an average net price of more than $15,000 annually. Thus the New America Foundation asks, "Why does Temple ask the lowest-income, in-state freshmen to pay an average net price that equals more than half of their families' yearly earnings?" The answer is telling: a combination of less state funding and an obsession with *U.S. News & World Report* rankings.[35]

If these statistics leave a shadow of doubt, *Wall Street Journal* writer Daniel Golden dispels the myth that college admissions in the United States are meritocratic in his book, *The Price of Admission.*[36] Based on myriad interviews with college administrators, Golden concludes that many colleges and universities intentionally overlook low-income students because they do not represent a potentially wealthy alumni base.[37] Second, he reveals that socioeconomic diversity counts least in admissions; administrators are willing to "sacrifice the interests of low-income students" in order to create more racial, ethnic, and gender diversity. These goals are achieved by targeting middle- and upper-class racial minority students, female athletes, and affluent international students.[38] Moreover, many Whites from middle- and high-income families benefit from affirmative action to a larger degree than low-income and minority students. As Golden maintains:

> At least one-third of the students at elite universities, and at least half at liberal arts colleges, are flagged for preferential treatment in the admissions process. While minorities make up 10 to 15 percent of a typical student body, affluent whites dominate other preferred groups: recruited athletes (10 to 25 percent of students); alumni children, also known as legacies (10 to 25 percent); development cases (2 to 5 percent); children of celebrities and politicians (1 to 2 percent); and children of faculty members (1 to 3 percent).[39]

Students who have such "hooks," in the parlance of admissions officers, obtain profound preferences in the admissions process. Legacies, who tend to come from affluent families, are two to four times more likely to be admitted to elite schools than other applicants even though they are often less qualified.[40] Recruited athletes get a similar boost. Unfortunately, the idea that sports provides a vehicle by which poorer students "get a chance" is also a myth. Golden cites a study of nineteen Ivy League schools and liberal arts colleges that found that only 6 percent of recruited athletes come from the lowest income quartile.[41] All of this is happening while many universities turn down highly qualified low-income candidates in favor of less qualified, more affluent candidates. This "need sensitive" admissions process, as it is commonly called, takes into account the applicant's financial status. Thus, talented low-income students are cast aside in order to meet budgets and to court potential donors.[42] Unfortunately, some institutions that utilized need blind admissions in the past have recently abandoned it.[43]

In spite of this bleak situation, the news is not all bad. To reiterate, the New America Foundation and others have lauded the "extraordinary efforts" of a small number of institutions that have successfully opened their doors more widely to economically disadvantaged students. For example, Franklin and Marshall increased its Pell students from 5 percent to 17 percent in just three years. The college's board of trustees decided to end non-need-based aid and to dramatically increase need-based aid. The board also intentionally recruited a president who would further the goal of creating more diversity among its student body. Dan Porterfield assumed the presidency in 2010 and created the Next Generation Initiative, with numerous programs targeting first-generation, low-income students such as F&M College Prep, which has graduated more than 150 high school juniors from its summer program, with 90 percent of them going to college (25 percent have attended Franklin & Marshall). Porterfield is widely recognized as a leader in promoting college access.[44] According to the New America Foundation, "strong leaders" at Amherst, Cooper Union, Grinnell, the Massachusetts Institute of Technology, Smith, and Vassar have also made concerted efforts to create more socioeconomically diverse campuses, placing them among 25 High-Pell, Low-Net-Cost private institutions.[45] Once economist Catherine Hill Bond took over Vassar's presidency in 2006, for example, she adopted need-blind admissions, eliminated loans from aid packages for families earning under $60,000, and spearheaded efforts to recruit talented low-income students. These efforts raised the number of Pell recipients attending Vassar, from 12 percent to almost 20 percent.[46] Grinnell College also has exhibited robust commitment to socioeconomic diversity via increased need-based aid, recruiting, and community partnerships. Grinnell has explicitly linked its commitment to socioeconomic diversity with long-standing historical commitment to progressivism and "social responsibility."[47] Some public institutions have also maintained or enhanced their commitment to serving low-income students. The New America Foundation lists forty-eight among the "best of the best" for enrolling more than 50 percent Pell recipients and for keeping the average net tuition below $10,000 for these students.[48] As I will discuss below, some Catholic colleges either admit high numbers of Pell recipients, or keep the cost down for low-income students, or achieve both goals. It can be done.

Such positive examples amidst the overall negative picture demonstrate that institutions can make choices to move toward expanding access. They are not in a "straightjacket" caused by rising educational costs, stagnant wages for many families, persistent economic inequality, etc. Institutions demonstrate which values they espouse when deciding how much aid and to whom to allocate it.

The trends described above have tremendous significance for several reasons. Even if a college degree no longer guarantees good pay (as mentioned in Chapter 2), social class and economic well-being is still significantly determined by educational attainment in the United States. For example, the College Board reported in 2016 that bachelor's degree holders earned 65–70 percent more than high school graduates on average. This income premium for male and female college graduates has reportedly more than doubled over the last thirty years.[49] According to one recent estimate the income premium for a BA amounts to about $32,000 more annually, or roughly $1,383,000 per lifetime.[50] A college degree is also a major engine for "intergenerational income mobility."[51] Moreover, education is intrinsically a good that all persons, regardless of socioeconomic status, should be able to enjoy. For this reason, Catholic social teaching, along with organizations such as the United Nations, has promoted the right to education in numerous documents and treaties.

The Right to Education in International Agreements

I cannot offer an exhaustive treatment of the right to education here.[52] However, briefly examining some of its historical roots in key international agreements will locate the discussion in a broader political context and facilitate useful comparison with Catholic teaching on the right to education.[53]

The 1948 *UN Universal Declaration of Human Rights* posited that everyone has "the right to education."[54] Notably the Declaration states that only elementary and "fundamental" education must be free, while "technical and profession education" must be "equally accessible to all." This formulation obfuscates whether or not the right to education applies to university-level education. It also fails to spell out what must be done and by whom in order to provide equal access. *The International Covenant on Economic, Social and Cultural Rights* of 1966 clarified the meaning and scope of the right to education. It stipulates, among other things, that "higher education shall be made equally accessible to all, on the basis of capacity, by every appropriate means, and in particular by the progressive introduction of free education."[55] In other words, free primary education should be realized as a right immediately and access to secondary and higher education must be made available "progressively."[56]

Later documents have reaffirmed that the right to education pertains to primary, secondary, and higher education.[57] The *Framework for Priority Action for Change and Development of Higher Education*, which was adopted with the *World Declaration on Higher Education for the Twenty-First Century* by UNESCO in 1998, ranks among the most important. According to this document, the UN Universal Declaration mandated that governments must establish the necessary "legislative, political and financial frameworks" to ensure that "equal access on the basis of merit" to higher education becomes a reality. Furthermore, "no one can be excluded from higher education or its study fields, degree levels and types of institutions on grounds of race, gender, language, religion, or age or *because of any economic or social distinctions or physical disabilities*."[58] Moreover, universities must "actively facilitate" both access and success in higher education for "special target groups," which include the economically disadvantaged. Institutions of higher learning should foster this as broadly as possible by creating a "seamless system" with early childhood, primary, and secondary educational schools.[59]

Many US institutions of higher learning are largely out of touch with realities and problems in their local communities, as Golden persuasively contends.[60] Therefore, the *World Declaration on Higher Education* calls for nothing short of a radical restructuring of the relationship between US colleges and universities and various actors in their communities in order to make it truly possible for all persons with the capacity to obtain college degrees. According to the *World Declaration*, universal access to higher education benefits disadvantaged individuals and society as a whole, as these learners bring their unique experiences and untapped talent to the task of development.[61]

Admittedly, the enforceability or "bite" of the aforementioned agreements concerning the right to higher education is tenuous, particularly in the United States. The United States still has not ratified *The International Covenant on Economic, Social and Cultural Rights*. Powerful currents in US history and culture have dismissed the existence of such rights.[62] The Constitutional basis of the right to education, at all levels, remains a contentious debate.[63] However, as I have argued throughout this book, Catholic higher education must adopt Catholic social teaching as its normative framework. Catholic social teaching holds that rights are not bestowed on human beings by governments by dint of their citizenship. Rather, human rights inhere in the nature of the human person, and are ultimately God-given. Human rights are required for the protection of the dignity of the human person.[64] This includes the right to education.

The Right to Education in Modern Catholic Social Teaching

Catholic social teaching has undergone an evolution on the right to education. Pope Leo XIII did not speak of a "right" to education, but he lauded the generosity of Catholics that made education for those "of slender means" possible.[65] Pope Pius XI referred to the right of all children to receive proper moral and spiritual education. However, he mainly emphasized the right and duty of parents and the church to provide that education, while the state should support, and when necessary, "supplement their work" with its own educational institutions.[66] In his 1942 Christmas Radio Message, Pope Pius XII shifts to locating a general right to education among the "fundamental rights of the person." He also maintains that the church envisions a "social order" that promotes among other things "higher education for children of the working classes" who demonstrate exceptional aptitude, character, and commitment to the common good.[67] Pope John XXIII articulates the Catholic position on the right to education and its basis more lucidly than any other pope in his 1963 encyclical, *Pacem in Terris*. It is worth quoting the entire passage:

The natural law also gives man [sic] the right to share in the benefits of culture and therefore a right to a basic education and to technical and profession training in keeping with the stage of the educational development of the country to which he belongs. Every effort should be made to ensure that persons be enabled, on the basis of merit, to go on to higher studies, so that, as far as possible, they may occupy posts and take on responsibilities in human societies in accordance with their natural gifts and the skills they have acquired.[68]

Vatican II's Pastoral Constitution on the Church in the Modern World, *Gaudium et Spes*, enumerated the right to education among other rights and endorsed educational equity for women.[69] The declaration also contended that the "gifted" among "the social groups of every people" should be able to attain higher education so they can contribute to society in accordance with their abilities and preserve their group's culture.[70] However, *Gaudium et Spes* does not clearly postulate that higher education is a right due to all persons in justice.

Vatican II's Declaration on Christian Education *Gravissimum Educationis* contains a specific section on the "meaning of the universal right to an education."[71] There is no mention of higher education. However, *Gravissimum Educationis* maintains that one's educational opportunities should cohere with factors such as ability, goals, and the "culture and tradition of one's country." Moreover, Catholic schools have an obligation to "fulfill their function in an increasingly more adequate way, and especially in caring for the needs of those who are poor in the goods of this world."[72] The Declaration calls upon both pastors and the faithful to "spare no sacrifice" in fulfilling this duty. Colleges and universities should make education "readily available to students of real promise, even though they be of slender means."[73] This mandate particularly applies to students from developing nations.

In *Populorum Progessio* (1967), Pope Paul VI decried educational imbalances between nations and maintained that people from less developed countries should be able to seek advanced training in highly developed countries (no. 67). He also claimed that primary education is the most important means to and a goal of development (no. 35). Although St. Paul VI did not call basic education a right, he did state that "lack of education is as serious as lack of food" (no. 35). The encyclical does not explicitly discuss higher education.

Pope John Paul II, a former university professor, listed the lack of access to higher education among the many "scourges" that afflict the poor and marginalized in his encyclical *Sollicitudo Rei Socialis*.[74] He lamented that this occurs in the "Second World," "Third World," and the "Fourth World"—i.e., the large tracts of poor in affluent countries. Elsewhere, the pope called education a "primary human right," which the church and civil society must promote.[75] He also posited education as a necessary condition of the right to human fulfillment. John Paul II was clearly dismayed that more progress had not been made in realizing the right to education for all. He maintained that in many parts of the world educational opportunities for the poor are disappearing. In his view, lack of access to primary education is a particularly egregious violation of human dignity. Affluent countries often set up an apartheid-like system that provides top-notch higher and secondary education for elites, while devoting preciously few assets to basic education for all.[76] Drawing on Thomistic natural law, John Paul II argued that education is a fundamental human right because it is necessary for the human person to become fully human.[77]

In remarking on the Catholic university's obligation to pursue social justice and the church's commitment to the "integral growth of all men and women," John Paul II stated in *Ex Corde Ecclesiae*:

> Every Catholic University feels responsible to contribute concretely to the progress of the society within which it works: for example it will be capable of searching for ways to make university education accessible to all those who are able to benefit from it, especially the poor or members of minority groups who customarily have been deprived of it. A Catholic University also has the responsibility, to the degree that it is able, to help to promote the development of the emerging nations.[78]

While this falls short of positing that the poor have a right to higher education, with a corresponding duty of Catholic universities to fulfill that right, it moves toward obliging Catholic universities to do everything in their power to do so. It is the Gospel, according to John Paul II in *Ex Corde*, which calls them to this task.

Like John Paul II, Benedict XVI insisted that Catholic schools must be "accessible to people of all social and economic strata."[79] However, he did not mention a right to higher education in his speech at the Catholic University of America. Earlier in his papacy Benedict stressed the urgency of realizing the right to education on a much greater scale given the complexities of globalization. Once again he did not refer explicitly to higher education.[80]

Pope Francis has frequently championed the right to education, prompting one journalist to ask if he might be "the world's most important education advocate."[81] For example, in a dialogue with educational leaders from around the world in Rome, the Pope lamented that "education has become too selective and elitist. It seems that only people or persons who have a certain level or who have a certain capacity have a right to education." He went on to say, "but certainly all children and all young people have a right to education." He urged these educators to actualize "the 14 works of mercy . . . in education."[82] At the United Nations Francis insisted that promoting integral human development and human dignity "presuppose and require" the right to education.[83] In an address at the Pontifical Catholic University of Ecuador in Quito, he told students that their "time of study" is both "a right" and "a privilege."[84] Thus, the current Pope has more clearly expressed that there is a right to higher education than many of his predecessors, albeit not in an encyclical.

The United States Conference of Catholic Bishops has echoed what the universal teaching of the magisterium held regarding the right to education. The American bishops have endorsed the right to education on numerous occasions.[85] In their 2003 pastoral *Faithful Citizenship*, they stated:

> All persons, by virtue of their dignity as human persons, have an inalienable right to receive a quality education. We must ensure that our nation's young people, especially the poor, those with disabilities, and the most vulnerable, are properly prepared to be good citizens, to lead productive lives, and to be socially and morally responsible in the complicated and technologically challenging world of the twenty-first century. We support the necessary initiatives that provide adequate funding to educate all persons no matter what school they attend—public, private, or religious—or their personal condition.[86]

The bishops have argued that American society needs to make a much more concerted effort to realize the right to education for the poor.[87] They also heralded Catholic schools as a model for providing quality education for the poor.[88] The bishops stated that Catholic schools serve as one of the nation's "best anti-poverty programs" by offering an excellent education, "moral truth," and "discipline" to impoverished communities.[89]

Furthermore, they have pledged "to make Catholic schools models of education for the poor."[90] A good deal of evidence supports the contention that Catholic primary and secondary education empowers the poor, who would otherwise have little chance to receive quality education, particularly in inner cities.[91] This chapter asks whether or not this is the case at the tertiary level as well. Although the bishops have never unequivocally stated that access to higher education is a right of the poor, it would make little sense to exclude the more than 220 Roman Catholic colleges and universities in the United States from the "models of education for the poor" that the bishops envision in their pastoral *Economic Justice For All*.

To summarize, modern Catholic social teaching has unequivocally endorsed the right to education. Yet, official Catholic social teaching has not postulated clearly enough that the fulfillment of the right to education requires equal and affordable access to *higher education*. John XXIII's statement in *Pacem in Terris* comes the closest, but remains ambiguous about whether or not universal access to higher education is a desirable good or a human right. Pope Francis's remarks in Quito are unambiguous, but they do not have the same authoritative weight as papal teaching in an encyclical. For one reason or another, official Catholic social teaching has not specified the meaning and scope of the right to education as lucidly as the above-mentioned international agreements. These agreements have reiterated the need to make access to higher education a realizable right, spelled out who bears the duty to enable its fulfillment, and described ways these duty-bearers should go about accomplishing this task. In spite of this lacuna in CST, the strong endorsement of the right to education in general, coupled with other key themes such as solidarity, participation, and the option for the poor, leads to the conclusion that higher education is a right to be enjoyed by all in Catholic social teaching. According to Catholic social teaching, institutions should help especially the poor to realize this right. For Catholic institutions, this obligation arises out of their raison d'être. The following section will unpack this claim.

The Right to Higher Education as a Requirement of Solidarity and Precondition of the Right and Duty of Participation

As I discussed earlier, the universal teaching of the magisterium unequivocally requires solidarity with the poor. The church itself must embody solidarity with the poor as a sign of its "fidelity to Christ," as Pope John Paul II argued.[92] John Paul II described the church's preferential option for the poor in *Sollicitudo Rei Socialis* as "the option or love of preference for the poor. This is an option, or a special form of primacy in the exercise of Christian charity, to which the whole tradition of the Church bears witness. It affects the life of each Christian inasmuch as he or she seeks to imitate the life of Christ, but it applies equally to our social responsibilities and hence to our manner of living, and to the logical decisions to be made concerning the ownership and use of goods."[93] The pope stated that ignoring the growing numbers of poor in our world would be akin to the "rich man" ignoring Lazarus the beggar, whom he encountered every day outside of his gate (see Luke 16:19–31). According to John Paul II "a wealthy minority" today bears responsibility for denial of the rights of the poor because their avarice demands more and more at the expense of the needy.[94]

This option for the poor must be translated into concrete social and economic policies designed to combat the evil of poverty. As John Paul II maintained, local groups must decide which institutional reforms are most needed in order to rectify the "scandalous" situation of the poor in myriad parts of the world, including so-called "developed" countries like the United States.[95] Furthermore, the rights of the poor, such as the right to adequate nutrition, health care, and education must be given the highest priority in economic policy-making and financial planning. Prioritization of the rights of the poor follows from the church's ancient teaching on the "universal destination of goods." In other words, God has created all things to serve all God's children. This principle requires societies and all their institutions to acknowledge the social function of private property, which means that private property must be used to serve the common good, not only the prosperous.[96] Moreover, just as Jesus called Zaccheus the tax collector to immediate conversion, (see Luke 19:1–10) following Christ requires answering the "shout and cry" of the poor today by recognizing their just claims on society now, not some time in the future.[97] In short, the justice of the entire economy and individual economic policies is determined by its effects on the poorest members of society, as the United States Conference of Catholic Bishops contended.[98]

If solidarity with the poor and promoting social justice is not an "option," but rather "a constitutive dimension of the preaching of the Gospel," Catholics must ask of themselves and their institutions, "What does solidarity with the poor and oppressed require in the US context?"[99] Realizing the option for the poor in the US context undoubtedly requires the promotion of many forms of justice and numerous human rights. This chapter focuses on just one: the right to educational achievement that allows for the full participation in the life of the community. In the US context, and elsewhere for sure, solidarity with the poor demands making higher education accessible so that they can escape marginalization and the cycle of poverty.[100]

Solidarity with the poor cannot be achieved solely through acts of charity. According to Catholic social thought, solidarity strives to enable the poor and the marginalized to become full members of the community. In other words, it seeks to procure the right to participation for all, a right that Catholic social teaching upholds.[101] Catholic social teaching views the right to participation as the precondition of all other rights; without it, the realization of all other rights remains in jeopardy.[102] Moreover, Catholic social teaching posits a connection between economic deprivation and the denial of the right to participation:

> Unless combated and overcome by social and political action, the influence of the new industrial and technological order favors the concentration of wealth, power and decision-making in the hands of a small public or private controlling group. Economic injustice and lack of social participation keep a man [sic] from attaining his basic human and civil rights.[103]

In short, solidarity must be embodied in policies and institutions that promote the participation of the oppressed as agents of personal and social change.[104] Modern Catholic social teaching has continually specified the rights necessary for human dignity and flourishing in the context of particular historical, social, political, and economic conditions.[105] For example, the horrific plight of workers during the Industrial Revolution led to support for labor rights in modern CST.[106] This method of "reading the signs of the times" yields the conclusion that today's social and economic conditions in the United States necessitate including the right to higher education among those rights due to the poor in justice. Because of the nature of the US economy and contemporary society, the poor should be able to attain a college education to ensure this kind of participation.

Experts widely recognize education as one of the primary vehicles for attaining "human capital." Skills, education, knowledge, and health constitute the core elements of human capital, which has become "the dominant factor of production—not just an important adjunct to physical capital."[107] According to the World Bank's 2019 World Development Report, human capital helps individuals to reach their full potential and has broad benefits to society. The greater the accumulation of human capital, the more people tend to be healthier, productive, politically engaged and able to "adapt faster to technological change." More skilled workers that can utilize "machines, not fear them" will succeed in the global economy. Furthermore, people with more human capital are equipped with "sociobehavioral skills such as an aptitude for teamwork, empathy, conflict resolution, and relationship management." Human capital therefore underpins "social cohesion" and one's ability to participate in society.[108] People often find themselves in the throes of a cycle of poverty without the human capital acquired through education, which enables them to participate freely and equally in the market, and more broadly in the "polis."[109] Without the proper training, skills, and knowledge, people tend to be relegated to the sidelines of the market and the society as a whole.[110] As the economist Amartya Sen puts it, educational deficiencies seriously detract from the ability to attain freedoms that all persons wish to enjoy, such as political participation, economic activity, literacy, numeracy, and health.[111]

After World War II American higher education increasingly functioned as the engine of social mobility in the United States.[112] In other words, higher education began to level the "human capital" playing field. However, as I indicated above, low-income students in recent decades have less access to higher education and the social mobility it affords. Given the importance of human capital in today's knowledge-based society, it should come as no surprise that college enrollment is one of the biggest predictors of the ability to escape "inherited" poverty.[113] MIT economist David Autor attributes growing economic inequality largely to "the dramatic growth in the wage premium associated with higher education and, more broadly, cognitive ability."[114] Furthermore, the US pays the highest premium for higher education and cognitive skills in the developed world.[115] Getting a job in the first place increasingly requires some type of postsecondary education, as experts have predicted 65 percent of jobs require it.[116]

Succinctly stated, access to higher education, though not a guarantee, greatly assists poor people to escape the poverty trap. Enrolling in college "inoculates" an individual against the plague of poverty, while finishing a BA provides even greater immunity.[117] In the US, where educational attainment is strongly linked to both family income and one's own future income, the cycle of poverty is clear: If you come from a poor family, you are much less likely to obtain a college degree. This also means that you are much more likely to endure poverty than your counterparts from affluent backgrounds.

In addition to the necessity of the procurement of the right to education for the achievement of economic freedoms, such as the ability to escape poverty, the poor must be able to attain higher education in the United States in order to exercise political liberty. Because of the strong link between economic status and educational achievement, the economic disadvantages that arise due to a lack of a college education vitiate true political liberty for all in the United States. As John Rawls argued in *A Theory of Justice*, in a democracy that allows for vast inequalities of wealth and property, all people do not have the same "fair value of political liberty."

> Political power rapidly accumulates and becomes unequal; and making use of the coercive apparatus of the state and its law, those who gain the advantage can often assure themselves of a favored position. Thus inequities in the economic and social system may soon undermine whatever political equality might have existed under fortunate historical circumstances.[118]

According to Rawls, for a democracy to truly allow for the fair value of political liberties, private ownership and the means of production, property, and wealth must be "widely distributed." This is necessary because the wealthy have a greater likelihood of influencing politicians and political parties, whose campaigns are privately financed. They also have more opportunity to advance their interests by controlling the media and influencing those who may pass laws that further their interests.[119] In other words, not having a college degree seriously detracts from the ability to have a voice in society. The disadvantage of the poor in the political sphere in turn makes it unlikely that their economic, social, and cultural needs and interests will be represented in government and public policymaking.[120] Thomas Jefferson presciently realized this. Therefore, he advocated expanding access to higher education so that citizens could "develop the critical analytic skills necessary for formulating opinions and making decisions" necessary for the protection of their rights and the flourishing of democracy.[121]

In these circumstances, solidarity, which seeks to empower the poor in order to escape marginalization, requires the fulfillment of the right to education. The poor have a right to participate fully in all cultural, political, economic, and social spheres of society. Given the relationship between educational attainment, economic status, and access to these other spheres in American society,[122] the poor must be able to take their place at well-resourced US colleges and universities. In addition to the ability of individuals to escape poverty, if more members of underrepresented groups populate our university halls, they in turn will be more likely to defend the rights of the poor and oppressed through social and political advocacy. In this way, communities of solidarity will be born, in which all members can "carry one another's burdens."[123]

Given CST's commitment to solidarity and the option for the poor, Catholic universities should excel in providing high-quality education for the poor. I have argued in the current US context, access to higher education constitutes a right, not just a desirable good. Roman Catholic universities, along with other governmental and nongovernmental entities, bear a duty to enable the fulfillment of this right, particularly among the poor. As was discussed above, far too many American colleges and universities have failed to uphold this duty. Have Roman Catholic colleges and universities succeeded to a greater degree? The following section will assess selected Catholic colleges and universities in this light. This assessment is a preliminary attempt to determine whether or not current admissions and retention practices and policies cohere with Catholic social teaching on the right to education of the poor. Given some of the complexities of college admissions and the economics of higher education, this discussion is meant to be a "conversation starter," rather than a final judgment. My analysis may overlook or oversimplify some important issues, which will require further examination. Nonetheless, given Catholic teaching on the right to education, administrators, trustees, faculty, staff, and students at all Catholic colleges and universities must give serious and sustained attention to the issues raised here.

US Catholic Colleges and Universities and the Right to Education of the Poor

Historically, access to education for the poor represented a core element of the mission of many Catholic colleges and universities. For example, education of the poor has been a hallmark of the Christian Brothers, who were founded three hundred years ago by St. John Baptiste de La Salle (1651–1719). De La Salle made this a central part of the order's mission at its inception. In the vow of 1694, he and eleven other Christian Brothers promised "to keep together and by association gratuitous schools, wherever I may be, even if I were obliged to beg for alms and live by bread alone."[124] The contemporary mission statement of the Christian Brothers, as well as mission statements of their schools such as LaSalle University, reflects this ideal.[125]

Like de La Salle, the founder of the Society of Jesus, Ignatius of Loyola (1491–1556), insisted that the order's schools remain accessible to the poor. Jesuit schools had special housing for the poor so that they could be afforded an education.[126] In 1986 the Superior General of the Jesuits, Fr. Peter-Hans Kolvenbach, commissioned an international group of Jesuits to produce "The General Characteristics of Jesuit Education." This document states that the Society of Jesus has made a "preferential option for the poor." Jesuit schools should embody the option for the poor "both in the students that are admitted and in the type of formation that is given."[127] Concretely, every Jesuit school should do "what it can to make Jesuit education available to everyone, including the poor and the disadvantaged."[128]

St. Katharine Drexel (1858–1955) also saw the need to provide access to education for the disadvantaged, creating schools for Native Americans and Black Catholics in the early twentieth century. Her crowning achievement was the founding of Xavier University of Louisiana in 1925, the first and only Catholic institution of higher learning for Blacks in the United States.[129] Venerable Catherine McAuley (1778–1841), who founded the Sisters of Mercy in 1831 in Ireland, recognized the duty to serve and educate the poor because of Jesus's "tender love for the poor."[130] She created numerous schools for poor women so they could gain the skills to overcome poverty. In that spirit, the 2004 Conference for Mercy Higher Education document *Mercy Higher Education: Culture and Characteristics* names "promoting compassion and justice to those with less, especially women and children," one of the four "hallmarks" of Mercy higher education. The document identifies "scholarship programs that reach out to the most marginalized" as a key means of maintaining this characteristic.[131]

By contrast, the majority of the students today at many Catholic colleges and universities come from affluent backgrounds, while most of the nation's and the world's poor remain excluded from their halls. Of course, there are exceptions at every institution; a relatively small number of scholarships bring poorer students to many Catholic campuses. On the other hand, some Catholic colleges and universities have been more successful than others in recruiting, admitting, and retaining economically disadvantaged students.

Table 1 below lists the ten wealthiest US Catholic colleges and universities. Given their superior financial resources over other Catholic institutions it is reasonable to start by asking how they fare in terms of promoting the option for the poor and the right to education. Unfortunately, few have large numbers of Pell recipients, according to the latest available data (2016–17).[132] For example, the University of Notre Dame's endowment dwarfs all other Catholic institutions at more than $10 billion, yet less than 10 percent of its first-year students are Pell grantees. The Education Trust deems five of the wealthiest Catholic colleges and universities "engines of inequality" because they "fall in the bottom five percent of institutions for their enrollment of students from working-class and low-income backgrounds."[133] In other words, the Pell enrollment rates for first-year students at Notre Dame, Boston College, Georgetown, Villanova, and Santa Clara are among the lowest five percent nationally. This is the case even though their endowments rank among the top ten for Catholic institutions of higher learning and are among the largest 175 of any type of higher educational institution.[134]

The lack of economic diversity is not confined to the wealthiest or most selective Catholic institutions. For example, Providence College, Fairfield University, Saint Joseph's University, and Loyola College of Maryland occupy four of the ten lowest rankings in *U.S. News and World Report*'s "Economic Diversity" index for the Regional Universities North category. At each school between 12 and 13 percent of undergraduates are Pell recipients.[135]

In addition to low Pell enrollments, other indicators should raise concerns for the wealthiest (and other) Catholic institutions. The Opportunity

Table 1. Catholic Institutions of Higher Education with the Largest Endowments

Institution	Endowments (FY 18 $000)	Average Net Price after Grants	Average Net Price for Low-Income Students ($0–30K)	% Pell Recipients among Freshmen	% Pell Recipients among Undergrads	Average Institutional Grant Aid	Average Freshmen Student Loan (all sources)
University of Notre Dame	$10,727,653	$26,683	$9,478	9.9%	10.2%	$36,897	$6,150
Boston College	$2,477,700	$27,167	$5,549	11.9%	12.4%	$36,131	$4,027
Georgetown University	$1,769,557	$26,625	$6,112	12.5%	12.0%	$38,784	$6,518
Saint Louis University	$1,222,688	$33,222	$21,970	18.8%	12.1%	$21,410	$8,003
Santa Clara University	$979,248	$37,657	$16,963	8.9%	10.9%	$23,674	$6,609
College of the Holy Cross	$784,264	$26,965	$9,169	15.5%	15.2%	$32,878	$6,423
St John's University (N.Y.)	$756,099	$26,582	$24,095	43.3%	28.4%	$21,469	$7,456
Fordham University	$729,179	$38,008	$24,248	19.1%	19.9%	$23,907	$8,603
Villanova University	$715,650	$33,270	$19,284	13.1%	12.0%	$27,699	$8,611
Marquette University	$668,567	$33,502	$18,674	17.5%	15.5%	$16,575	$9,116

Source: The Education Trust, College Online Database at http://www.collegeresults.org/default.aspx and 2018 NACUBO-TIAA Study of Endowments at https://www.nacubo.org/Research/2019/NACUBO-TIAA-Study-of-Endowments

Project data indicates that more students hail from the top 1 percent of *household income* than the bottom 60 percent combined at Notre Dame, Georgetown, Boston College, and Villanova (Table 3). Many "elite" secular institutions exhibit this kind of "preferential option for the rich," but Catholic institutions need to ask whether or not these demographics cohere with CST, particularly the preferential option for the poor. Some of the ten wealthiest Catholic institutions, like St. John's University in New York, appear much more favorably in light of this CST principle, with many more low-income students than members of the economic upper echelon (Tables 2 and 3). Others fall somewhere in between. For example, College of the Holy Cross, considered "elite" based on selectivity, has made strides in providing greater access over the last decade and now has more than 15 percent Pell recipients (Table 1). Holy Cross also recently joined the American Talent Initiative, which aims to educate 50,000 more talented low-income students at schools with the highest graduation rates nationally by 2025.[136] However, 13.1 percent of Holy Cross students come from the top 1 percent income bracket, 15.5 percent from the bottom 60 percent, and only 4.1 percent from the bottom 20 percent (Table 3).[137] Fordham and Marquette have even more Pell recipients than Holy Cross (Table 1) and much lower ratios of students from the top income percent to students from lower income backgrounds (Tables 2 and 3). Admittedly, the data from the Opportunity Project on the ratios of income groups can be interpreted in various ways and is now several years old. Nonetheless, Catholic colleges should use this type of data to consider if the socioeconomic profile of their student bodies reflects a determination to embody the option for the poor.

Unfortunately, very few Catholic institutions rank among the leaders in providing a *low-net-cost* education for large numbers of Pell recipients. For example, only Calumet College of Saint Joseph and the University of Holy Cross in Louisiana earned the distinction of High-Pell, Low-Net-Cost in The New America Foundation's most recent report including private institutions, which was published in 2016.[138] It should be noted, however, that some Catholic institutions are High-Pell, but miss the designation of Low-Net-Cost because they charge a net price only slightly above the $10,000 threshold used in the report. Among such schools are Saint Peter's University, Saint Joseph's College-New York, Fontbonne University, University of Mary, Madonna University, and Mercy College.[139]

Table 2. Wealthiest Catholic Institutions vs. Elite Colleges with High Enrollments of Low-Income Students

Rank among Elite Colleges	Institution	Pct. from Bottom 40%
–	Saint John's University (N.Y.)	27.4
1	University of California, Los Angeles	19.2
2	Emory University	15.9
3	Barnard College	15.3
4	New York University	14.3
5	Vassar College	13.8
6	Bryn Mawr College	13.7
7	Massachusetts Institute of Technology	13.5
8	University of Miami (Fla.)	13.1
9	Brandeis University	12.9
–	Fordham University	12.7
31	College of the Holy Cross	9.5
–	Saint Louis University	9.2
–	Santa Clara University	7.7
49	Boston College	7.4
50	Georgetown University	7.1
–	Marquette University	7
68	Villanova University	5.7
76	Notre Dame	4.4

Source: "Mobility Report Cards: The Role of Colleges in Intergenerational Mobility," The Equality of Opportunity Project[140]

On the other hand, many Catholic institutions are considered Low-Pell, High-Net-Cost, including several Catholic schools with the largest endowments. The Catholic University of America, Fairfield University, University of Dayton, Saint Joseph's University, Santa Clara University, Villanova University, Loyola University of Maryland, Boston College, and Stonehill College all appear on the 2016 list. Each school had between 11 percent and 15 percent Pell recipients and charged them a net price ranging between $29,000 and $15,000 annually.[141]

In recent years observers have decried the high net cost at many Catholic institutions, whose social teaching holds that "poor people have the

Table 3. Ratio of Students from the Top 1% and Bottom 60% of Household Income

Rank (top 1% / bottom 60% ratio)	Institution	The Top 1% ($630K+)	The Bottom 60% (<$65K)
1	Washington University in St. Louis	21.7	6.1
2	Colorado College	24.2	10.5
3	Washington and Lee University	19.1	8.4
4	Colby College	20.4	11.1
5	Trinity College (Conn.)	26.2	14.3
6	Bucknell University	20.4	12.2
7	Colgate University	22.6	13.6
8	Kenyon College	19.8	12.2
9	Middlebury College	22.8	14.2
10	Tufts University	18.6	11.8
12	Georgetown University	20.8	13.5
13	Notre Dame	15.4	10
24	Villanova University	15	12.4
32	Boston College	16.1	15.2
45	Santa Clara University	14.4	15.9
49	College of the Holy Cross	13.1	15.5
110	Marquette University	7	16.1
117	Fordham University	8	20.6
154	Saint Louis University	5.4	19
764	Saint John's University (N.Y.)	<1	47.8

Source: "Mobility Report Cards: The Role of Colleges in Intergenerational Mobility," The Equality of Opportunity Project first claim on limited resources."[142] In this regard, Paul Moses reported that in 2014 "five of the 10 most expensive private universities for low-income students, and 10 of the top 28, are Catholic." He also noted that the Catholic University of America charged the most expensive net price to poor students among all private institutions, at $30,770.[143] Even some of the richest Catholic institutions charge close to $20,000 or more to the students least able to pay (Table 1).[144] Another journalist pointed out that low-income students at more than half of all Catholic institutions are saddled with upwards of $20,000 in federal loans after graduation.[145] In short, Catholic colleges and universities have come under scrutiny for not doing enough to serve the needs of poorer students. In many cases, this criticism warrants renewed and more vigorous efforts to create greater access to more affordable education for the poor.

Notre Dame, Georgetown, and Boston College have increased resources in recent years to assist the small number of matriculated low-income students by providing a relatively low net price. These Low-Pell, Low-Net-Cost Schools charge them $9,500, $6,500, and $5,500 respectively. Boston College uses need-blind admissions and a generous need-based aid program to meet full demonstrated financial need.[146] These policies appear to have enabled Boston College, once considered High-Net-Cost by New America Foundation, to move to Low-Net-Cost for the neediest students in just a few years. In 2015 Notre Dame designated $20 million to bear the entire cost of attendance for low-income students.[147] Georgetown matches donors with needy students to provide them with full tuition scholarships, promising to meet the "full financial need" of every student.[148] Though Villanova's net cost remains high, the university has instituted a scholarship program for needy students from the Archdiocese of Newark thanks to a $10 million gift.[149] All of these initiatives are laudable and move these institutions toward greater fidelity to CST. However, they still have more work to do in order to measure up to those outstanding High-Pell, Low-Net-Cost private (and highly selective) institutions like Wellesley College, Amherst College, Williams College, Pomona College, Columbia University, and Princeton University (Table 4).[150]

Many highly selective High-Pell, Low-Cost institutions have substantially larger endowments than most of their Catholic peers. However, the

Table 4. Select High-Pell, Low-Net-Cost Highly Selective Institutions[151]

Institution	Endowment (FY 18 $000)	Average Net Price after Grants	Average Net Price for Low-Income Students ($0–30K)	% Pell Recipients among Freshmen	% Pell Recipients among Undergrads
Williams College	$2,749,653	$18,167	$1,910	22.0%	18.6%
Princeton University	$25,917,199	$17,732	$2,469	16.8%	15.3%
Vassar College	$1,082,831	$21,933	$5,585	22.6%	23.9%
Pomona College	$2,273,707	$18,140	$5,739	22.0%	19.5%
Massachusetts Institute of Technology	$16,529,432	$21,576	$5,968	15.5%	17.4%
Amherst College	$2,377,537	$19,055	$6,228	21.0%	23.3%
Wellesley College	$2,105,212	$20,013	$8,357	20.2%	18.5%
Columbia University	$10,869,245	$22,973	$9,481	17.5%	22.4%
Franklin and Marshall College	$352,131	$23,182	$11,849	19.1%	18.5%

Source: The Education Trust, College Online Database at http://www.collegeresults.org/default
.aspx

example of Franklin and Marshall demonstrates that institutions can achieve relatively high Pell percentages and relatively low net price even with a modest endowment, compared to the ten wealthiest Catholic institutions (Tables 1 and 4).[152] Furthermore, a number of smaller, less well-endowed Catholic institutions outperform them using what might be called the "option for the poor metric," even though they have fewer resources. As mentioned above, a few Catholic institutions are High-Pell, Low-Net-Cost, with another group of High-Pell schools with net costs close to the Low-Net-Cost threshold. In addition, institutions like Christian Brothers University, LaSalle University, and Loyola Marymount University all admit many more low-income students than the wealthiest Catholic institutions. Smaller schools such as Trinity University in Washington DC, Mount Saint Mary's in California, and Saint Peter's College in New Jersey have even more low-income students (Table 5). In other words, in many cases "those with less are doing more," which seems to turn Jesus's injunction "from the one who has been entrusted with much, much more will be asked" (Lk 12:48, NIV) on its head.

In short, most Catholic colleges and universities attempt to provide access to some students of lesser means. However, many Catholic institutions must do more to become a "model of education for the poor," in the words of the United States Conference of Catholic Bishops. In particular, the wealthiest and most selective Catholic institutions must work harder to recruit, admit, and graduate talented low-income students without asking them to pay a prohibitive net cost and saddling them with massive debt. The final section of this chapter will ponder some ways to make progress in the "option for the poor" rankings.

Normative Conclusions and Future Directions

In today's market-driven academy, Catholic institutions must be as "wise as serpents and innocent as doves" (Matthew 10:16 NRSV). In other words, they must carefully balance the need to be financially sound and institutionally competitive with the mandates of Catholic social teaching. For certain, this is no easy task. But the fact that many Catholic colleges and universities mirror secular institutions of higher learning in myriad ways, including the denial of access to the poor, should raise serious concerns. As discussed in Chapter 1, US Catholic universities will have difficulty remaining faithful to their mission and identity today if they operate like corporations, i.e., by measuring success according to profit margins and status. In regard to access for economically disadvantaged students, it is worth recalling David Hollenbach's admonition:

> It is certainly true that the board members are aware of the dangers of private institutions pricing themselves out of the educational market, and a number of them are desirous of guiding their institutions in ways that respond to the needs of the poorer segments of American society. But it is also true that the link between the goals they set for the universities and a vision of economic success is a strong one. On the

Table 5. Select High-Pell Catholic Institutions

Institution	Endowments (FY 18 $000)	Average Net Price after Grants	Average Net Price for Low-Income Students ($0–30K)	% Pell Recipients among Freshmen	% Pell Recipients among Undergrads	Average Institutional Grant Aid	Average Freshmen Student Loan (all sources)
Loyola Marymount University	$471,841	$40,946	$28,279	18.5%	19.9%	$16,607	$8,620
Saint Mary's College of California	$180,474	$35,696	$26,031	22.8%	24.1%	$22,211	$8,018
Saint Joseph's College-New York	N/A	$16,831	$12,514	35.1%	32.3%	$9,967	$6,298
La Salle University	$85,074	$26,772	$27,990	46.0%	39.6%	$25,642	$8,706
Mount Saint Mary's University (Calif.)	N/A	$27,134	$24,412	67.4%	58.7%	$15,787	$4,059
Madonna University	N/A	$14,810	$10,118	30.9%	32.2%	$9,596	$6,032
Saint Peter's University	N/A	$14,734	$10,472	66.4%	59.0%	$20,263	$5,841
University of Mary	$41,158	$16,746	$14,174	21.7%	18.8%	$7,782	$8,288

(continued)

Table 5. (continued)

Institution	Endowments (FY 18 $000)	Average Net Price after Grants	Average Net Price for Low-Income Students ($0–30K)	% Pell Recipients among Freshmen	% Pell Recipients among Undergrads	Average Institutional Grant Aid	Average Freshmen Student Loan (all sources)
Fontbonne University	N/A	$20,295	$16,661	32.6%	34.6%	$14,530	$7,665
Christian Brothers University	N/A	$16,660	$8,354	37.0%	38.4%	$17,626	$6,038
Saint Xavier University	N/A	$15,448	$12,692	62.4%	53.3%	$16,785	$6,414
Trinity Washington University	N/A	$16,113	$15,401	80.7%	69.5%	$9,973	$5,800
Mercy College of Ohio	N/A	$18,181	$16,153	30.8%	43.7%	$3,705	$6,362
Our Lady of Holy Cross College	N/A	$13,212	$11,706	46.4%	41.6%	$2,261	$5,602
Calumet College of Saint Joseph	N/A	$11,346	$10,610	53.6%	44.2%	$6,056	$5,748

Source: The Education Trust, College Online Database at http://www.collegeresults.org/default.aspx

basis of my limited experience both on the faculty of my home institution and as a board member at two other Catholic colleges, I think there is at least some foundation for suspicion that the pursuit of institutional advancement at the best Catholic universities can be a tool serving the self-interest and privilege of the powerful.

Hollenbach notes that even leaders of Catholic universities sometimes value elite status over remaining true to their mission to serve the poor, while this tendency is "virtually total" among most undergraduates.[153] In short, those Catholic universities that have achieved elite status have often done so at the expense of being faithful to the call to solidarity and the option for the poor.[154] Peter-Hans Kolvenbach, SJ, offered similar warnings and critiques. He fears that students, administrators, faculty, and trustees are sometimes indifferent, or even hostile to the mission of Jesuit universities. In his view, it is imperative that Catholic, Jesuit colleges and universities resist the commodification of education and avoid the "danger of elitism." In his words, "it is necessary to discern and to make a choice for the kind of greater service which we intend to give to Church and society through our universities."[155]

While no simple formulas exist, the many Catholic colleges and universities that claim "preeminence" as one of their goals should heed these admonitions as they move forward into the future. Some Catholic universities, such as Notre Dame, Georgetown, and Boston College, have already achieved elite status among US institutions of higher learning. They rank among the nation's best universities according to *U.S. News & World Report*. Their endowments are among the nation's top 100. Yet, as demonstrated above, they fail to rank among the leading "elite" institutions for prevalence of low-income students and low net cost for those students. A number of Catholic institutions, which are excellent schools in other ways, have failed in this aspect of their mission. However, Catholic institutions are called to be "signs of contradiction" by exhibiting a countercultural insistence on equity in access to higher education. It is all the more imperative in the light of recent indictments of more than fifty individuals for bribes and cheating to "guarantee" children of wealthy parents admission to elite institutions.[156] Catholic institutions need to do more to open their doors to disadvantaged students out of fidelity to their mission, apart from and before lawmakers enact proposals forcing them to do so.[157]

In conclusion, this chapter offers several practical proposals that might aid in the continual and greater embodiment of the right to education, the principle of solidarity, and the option for the poor at Catholic colleges and universities. This list does not pretend to be exhaustive. Nor does it claim to be definitive. Rather, some suggestions are offered here that admissions and enrollment experts, along with other interested constituencies at Catholic institutions, would need to consider thoroughly. Some of them have been tried and tested already at some institutions.

More Aggressive Recruiting of Low-Income Students

The standard argument against recruiting low-income students at selective institutions rests on the assumption that these students cannot meet the rigors of a demanding college education. Many if not most students in this category attend underfunded public schools that do not prepare them for the challenges of college education. In addition, perhaps more significantly in the minds of some administrators, bringing in such students will lower the university's rankings, which are based in part on indicators such as SAT scores.[158]

There are several problems with this line of thinking. For starters, many college students from affluent backgrounds are *de facto* under-prepared and/or underqualified. As Golden reveals, preferences for legacies, athletes, children of faculty and wealthy current or potential donors often result in underqualified students being admitted to many of the nation's selective and highly selective universities. Even though their high school grade point averages, SAT scores, and other variables tend to be significantly lower than the average at many schools, these students enjoy the advantage of affirmative action.[159] While some people already knew about the unfair advantages involved in admissions, the FBI's 2019 "Operation Varsity Blues" has evinced to the public the radical and sometimes illegal lengths that some elites, and some university officials, will go to in order to ensure spots for students already of great means and privilege. These "admits" damage the overall academic profile of the students body.[160]

Thus, claiming that admitting low-income students will detract from a putatively judicious and meritocratic admissions process no longer seems defensible. Administrators and admissions officers should at least be willing to apply the same flexibility to economically disadvantaged students.[161]

In fact, CST points toward a) making admissions standards more transparent and b) curtailing or eliminating preferences in favor of those more coherent with the principles of solidarity and the option for the poor.[162]

Bowen, Kurzwell and Tobin have made a compelling case for giving preferences in admissions based on socioeconomic status, as opposed to other types of nonacademic preferences. In their extensive study of equity issues in American education, they argue that:

1. Many of the best students at US colleges and universities have historically been from low-income families.
2. Students from economically challenged backgrounds enhance the learning environment because they help other students to understand people from their life situations.
3. Real opportunities for people from low and middle class backgrounds must exist and people must believe they can obtain them for democracy to flourish in any society.
4. Students from low-income backgrounds have overcome great hardships to become viable candidates at all.
5. These students do not under-perform; they generally do very well given their level of academic preparedness.[163]

These reasons complement the Catholic perspective of the option for the poor, which demands making room for the disadvantaged at all Catholic institutions of higher learning. While this chapter emphasizes socioeconomic disadvantage, a following chapter will extend my argument to racially minoritized students.

In addition to creating admissions preferences for low-income students, the premium that many institutions place on standardized test scores in the admissions process also needs to be reconsidered. Researchers contend that SAT scores in particular have racial and class biases and that wealthier students do better on such tests.[164] Given the built-in bias of the test, the additional fact that low-income students cannot afford expensive SAT coaching courses, and that the predictive value of the test is questionable,[165] discounting applicants from low-income backgrounds based on test scores is unfair. The evidence indicates that these tests often create a barrier that causes talented, low-income students not even to apply. These students exceed the qualifications for admissions at most schools, but are often overlooked because they are a financial "liability," as Golden revealed.[166] According to one study, approximately one-fourth of the best high school students from low-income families do not attend college within two years of graduating. Those who do matriculate tend to attend colleges whose admission standards fall below their achievement levels.[167] Another study indicated that of the 25,000–35,000 estimated high-achieving, low-income students in the US, "the vast majority . . . do not apply to any selective schools."[168] A 2009 study by Princeton sociologist Thomas Espenshade and statistical programmer Chang Young Chung predicted a 30 percent increase in Black, Latino/a, and low-income students by making the SAT optional. Their predictive modelling claimed to "show unambiguously" that such increases in diversity would take place. Moreover, making the SAT optional would raise the average GPA of incoming students.[169] A more recent study using data from almost one million student files from a diverse array of institutions confirmed gains in low-income students at 50 percent of test-optional institutions and increases in underrepresented minority students at two-thirds of such institutions.[170]

A growing number of institutions have gone test-optional in the hopes of attracting low-income, first-generation, and underrepresented minority students. Colleges such as Bowdon and Bates went test-optional almost forty years ago.[171] The College of the Holy Cross (2005), Providence College (2006), and Merrimack College (2007) were among the first Catholic institutions to make reporting test scores optional.[172] Schools like Smith and Wake Forest have followed suit, citing the test's inability to predict academic success and its correlation with household income, parental education, and race.[173] Today more than a thousand colleges and universities nationally are test optional, with one every ten days announcing the change in their admissions policies in 2019.[174] In 2018, the University of Chicago, one of the nation's most selective institutions, announced it would adopt a comprehensive plan to attract more talented low-income students. This plan includes going test optional. As the vice president for enrollment stated: "It was time that we looked at the application process and made sure it was fair for everyone. . . . High-school counselors will tell you about a kid who would be a perfect fit for Chicago, who's not a good tester but who's talented in other ways, but who chose not to apply." He also contended that the university analyzed lots of data and concluded that test scores had little correlation to student performance, but rather high school transcripts "tell such a powerful story." Other institutions have determined that "high school transcripts and rigor of courses" more robustly predict success in college.[175]

Changing the admissions criteria is important, but not a panacea. The test-optional schools with the largest increases in socioeconomic diversity amplify recruiting and retention of low-income students and increasingly channel aid dollars to them.[176] Breaking down the walls between a large pool of superb talent among the economically disadvantaged and colleges is crucial, as colleges and universities have historically done less recruiting in schools in low-income areas. Fortunately, nonprofits such as Quest-Bridge and College Advising Corps now link bright students of lesser means with highly selective institutions. These agencies serve a dual purpose: They help these students aspire to schools they might imagine to be beyond their reach and expose them to good, but unfamiliar schools. At the same time, it facilitates recruiting these students for schools that in the past have had difficulty finding them. And they have had impressive results. QuestBridge helped three hundred students enroll at Stanford in one year alone, with high enrollment rates at colleges like Amherst and Pomona as well.[177] Among Catholic institutions, only the University of Notre Dame is currently listed as one of their partner institutions.[178] Another organization called CFES Brilliant Pathways, founded by a former admissions officer at Harvard and Middlebury, boasts helping "100,000 low-income students get to and through college."[179] Currently seventeen Catholic colleges and universities have pledged to admit and serve first-generation students (who often come from low SES backgrounds) by partnering with Strive for College. This organization sponsors free test preparation and the "I'm First" initiative, which celebrates the accomplishments of "first-gen" college students thereby helping them overcome the stigma and isolation they may feel on campuses.[180]

More Catholic colleges and universities struggling to enroll low-income students should avail themselves of such organizations, which could help them attract talented students who desire a solid liberal arts education and a university that rigorously explores questions of faith, provides rich opportunities for spiritual development, and promotes social justice. The commitment to the right to education for the poor should be more prominently articulated and clearly displayed in admissions policies and mission statements. This would send a clear signal to talented students of lesser means that they too deserve a place at Catholic colleges and universities.

Loyola University of Maryland has taken another fruitful approach to finding talented students: They have looked among their employees. The faculty, admissions officers, student development, the career center, the Center for Community Service and Justice, human resources, and academic development all contribute to the Maguire scholars program, which entails seminars and support services to prepare employees for applying, matriculating, and succeeding at Loyola. Mentors continue to walk with the students throughout the college experience. As of August 2013, twenty-two employees had matriculated, most of whom have maintained a 3.0 GPA or better. According to one Loyola HR Specialist, this program reflects Loyola's commitment to justice and *cura personalis*, or care of the whole person. It also fosters employee retention.[181]

In 2015 Loyola University Chicago opened Arrupe College, a two-year institution that is "specifically designed for students who have the capacity to go to college but who need extra support," according to its president Stephen Katsouros, SJ.[182] In 2013, the superior general of the worldwide Society of Jesus, Adolfo Nicolás, expressed concern that Jesuit colleges and universities "were becoming too elite." Arrupe College addresses this concern, as all of its students who are Pell-eligible pay no more than $2,000 a year, and receive support that many low-income students elsewhere are not afforded.[183] The retention rates and graduation rates are well above national averages for two-year colleges. Moreover, almost half of their students have completed a bachelor's degree within four years. In other words, this model of a two-year college for low-SES students has been successful and has been adopted at St. Thomas University in Minnesota.[184] Institutions like Arrupe College and The Dougherty Family College serve as remarkable countersigns to corporatized higher education and its priorities, and are worthy of emulation. However, they should not replace striving toward greater fidelity to the option for the poor at all types of Catholic institutions of higher learning, as the scope of the problem requires an "all hands on deck approach."[185] Separate colleges for low-SES students, both admirable and necessary, should not assuage the consciences of corporatized Catholic institutions seeking elite status and continually operating country-club like campuses.

Finally, recruiting economically disadvantaged students to all Catholic colleges and universities must involve increased commitment to need-based scholarship aid for them, without heavily burdensome loans. Catholic institutions must eschew the tendency to use more aid money to attract students who score high on the SAT to boost average SAT scores, which gives universities an edge in rankings.[186] However, as was argued in Chapter 1, Catholic universities should not be preoccupied with "success" measured in such terms, nor should their alumni be concerned with their "status" on such lists. Rather, they should take pride when their institutions provide access for as many economically disadvantaged students as possible. Toward that end, universities and their alumni should prioritize need-based aid in their financial planning and giving. In addition to the examples mentioned above, Santa Clara University's Hurtado Scholars Program, funded by the Jesuit Community of Santa Clara, has granted fifty student scholarships to the university, all of whom are for undocumented immigrants.[187] Such examples move in the right direction, but need to be implemented on a much larger scale at Catholic colleges and universities across the nation.

Fostering a Social, Educational, and Financial Environment Conducive to Learning for Economically Challenged Students

Many of our nation's universities have become bastions of wealth and privilege. This environment intimidates and alienates students who have suffered economic hardship and the social stigma attached to it. As was mentioned earlier, they often question whether or not they are qualified to attend such "prestigious" institutions. They often feel lost socially because they do not have all of the amenities of their peers: the fancy car, the iPad and/or MacBook Air, the expensive Vineyard Vines or Lululemon outfits, etc. As a working-class, first-generation student at a Catholic university full of wealthy students who went on extravagant spring break trips, I can relate to the student experience scholar Anthony Abraham Jack describes. Based on numerous interviews, he notes that "low-income students feel like outsiders who don't belong on campus." Witnessing gaggles of students wearing $650 Canada Goose jackets while the university pays you to clean their filthy dorm rooms and bathrooms can be humiliating.

Moreover, while classmates are enjoying themselves skiing, hiking, or lounging in exclusive places, you may be struggling to find food on your campus, as "only one in four" universities keep student cafeterias open. In other words the country club environment of many of our campuses seems tailor-made for wealthy students, and extremely unwelcoming for low-income students. As Jack describes in his groundbreaking study *The Privileged Poor*, these class dynamics also intersect with racial barriers to feeling welcome at elite institutions (a topic I take up later in this book).[188]

Faculty and staff may add to the problem by harboring, sometimes subconsciously, negative stereotypes of students from poor backgrounds; they may see these students as lacking in the cognitive and linguistic abilities and "cultural knowledge" that their affluent students possess. These stereotypes can rear their ugly heads in class discussions. Students who have internalized some of these stereotypes often fear raising their voices in discussion, for fear of failure and ostracization. Faculty members sometimes lack the patience and/or understanding to welcome perspectives "from the margins," i.e., from students of underrepresented groups or nationalities who may speak or think differently. Eurocentrism, for example, sometimes leads professors to discount or ignore other ways of knowing and expressing insight.[189] This particularly discourages and offends students from Africa, Latin America, Asia, and American students of non-European roots (as I will discuss in Chapter 5). Even if faculty do not actively mistreat students from low-SES backgrounds, they may fail to understand the obstacles such students face. Unlike their wealthier counterparts, low-SES students often "find the collegiate style of interacting with faculty unsettling."[190]

Catholic universities have an obligation to combat these tendencies. First, the Christian tradition at its best has always challenged unbridled affirmations of materialism and hedonism. The list of such prophets is long, going back to figures such as St. Basil and St. John Chrysostom, not to mention Jesus himself. More recently Pope Francis has forcefully critiqued the materialism that undergirds much of contemporary culture and economic life.[191] Catholic universities should not acquiesce in the face of some of their students' desire to live "as if God did not exist," to use John Paul II's description of the consumerist way of being. Challenging the false notion that students and their families are entitled to all the luxuries they can afford rests squarely within the mission of Catholic universities. A more vocal, prophetic stance on this issue might assist students from economically challenged backgrounds in overcoming their sense of inferiority.

Second, Catholic institutions of higher learning must insist that their faculty, staff, and administrators seek to understand why the "haves" and "have-nots" exist in our globalized world. Time and again John Paul II called for "globalization with solidarity, globalization without marginalization." As was mentioned earlier, he and Paul VI both argued that affording students from economically disadvantaged nations a chance to study is inherent to the mission of the Catholic university. Faculty must, therefore, welcome and assist such students in their studies in every way possible. One way of doing this is for White, US-born faculty to avoid the tendency to see "our way of being" and "our way of knowing" as superior to those from other parts of the world and marginalized groups in our own country.

Finally, while Catholic institutions assist students who enter the university with educational challenges due to their background, they must earnestly consider whether they are doing everything possible. Recruiting is one part of the equation; retaining low-income students is another crucial part of the option for the poor in higher education. If some of the low-income students do struggle due to academic, social, or financial reasons, Catholic institutions have a duty to aid them in every way possible. The nationally recognized No Excuses Poverty Initiative at Amarillo College in Texas has shown that wide-ranging support such as subsidies for rent, child care, transportation, and free food and clothing can make the difference between a student's completing a college degree and escaping poverty, or not.[192]

The Georgetown Scholarship Program and the Community Scholars Program move toward this kind of institutionalized solidarity with students from low-income backgrounds. The GSP assists about 10 percent of Georgetown's undergraduate population. In addition to academic and financial support, these programs recognize that students from this background often feel stigmatized or "out of place" and helps them to cope with these feelings.[193] Villanova University's Center for Access, Success and Achievement (CASA) has a dedicated full-time staff and graduate assistants offering mentorship, tutoring, life skills coaching, and other services including a summer enrichment program prior to matriculation and a first-generation student celebration week. CASA also created a fund "to provide . . . students with all of the opportunities their college peers experience without exclusions that are a result of financial hardship."[194] Loyola University Chicago has taken steps to help make higher education a possibility for DACA-eligible students, including creating a scholarship fund with fees the student body has chosen to pay.[195] These types of initiatives present challenges, both financially and logistically, and require dedicating resources to them. However, solidarity with students who may struggle financially, socially, or academically calls for nothing short of this. Moreover, federal funding can defray the cost of such programs. Saint Peter's College, for example, received a $2.8 million federal grant designated for Hispanic-serving institutions (HSIs). The money was dedicated to establishing an English Language Center to tutor students who may need it and to develop programs "tailored to the unique strengths and needs of low-income and minority students."[196]

Creative Development and Fundraising Appealing to Catholic Mission and Identity

Divesting themselves of the assured alumni base of legacies and "development cases" in order to make room for the poor, Catholic universities will likely incur financial losses, at least in the short term. However, as Golden illustrates in *The Price of Admission*, there is more than one way to court wealthy donors. Several colleges and universities have demonstrated that eschewing legacies and other preferences need not lead to financial ruin. Schools like Cal Tech and Berea College have enormous endowments, maintain the highest academic standards, and have very large numbers of low-income students. They have achieved their goals by creatively appealing to the mission of their schools in their fundraising: The best and the brightest deserve first-rate college education, even if they are poor.[197] Golden points out that many wealthy people still believe in this ideal, and dislike the fact that many elite schools have become little more than networks for the rich and powerful. Therefore, even though they have no particular affiliation with Cal Tech, known for its superior education in math and science, or Berea, a highly ranked liberal arts college almost exclusively for low-income students, they prefer to donate to these schools. As a result, Berea has generated one of the largest endowments in the country. At $862 million, Berea is twenty-second in the country for endowments per capita.[198] Astoundingly, nearly 80 percent of Berea's students are Pell-eligible.

Catholic institutions should glean important insights from the practices and successes of these schools. They disprove the idea that an institution needs to jettison or curtail its ideals for the sake of remaining financially solvent. They also reveal that donors are willing and eager to contribute to institutions that have an egalitarian and social justice orientation. Catholic universities are well-poised to capitalize on the good will of such philanthropists. As this chapter has revealed, equity, solidarity, and a preferential option for the poor are at the heart of Catholic social teaching.

Some alumni at Catholic institutions are dismayed by the increasing preponderance of affluent students among the student body.[199] At many institutions alumni have already generously funded scholarships to make college accessible for students of lesser means. In addition to appealing to such alumni by boosting the enrollment of low-income students, Catholic colleges and universities must seek out donors who are not affiliated with their institutions, but who share the values and principles of the Catholic social tradition. Although many Catholic schools have loyal alumni who support them financially, their alumni bases are often too small to fund the changes called for in this chapter and to fully address the scale of the problem.[200] Berea does this by sending students as well as staff on the road to seek out such donors. Their first-hand accounts of the importance of their Berea education often convince potential donors that they are making worthwhile and socially responsible investments. Cal-Tech invites donors to campus for lunch with scholarship students to achieve the same effect.[201] At Catholic institutions, this could be a way of sharing in the mission and identity of the school and building relationships of solidarity. Catholic colleges and universities should describe the significance of such encounters by appealing to the language of Catholic social teaching and their founding orders. This evinces the need to hire admissions and development officers, along with faculty and administrators, who understand and embrace the ideals of Catholic social teaching. Not only is it important that key decision-makers adopt policies and strategies conducive to embodying solidarity with the poor, it is also imperative that they can discuss those policies and strategies with potential donors in the language of Catholic social thought. This does not imply that all such personnel need to be Catholic. However, they should affirm ideals of Catholic social teaching such as solidarity and the option for the poor and be willing to learn about the Catholic social tradition.[202]

In addition to private funding, as much federal and state funding as possible must be garnered for tuition discounts for low-income students. A handful of Catholic institutions participate in programs such as ACT 101 in Pennsylvania, which provides funding for tuition discounts and retention programs for low-income students.[203] University presidents, provosts, and trustees should make a concerted effort to lobby policy makers in Washington and state capitals for more generous Pell grants and other forms of federal and state aid specifically targeted at low-income students. Federal and state funding has fluctuated in recent decades, and has not kept pace with the rising costs of tuition. As of this writing the maximum Pell grant is $6,195.[204]

If funding for low-income students falls short (as it inevitably will) after exhausting these possibilities, Catholic universities will need to assess their budgetary spending scrupulously. Difficult trade-offs and sacrifices will need to be made in order to fulfill the option for the poor and the right to education of low-income students. For example, just as in the case of justice for adjunct faculty, tenured faculty members might need to consider foregoing some of their research funds in order to promote this greater good. Trustees and high-ranking administrators will need to discuss the salaries of the latter in light of Catholic principles. In 2012 Georgetown's president John DeGioia demonstrated such thinking by donating a one-time bonus of $400,000 to the Georgetown Scholarship Program.[205] Expansion and updating of facilities, as well as costly athletics budgets, should also be carefully weighed against the need to provide access for low-income students. In short, the desire to be preeminent must never be divorced from these considerations. Rather, preeminence should be redefined to include access to education for the poor as one of the primary benchmarks at Catholic institutions.

Faculty, Religious Community, and Student Involvement in Admissions

In addition to the aforementioned proposals, involving faculty and members of the religious communities affiliated with Catholic colleges and universities in the admissions process may prove to be helpful. Golden's research indicates that when faculty members are involved in admissions, nonacademic preferences such as legacy status or "development potential" are weighed much less. Faculty members tend to want the best students possible in the classroom and are less concerned about appeasing current or actual donors.[206] In the case of Catholic universities, faculty who understand the Catholic call to solidarity and the option for the poor in education should be involved in admissions. They should advocate for students from low-income backgrounds (and as discussed in Chapter 5 racially minoritized students) in admissions decisions. They should insist that those who clearly meet the standards but cannot afford the costs be admitted and that every effort be made to meet their financial need. The same applies to members of religious communities affiliated with Catholic universities and students who care about the mission and identity of the university. At the very least, they should be conversation partners in the admissions process.

Strengthening Partnerships with Local Schools, Communities, and Parents

Clearly if low-income students are to reach the university in much greater numbers, sweeping reform at the primary and secondary levels must happen. Students from poor urban and rural areas are not nearly afforded the same quality of education at the primary and secondary levels as their affluent counterparts.[207] This is one of the reasons they do not have the same likelihood of attending college. Thus, the US needs to work toward the "seamless system" of education called for in international agreements on the right to education. Universities should aid primary and secondary schools in developing better educational programs in school districts where funding and dedicated, well-trained teachers are lacking.

Some Catholic institutions of higher learning already do this to one degree or another. Saint Joseph's University, for example, has a partnership with Samuel Gompers Elementary School, where professors tutor students in after-school programs. The Ignatian College Connection at Saint Joseph's works closely with families of recruited students (about ten to fifteen annually), which builds a sense of trust and community. Georgetown's Institute for College Preparation maintains a "KIDS2College" program, which provides sixth graders in DC public schools with a college awareness program. Starting in the seventh grade, students can enter the ICP enrichment program, which includes academic classes on Saturdays and summer courses at Georgetown. The program staff and volunteers also help with test preparation and guide students through the daunting college application process (as a first-generation college grad, I know firsthand how daunting it can be!).[208] While only 58 percent of DC public school students finish high school, 98 percent of ICP participants graduate. An impressive 97 percent go on to college. Inspired by the Harlem Children's Zone, Seattle University's Youth Initiative uses a multipronged approach to promoting transformation in the surrounding Bailey Gatzert neighborhood. Partnering with local schools from pre-K onward and community organizations, the Youth Initiative attends to the whole range of needs of local children and their parents in order to promote full human flourishing, which includes college preparedness for students.[209] Other Catholic institutions of higher education undoubtedly aspire to embody CST in a similar way. Those that do not should look at some of these successful models and determine what they might emulate. Perhaps Catholic colleges and universities can help replace financially insolvent urban archdiocesan schools with more Cristo Rey schools. Founded in 1990, the Cristo Rey network exclusively serves low-income students and now has thirty-two schools with over eleven thousand students. The results have been impressive: "Not only do most Cristo Rey graduates enroll in college; they also graduate college at more than double the expected rate for low-income students."[210] In short, the links between Catholic universities and primary and secondary schools should be deepened as much as possible in order to bring more students from economically blighted areas into the halls of these universities. Catholic social teaching on the right to education, solidarity, and the option for the poor mandates this outreach.

Socially Responsible Investment, the
      Stewardship of University Resources,
      and Integral Ecology

On a cold but sunny afternoon in late fall of 2012 I had my first opportunity to see the fabled "Word of Life" mural, commonly named "Touchdown Jesus."[1] I had heard much about it from proud "Domers." Imposing in size and visible from inside the famed Notre Dame football stadium, the mosaic conveys the impression that Jesus, the Lord of Life, has dominion over everything the nation's flagship Catholic university does.

While I enjoyed my tour of the beautiful campus, my first opportunity to visit the University of Notre Dame was not a pleasant one. I knowingly walked into a briar patch. Students, faculty, and staff at the university had been waging a contentious divestment campaign there from 2007. I was invited to campus to opine on the matter from the standpoint of Catholic moral theology. Those opposing the university's investment in HEI, a private equity that used investment funds from several large universities including Notre Dame to purchase hotels around the country, contended it conflicted with Catholic social teaching. Their concern stemmed from multiple allegations of mistreatment of workers at HEI owned and/or operated hotels.[2] Several universities had already chosen to divest from HEI. For example, Brown University's Advisory Committee on Corporate Responsibility in Investment Policies released a statement explaining its decision to divest from HEI. It stated that "a persistent pattern of allegations involving the company's treatment of workers and interference with their efforts to unionize, combined with repeated settlements [mediated by the National Labor Relations Board], raised serious questions whether Brown's continued association with HEI would be consistent with the ethical principles governing the university's investments."[3]

The UNITE HERE union, which represents American and Canadian workers in the hotel and other service industries, surveyed staff at HEI hotels about their working conditions in 2011.[4] In many cases, the workers' responses revealed that their dignity and rights as workers, according to CST, had been violated.[5] For example, the vast majority of workers reported not being paid a living wage. In addition, more than 80 percent of respondents indicated that their employer did not offer an affordable health care plan. According to CST, access to decent and affordable health care is a "fundamental human right."[6] In the contemporary US context, the duty to enable the fulfillment of this right rests primarily on employers.[7] Respondents also overwhelmingly indicated they believe that their hotels did not protect their right to health and safe working conditions. Almost 56 percent responded that they or one of their coworkers "ha[d] been treated differently or unfairly because of race, ethnicity, age, gender or religious views." Another 37 percent maintained that management did not take "appropriate steps when a case of discrimination is reported." Finally, the rights to unionize and to collective bargaining, which CST considers indispensable to worker justice and the common good, appeared to be in jeopardy for many workers. Almost 60 percent of respondents claimed that workers were not free to join a union without reprisal. Approximately 75 percent said their employer did not respect the right of workers to bargain for their wages and benefits. In light of these conclusions, I produced a report that assessed whether or not Notre Dame's investment in HEI conflicted with Catholic moral theology.[8] The report took as its point of departure John Paul II's statement that the decision to invest or not to invest in an entity "is always *a moral and cultural choice*," which cannot be justified solely by the desire to maximize profit.[9]

Before my scheduled talk, a group of faculty, staff, and students dedicated to the cause gathered on campus with two HEI hotel workers from California and a UNITE HERE organizer. We listened as they told their stories of hardship and what can only be called abuse. They assured us that their experiences were not anomalies; their contention corroborated the repeated charges of mistreatment recorded in the UNITE HERE study. Two faculty members and the two hotel workers gave brief presentations after my lecture. The academics laid out the intellectual and moral case against Notre Dame's investment in HEI. However, the voices of the workers resonated much more powerfully.[10] Luz, a housekeeping supervisor at a hotel in San Diego spoke boldly: "These people treat us like machines or like animals. And I'm not a machine, I'm a human being, and I have feelings. And that's why we went to look for help."[11] She went on to say that as a Catholic university, Notre Dame should not invest in HEI.

Subsequently, 122 signatories from the university sent a letter to the president requesting that Notre Dame end its financial relationship with HEI. In addition, UNITE HERE circulated an online petition that was signed by more than one hundred Catholics activists and one active bishop. Brown University and several others had already announced their intention not to reinvest with HEI due to concerns about labor. While the Notre Dame administration did not acknowledge the violations of workers' rights at HEI hotels, and could not divest its funds because of private equity rules, it did state that it would not reinvest in the HEI fund again.[12] The participants of the campaign at Notre Dame considered this a success. More importantly, in December 2013 HEI reached an agreement with UNITE HERE, which promised to improve the lives of workers like Luz.[13] In my estimation, there is good reason to believe that the campaigns at Notre Dame, Brown, and other universities played a role in bringing about this development, along with the courageous protests of the workers themselves.[14] The students, faculty, and staff involved in the campaign at Notre Dame had put Catholic social teaching into action, and it made a difference.

The Duty of Just Stewardship of Financial Resources

All Catholic institutions of higher learning have endowments. Some are large, making these universities major investors, while others are small.[15] Regardless of the size of its endowment, all Catholic institutions have responsibilities as investors rooted in Catholic social teaching. While boards of trustees have a fiduciary responsibility to maintain the financial stability of a university, a Catholic institution has moral duties that go beyond its solvency.

According to the magisterium, Catholic social teaching applies to all areas of economic life, including investments.[16] As Saint John Paul II contended, "It is . . . necessary to create life-styles in which the quest for truth, beauty, goodness and communion with others for the sake of common growth are the factors which determine consumer choices, savings and investments. . . . Even the decision to invest in one place rather than another, in one productive sector rather than another, is always *a moral and cultural choice*."[17] Pope Benedict XVI expanded on this notion in his 2009 encyclical on the global financial crisis, *Caritas in Veritate*. He commended initiatives such as efforts to create "ethical accounts and investment funds," as well as "ethical financing" such as micro-lending. However, he warned that such efforts sometimes either use a hollow understanding of "ethics" or falsely imply that other spheres of economic activity stand outside of morality and ethical scrutiny. On the contrary, he argued that there must be a "sound criteria of discernment" for judging the ethics of financial decisions and that CST "can make a specific contribution, since it is based on man's [sic] creation 'in the image of God' (Gen 1:27), a datum which gives rise to the inviolable dignity of the human person and the transcendent value of natural moral norms." Moreover, Benedict contended that "efforts are needed . . . not only to create 'ethical' sectors or segments of the economy or the world of finance, but to ensure that the whole economy—the whole of finance—is ethical, not merely by virtue of an external label, but by its respect for requirements intrinsic to its very nature." Furthermore, CST clearly insists that "the economy, in all its branches, constitutes a sector of human activity." Therefore, it must be guided by the proper moral considerations.[18]

The United States Conference of Catholic Bishops also explicitly treated the moral responsibilities of individual and institutional investors in *Economic Justice for All*. Echoing papal teaching, the bishops maintained that "on the parish and diocesan level, through its agencies and institutions, the Church employs many people; it has investments; it has extensive properties for worship and mission. All the moral principles that govern the just operation of any economic endeavor apply to the church and its agencies and institutions; indeed the church should be exemplary."[19] The bishops recognized that managers of corporations have a duty to create returns for investors. However, "morally this legal responsibility may be exercised only within the bounds of justice to employees, customers, suppliers, and the local community."[20] The USCCB elaborated on these general norms in its 2003 "Socially Responsible Investment Guidelines" (which will be discussed below).

The Sisters of Charity, the Sisters of St. Francis, the Christian Brothers, and other Catholic communities have developed their own socially responsible investment (SRI) policies and practices over the last several decades.[21] As a member of Villanova University's Committee on Social Responsibility Proxy Votes and the Committee for Socially Responsible Investment of the Maryland Province of the Society of Jesus from 2008–10, I have obtained an insider's view about how such policies are designed and implemented within religious orders and at Catholic universities. Good work informed by the Christian faith is being done in this area.

For example, the Society of Jesus aptly considers socially responsible investment "a work of structural justice."[22] Already in the 1970s Jesuit universities such as Georgetown and Loyola University Chicago established standing SRI committees to monitor whether or not their universities' investments cohere with CST. The Interfaith Center for Corporate Responsibility, Investor Advocates for Social Justice (formerly Tri-State Coalition for Responsible Investment), and the National Jesuit Committee for Investment Responsibility have assisted Catholic institutions in both developing and carrying out SRI policies for decades.[23] More recently a group of Catholic finance executives formed Catholic Investment Services, which currently manages more than $200 million dollars for Catholic schools, universities, hospitals, religious orders, dioceses, etc. in accordance with "Catholic principles."[24] Moreover, religious investors have been listed as the largest group of SRI practitioners in the United States.[25] In August 2015, the S&P Dow Jones Indices even established the S&P 500 Catholic Values Index, which enables Catholics to invest in accordance with the USCCB's socially responsible investment guidelines.[26]

Despite these positive developments, some employees at Catholic institutions do not yet recognize the need to bridge the worlds of finance and investing and the principles of Catholic social teaching. According to Douglas Demeo, a former manager of SRI mutual funds, most administrators at Catholic institutions exclusively focus on return on investment.[27] However, some Catholic organizations have recognized the call to be just stewards, which obliges Catholics to receive "God's gifts gratefully, cultivate them responsibly, share them lovingly in justice with others, and return them with increase to the Lord." Like the beautiful image of "the Word of Life," just stewards recognize God as the source of all things and hear Jesus's call to discipleship in every aspect of their lives.[28] Socially responsible investment policies represent a way forward on the path of economic discipleship.

The ABCs of Socially Responsible Investment

SRI entails the tripartite strategy of community investing, "screening" for investments that violate or promote the values of the investor, and shareholder advocacy.[29] Ideally, Catholic institutions decide to invest, not to invest, continue to invest, or to divest from a particular entity based on whether or not the investment promotes both a reasonable return and "social change consistent with the Christian vision of justice and compassion."[30] Given CST on the use of financial resources, a Catholic institution of higher learning must address a number of issues in order to "exercise faithful, competent and socially responsible stewardship in how it manages its financial resources."[31]

Investing always runs the risk of abetting corporations that sometimes, or often, harm individuals, communities, and the environment. Yet, Catholic moral teaching does not preclude investing in corporations, even those that commit such harm. How can this be the case? Catholic moral theology holds that we cannot escape some degree of co-responsibility for the myriad sinful practices and structures in the contemporary world. For example, if I purchase clothing, electronic goods, food, or any other item made or harvested in a workplace where workers' dignity and rights (to safe working conditions, a just wage, etc.) are violated, I am in some way complicit with the exploitation of workers. I am cooperating in evil.[32] Paying tax dollars to a government that uses them to engage in warfare using illicit weapons of war such as cluster bombs also enmeshes me in evil.[33] Voting for a politician who does not uphold the sanctity of every human life in all of its stages also constitutes cooperation in evil.[34] However, cooperation in evil is considered "material" and permissible according to Catholic teaching if: (1) the cooperator does not intend the evil perpetrated by the primary agent with whom she or he "cooperates"; (2) doing so serves a proportionate good; (3) the "temporal, geographic and causal proximity" from the evil act is remote enough; and (4) scandal will not be caused.[35] In cases of formal cooperation in evil, the cooperator shares the intention of the wrongdoer. In other words, the cooperator intends to advance the evil committed by the evildoer. Importantly, formal cooperation in evil can exist "even though the cooperator denies intending the wrongdoer's object, [yet] no other explanation can distinguish the cooperator's object from the wrongdoer's object."[36]

The USCCB applies the principles of cooperation and toleration of evil to their guidelines on investment.[37] These principles allow for holding shares in a company that represents "a mixed investment," in which "socially beneficial activities and socially undesirable or even immoral activities are often inextricably linked in the products produced and the policies followed by individual corporations." The policy further specifies that "investments of this type may be tolerated, after careful application of the principle of cooperation and the duty to avoid scandal, so long as the Conference engages" actively in shareholder advocacy that has "a reasonable hope of success for corporate change." The bishops give specific examples requiring an "absolute exclusion" of investments, such as companies directly involved in abortion. In this case the evil involved in investing is too closely intertwined with a gravely immoral industry that serves no good purpose. In other words, no proportionate good can be served by investing in such a corporation. The bishops also enumerate a number of permissible investments in corporations or industries that engage in activities contrary to Catholic teaching while serving some other morally licit purposes, with the proviso that shareholder advocacy is undertaken to promote positive change. This policy presumes that the industry in question can abandon its unethical practices. For example, the USCCB will "actively promote and support shareholder resolutions directed toward avoiding the use of sweatshops in the manufacture of goods" and those that "promote generous wage and benefit policies and adequate worker safety guidelines."[38] In other words, it is never justified to participate directly in the exploitation of a worker, for any reason whatsoever, because church teaching considers it an "intrinsic evil."[39] Such acts can never be "ordered to God" because they radically denigrate the dignity of the human person.[40]

However, the indirect participation by investing in a corporation that exploits workers may be allowable *under certain circumstances.*[41] To reiterate, such an investment must not give rise to scandal and there must be "a reasonable hope of success for corporate change." When it appears impossible to engage a corporation in order to encourage change consistent with CST, another approach must be taken. Here the bishops appeal to the principle "do no harm and avoid evil." In such a scenario, two options remain: (1) "refusal to invest in companies whose products and/or policies are counter to the values of Catholic moral teaching or statements adopted by the Conference of bishops"; or (2) "divesting from such companies." If divestment is undertaken, prudence must be used to determine how to mitigate the negative impact and unintended consequences of this action.

Although it now appears to be defunct, Loyola University Chicago's previous "Statement on Shareholder Advocacy Committee Activities" reflected the USCCB's guidelines, albeit in a more streamlined fashion. The statement expressed the preference for active engagement via shareholder advocacy in order to promote the values of CST. Nonetheless, the policy cited *Economic Justice for All*'s approval of divestment when it "appears unavoidable" and is "done after prudent examination and with a clear explanation of the motives." Thus, the university approved divestment "as a strategy of last resort."[42] The statement further specified when divestment should be pursued. Succinctly stated, when all other means such as shareholder advocacy and dialogue cannot persuade a company to improve its "negative, harmful and unrecoverable impacts" during a reasonable amount of time, divestment and avoiding future investment in the company shall be recommended by the committee to the University.[43] In other words, if there is no other way to ensure that the university's investments are "consistent with Jesuit, Catholic social teachings and the values inherent to its mission of the service of faith and promotion of justice," divestment should be utilized "as a tool of shareholder advocacy."[44] Sometimes making a prophetic statement through divestment may be the most effective way for Catholic investors to promote the values of CST. Thus, Catholic universities' SRI policies should admit of the possibility and necessity of divestment in some cases.

Catholic Universities as Socially Responsible Investors and the Fullness of CST

Almost twenty years ago some Catholic fund managers began screening out investments in companies that supported abortion, pornography, or other evils that violate the church's teaching on sexual morality. In his book *Good Returns: Making Money by Morally Responsible Investing*, George P. Schwartz discusses the Ave Maria Funds, which he cofounded in 2001 and which has since become "the largest family of Catholic mutual funds in operation." They are designed to help investors "get good returns" without investing in corporations that violate certain core teachings of the Catholic Church. Schwartz touts the fact that all of these funds "screen out . . . companies that support abortion or pornography."[45]

It is certainly appropriate for Catholic investors to screen out such companies, whose products contradict important church teachings.[46]

However, the students and faculty at Notre Dame rightly understood that Catholic investors should be accountable to the full range of Catholic social teaching, which includes but goes beyond evils such as abortion and pornography. While it is encouraging that Catholic institutions have developed screens to eliminate investments in companies that produce abortifacients or pornography, CST on workers' rights and other issues such as weapons of mass destruction, the environment, racial and gender discrimination, and access to pharmaceuticals should also inform what Catholic institutions do with their money, as the USCCB maintains.[47] Saint John Paul II clearly condemned prioritizing the "criterion of maximum profit" over "the objective rights of the worker—every kind of worker: manual, or intellectual, industrial or agricultural, etc." In his words, the rights of workers "must constitute the adequate and fundamental criterion for shaping the whole economy."[48] This is why the USCCB guidelines urge "promot[ing] and support[ing] shareholder resolutions to promote generous wage and benefit policies and adequate worker safety guidelines."

In my judgment, CST on workers' rights calls Catholic institutions to go further, as exploitation of workers is considered intrinsically evil in Catholic teaching.[49] In the words of Pope Francis, the exploitation of workers is a "cancer" which must be combatted until its demise.[50] According to the pope, employers who do not offer employees decent salaries, job stability, or health benefits are "bloodsuckers." Profiting by exploiting workers constitutes "mortal sin." Francis reminds us of the relevance of the words from the Letter of St. James (Jas. 5:1–6): "Behold, the wages you withheld from the workers who harvested your fields are crying aloud; and the cries of the harvesters have reached the ears of the Lord Almighty."[51] He also chastised business owners who lay off workers and maximize profit by using cheaper sources of labor in other countries. In his view, they are not entrepreneurs but "speculators" and "traders," who are "today . . . selling their people; tomorrow they will be selling their own dignity."[52] Given these teachings on workers' rights, companies that violate workers' rights and show no hope for changing their practices should also be screened out from a Catholic institution's investments. As a group of Catholic business leaders in Chicago correctly stated: "The rights of all employees of the company to earn a living wage is at least as important as the right of owners/investors to earn a reasonable rate of return on their investment in the company."[53] Therefore, a Catholic institutional investor should encourage companies in which they invest to work steadily toward paying all workers a living wage. The Catholic investor should also insist that necessary adjustments are made in order to improve workplace safety. Any allegations of discrimination based on race, ethnicity, gender, sexual orientation, religion, or preference for a union should also be addressed in discussions between Catholic investors and companies in which they hold shares.

When shareholder advocacy cannot produce change, refusal to invest or divestment is the only way to convey that worker exploitation is unacceptable. In addition, Catholic institutions should follow the USSCB guidelines by excluding investment in companies that practice racial or gender discrimination. Catholic universities should emulate this stance, as well as the USCCB's pledge to invest in companies that promote racial and gender parity via inclusion of women and racial minorities on their corporate boards, equal pay for equal work policies, etc.[54]

As I argued in the case of Notre Dame's investment in HEI, a Catholic institutional investor should contemplate whether or not investing in a company that repeatedly violates CST and on a large scale creates scandal. Earlier in this book I discussed the Catholic notion of scandal and maintained that union busting on Catholic campuses may give rise to scandal. In the case of investing, that scandal might arise if the Catholic investor could not demonstrate a reasonable chance of convincing the corporation involved to abandon its practices that conflict with Catholic social teaching. In this scenario, there would be no other justifiable reason to invest in this corporation, as a profitable return alone does not suffice, according to CST. As leading theorist of critical pedagogy Henry Giroux maintains, universities are "all too willing to define higher education as a business venture, students as consumers and investors, and faculty as a cheap source of labor. Left to the logic of the market, education is something that consumers and investors now purchase for the best price, deal, and profit."[55] A university's investments either ratify or challenge the status quo, the neoliberal corporatized university. Catholic universities run the risk of causing scandal when their investments simply mirror profit-seeking capitalists.

For example, would the USCCB—or a Catholic university—investing in Walmart or Nike cause scandal? The answer depends on whether these companies seriously attempt to do everything they can to improve the lives of workers they either employ directly or indirectly in their supply chain. In the past, reputable NGOs have provided ample documentation of these corporations' failing to ensure consistently that the rights of workers are respected. Walmart, for example, has faced longstanding serious allegations of abusive practices, including denying the right to unionize, wage theft, and abysmal working conditions in its retail stores and supply chain factories.[56] According to one comprehensive report, "the exploitative approach was there from the start" in Walmart's labor practices.[57] Nike also has a "checkered history," according to Professor John Kline of Georgetown University's School of Foreign Service.[58] Given the ongoing concerns about Nike's business practices and widespread abuse of workers in its supply chain, the numerous Catholic colleges and universities that invest in or hold contracts with Nike should carefully examine as much evidence as possible.[59] I cannot undertake an exhaustive analysis here, but a brief overview of the concerns should encourage further investigation.

According to Kline, Nike has taken some positive steps in the past, but appears to have regressed recently.[60] Nike has decreased its environmental impact in some ways.[61] In addition, Nike became the first large manufacturer to release its list of its suppliers, took steps to eradicate child labor, and implemented some safety improvements in its supply chain after public outcry over children making its soccer balls.[62] However, wages remain extremely low for most workers that make their products, while dangerous and abusive conditions remain in the supply chain, according to multiple sources.[63] A 2018 report by the Clean Clothes Campaign stated that workers in Nike's supplier factories in Indonesia, Cambodia, and Vietnam earn only 2.5 percent of the cost of each pair of Nike shoes, which is 30 percent less than in the 1990s. Nike has shifted production to these three countries away from China, where wages have risen. In these three countries, garment workers generally earn 45 percent to 65 percent below a living wage. This report discloses how the "lean management" system used by Nike and Adidas precludes its suppliers from paying a living wage in spite of growing revenues for both shoe makers that would enable them to "pay living wages across their supply chain" if they saw it as a "priority."[64] Nike touts a 2018 study that showed modest gains in wages for workers as a result of its "lean" principles, which tie wage increases to greater transparency about the relationship between productivity and the wage structure.[65] However, the study's authors also concluded that "external efforts" such as investigative journalism, consumer campaigns, labor unions, and collective bargaining play a crucial role in "protect[ing] wage gains" and "ratchet[ing] up conditions over time."[66]

Nike's search for the cheapest labor source has a long history. In his book *University of Nike*, Joshua Hunt maintains that "exploiting Asia's cheap labor market" represents "one of the company's founding principles."[67] Activist and educator Jim Keady first started his campaign against low wages and poor working conditions in Nike's supply chain with his 2001 documentary *Behind the Swoosh*. He resigned from his position as a soccer coach at St. John's University in 1998 because he refused to wear Nike per his contract requirement. He explained that his decision was matter of fidelity to Catholic social teaching on the dignity and rights of workers.[68] Keady continues to visit campuses across the country to urge students to boycott Nike.[69] In a 2015 lecture at Georgetown, he argued that workers who earn about $1.25 a day making Nike shoes would have to toil for over nine years to earn what Nike's premiere endorser Lebron James makes in one game.[70]

In recent years, some students and faculty at Georgetown and Villanova University, among other schools, reproached Nike for its poor record on workers' rights.[71] After Nike denied the Worker Rights Consortium access to its factories in 2015, the presidents of both universities reportedly contacted Nike, requesting that the corporation cease denying access.[72] The WRC, founded in 2000, "assesses factories *for universities and colleges,* to determine whether they are in compliance with *universities'* licensing standards."[73] According to the Catholic Labor Network, eighteen Catholic colleges and universities belong to the Worker Rights Consortium.[74] The WRC has informed its partner colleges and universities about egregious labor practices at Nike's factories in Indonesia, the Dominican Republic, Mexico, Thailand, El Salvador, Honduras, Vietnam, and Bangladesh. These violations include "physical abuse of workers, forced overtime and failure to pay legally mandated compensation (among other abuses)," in addition to "discriminatory firings of pregnant workers," "unlawful assignment of physically dangerous tasks to pregnant workers" and "many other examples."[75] A letter signed by more than six hundred university professors insisted that Nike must recognize the right of colleges and universities to designate the WRC as their representative to help them enforce their codes of conduct.[76] Georgetown eventually let one of its contracts with Nike expire because of the company's stonewalling of the WRC.[77] Nike has cooperated with the WRC in the past, but one of the company's founders has allegedly tried to "pressure Nike's partner schools into ignoring the WRC." Instead, he tried to steer them "towards the relatively toothless" and purportedly more industry-friendly Fair Labor Association.[78]

In 2017 the University of Washington and Georgetown University separately brokered agreements with Nike that required the company to give the WRC access to its supplier factories in a timely fashion upon written request. Industry observers and the universities themselves touted these contracts as breakthroughs in the efforts of universities to ensure compliance with their codes of conduct by suppliers.[79] WRC executive director Scott Nova thanked Georgetown for its "leadership" and "the engagement of other universities" for helping to ensure that the WRC "will be able to effectively conduct factory investigations, and seek remedial measures when needed, at any Nike supplier factory that makes goods bearing the names of universities and colleges affiliated with the WRC."[80]

This agreement represents a positive step between Nike and universities that take workers' rights seriously. It reveals that when students, staff, faculty, and administrators at universities collectively engage suppliers like Nike around workers' rights, they can make a difference.[81] However, the agreement itself, while strong in many ways, still falls short of reflecting CST fully. It does not appear to demand, for example, that Nike requires its suppliers to pay a living wage, which is almost 350 percent higher than the minimum wage in the Dominican Republic, for example.[82] Georgetown's contract includes the labor standards created by IMGCL, a third-party that manages many collegiate licensing agreements. With regard to wages, the IMGCL protocol states that "licensees shall pay employees, as a floor, at least the minimum wage required by local law or the local prevailing industry wage, whichever is higher, and shall provide legally mandated benefits."[83] Georgetown's own code of conduct, which Nike has apparently not signed, more robustly stipulates that "licensees shall report annually on their efforts to achieve a living wage standard for employees and contracted or subcontracted employees engaged in the production of licensed articles." In addition, the university "reserves the right to require licensees to pay a living wage to employees involved in the production of its licensed articles if and when sufficient production facilities that meet this standard become available with an independent system to monitor compliance."[84] This language comes close to the ideal of CST and is commendable, especially while other Catholic universities fail to even mention a living wage.[85] However, all Catholic universities, including Georgetown, must continually scrutinize whether their most recent agreements ensure that all workers making collegiate products with the Nike logo are actually afforded their rights to a living wage, health benefits, freedom of association, and all the other rights demanded by CST.[86] In 2018, for example, the WRC reported to its affiliated universities that Nike relocated between two and three thousand jobs from Indonesia, while declining to meet with the union representation of the workers.[87] Catholic institutions must also consider why Alta Gracia, a factory in the Dominican Republic that makes collegiate apparel and is available on a growing number of Catholic campuses, has been able to pay all of its workers a living wage and to provide health care benefits while suppliers of the highly profitable Nike cannot.[88] Catholic universities dealing with Nike should adopt the unequivocal language of the WRC model code, which requires a "dignified living wage for workers and their families" and specifies its details.[89] Catholic institutions should also take notice of Nike's reportedly discriminatory treatment of female athletes who become pregnant.[90]

If sustained efforts on multiple fronts to convince corporations such as Nike and others to eliminate deleterious labor practices and to completely embrace transparency have failed, investment in them would give rise to the charge of hypocrisy in the church and possibly create scandal. How could Catholic institutions justify turning a blind eye to abuse of workers when the church proclaims justice for workers because *Jesus himself was a worker* who devoted most of "his life on earth to *manual work* at the carpenter's bench" and, as Francis maintains, exploitation of workers is a mortal sin?[91] As I pointed out earlier in this book, many of my students have contended that learning about Catholic social teaching is futile if Catholic institutions do not attempt to live up to the tradition's own ideals. Young people have become disillusioned by a church whose institutions blatantly violate its own teachings. In the case of a corporation not willing to address concerns about abuse of workers, or discrimination, or human rights violations, or despoliation of the environment, any Catholic institutional investor ought to seriously consider divestment after it has exhausted all other options to promote change. Prior to investing, it is incumbent upon Catholic investors to find out as much as possible about a corporation's practices through careful research. SRI committees at some Catholic universities already do this.[92] As Catholic tradition holds, ignorance cannot excuse complicity in evil when the sinner could have reasonably known about the transgression.[93]

The same principles should apply to the acquisition of money through donations, university partnerships with government agencies and corporations, corporate sponsorships, and other sources. Corporatized US universities have not only appropriated resources from governmental agencies such as the CIA or industries like tobacco, they have also sometimes wittingly or unwittingly used them for diabolical purposes. For example, researchers at more than fifty universities conducted experiments funded by the CIA in the 1950s and 1960s aimed at "developing more effective methods of interrogation and torture."[94] Universities have also colluded with pharmaceutical companies in research that caused consumers to pay more than necessary for drugs or potentially to suffer from harmful consequences because of suppressed or falsified data from clinical trials.[95] However, even if colleges and universities use the resources gained for morally legitimate purposes, the ethical status of the source must also be considered. In other words, universities must evaluate both how the source obtained its resources and whether the donor or contractor engages in actions that violate core Catholic teachings. In this connection, Pope Francis has said that donations to charity cannot excuse employers who do not treat their workers with justice and mercy. Furthermore, he bluntly stated that "the People of God don't need their dirty money but hearts that are open to the mercy of God." According to the Holy Father, the church cannot accept the "fruit of the blood of people who have been exploited, enslaved with work which was under-paid."[96] The Christian tradition's concern for how money is acquired dates back to the Bible itself. As Sandra Ely Wheeler points out, in numerous biblical passages dealing with wealth "unjust distribution is condemned, along with unjust accrual and unjust use."[97] For example, the ninth-century BCE prophet Isaiah condemns wealthy landowners in Israel and Judah for obtaining property at the expense of the poor and the rich using "unjust laws" to "deprive the poor of their rights" (Isa 10:2). Isaiah decreed that God would inflict upon Israel and Judah the punishment of foreign captivity because of their economic injustice.[98] Echoing the great Hebrew prophets Isaiah and Amos (see Amos 2:6–8), the Letter of James (5:1–6) presents one of the strongest indictments in the New Testament of the wealthy who achieve their fortune by exploiting and oppressing the poor (NIV):

> Now listen, you rich people, weep and wail because of the misery that is coming on you. ²Your wealth has rotted, and moths have eaten your clothes. ³Your gold and silver are corroded. Their corrosion will testify against you and eat your flesh like fire. You have hoarded wealth in the last days. ⁴Look! The wages you failed to pay the workers who mowed your fields are crying out against you. The cries of the harvesters have reached the ears of the Lord Almighty. ⁵You have lived on earth in luxury and self-indulgence. You have fattened yourselves in the day of slaughter. ⁶You have condemned and murdered the innocent one, who was not opposing you.

Later Christian figures such as Basil the Great (c. 330–79) reiterated this concern. In his well-known sermon on Luke 12:13–31, he deplored the fact that some in his congregation tried "every trick" to acquire wealth by cheating others. To those Christians he offered this admonition: "For well worthy of destruction are the barns of injustice. Tear down with your own hands what you have unjustly built up."[99]

When universities receive donations or resources, such as free athletic equipment, endowed professorships, or research grants from companies, governmental agencies, or individuals that exploit people, these universities are ensnared in evil. To use Cathleen Kaveny's language, they "appropriate evil." Benefiting from the evil of another person or institution can blunt our sensitivity to injustice and distort our consciences. Those who appropriate the benefits of another's evil often engage in rationalization and "self-deception." As Kaveny states, "it is tempting to so accustom ourselves to the benefits that flow from appropriation that we would be inclined to decide against taking steps to eliminate the wrongdoing if the opportunity presented itself."[100] Taking resources that are the fruits of injustices tarnishes a Catholic institution's reputation and diminishes its ability to be a force for good.

For decades the athletics industry has lavished free gear and monetary goods, including coaches' compensation, on universities that market their products for them. Hunt reports that beginning in the 1970s, Nike started paying college coaches from top athletics programs such as Georgetown,

Kentucky, and St. John's. Competitors such as Adidas and Puma quickly followed suit.[101] In 2016 the University of Michigan landed the largest Nike contract to date at $169 million, which was eclipsed by the University of Texas deal at $250 million.[102] In 2014 Notre Dame "bucked the Nike trend" by signing a contract with Under Armour. The deal is reportedly worth $90 million "in cash, stock, and merchandise" in exchange for the athletics programs wearing the brand gear.[103]

Numerous Catholic colleges and universities and their employees prefer to do business with Nike.[104] In 1986 Nike "was cutting $100,000 deals with coaches" at Georgetown, St. John's, and other basketball programs according to Hunt.[105] According to another source, Georgetown men's basketball coach John Thompson III received base compensation for an endorsement deal from Nike of $200,000, plus bonuses based on his team's performance in addition to his university-paid salary.[106] Although Georgetown was one of the earliest to form a relationship with Nike, the company now provides free gear to many Catholic institutions, which all team members and coaching staff must wear.[107] However, this comes at a cost. When I was a varsity athlete, our rowing team had no corporate sponsorships (some rowing teams now wear Nike, for example). We were expected to raise money to pay for our own uniforms. We hand delivered small refrigerator rentals and held erg-a-thons from morning until midnight. Perhaps some today would see this as an undue burden, but it allowed us the freedom to have input regarding who made our uniforms, thereby preserving our agency as young adults. Today's intercollegiate athletes and athletics staff are often forced to be "walking billboards" for their university's corporate supplier. Such coercion may constitute a violation of their freedom of conscience and freedom of religion if these students believe the supplier's business practices violate their moral values. The athletes at Georgetown who protested wearing Nike gear at Georgetown made such a case.[108] No Catholic institution should compel its students to advertise a corporation if those students embrace CST on the dignity and rights of workers. Forcing students to wear a brand that they have earnestly determined grossly mistreats workers flouts Catholic doctrine on freedom of religion and freedom of conscience. As the Second Vatican Council's Declaration on Religious Freedom maintains, the dignity of the human person demands that all people "are to be immune from coercion on the part of individuals or of social groups and of any human power, in such wise that no one is to be forced to act in a manner contrary to his own beliefs, whether privately or publicly, whether alone or in association with others."[109]

If the earlier assessment of Nike's business practices remains accurate, Catholic universities that benefit from the company's largess are appropriating evil. This may also be the case with Catholic universities contracting with Under Armour, Adidas, and other athletic apparel companies, which may also exploit workers in their supply chain. At a minimum, these institutions should undertake research concerning the labor practices of the companies to discern whether or not they are appropriating the fruits of gross injustices. If they choose to continue to do business with a company after finding out about morally illicit practices such as paying poverty wages or unionbusting, Catholic moral teaching mandates determined engagement with the company to provoke change. To reiterate, some cases may require taking a prophetic stance by severing the relationship if the company's immoral behavior proves incorrigible. Catholic institutions should also make the terms of deals with these companies publicly available, in the same way public institutions must report them.[110] This is a matter of respect for the right to participation, which according to CST affords all members of a community a meaningful role in decisions that affect them or the community as a whole, including what kind of moral community they want to form and how they relate to other communities.

As stated above, Catholic colleges and universities should also scrutinize the sources of charitable donations. Obviously, donations from companies that produce abortifacients or illicit weapons of war such as landmines and cluster bombs would be out of bounds.[111] However, just as in the case of investments, the problem extends beyond these industries. In this vein, Catholic moral theology calls into question the recent large donations from the Charles Koch Foundation to the Catholic University of America (more than $11 million), Creighton University (over $2 million), and other Catholic institutions.[112] According to the Foundation website, at least twenty-five other Catholic colleges and universities have accepted money from the foundation.[113] Why might this be problematic? Anthony Annett, a Catholic economist and climate change and sustainable development advisor at the Earth Institute at Columbia University, argues that the Koch brothers' staunch libertarianism, climate-change denial, and unethical business practices squarely contradict Catholic social teaching.

He contends that accepting this donation conflicts with the university's mission.[114] In a letter to CUA administrators, more than fifty Catholic academics, with a former university president and USCCB staffers among them, decried the "stark contrast between the Koch brothers' public policy agenda and our Church's traditional social justice teachings." Their letter specifically cites ways in which the Koch brothers' activities have undermined the church's support for the right to unionize, universal access to healthcare, equitable tax policies, addressing climate change, and regulation of the economy "in the service of the common good."[115] Students on numerous US campuses, including Boston College, have also started an "UnKoch My Campus" campaign to sever ties with what they perceive to be an unethical source of funding.[116] Rendering a definitive judgment on this case exceeds the scope of my analysis here. However, these are serious allegations, which numerous sources appear to corroborate.[117] I raise attention to it here to say that Catholic universities must thoroughly investigate such claims before accepting significant donations in order to avoid taking "blood money" and possibly causing scandal. Although development offices cannot examine how every donor's income has been derived, they can investigate the largest, which more deeply implicate them in any possible immoral and even illegal ways donors have harvested the fruits of injustice at the expense of the poor, the oppressed, and the planet.

I have argued that when it comes to the refusal to invest and acquire money in immoral ways, Catholic universities should not focus on a narrow set of issues. In this regard, they should emulate the approach taken by some of the religious orders, whose SRI policies demonstrate concern for the fullness of CST. Many Catholic universities that do have SRI policies remain at the level of vague principles. Boston College, for example, states that "the management of its investments . . . reflects the ethical, social, and moral principles inherent in its mission and heritage. In particular, the University is firmly committed to the promotion of the dignity of the individual, personal freedom, and social justice." In addition, periodic review of the University's investments will be undertaken so that "gains from investments will not be derived from fraud, abusive power, greed, or injustice."[118] Seattle University states: "Consistent with the university's Jesuit Catholic values, the [Investment] Committee will consider the university's commitment to ethics and social responsibility in making investment decisions. While the committee remains committed to its fiduciary duty to the university's long-term financial growth and sustainability, it also recognizes the value of nontraditional investment opportunities in providing a reasonable return as well as furthering the university's mission and values."[119] Georgetown University's Principles and Operating Guidelines for the Committee on Investments in Social Responsibility specifies to a greater degree, by ruling out investments in companies that are "substantially involved in the provision of abortion services" and by calling for avoidance of investments "in companies that have demonstrated records of widespread violations of human dignity." Examples include companies "that are directly and significantly involved in the production of weapons that are intended to be used for indiscriminate destruction" and companies with practices that have "an extremely deleterious effect on the environment." In 2017, this statement undergirded a student proposal to divest from the private prison industry, which the university board approved.[120]

Such statements are welcome steps in the right direction, but even greater specificity can help ensure that a university's investments reflect the fullness of CST rather than selective adherence to it. In other words, abstract statements are likely to give too much "wiggle room" for investments that violate CST in some way and generate time-consuming debate among those responsible for implementing the policy. A clear and detailed policy will make the job of decision makers easier and the process more efficient, something that busy members of university committees should appreciate. Moreover, it is important to specify precisely who will determine how to implement the policy (more on this below). An advisory board akin to Loyola's former Shareholder Advocacy Committee or Georgetown's Committee on Investments and Social Responsibility should undertake this task. The board should ideally contain members with expertise in finance, labor law, environmental studies, and Catholic social teaching (as is recommended by Georgetown's policy).[121] A Catholic institutional investor could also avail itself of an organization such as the Responsible Endowments Coalition, which assists universities that lack experience in this area.[122] In accordance with the principle of participation, a Catholic investor should be open to perspectives from all stakeholders at the institution, while recognizing that ultimately the university's president and board of trustees hold responsibility for all investments. Respect for the principle of participation requires providing all members of the university community, and preferably the broader public, with the knowledge of the SRI policy and the investments. Posting them publicly on the website would best serve this end.[123]

The investment criteria of the Adrian Dominican Sisters exemplify an approach that broadly takes account of CST and provides much greater specificity than most Catholic university SRI policies. It is worth examining here as it could provide a useful template for Catholic universities. For starters, the criteria explicitly promote investing in entities that respect the rights and dignity of the worker: "We promote the protection of human dignity and human rights in the global economy to fair labor practices throughout the global supply chain, including: the right to organize; adequate benefits; prohibition of child labor; safe working conditions; empowerment of employees through training and development; and participatory decision-making, including management and board membership. We discourage investment in corporations which are known to be discriminatory in their policies related to hiring, wages, promotions and governance due to prejudices in the areas of gender, age, race, religion, culture, advocacy, disability, sexual orientation or political affiliation." In addition, the criteria call for avoiding investments in the global military industrial complex, excluding "any company that derives more than 4 percent of its revenues from military systems-related contracts and/or any of its revenues from nuclear weapons systems-related contracts." The criteria equally insist on investing in companies that produce renewable energy and avoiding companies that wreak havoc on the environment by producing nuclear energy, "disposing of hazardous waste improperly," polluting water, land and/or air without taking "corrective measures," destroying "the land by mountain-top mining, clear cutting timberland, or harvesting rainforests," or producing "hazardous/toxic chemicals, ecologically destructive herbicides and/or pesticides." The criteria also eschew investing in companies that deteriorate "quality-of-life," such as tobacco companies, for-profit health providers, and financial institutions that practice "predatory lending" and create loans that "undermine a country's socio-economic development."[124] The Adrian Dominican Sisters also engage in community investing in order to make a positive impact on communities, particularly those of the marginalized. Since 1979 they have invested approximately $26 million in 478 such investments, "to promote social, economic and environmental justice."[125] These "alternative" or community investments include community banks and credit unions, affordable housing, fair trade farmer coops, and the global cooperative and social investor Oikocredit. The Adrian Dominican Sisters were also the first lender to Equal Exchange, which has become one of the leading importers of fair trade coffee and other goods from small farmer cooperatives.[126]

The Christian Brothers Investment Services (CBIS), an investment firm that manages $6 billion according to Catholic Responsible Investing (CRI) principles, also applies a wide-ranging set of criteria to determine the moral permissibility of investments.[127] The company utilizes four screens: "life issues" (abortion, abortifacients, contraception, and embryonic stem cell research), pornography, "violence and militarism," and tobacco. CBIS director Daniel Nielsen has helpfully explained some of the complexities involved in applying these criteria.[128] For starters, he correctly maintains that applying the principle of cooperation with evil involves making "prudential judgments" that may yield different conclusions among different investors. In Catholic ethics prudential judgments are made when an individual or a group attempts to apply a particular principle or value of CST to a concrete case, using the best available data pertaining to the case.[129] For example, a Catholic investor must use prudential judgment when determining whether or not the corporation will be amenable to bringing its practices in line with CST in the future, based on its past history, current practices, and stated aims. In other words, prudential judgment is necessary to determine whether there is a "reasonable hope of success for corporate change," to advert to the USCCB guidelines language once again. According to Nielsen, CBIS "focuses on different levels of cooperation with evil," thereby screening out illicit forms such as investing in a company that produces abortifacients, and permitting investments in some companies that produce weapons. In this vein, CBIS precludes investments in landmine manufacturers, which produce weapons that indiscriminately kill innocent human beings. On the other hand, CBIS allows for investments in companies that create guns used exclusively for police work. CBIS also has included investments in companies such as BP and Royal Dutch Shell, which may appear controversial, especially given Pope Francis's call in his landmark encyclical Laudato Si to "progressively replace" fossil fuels "without delay" to address climate change.[130] However, according to Nielsen these investments are permissible given that

CBIS and other investors filed shareholder resolutions that after years led both companies "to issue public reports in 2015 and 2016 on their efforts to address climate change."[131] In other words, according to the prudential judgment of CBIS and other religious investors, shareholder advocacy has a reasonable hope of success to get these companies to deal responsibly with climate change. This is obviously a complex matter. Other Catholic analysts disagree with that prudential judgment, as I will discuss below in more detail.

Regardless of this particular assessment, Catholic investors must decide how in good conscience they can address the problem of global climate change, one of the "principal challenges facing humanity in our day" according to Pope Francis, through their investment policies and by any other means available to them.[132] In *Laudato Si*, the Pope points to a number of simple practices that individuals and organizations such as universities can adopt: "avoiding the use of plastic and paper, reducing water consumption, separating refuse, cooking only what can reasonably be consumed, showing care for other living beings, using public transport or car-pooling, planting trees, turning off unnecessary lights, or any number of other practices."[133] Many Catholic institutions have already incorporated such steps in order to "green" their campuses. They are appropriate and will be discussed in more detail below. However, some administrators and students alike have acknowledged that more can and must be done on the level of institutional investments.

The Case of Fossil Fuels and Stewardship of the Environment

In recent times several Catholic universities have chosen to make prophetic statements through divestment from companies causing environmental destruction. In 2009 Santa Clara University students, for example, prompted the university president to divest from Massey Energy because of its practice of mountaintop removal in Appalachia, which creates disastrous environmental and human costs.[134] The University of Dayton became the first Catholic university to completely divest from coal and fossil fuels in 2014. In a statement explaining the decision, university president Dan Curran stated: "We cannot ignore the negative consequences of climate change, which disproportionately impact the world's most vulnerable people. Our Marianist values of leadership and service to humanity call upon us to act on these principles and serve as a catalyst for civil discussion and positive change that benefits our planet."[135] The University of Dayton has since become a leading advocate for divestment from fossil fuels and investing in renewable energy, sponsoring a major conference on the topic in the fall of 2015.[136]

Conversely, some Catholic universities have consciously rejected divestment from fossil fuels. For example, in 2019 Creighton University rejected a proposal endorsed overwhelmingly by the student body in order to "achieve long-term returns."[137] In 2015 Georgetown announced its plans to partially divest, targeting only those coal companies that it considers the worst environmental polluters. The university did go further in 2020, moving to "prudently divest from fossil fuel companies."[138] After a six-year student-led campaign during which the administration resisted divestment from fossil fuel, Seattle University announced the decision "to fully divest the marketable portion of the endowment from any investments in companies owning fossil fuel reserves" by 2023.[139] However, the Sustainable Student Action group saw the announcement as a partial victory, as the university did not commit to divesting from companies that "extract, process, and transport fossil fuel."[140] In short, Catholic universities generally concur with Pope Francis's plea to halt climate change and environmental despoliation. They do not agree, however, on the most appropriate means for achieving this goal.

The decision of whether or not to divest from fossil fuels depends on a number of factors. First, many faith-based investors believe that engaging companies through shareholder resolutions and proxy voting can produce positive change. As Mary Ellen Foley McGuire points out, owning even a small portion of the company's stock entitles investors to attend shareholder meetings and/or vote via proxy votes on shareholder resolutions delivered to them by mail.[141] "As an owner, you have the legal right (actually, a responsibility) to act if directors fail in their duty to represent your interest. At the same time, your status as an owner gives you certain ethical obligations as regards the policies and procedures by which the company operates."[142] Along with the CBIS, the Catholic Tri-State Coalition, and its partners in the Interfaith Center on Corporate Responsibility, utilized this approach to cajole Massey energy into doing less harm to the environment. These groups believe that divestment leaves Massey "little incentive to change its practices." As I stated above, Seattle University explicitly agreed with this contention. The ICCR also points to successes through shareholder advocacy such as coaxing Coca-Cola to improve working conditions at its factories in Columbia.[143]

In some cases, investors cannot use shareholder resolutions and proxy voting. Investors in private equity funds do not have recourse to these common forms of shareholder advocacy used in publicly owned corporations.[144] This was the case with Notre Dame's investment in HEI. However, a United Nations report on responsible investment in private equity argues that although asset managers "have complete discretion over investment decision-making and ownership activities" in private equity, investors have several avenues for discussing "environmental, social and corporate governance issues."[145] Bigger Catholic institutions such as the University of Notre Dame, which had a $10.7 billion endowment as of 2018, might have "much more leverage to influence corporations" than individual investors.[146] In short, there might be reasons to hope that holding onto an institution's investments can help to produce goods that outweigh the evil involved in investing in private equities.

On the other hand, experts have offered considerable grounds for abandoning hope with regard to fossil fuels. They argue that the scientific evidence demands an almost complete abandonment of harvesting fossil fuels from the earth in order to adequately address climate change. In other words, Catholic investors are morally required to call for the abandonment of the raison d'être of these companies. It is naïve to assume that shareholder advocacy might get them to relinquish their primary practices.[147] There is little evidence that coal, oil, and gas companies are willing to do what it takes to stem climate change, for example by switching completely to renewables.[148] Moreover, fossil fuel companies have successfully fought against shareholder advocacy for years, either by getting the SEC to deem resolutions invalid or by waging propaganda wars against them. Even the most determined and experienced groups such as the Tri-State Coalition for Responsible Investments and ICCR are undertaking a Sisyphean task against corporate giants like Exxon, ConocoPhillips, and Chevron, which continue to prioritize the bottom line and not the environment.[149] Sister Patricia Daly, who is on the forefront of this battle, acknowledged in reference to Exxon that "decades have been lost in the fight against climate change, due in part to our company's campaign of disinformation."[150]

Therefore, many Catholic scholars are advocating divestment from fossil fuels altogether and reinvestment in renewable energy sources as the course most consistent with Catholic teaching.[151]

Local Efforts to Green Campuses

Already in 2006 US institutions of higher education pledged to advance environmental sustainability and to address climate change by adopting the American College and University Presidents' Climate Commitment (ACUPCC). A number of Catholic university presidents became charter signatories.[152] Catholic social teaching requires that Catholic institutions take "micro-level actions" and promote systemic-level changes to promote sustainability. Investment policies serve the latter goal. Reducing their carbon footprint fulfills Catholic universities' obligations on the former level. Since the ACUPCC, many more Catholic colleges and universities have pledged to implement sustainability policies. In the summer of 2015 about one hundred US Catholic university presidents signed a declaration to support the ecological vision of Pope Francis's *Laudato Si*. They were joined by roughly eighty representatives from Catholic universities around the world and the Association of Catholic Colleges and Universities, the Association of Jesuit Colleges and Universities, the Association of Franciscan Colleges and Universities, and the International Federation of Catholic Universities based in Paris. In an excerpt from the declaration, they stated:

> We commit ourselves as leaders in Catholic Higher Education to work together regionally and globally, through all the means available to and appropriate for our colleges and universities as institutions of higher learning, to study, promote, and act on the ideals and vision of integral ecology laid out by Pope Francis. . . . More specifically, we commit ourselves as leaders in Catholic Higher Education globally to integrate care for the planet, integral human development, and concern for the poor within our research projects, our educational curricula and public programming, our institutional infrastructures, policies and practices, and our political and social involvements as colleges and universities.[153]

Thirty-two Catholic colleges and universities have also taken the St. Francis Pledge, which was created by the Catholic Climate Covenant along with a helpful "toolkit" for implementing its five pillars: "Pray, learn, assess, act, and advocate" on behalf of climate change.[154]

Many Catholic colleges and universities have taken action and impressively "greened" their campuses.[155] Some can proudly claim that they have been recognized by external bodies for these efforts. For example, Villanova University was designated the "green business" of the year by the local Chamber of Commerce. Among the university's achievements recognized by the award were its five LEED-certified buildings, hydration stations to eliminate plastic bottles, and ionized water cleaning technology, which reduces waste materials and toxic chemical use. Villanova also decreased its greenhouse gas emissions and instituted several academic programs and degrees focused on sustainability.[156] All of its trash is converted to electricity by a waste-to-energy facility, while 41 percent of waste is recycled or composted.[157] About one quarter of the food consumed on campus is grown locally and/or organically.[158] Other schools, such as Seattle University, where community members can grow their own food in two gardens and 72 percent of all campus waste is either composted or recycled, boast similar policies and awards.[159] In 2019 the University of San Francisco remarkably achieved carbon neutrality, even though it had earlier set a target date of 2050. On the road to becoming one of the "greenest" Catholic campus in the country, changes included a 30 percent reduction of water usage, environmentally-friendly cleaning supplies, channeling two-thirds of campus waste toward reuse, recycling, or composting, energy-producing micro turbines on campus, and "purchasing mission-driven carbon offsets."[160]

Creating green campuses has become fashionable, with a number of organizations ranking and showcasing the best performers. Loyola University Chicago ranks fourth among "America's Greenest Colleges" according to the renowned environmental NGO the Sierra Club. Loyola has distinguished itself as the only Catholic university to crack the list of top ten "coolest schools." The Sierra Club touts Loyola's "extensive recycling and composting programs." It also states that Loyola's "new Institute of Environmental Sustainability offers five environmental bachelor's programs (with two more coming soon), aquaponics facilities, Chicago's biggest geothermal facility, and a lab in which students learn how to make biodiesel—and soap!—from excess vegetable oil. It also has a 3,100-square-foot research greenhouse . . . where students learn about urban agriculture."[161] Beyond

Loyola, eleven other Catholic institutions made the Sierra Club's 2014 list of 173 "coolest schools."[162] The Sierra Club evaluates schools according to sixty-eight criteria, ranging from relatively low-cost sustainability solutions such as bike-sharing programs and having a student sustainability group, to more costly interventions such as converting to reliance on renewable energy sources. Schools receive points in each of the sixty-eight areas, with the more demanding sustainability initiatives weighted more heavily.[163]

Princeton Review profiles even more environmentally responsible schools in its *Guide to 353 Green Colleges* (2015).[164] It particularly highlights the schools it ranks among the "Top 50 Green Colleges." Three Catholic institutions received this distinction: Santa Clara University (no. 19), Saint Michael's College (no. 39), and Loyola University Chicago (no. 43). Many more made the overall list. Princeton Review selects data from STARS, the Sustainability Tracking, Assessment, and Rating System, which the Association for the Advancement of Sustainability in Higher Education (AASHE) administers.[165] Universities report their data to STARS, then Princeton Review culls the data to rate the schools on its list. The data pertains to areas such as low-impact dining, clean and renewable energy, waste diversion, indoor and outdoor air quality, and whether or not the university has a committee on investor responsibility.[166] It is interesting to note that STARS 2.0 includes a subcategory that "recognizes institutions that are advancing diversity and affordability on campus and are working to promote environmental and social justice." This area valorizes making higher education accessible for low-income students and creating a diverse student body and faculty (I discuss the importance of this in the next chapter).[167]

STARS 2.0 also has a Wellbeing and Work subcategory, which asks universities to report if they have "sustainable compensation standards, guidelines or policies" for their employees. STARS 2.0 states that it "recognizes institutions that have incorporated sustainability into their human resources programs and policies to positively affect the health, safety and wellbeing of the campus community."[168] The STARS 2.1 rating system amplified the importance of work policies, with particular emphasis on paying all employees a living wage: "This credit recognizes institutions that ensure that their lowest paid workers earn a living wage. Poverty, or the inability of current generations to meet their needs, is a sustainability challenge even in highly developed countries. By providing employees wages and benefits that meet basic needs, a university or college can enfranchise its entire workforce so that each individual can contribute positively and productively to the community."[169] Unfortunately, however, neither Princeton Review nor the Sierra Club uses these subcategories in creating its lists of green schools.

In my judgment, care for the environment is perhaps the area where numerous Catholic universities have best embodied Catholic social teaching, even if Catholic institutions could strive to do more. More than a few Catholic universities have undertaken serious action in order to promote environmental sustainability, not just made lofty statements and signed platitudinous pledges. In addition to those efforts I have already mentioned, it is worth pointing to just a few of the many other laudable initiatives implemented on Catholic campuses. At Santa Clara University, almost half of the university's energy comes from renewable sources.[170] Three photovoltaics have been installed on the top of structures. More than 80 percent of water used to maintain the landscape is recycled water. The university has decreased greenhouse gas emissions by 40 percent since 2005.[171] Saint Michael's College in Vermont requires all of its students to take a course dealing with sustainability.[172] Its partnership with Efficiency Vermont has made it financially feasible to make myriad lighting and technology efficiency improvements and to reduce its electricity usage by more than 3.1 million kWh annually. In addition, the college collects 270,000 kWh annually from its nearby solar array.[173] Like many other Catholic colleges and universities, Saint Michael's exhibits shining examples of fulfilling Catholic social teaching on care for God's creation.

One wonders, though, why university leaders have been willing to commit themselves to this issue, while reluctant to move on some others. For example, would one hundred Catholic university presidents sign a declaration on the rights of all workers on college campuses that would reflect Catholic social teaching on the right to unionize and to a living and just wage? What about a solemn pledge to enact the option for the poor in recruiting, admissions, financial aid, and retention policies? This discrepancy might create the impression, fairly or not, that Catholic university leaders have undertaken initiatives on sustainability and climate change because they are trendy and in the spotlight today. Mention of Princeton Review Green campus status can serve as a marketing tool, much like a university's ranking in *U.S. News & World Report*'s Top Colleges and Universities list. No such list exists regarding respect for workers' rights or an institution's record on racial and gender equity. *U.S. News* did implement an economic diversity ranking several years ago, but it has not gotten the media attention the green campus lists have garnered. For example, the College Sustainability Report Card was featured in the *New York Times Magazine*.[174] There is also evidence that market pressures may contribute to universities going green. A senior vice president from the Princeton Review noted that "among 10,116 college applicants who participated in our 2014 'College Hopes & Worries Survey,' 61 percent said having information about a school's commitment to the environment would influence their decision to apply to or attend the school." Rachel Gutter, director of the Center for Green Schools at the U.S. Green Building Council concurred, stating that sustainability policies represent "an important deciding factor for today's four-year college bound students."[175]

It is true that recently the media has reported increasingly on the adjunct situation, as I discussed earlier in this book. In addition, more news stories about the lack of economic diversity among students at US colleges and universities are also appearing.[176] Only time will tell if this attention spurs more dramatic action by Catholic university leaders on these issues. It is also reasonable to speculate whether sustainability practices that actually save universities money are more likely to be adopted than paying to do the right thing. For example, Saint Michael's reportedly has saved $168,000 annually on energy costs by adopting its green energy practices.[177] On the other hand, paying adjunct faculty will cost colleges and universities, even if some scholars have exaggerated the cost of promoting just compensation for adjunct faculty. To reiterate, moving toward respect for the rights of part-time faculty may not cost as much as some are inclined to think.[178]

CST on Integral Ecology: "Everything Is Interconnected"

In thinking about which areas of CST to implement, Catholic universities cannot simply prioritize according to convenience, cost efficiency, or popularity. They should not take pride in sustainability efforts while allowing a corporate culture that denies workers the right to unionize or to earn a living wage, for example. Rather, policies such as those relating to sustainability must be considered in conjunction with those dealing with issues such as racial and gender equity, workers' rights, and access to education for the poor. CST does not permit seeing such issues in isolation from one another. As Pope Francis stated in *Laudato Si*, "everything is interconnected" (no. 70).

Standing on the shoulders of giants like St. Augustine and St. Francis of Assisi, Pope Francis's encyclical on the environment builds on the long-standing obligation of care for God's creation in the Catholic tradition. Christian teachings requiring us to appreciate and care for the natural world can be traced back to the Bible.[179] In the 1980s, the United States Conference of Catholic Bishops already called our attention to the "moral dimensions of energy policy."[180] In 1990 Pope John Paul II maintained that world peace was threatened by, among other things, a "lack of due respect for nature."[181] Pope Benedict became known as the "Green Pope" for his repeated calls for us to be "guardians of life and creation."[182]

Pope Francis thus stands in unity with his predecessors and adds a new sense of urgency to the environmental crisis. He wants to impress upon the world that the time to act is now. We can no longer wait, as the science is clear about the severity of the problem. We must undertake changes, both in our personal lives and on the level of policy, to promote a sustainable and just future for all of our children and grandchildren. The fact that Pope Francis has issued the first-ever papal encyclical on creation care indicates how important it is for us to reflect on the moral dimensions of the environment.

As a pastor and leader of the worldwide Catholic Church, Pope Francis feels compelled to address the moral issues arising from climate change and other forms of destruction of the environment. Catholicism stresses that the natural world is a gift from God, and Francis wants to remind us that it is not ours to plunder. Rather, God has entrusted us with the duty of caring for all of creation. Right relationship with God requires right relationship with all of God's creation.[183] Moreover, Pope Francis rightly has emphasized that the poor in particular suffer most from the effects of climate change and environmental degradation. We must abandon the "throwaway culture" that promotes overconsumption, gives rise to environmental degradation, and fails to recognize the dignity of the world's poor.[184] Caring for creation is a requirement of the Catholic Church's option for the poor; promoting environmental responsibility necessarily includes advocating for the rights of the poor.[185] In short, Pope Francis's encyclical shines a much-needed spotlight on environmental issues, which have clear moral dimensions and ramifications for the plight of the world's poor. According to CST, concern for the common good must include concern for the environment. Concern for the environment necessarily entails concern for human rights, especially the rights of the poor, who are disproportionately harmed by climate change and environmental degradation.

This "integral ecology" of CST generally and of Pope Francis specifically echoes Saint John Paul's emphasis on human dignity.[186] Pope Francis maintains that "since everything is closely interrelated, and today's problems call for a vision capable of taking into account every aspect of the global crisis . . . we [must] now consider some elements of an integral ecology, which clearly respects human and social dimensions."[187]

Whether we are dealing with White supremacy and racism, economic injustice, environmental despoliation wrought by humans, or imperialism or other forms of oppression, the root is what Augustine called *libido dominandi*, the lust for domination.[188] The Christian tradition rightly challenges all people to renounce this disordered desire and to acknowledge their sinfulness in the face of the Almighty Creator—the One who creates, unites, and calls upon us to save ourselves and the planet from self-inflicted destruction. Pope Francis is absolutely right: "We are not faced with two separate crises, one environmental and the other social, but rather one complex crisis which is both social and environmental. Strategies for a solution demand an integrated approach to combating poverty, restoring dignity to the excluded, at the same time protecting nature."[189] We learn from the Genesis creation narrative and the story of Cain and Abel that dealing with the environmental crisis is "inseparable from fraternity, justice and faithfulness to others."[190]

Francis bemoans a kind of "green rhetoric" that fails to acknowledge that a "true ecological approach always becomes a social approach."[191] Earlier, Saint John Paul II had put the matter starkly. He maintained that any concern for the environment without deep interest in "human ecology" remains morally suspect:

In addition to the irrational destruction of the natural environment, we must also mention the more serious destruction of the *human environment,* something which is by no means receiving the attention it deserves. Although people are rightly worried—though much less than they should be—about preserving the natural habitats of the various animal species threatened with extinction, because they realize that each of these species makes its particular contribution to the balance of nature in general, too little effort is made to *safeguard the moral conditions for an authentic "human ecology."* Not only has God given the earth to man [sic], who must use it with respect for the original good purpose for which it was given to him, but man too is God's gift to man. He must therefore respect the natural and moral structure with which he has been endowed. In this context, mention should be made of the serious problems of modern urbanization, of the need for urban planning which is concerned with how people are to live, and of the attention which should be given to a "social ecology" of work.[192]

Laudato Si echoes these words: "Questions of justice" must be included in any approach to environmental ethics, so that *"both the cry of the earth and the cry of the poor"* can be heard.[193] Pope Francis points to the denial of the rights of the poor to a safe, clean, and beautiful environment. But he also maintains that "every violation of solidarity" and the denial of the rights of the poor to a living wage, healthcare and other goods harm the environment itself.[194] Succinctly stated, "we urgently need a humanism capable of bringing together the different fields of knowledge, including economics, in the service of a more integral and integrating vision."[195] To put it another way, Saint Paul VI said that if you want peace, work for justice. Saint John Paul II added that if you want justice, defend life. Pope Francis reminds us that to defend life and justice we must care for the earth and share its resources equitably.

As was mentioned above, AASHE's STARS rating system reflects CST's concern for sustainability of the earth and the wellbeing of its inhabitants. In other words, the emphasis on the rights and dignity of workers within the larger framework of sustainability and environmental concern reflects the "integral ecology" of CST. In this paradigm, policies relating to sustainability must be considered in conjunction with those dealing with issues such as racial and gender equity, workers' rights, and access to education for the poor. CST does not permit seeing such issues in isolation from one another. Thus, by participating in STARS 2.1 Catholic universities can demonstrate how they have moved toward embodying the integral ecology that they affirmed in the pledge they signed to support *Laudato Si* in 2015. Some schools already seek the STARS certification from AASHE, but more could join them. Catholic universities that rightfully commit themselves to sustainability and care of the environment must also earnestly pursue a "social ecology of work" that respects the rights to a living wage and freedom of association, education that empowers the marginalized, and a milieu that fosters equity for those historically oppressed and excluded in society broadly and at universities in particular.

5 Racial Inclusion and Justice at Catholic Colleges and Universities: From Tokenism to Participation

I had never heard the song "Plenty Good Room" before. I had also never encountered an academic beginning a lecture by singing. Thus, I was taken by surprise one evening in the beautiful University chapel of Saint Joseph.

Joseph A. Brown, SJ, PhD, a Jesuit priest and highly accomplished scholar and poet, joined our university community as the holder of a prestigious chair in 2009. His Chair's lecture treated us to his mellifluous voice and powerful words—words that have stuck with me ever since. In addition to his sharp intellect and penchant for the aesthetic, Father Brown does not mince words. In his lecture he challenged those of us in the audience, particularly those of us who are White, to consider the fact that while people of color are present at our universities, there really isn't "room at the table" for them. In other words, very often their presence amounts to tokenism, rather than to equal partnership in all aspects of the life of the university.[1] Even if there is "plenty good room" for people of color at our universities, they cannot "just choose [their] seat and sit down," as the popular spiritual counsels. The vast majority of important decisions are made by White administrators and White board members, while precious few people of color hold positions of power in our universities.[2]

Although Fr. Brown is correct, I would add one caveat. Very often women and members of the LGBTQ community also do not have seats at the table when the most pressing issues are decided at our universities. Many stakeholders have undeniably done much good work to diversify Catholic university communities and to make them more welcoming and inclusive to all people. In what follows, I refer to some of the most promising means.[3] Some institutions have been more successful than others. In all cases, much remains to be done. Unfortunately, just as I have shown in previous chapters, particular practices and underlying assumptions of the corporatized model of higher education impede making greater progress in creating truly inclusive and participatory educational communities.

The remaining chapters of this book will discuss some of the obstacles that hinder people of color, women, and members of the LGBTQ community from fully participating in the common good of our educational communities. The challenges facing each of these groups warrant separate book-length analyses. However, I can only provide here an impetus for further conversation.

The thread from Catholic social teaching that holds the concerns of these groups together is the unassailability of human dignity and the right to participation. The right to participation, as I have discussed in earlier chapters, requires enabling all people to "sit down at the table" as equals in our educational communities, rather than simply just welcoming minoritized peoples into White supremacist domiciles.[4] Solidarity in the Catholic tradition requires promoting the full participation and rights of the marginalized, not just tolerating their presence or charitably accepting them into our institutions.[5] Solidarity, which is a contemporary expression of Jesus's love commands according to Catholic Hispanic theologian Ada María Isasi-Díaz, must extend to all people, especially the disadvantaged.[6] In our society, this includes people of color, women, and LGBTQ persons. Solidarity requires transforming our educational institutions, jettisoning the White supremacy of society that still maintains "relationships of white cultural, political, and social dominance."[7] St. John Paul II contended that racism "constitutes a serious offence against God." As he put it, *"every upright conscience cannot but decisively condemn any racism, no matter in what heart or place it is found."*[8]

Hateful prejudice and overt discrimination obviously preclude equal participation in a community. As I shall discuss, members of historically marginalized groups unfortunately encounter overt bigotry sometimes on our campuses, with a disturbing uptick in recent times. The White supremacist rally on the University of Virginia's campus on August 14, 2017, painfully reminds us that universities can become bastions of hatred and even violence.[9] However, people of color likely more often face what is called aversive racism. Catholic theologian Marvin Krier Mich states that aversive racists uphold White supremacy while not directly discriminating against racially minoritized persons. Rather, the aversive racist

"ignore[s] the existence of black people" and when necessary feigns acceptance of them.[10] Psychologist Derald Wing Sue and his colleagues have
produced a taxonomy of racism, in which they maintain that aversive racists consciously affirm "egalitarian values" but operate with "antiminor-
ity feelings" subconsciously.[11] According to Mich, aversive racism "could
fit the behavior of many American Catholics."[12] Unfortunately, some research has shown that Catholics are no less racist than the general population and in some ways exhibit racist attitudes more often than the
religiously unaffiliated.[13]

In my judgment, this notion of aversive racism can be extended to include aversive sexism, homophobia, and transphobia. Although hard to
measure, this form of prejudice is present on our campuses (as I will discuss below). There is yet another understanding of racism germane to the
subject of this book. Catholic ethicist Fr. Bryan Massingale has aptly described racism as a culture, or "an underlying set of meanings and values
attached to skin color, a way of interpreting skin color differences that pervades the collective convictions, conventions, and practices of American
life." This culture, Massingale continues, has both "interpersonal and systemic effects" and undergirds White privilege in our society.[14] "Racism
functions as an ethos, as the animating spirit of US society, which lives
on despite observable changes and assumes various incarnations in different historical circumstances."[15] Perhaps a simile encapsulates the meaning of this understanding of racism: It is as if a toxin exists in the air that
only affects minorities. It affects their breathing, but not the breathing of
Whites, who retain their ability to breathe freely. This "toxin" was created over centuries by Whites who perpetuated racial injustices—many
of which were codified by laws—and White supremacy. It continues to
plague minorities while most Whites are unaware of it.[16] As Massingale
puts it, racism is "an underlying dynamic that remains constant despite
significant watersheds and shifts, and that morphs to assume new forms
and manifestations."[17]

This racism is also largely "unconscious." Whites are generally unaware
of the ways in which they have been conditioned by racism, a "largely
unconscious or preconscious frame of perception," and the forms of racial
advantage (White privilege) that they continue to enjoy in contemporary
society.[18] This includes the "institutional racism" that has been embedded in our society's institutions. According to Cardinal Francis George,

People who assume, consciously or unconsciously, that white people are superior create and sustain institutions that privilege people like themselves and habitually ignore the contributions of other peoples and cultures. This "white privilege" often goes undetected because it has become internalized and integrated as part of one's outlook on the world by custom, habit and tradition. It can be seen in most of our institutions: judicial and political systems, social clubs, associations, hospitals, *universities*, labor unions, small and large businesses, major corporations, the professions, sports teams and in the arts . . . in the Church as well.[19]

I argue that this kind of racism—cultural, unconscious, and institutional—as well as an analogous type of sexism, homophobia, and transphobia, persists at Catholic colleges and universities despite well-intentioned efforts to overcome them. The vast majority of people at these institutions eschew the kinds of overt, historical discrimination that once plagued our society, such as banning minoritized people and women from higher education. However, more subtle forms of discrimination continue to be embedded in the policies and practices of institutions of higher learning in the United States. This chapter will discuss some of them and will marshal resources from the Catholic social tradition to consider ways of overcoming them. In doing so, I will also locate the "growing edge of the tradition"—to use a phrase from John Courtney Murray, SJ—to describe areas in which church teaching stands in need of reflection and reform.[20]

Racial Justice and Equality on Campus: Some Statistics

In discussing the need to eradicate sexism and racism both within society broadly and within the church as well, Rick Malloy, SJ, contends that surveys have repeatedly indicated that "people of color feel uncomfortable" on Catholic campuses. In his book *A Faith That Frees: Catholic Matters for the 21st Century*, Malloy recalls a Latina visitor to the university saying "this place looks like a plantation." She noted that almost all of the faculty, students, and staff were White, while those who serve them food and clean their buildings are African American.[21] As Malloy contends, it is not that Catholic institutions of higher learning are overtly racist. Sincere and concerted efforts have been made to increase the presence of minorities among the students, faculty, and staff. Earnest attempts have been made to address racism on many campuses. Yet many people of color still do not feel welcome, even though Catholic teaching demands creating a welcoming environment and promoting racial equity and justice at all Catholic institutions.

In 1979 the United States Conference of Catholic Bishops issued a landmark document on racism entitled *Brothers and Sisters to Us*. The bishops condemned the "radical evil" of racism in the strongest terms, maintaining that "the Church cannot remain silent about the racial injustices in society and its own structures."[22] Racism is a sin that denies the fundamental truth revealed in the incarnation of Jesus Christ—namely, that all human persons are equally imbued with dignity. It disregards the fact that all persons are created in the image of God. Racism also "mocks" the teaching of Jesus to "treat others the way you would have them treat you."[23] Every Christian is obligated to undertake a "radical transformation" in both their personal lives and in "the structure[s] of society" in order to dismantle racism in all its forms.[24] The bishops advocated a "continuing dialogue throughout the Catholic community and the nation at large" and an examination of conscience on all levels of the church in the United States regarding "attitudes and behavior towards blacks, Hispanics, Native Americans, and Asians."[25] The duty of all Catholics to evangelize, which requires "bringing consciences, both individual and social, into conformity with the Gospel," must entail continually working to overcome the persistent forms of racial injustice in American society.[26]

The bishops advocated a number of concrete proposals to eradicate racial injustice. They urged, for example, an "effective affirmative action program in every diocese and religious institution." Furthermore, they specifically stated that Catholic schools and universities should ensure that their employment policies adhere to CST on "justice for workers and respect for their rights." The bishops acknowledged that Catholic institutions have not always lived up to the church's teaching in these areas, while exhorting them to do better. That was in 1979. Twenty-five years later the USCCB commissioned a research report to examine the reception of the teaching in *Brothers and Sisters to Us*. Unfortunately, the report concludes that many of the bishops' recommendations from the 1979 pastoral remained unrealized. I have discussed the sobering conclusions in detail elsewhere.[27] A few particular findings are especially pertinent to my arguments here. The bishops contended in their pastoral that Catholic educational institutions must retain their historic dedication to education of the poor and marginalized. For over a century, Catholic schools had provided an excellent educational milieu for many Blacks, Hispanics, Native Americans, and Asians. Therefore, "no other form of Christian ministry has been more widely acclaimed or desperately sought by leaders of various racial communities."[28] With regard to this contention, the twenty-fifth anniversary report lamented that 50,000 fewer African American students attended Catholic elementary and high schools than in 1979. In addition, Black or African American students represented only 6 percent of the student body at Catholic colleges and universities. Blacks or African Americans comprised significantly higher proportions of the student body at public institutions (11 percent), for-profit institutions (15.6 percent), and Protestant universities (13.4 percent). The authors of the report cited prohibitive tuition costs as the primary reason for the underrepresentation of Blacks and African Americans at Catholic colleges and universities. To make matters worse, Black or African American faculty members were even less prevalent, creating a dearth of "role models" for Black and African American students. At that point less than 2 percent of full-time faculty members were Black or African American.[29]

While some progress has been made in the last two decades in recruiting scholars of color to Catholic colleges and universities, the most recent data available do not provide a cause for celebration.[30] According to data from the US Department of Education's Integrated Postsecondary Education Data System (IPEDS) for academic year 2013–14, only 3.38 percent of all tenure-track or tenured faculty are Black or African American at the 166 Catholic colleges and universities with a tenure system. Among the most recently hired faculty, the proportion of Blacks or African Americans represented is slightly more encouraging, at 4.42 percent. Still, the numbers are not impressive: on average only two tenure-track Black or African American professors (329 out of 7,436 total tenure-track professors) work at these Catholic institutions. There are 508 African American professors who have achieved tenure at these same institutions, which is an average of three on each campus or 2.93 percent of all tenured professors (17,322 in total).[31] Hispanics and Latinas/os also continue to be underrepresented among faculty at Catholic colleges and universities. They represent only 4.37 percent of all tenure-track or tenured faculty at Catholic institutions of higher learning. On the average Catholic campus there are about two Hispanic or Latino/a faculty members climbing the tenure ladder. About four have earned tenure.[32]

These statistics show that Catholic institutions lag behind other institutions of higher learning in employing minority faculty, albeit slightly. According to the US Department of Education, Whites made up 79 percent of all full-time faculty at all degree-granting colleges and universities. Blacks or African Americans comprised 6 percent of full-time faculty, while Hispanics and Latinos/as represented 5 percent. Asian/Pacific islanders were 10 percent. American Indian/Alaskan natives represented only 1 percent. The prevalence of Blacks or African Americans and Hispanics or Latinos/as was lowest among full professors, at 3 percent respectively. Their representation at lower ranks was higher: 6 percent for Blacks or African Americans and 4 percent for Hispanics or Latinos/as at the associate professor level; 7 percent for Blacks and African Americans and 4 percent for Hispanics or Latinos/as at the assistant professor level.[33] Generally speaking, all types of higher education institutions have not done a good job of hiring and retaining tenure-track faculty members from underrepresented minoritized groups, not just Catholic colleges. A recent study from the TIAA Institute indicated that although the percentage of underrepresented minoritized people among all faculty members grew from 9 percent to 13 percent between 1993 and 2013, they hold only 10 percent of all tenured jobs.[34] In 1993 about 42 percent of all minoritized faculty members were part-time. By 2003 that proportion swelled to 58 percent.[35] In other words, minoritized faculty members entering the academy during that period had a strong likelihood of joining the academic precariat given that their greatest gains came among part-time and nontenure-track positions.[36]

A handful of Catholic institutions have been relatively successful in hiring and tenuring Black or African American and Hispanic or Latino/a faculty members. For example, at the University of San Francisco 9.8 percent of all tenure-track faculty members are Black or African American and 9.8 percent are Hispanic or Latino/a. At the University of San Diego, 11.8 percent of tenure-track faculty are Hispanic. DePaul's tenure-track faculty consists of 10 percent Hispanics or Latinos/as and 6.7 percent Blacks or African Americans. At Trinity University Washington, 50 percent of tenure-track faculty is African American (8 out of 16). Roughly the same proportion of tenure-track faculty at St. Peter's University is African American (10 out of 19). Xavier University of Louisiana, the nation's only Catholic historically Black institution, boasts that 26 percent of all tenure-track faculty are Black or African American (19 out of 73). At Loyola Marymount University, 15 percent of tenure-track faculty are Asian, 11.8 percent are Black or African American, and 12.9 percent are Hispanic or Latino/a. Among tenured professors, 10.4 percent are Hispanic or Latino/a, 9.8 percent are Asian, and 4.3 percent are Black or African American. Starting in 2008, Loyola of Marymount undertook a series of deliberate initiatives to diversify its faculty, which appear to have borne fruit.[37] There may be a few other positive examples, but for the most part the remaining Catholic colleges and universities mirror the rather discouraging percentages for Catholic institutions as a whole.

Given the statistics, no one can claim that Catholic institutions are significantly worse at attracting and retaining full-time faculty members from minoritized groups. However, neither can anyone say that as a whole they are better, even if there are some encouraging exceptions. In other words, higher education in the United States generally underemploys faculty of color, and Catholic institutions are no exception. At 12 percent and 18 percent of the US population respectively, Blacks and Hispanics are underrepresented among full-time faculty members at our nation's universities. Whites and Asians, who make up 62 percent and 6 percent of the population respectively, have secured full-time faculty positions in proportions greater than their share of the overall population.[38]

Minoritized groups, particularly Blacks and Hispanics or Latinos/as, are also still underrepresented among the student bodies of today's colleges and universities. The racial composition of student bodies at Catholic colleges and universities largely mirrors that of all four-year private institutions of higher learning nationally. According to a recent article in *The National Catholic Reporter*, about 60 percent of all students at Catholic colleges and universities are White. Hispanics comprise 10.65 percent, while Blacks or African Americans represent 9.39 percent and 5.11 percent are Asian. Other groups such as native Hawaiians or other Pacific Islanders, along with American Indians or Alaskan natives, make up less than one half of 1 percent. About 7 percent falls into the category "race/ethnicity unknown."[39] The numbers at all private nonprofit four-year institutions look very similar.[40]

Some progress has been made in attenuating racial disparities in higher education enrollment. The rate of matriculation of Blacks and Latinas/os to degree-granting postsecondary institutions has increased substantially over the last several decades, growing much faster than Whites and diminishing the racial gap.[41] By 2012 the college enrollment rate of recent Hispanic high school graduates between the ages of eighteen and twenty-four reached 49 percent, surpassing Whites (47 percent) for the first time. By then the enrollment rate of Black high school graduates, at 45 percent, also approached that of Whites. The enrollment rate for the same cohort of Asians is 66 percent.[42] At this point, the postsecondary enrollment gap between high school graduates from high-income families and low-income families (82 percent versus 52 percent) far exceeds the gap between students who are White, African American, and Latinos/as.[43]

While the positive signs noted here are encouraging, they do not convey the whole story. Blacks and Latinas/os still have higher high school dropout rates than Whites (10 percent, 15 percent, and 5 percent respectively), even as dropout rates have fallen for each group over the last forty years. Blacks and Latinas/os are also more likely to leave college and less likely to graduate with a bachelor's degree than Whites, even if their parents earned a bachelor's degree.[44] Furthermore, two researchers from Georgetown University have argued that "the postsecondary system is more and more complicit as a passive agent in the systematic reproduction of White racial privilege across generations."[45] They find that White students are increasingly overrepresented at the 468 most prestigious and selective four-year colleges and universities. Blacks and Latinas/os, on the other hand are "more and more concentrated in the 3,250 underfunded, open-access, two and four year colleges."[46] In 2009, Whites constituted 68 percent of the college-age population, but they held 75 percent of the seats at the top 468 colleges and universities. Conversely, African Americans and Hispanics represented 33 percent of the college-age population (15 percent and 18 percent respectively), but held only 15 percent of those seats. Surprisingly, the share of seats held by African American and Hispanic students at the best schools *declined* relative to their share of the overall college-age population from 1995 to 2009 by 3 percent. Whites on the other hand saw an increase of 4 percent. Only 13 percent of newly-enrolled Hispanic students and 9 percent of Black students attended the most selective colleges and universities. Among Whites, growth in freshman enrollment occurred overwhelmingly (86 percent) at the 468 most selective institutions.[47]

Carnevale and Strohl put the matter starkly: "Whites captured the growth in the top 468 colleges, while shifting out of the open-access institutions. African Americans and Hispanics moved into the seats vacated by whites in the open access institutions."[48] Succinctly stated, class and race intersect in ways that make attending one of the most selective institutions very unlikely if you are poor and a person of color, and much more likely if you are White and wealthy.[49] This is not just sour grapes; there are real consequences to these trends. The less selective institutions spend much less on instructional costs than the 468 most selective schools: $6,000 per student on average versus $13,400 (the eighty-two most selective schools spend a whopping $27,900). This higher spending in the most selective institutions correlates with higher graduation rates, greater likelihood of acceptance to graduate programs, and greater lifetime earnings. Carnevale and Strohl also maintain that more instructional spending leads to greater employment of full-time faculty, who generally have more time to devote to mentoring students than the itinerant adjunct faculty member.[50]

In addition, the vast majority of our nation's most powerful political leaders have graduated from the most selective colleges and universities.[51] In my judgment, a student may certainly learn well and succeed as a graduate of a less selective institution. However, she or he is much less likely to enter the ranks of powerful elites in the United States, thereby gaining the ability to enact legal and institutional change for minorities. Economist Alan Krueger has confirmed that the earnings boost for minorities and low-income graduates of elite institutions is substantial (though it is not for White middle- and upper-class students).[52] This fact particularly matters to groups such as Latinas/os, African Americans, and Native Americans, who continue to be disproportionately plagued by poverty.[53] For all of these reasons, Carnevale and Strohl accurately maintain that our system of higher education reifies White privilege.

Although Carnevale and Strohl make compelling arguments, they overlook that some elite institutions of higher learning have increased the diversity of their student bodies. For example, *U.S. News and World Report* ranks Stanford, MIT, UCLA, Rice, Berkeley, Rutgers (Newark and New Brunswick), and Columbia among the thirty most diverse national universities in the nation. These schools are often considered diverse because of the large population of Asian-American students.[54] Nonetheless, the *Journal of Blacks in Higher Education* has praised some of these institutions for demonstrably increasing the proportion of Black students among their incoming classes. In their annual survey of the thirty top research universities in the country, they list Columbia (12.9 percent), Stanford (11 percent),

Harvard (10.9 percent), Yale (10.9 percent), Emory (10.8 percent), Vanderbilt (10.8 percent), Duke (10.7 percent), University of Pennsylvania (10.2 percent), and MIT (9.6 percent) with the largest percentage of Black students in their most recent entering class.[55] For the most recent IPEDS data available, 16 percent of enrolled students at MIT and Stanford were Hispanic or Latino/a, 13 percent at Columbia, 11 percent at Yale, and 10 percent at University of Pennsylvania and Harvard.[56] A few elite schools have had a non-White majority student body for some time.[57] This year among Harvard's admitted students were 14.6 percent African Americans, 11.6 percent Latinos/as, and 1.9 percent Native Americans.[58] In short, Latinas/os and Blacks are still underrepresented at these institutions relative to their larger share of the college-age population between eighteen and twenty-four years old (15 percent for Blacks and 18 percent Hispanic respectively).[59] However, the gap is less stark than at the 468 most selective universities in the United States taken as a whole.[60]

The most highly selective Catholic colleges and universities replicate the interlocking patterns of race, wealth, and selectivity of the country's 468 most selective universities. These Catholic institutions, with a few exceptions, have the least amount of racial diversity (recall I noted a similar trend in Chapter 3 with regard to the prevalence of low-income students). In this regard, Catholic antiracist theologian Alex Mikulich writes that the twenty-eight Jesuit colleges and universities in the United States celebrate their place among the most selective universities in the country. At the same time, they "tend not to acknowledge they are predominantly white." In his view, several factors contribute to their blindness to this fact: "ignorance, denial, fear of losing applicants and donors and the moral and practical conundrums such honesty presents to people shaped by predominantly white culture."[61] There is, however, considerable difference among the Jesuit universities. As the chart below indicates, the most selective (Georgetown, Boston College, College of the Holy Cross) are indeed among the least racially diverse Jesuit institutions and are predominantly White.[62] In fact, they are less racially diverse than Columbia, Harvard, Stanford, and MIT. Even some of the less selective schools, such as Rockhurst, Le Moyne, John Caroll, and Saint Joseph's are predominantly White institutions (PWIs). However, the student bodies at some Jesuit institutions are quite diverse. For example, Loyola University New Orleans, Saint Peter's University, Loyola Marymount, and University of San Francisco all have minoritized student populations approximately 50 percent or above. In 2008 Loyola University New Orleans received the Minority Access Role Model Award from Minority Access, Inc. The university was recognized for its diverse student body, which enrolled 36 percent racially minoritized students and 30 percent first-generation students two years in a row.[63] Although only 3 percent are African Americans, Santa Clara University, a highly competitive institution, is also a relatively diverse campus. Latinas/os comprise 19 percent and Asians comprise 20 percent of the student body.[64] In short, some Jesuit institutions have pursued and achieved a respectable level of diversity, while for others this goal represents a "work in progress."

The same can be said of Catholic colleges and universities taken as a whole. According to Barron's, Boston College, Holy Cross, Georgetown, Notre Dame, and Villanova belong to the "most competitive" institutions of higher learning. (See Table 2 below.) Black and Latino/a students are markedly underrepresented at these schools.[65]

One recent study concluded that Catholic institutions of higher learning are slightly more racially and socio-economically diverse than secular private institutions. However, they "continue to attract a relatively homogeneous group of students, especially when compared with public institutions." Moreover, minoritized students, women, older students, and students from lower socioeconomic backgrounds are "concentrated in less selective Catholic institutions."[66] Another study indicated the same pattern of scant racial diversity at the most selective and selective (and well-resourced) Catholic doctorate-granting institutions. Schools such as Duquesne University (88 percent), University of Dayton (87.9 percent), Marquette University (82.9 percent), St. Mary's University of Minnesota (80 percent), University of Notre Dame (75.5 percent), Boston College (70.5 percent), and the Catholic University of America (75.4 percent) have percentages of White students well above the share of the US college-age population that is White (62 percent). This study also found that the universities designated Hispanic-serving institutions (HSIs) because they had 25 percent or more Latino/a students also had the lowest graduation rates for that group. Conversely, the most selective Catholic institutions like Notre Dame and Georgetown had the smallest number of Hispanic students but the highest graduation rate.[67] This finding is consistent with the conclusion drawn by Carnevale and Strohl that minoritized students have

Table 1. U.S. Jesuit Colleges and Universities

Institution	Year	American Indian or Alaskan Native undergraduates Fall (%)	Asian or Pacific Islander undergraduates Fall (%)	Black, non-Hispanic undergraduates Fall (%)	Hispanic undergraduates Fall (%)	White, non-Hispanic undergraduates Fall (%)	Foreign/international undergraduates Fall (%)	Multiracial undergraduates Fall (%)	Race unknown undergraduates Fall (%)	Fall enrollment Undergraduate total (IPEDS)
Georgetown University	2013–14	0	0.09	0.06	0.08	0.57	0.13	0.04	0.04	7636
Fordham University	2013–14	0	0.09	0.04	0.14	0.61	0.06	0.03	0.03	8345
Loyola University Chicago	2013–14	0	0.11	0.04	0.13	0.61	0.03	0.06	0.02	10168
Boston College	2013–14	0	0.09	0.04	0.1	0.57	0.05	0.03	0.11	9698
Fairfield University	2013–14	0	0.02	0.03	0.08	0.7	0.02	0.01	0.15	3873
Loyola University New Orleans	2013–14	0.01	0.04	0.16	0.16	0.51	0.04	0.04	0.06	2946
Loyola Marymount University	2013–14	0	0.11	0.06	0.22	0.49	0.05	0.07	0	6205

(continued)

Table 1. (continued)

Institution	Year	American Indian or Alaskan Native undergraduates Fall (%)	Asian or Pacific Islander undergraduates Fall (%)	Black, non-Hispanic undergraduates Fall (%)	Hispanic undergraduates Fall (%)	White, non-Hispanic undergraduates Fall (%)	Foreign/ international undergraduates Fall (%)	Multiracial undergraduates Fall (%)	Race unknown undergraduates Fall (%)	Fall enrollment Undergraduate total (IPEDS)
Rockhurst University	2013–14	0	0.03	0.06	0.05	0.74	0.01	0.03	0.08	2241
Xavier University	2013–14	0	0.02	0.1	0.04	0.72	0.03	0.02	0.06	4620
Santa Clara University	2013–14	0	0.15	0.03	0.17	0.48	0.03	0.07	0.08	5435
University of San Francisco	2013–14	0	0.2	0.03	0.19	0.31	0.18	0.07	0.02	6392
Spring Hill College	2013–14	0.01	0.01	0.16	0.09	0.67	0.01	0.02	0.04	1292
Marquette University	2013–14	0	0.05	0.05	0.09	0.74	0.04	0.03	0.01	8365
Seattle University	2013–14	0.01	0.17	0.03	0.09	0.47	0.1	0.07	0.06	4608
Gonzaga University	2013–14	0.01	0.04	0.01	0.08	0.73	0.03	0.06	0.04	4896

Institution	Year									
Wheeling Jesuit University	2013–14	0	0.02	0.05	0.02	0.8	0.03	0	0.08	1180
College of the Holy Cross	2013–14	0	0.04	0.04	0.11	0.68	0.01	0.03	0.09	2912
Canisius College	2013–14	0	0.02	0.07	0.03	0.73	0.04	0.02	0.08	3084
Le Moyne College	2013–14	0.01	0.03	0.06	0.06	0.77	0.01	0.02	0.06	2785
Regis College	2013–14	0	0.06	0.21	0.11	0.46	0.01	0.02	0.13	1188
Saint Joseph's University	2013–14	0	0.03	0.07	0.05	0.79	0.02	0.02	0.03	5374
Saint Louis University	2013–14	0	0.06	0.06	0.03	0.7	0.05	0.04	0.05	12567
Saint Peter's University	2013–14	0.01	0.1	0.28	0.28	0.24	0.02	0.02	0.05	2484
University of Scranton	2013–14	0	0.03	0.02	0.07	0.81	0.01	0.02	0.05	3942
University of Detroit Mercy	2013–14	0	0.03	0.1	0.03	0.53	0.06	0.02	0.23	2888
Creighton University	2013–14	0	0.1	0.03	0.07	0.73	0.02	0.04	0.02	4076
John Carroll University	2013–14	0	0.02	0.05	0.04	0.83	0.01	0.02	0.04	3040
Loyola Maryland	2013–14	0	0.03	0.05	0.09	0.79	0	0.02	0.01	4004

Table 2. "Most Competitive" U.S. Catholic Colleges and Universities

Institution	Year	American Indian or Alaskan Native undergraduates Fall (%)	Asian or Pacific Islander undergraduates Fall (%)	Black, non-Hispanic undergraduates Fall (%)	Hispanic undergraduates Fall (%)	White, non-Hispanic undergraduates Fall (%)	Foreign/ international undergraduates Fall (%)	Multiracial undergraduates Fall (%)	Race unknown undergraduates Fall (%)
Boston College	2013–14	0	0.09	0.04	0.1	0.57	0.05	0.03	0.11
College of the Holy Cross	2013–14	0	0.04	0.04	0.11	0.68	0.01	0.03	0.09
Georgetown University	2013–14	0	0.09	0.06	0.08	0.57	0.13	0.04	0.04
University of Notre Dame	2013–14	0	0.06	0.04	0.1	0.71	0.04	0.04	0.01
Villanova University	2013–14	0	0.07	0.05	0.07	0.75	0.02	0.02	0.02

higher graduation rates at more selective universities with significant resources, even if their SAT scores were "substantially below the institutional averages at those schools."[68] Institutional resources matter, as they translate into more mentoring, smaller classes, and better learning outcomes (I will say more about this below).

To be certain, some fine Catholic institutions of higher learning have diverse student bodies in addition to the few Jesuit schools mentioned above. I can only highlight a few here. St. John's University in New York, listed as the third most diverse national university by *U.S. News*, has an undergraduate student population of 16 percent Asian, 15 percent Black, 16 percent Hispanic/Latino/a and 40 percent White. Trinity Washington University's student body is comprised of 71 percent Black students, 14 percent Hispanic/Latino/a students, and only 2 percent White. University of San Diego, a Barron's "highly competitive" school, has 19 percent Hispanic/Latino/a students, 6 percent Asian students, 3 percent Black and 55 percent White. At Xavier University of Louisiana, 77 percent of the students are Black, 10 percent are Asian, 2 percent are Hispanic/Latino/a and 4 percent are White. *Hispanic Outlook in Higher Education* ranks five Catholic universities among the top 100 institutions for Hispanics, based on the total number of enrollments and degrees granted in a given year: University of the Incarnate Word (Texas), DePaul, St. John's (New York) University, St. Mary's University (Texas), and Loyola Marymount.[69]

To summarize, minoritized students—particularly Blacks and Hispanics/ Latinos/as—remain underrepresented at the most selective Catholic colleges and universities. No doubt these schools have attempted to enroll and retain more minoritized students.[70] From the standpoint of Catholic social teaching this should be paramount. As Diane Cárdenas Elliot concludes in her study of student diversity at Catholic colleges, "there is a long history of racial and ethnic inequality in the United States, and higher education institutions should continue to embrace racial and ethnic diversity, not only for the benefit students derive, but also as a means for addressing historical inequalities."[71] The Catholic call to solidarity requires dismantling the obstacles to enrolling and graduating minority students, especially from the most marginalized groups. I will discuss some concrete steps that can be taken in this regard. First, I want to consider one of the biggest obstacles to creating an inclusive community for students and faculty of color— namely, virulent and odious racism on campus. Unfortunately, the last few years have clearly revealed that racism is alive and well at universities in the United States.

Racism on Campus since 2015

A feeling of alienation rather than full participation persists among many students of color on many college campuses. Although such protests happened in the past, a groundswell of campaigns against racism on campuses such as University of Missouri, Yale, Amherst, Georgetown, Boston College, DePaul University, and Seattle University occurred in 2015.[72] In a survey of 567 college presidents, almost 50 percent of them at four-year institutions, indicated that students on their campuses have "organized around concerns about racial diversity."[73] Moreover, students have presented concrete demands for change on no fewer than eighty campuses in recent years. Among them are Catholic institutions such as Boston College, Loyola University of Maryland, Notre Dame of Maryland University, Providence College, Santa Clara University, University of San Diego, and University of San Francisco.[74] Students have passionately engaged issues of racism and marginalization at Villanova University as well, calling for more diversity among faculty and in the curriculum, as well as other changes to make Villanova a more inclusive community.[75] Without a doubt, students at other Catholic colleges and universities have expressed concerns as well. Their voices and experiences echo the perspectives of Joseph Brown, SJ, and Rick Malloy, SJ, which we encountered at the beginning of this chapter.

In some cases, flagrant instances of racial discrimination and even violence triggered those feelings of alienation and anger among minoritized campus members. At Mizzou, for example, Black students received death threats.[76] Students at the University of Oklahoma and Duke endured racist chants. In addition, a noose was found hanging on Duke's campus.[77] A board of trustee member at one college reportedly displayed an image of Barack Obama with a noose around his neck.[78] Scores of racially-charged incidents have taken place all over the country.[79] In fact, college campuses and schools are the third most likely location for a hate crime to occur in the United States.[80] In 2013 alone there were 781 hate crimes at colleges reported to the police (with many more likely to have gone unreported).[81] According to the US Department of Education, racial harassment complaints doubled during the presidency of Barack Obama. In addition, a violent surge in hate crimes occurred on college campuses after the election of Donald Trump.[82] According to the Anti-Defamation League, college campuses saw a 77 percent uptick in White supremacist propaganda in 2017–18.[83] An egregious example horrified first-year Black students at the University of Pennsylvania, all of whom received messages via a social media app with "scheduled lynchings" from the pseudonymous sender "Daddy Trump."[84]

Sadly, Catholic institutions also struggle to eliminate virulent racism completely. After the 2008 election of Barack Obama, several Black students at LaSalle University were reportedly assaulted and subjected to racial slurs. At Saint Joseph's University, someone scrawled a stick figure in a noose on a dormitory wall.[85] In 2014, a screen projector at Saint Louis University displayed vile, hateful words about African Americans and homosexuals. A swastika was also constructed out of candles.[86] More recently, students at Fairfield University held a "ghetto themed party," where students apparently wore "baggy clothing, gold chains, fake baby bumps [and] blackface."[87] Unfortunately, such offensive "racially themed parties," which mock not only people of color but also immigrants and the poor, happen frequently on college campuses.[88] After the Trump election, abhorrent behavior occurred on Catholic campuses as well. For example, at Canisius College, two students posted pictures of a Black doll hung from a curtain rod.[89] An African American student reported she was knocked down by White students at Villanova, who chanted "Trump" in her face.[90]

In 2015, members of the student group called Eradicate Boston College Racism complained that the administration stifled their efforts to protest against racial disparities at the university.[91] Sixty-one faculty members signed an open letter defending the students, claiming that "today's governing approach to address racial disparities and marginalization at Boston College and the US is 'color-blind racism.' This phrase is defined by the idea that racism is largely a stain on the past, and that current racial disparities can be attributed to non-racial issues. . . . This 'new' racism goes unchallenged because it is hidden from plain sight, making meaningful discussion that leads to actionable political and policy changes near impossible."[92] At my own institution, a student lamented in the student newspaper that whether we like it or not, we've inherited the legacy of Vanillanova—the idea that our community is white, homogenous and bland. Even though the past decade has seen a steady increase in the number of multicultural students and faculty on campus, we can't seem to escape the nickname. To me, its persistence means we have to do more than just diversify our campus body—we also have to diversify our campus culture. . . . The culture of Villanova may not be completely purposeful, but it's not entirely accidental either. Take race, for example. Villanova, as an institution with a professed commitment to diversity, isn't trying to create a majority-white campus. Regardless, last fall, 75.9 percent of full-time undergraduates identified as white. Without anyone explicitly trying to create a campus that is three-quarters white, we somehow continually achieve it. It's not purposeful, but neither is it accidental.[93]

Students have expressed similar sentiments elsewhere in recent times. One Georgetown student put it this way: "There are two distinct Georgetowns. . . . Minorities are separate from whites and don't always feel welcome in campus organizations." A University of Notre Dame undergraduate baldly stated that "it's exhausting to be a black student at Notre Dame" because White students often have had little earlier contact with minorities, leading them to adopt negative stereotypes portrayed in the media.[94] Renowned Catholic ethicist Fr. Bryan Massingale has reported being repeatedly racially profiled by campus security at Marquette University and shunned by a colleague who did not recognize him when not wearing clerical attire.[95]

To reiterate, good work is being done on Catholic campuses to address problems of racism and inclusion.[96] However, a clear and pressing need exists to dig deeper into the historical roots of the problem and to implement broader, systemic solutions.

Higher Education's Historical Ties to Slavery and White Supremacy

In order to understand the pain and difficulties faced by people of color on American campuses, we need to understand and confront the historical connection between slavery, segregation, White supremacy, and US higher education. Craig Steven Wilder's book *Ebony and Ivory* elucidates how the system of higher education in the United States, and in the Americas more broadly, was literally built by slaves and with money from the slave trade. Slaves also maintained the college grounds and buildings. University-based academicians also concocted heinous ideologies such as so-called "racial science" and "theories of biological supremacy" to justify keeping Blacks in shackles or segregating them in later eras.[97] As Wilder reveals, the nation's earliest universities, Harvard, Yale, Brown, Columbia, and Princeton among them, all benefited from slavery.

Unfortunately, Catholics and their institutions in "the New World" also bear this stain. As Wilder writes, "Catholic clergy traded, bought, and sold Africans in the Atlantic markets, and forced them to labor on plantations, in mines, and in towns." Dominicans and Jesuits owned many "thousands of enslaved African people," who built and labored at their universities in Mexico, Peru, Colombia, and the Dominican Republic.[98] Since the publication of Wilder's book in 2013, much information has been disclosed about Georgetown University's connection to slavery. The Jesuits of Maryland, who had extensive plantations, already "relied upon a fully developed slave system" in the 1680s. According to the former dean of Georgetown University, Hubert Cloke, "the Jesuits were no better or worse" as slave owners. Wilder states that "the treatment of enslaved people on the Jesuit Farms was alarming."[99] In 1838 two presidents of Georgetown, William McSherry, SJ, and Thomas Mulledy, SJ, sold 272 slaves in order to save the University from insolvency.[100] Slaves owned by faculty and university officers toiled at Georgetown University for its first forty years. It is ironic that the university's motto "Utraque Unum" ("Both into One") comes from St. Paul's claim that Christ, "in his flesh . . . has made both groups into one and has broken down the dividing wall, that is, the hostility between us" (Eph. 2:14, NRSV). Like most North American Christians at the time, the learned Catholic community at Georgetown did not see a condemnation of slavery in Paul's statement that in "Christ there is neither Jew, nor Greek, slave nor free."[101]

In the fall of 2015, students demanded that Georgetown confront this history. As a first step, they insisted that the names of Mulledy Hall and McSherry Hall be changed. The administration agreed. In addition, Georgetown alumnus Richard J. Cellini funded the Georgetown Memory Project, which employs genealogists to help find the descendants of the slaves.[102] In 2015 the university created the Working Group on Slavery,

Memory, and Reconciliation. The university adopted the Working Group's recommendation to, among other things, grant the same admissions preferences to descendants of the slaves that children of alumni, faculty, and staff receive.[103] In June 2016 the university's president Dr. John DeGioia began meeting with some of the descendants. Although more than a dozen universities have acknowledged their ties to slavery, DeGioia is the first university president to personally meet with a descendent of slaves, according to Wilder.[104] In April 2017 the university issued a formal apology in the presence of descendants of the slaves during a "Liturgy of Remembrance, Contrition, and Hope."[105] Recently, Elizabeth and Shepard Thomas announced that they, descendants of slaves sold by the university, would matriculate to Georgetown in the fall of 2017.[106]

The complicity of Catholic institutions with slavery extends beyond Georgetown. The founders of St. Mary's Seminary of Baltimore used resources from Maryland slave plantations held by Catholic priests.[107] Wilder argues that the initial expansion of the Catholic Church out of Maryland in the higher education arena was financed by slave-holding prelates. Holy Cross, Saint Louis University, and Fordham all have financial ties to slavery.[108] It appears that Saint Joseph's University may have been paid for with proceeds from the sale of the 272 slaves as well.[109] In Wilder's words, "neither the Jesuits nor the antebellum Catholic Church disengaged from human bondage with the Maryland sale; rather, both follow the westward movement of plantation slavery in search of influence and affluence."[110]

In addition to the sin of slavery, Catholic and secular institutions alike were guilty of segregation. Apart from exceptions such as Middlebury, Amherst, Oberlin, and Berea College, the majority of higher educational institutions did not admit Black students. By the 1830s historically Black colleges and universities arose in order to give African Americans access to higher education. Slowly, historically White institutions granted access to Blacks.[111] Catholic universities, however, lagged behind. The first Blacks entered the Catholic University of America at the end of the nineteenth century, but this practice stopped and was not resumed until the 1930s.[112] Xavier University of Louisiana was founded by Sister Katharine Drexel in 1915 to serve racial minorities. In the 1930s Loyola University Chicago matriculated thirty Black students, more than any other US institution.[113] Villanova admitted two Black students in the 1930s, one of whom was reportedly denied admission to LaSalle University due to his race. Black students at Villanova could not live on campus and had to be Catholic.[114] However, it was not until the 1940s and '50s that African Americans finally could enter most Catholic universities on a widespread basis.[115] Georgetown University admitted Samuel Halsey, its first Black undergraduate student, in 1950. He died in 2012. He attended Georgetown 127 years after the first African American graduated from Middlebury College.[116] The first African Americans graduated from Notre Dame in 1947.[117] That is 121 years after Edward Jones, an African American, graduated from Amherst College.

In light of this deplorable history of exclusion in higher education, James Keenan, SJ, correctly maintains that "no group of people has been more continually unwelcome at the American university than African Americans." As he puts it, the American university practiced White supremacy by utilizing slaves, making money from their sale, and forbidding Blacks from attending.[118] Sadly Catholic universities perpetrated these injustices, in spite of the Gospel demands for radical egalitarianism and the fact that some popes had denounced slavery earlier.[119] Moreover, Catholic universities were not at the forefront of making higher education accessible to people of color after slavery ended.

Microaggressions and Racial Battle Fatigue in Higher Education

Undeniably, progress has been made since the first African Americans were admitted to Catholic universities. Yet, as indicated above, students and faculty across the nation continue to raise concerns about various forms of racism on campus. A growing body of academic literature describes, analyzes, and contests this state of affairs. One of the most damning and incisive works on the topic is appropriately entitled *Racial Battle Fatigue in Higher Education*. Drawing on the work of William A. Smith, the book's editors define racial battle fatigue (RBF) as "the anxiety experienced by racially underrepresented groups as well as those engaged in race work with a focus on the physical and psychological toll taken due to constant unceasing discrimination, microaggressions, and stereotype threat."[120] For example, faculty of color report that White students question their knowledge and expertise and doubt they are competent to be a university professor (in spite of their bona fides and accomplishments).[121]

Racial bias in students and colleagues hurts faculty of color—particularly those who challenge racism and White privilege—via negative student and peer evaluations.[122] According to Cleveland Hayes, such evaluations were used by colleagues to perpetrate an "academic lynching" against him because they did not appreciate his questioning of the "White social order."[123] Cheryl E. Matias, a Filipina scholar, lamented, "in order to survive RBF, I had recloseted racial humiliation after racial humiliation, knowing that the surveilling eyes of Whiteness would intensify with discipline and punishment if I dared to 'come out.'"[124] In her view, faculty of color are "forced to endure racism and white supremacy in the academic neoplantation."[125]

Fred A. Bonner II, who has written extensively on racism in the academy, maintains that Black faculty "feel the pressures of truncating aspects of their cultural selves to fit into templates that White academe deems appropriate."[126] Faculty of color often find themselves outside the collegial networks that help academics succeed in their guild.[127] In one study (from 2005) 60 percent of Black faculty reported feeling "marginalized in department meetings," with 90 percent stating this "had a moderate to strong effect on them."[128] Moreover, minoritized faculty perceive that their scholarship is devalued, particularly if it deals with diversity and inclusion. In addition, they often feel pigeonholed into areas and modes of inquiry that they would not otherwise pursue. As Dorinda J. Carter Andrews writes, "what it means to be a scholar is defined by neoliberal, colorblind White men."[129] Minorities sometimes experience threats to their academic freedom, particularly when racial battle fatigue erodes their ability to defend it.[130] In short, if minority faculty members are "lucky" enough to find jobs at PWIs, they are guests who must assimilate and adhere to the rules and regulations of their hosts: White faculty, administrators, and board members. They are not equal partners at the table.[131] As a group of Black scholars states, this constitutes tokenism: hiring Black professors "for window-dressing purposes" while "never really expect[ing] or . . . permit[ting] them to become fully included members of the faculty."[132] At the same time, many authors stress that Black and other minoritized faculty also disproportionately shoulder mentoring, committee work, and other university obligations. Given their small numbers, they are in high demand.[133] Serving as the "token voice of color" on committees creates what Amado Padilla has termed "cultural taxation."[134] The offices of minority faculty can be like "an oasis in the desert," as Fr. Brown puts it, for students who need a sympathetic ear, academic advising, and mentorship.[135]

Students of color also experience microaggressions and racial battle fatigue. Too often they find themselves being shadowed—or worse—by campus police, asked outrageous questions like whether or not they have ever been incarcerated, encounter racial slurs and jokes, amazement that a Latino/a student can speak English so well, asked to represent "the" Black or Latino/a or Asian perspective in discussions, dismissed by professors who do not appreciate their insights, and punished when they speak out against the perceived racism of their peers or instructors.[136] Many students also feel angry that their institutions gave them a counterfeit sense of diversity in their promotional materials. Once on campus, they find themselves alienated and struggling to connect with mentors and other students of color.[137]

Effects of RBF. Smith and his colleagues have emphasized that encountering racial battle fatigue has deleterious, devastating, and sometimes lethal physical, mental, and emotional consequences. Among them are "frustration, anger, hopelessness, headache, high blood pressure, insomnia, stereotype threat, social withdrawal, self-doubt."[138] RBF also manifests symptoms such as compromised immunity, nausea, mood swings, decreased mental acuity, and withdraw.[139] Some research indicates that racial battle fatigue may cause otherwise healthy African American women to give birth to their children prematurely.[140] Among pregnant Black women with university degrees, the infant mortality rate is almost three times higher than among similarly educated White women. Stress is a likely culprit.[141]

Noelle Witherspoon Arnold maintains that in the context of higher education, particularly in historically White institutions (HWI's), faculty of color continue to endure racial battle fatigue due to "racial microaggressive conditions."[142] Racial microaggressions are "brief and commonplace daily verbal, behavioral and environmental indignities, whether intentional or unintentional, that communicate hostile, derogatory or negative racial slights and insults to the target person or group."[143] Reflecting on his experience at numerous PWIs, Black scholar Mark Giles contends that faculty and students who experience racial microaggressions on campuses must confront the dissonance between reality and the individualistic, "simplistic propaganda" of corporatized universities, which advertise that "regardless of race, gender, or social class," your own hard work will determine whether or not you succeed.[144]

In addition to harmful health consequences, racial battle fatigue has negative effects on "material realities such as professional achievement, access to goods and services, and social mobility."[145] In short, racial battle fatigue can become a major obstacle to succeeding in the academy. Because of RBF and "idiosyncrasy and bias" in the tenure process, the turnover rate among racial minority faculty is about 50 percent.[146] In other words, almost half of African American and Latina/o faculty never obtain tenure. It is no wonder that such a large proportion of them choose to leave the academy, when they may feel "tokenized, stigmatized, left out or out of place" according to Witherspoon Arnold. The upshot is that the percentage of African American faculty will not reflect the percentage of African Americans among the American population for another 150 years.[147] Perhaps most distressing about racism and its pernicious effects in the academy is that they go largely unnoticed, even among higher education scholars. Shaun R. Harper, professor and director of the USC Race and Equity Center, has documented how scholars largely "rely on anything but racism" to explain racial disparities in "college access and student outcomes," as well as negative experiences among minoritized members of the campus community.[148] Many academics seem to be aware of racism "out there," but refuse to acknowledge its presence in our institutions.

Resistance to Diversity, Equity, and Inclusivity

What should be done to rectify this situation? On the one hand, universities have offices of diversity and inclusion, which create programs aimed at change. Many universities have chief diversity officers charged with spearheading the change. Yet, scholars of color believe that Whites on campus still do not understand the situation, nor do those colleagues accept the need for change. Leading scholar of racism Eduardo Bonilla-Silva maintains that most Whites fail to understand, or "pretend" they do not know, that "people of color are still treated as second-class citizens in the academy." He maintains that Whites on US campuses often tell people of color that they are "hypersensitive" when asked to confront the fact that their institution is "white oriented and white-led."[149] bell hooks writes that when people of color and their allies confront White supremacy, they "risk censorship" by those in power who accuse them of being "extremist" and "racist."[150] She furthermore contends that "teachers are often among the group most reluctant to acknowledge the extent to which White supremacist thinking informs every aspect of our culture including the way we learn, the content of what we learn, and the manner in which we are taught."[151]

The controversy at Providence College in 2016 around diversity and inclusion seems to validate the claims of Bonilla-Silva and hooks.[152] We should welcome debate about how to best promote a diversity that respects the cultures and perspectives of all community members. However, a professor invoking Orwell to dismiss inclusivity as a "political slogan" is unacceptable given the realities of racism and exclusion that I have described in this chapter.[153] More than one hundred Catholic scholars wrote an open letter to the university's president in the professor's defense. Their apologia surprisingly failed to mention the problem of racial discrimination on US campuses. It is one thing to "reframe the question of diversity," as Professor Esolen's learned supporters suggest. It is not, however, acceptable to gloss over the history of discrimination and marginalization of people of color and their cultures at US Catholic institutions of higher learning. The silence of these academics on these issues constitutes complicity. Fortunately, the President of Providence College responded by stating that he and others there "value and understand diversity" differently than Esolen.[154]

Indeed, the church has something to teach the larger society, as Esolen and his comrades state. I have argued that proposition throughout this book. However, to imply that the church can never learn from other "cultures" and reform itself, while standing "as boldly as the Cross upon that barren rock, opposing the world" is both ahistorical and inimical to the spirit of post–Vatican II Catholicism.[155] For example, while once eschewing political and civil rights, the church learned from the human rights movement and became one of its most forceful champions in the latter part of the twentieth century.[156] It also appreciated some of feminism's important insights about the oppression of women.[157] *Ex Corde Ecclesiae* explicitly charges Catholic universities with being "open to all human experience" and "ready to dialogue with and learn from any culture."[158] Catholic universities thereby serve the church, "enabling it to come to a better knowledge of diverse cultures, discern their positive and negative aspects, to receive their authentically human contributions."[159] St. John Paul specifically stated that the church "must become more attentive to the cultures of the world today and to the various cultural traditions existing within the church." Catholic universities must promote ecumenical and interreligious study for a "profitable dialogue between the gospel and modern society."[160]

Thus, to say that students calling for greater diversity in the curriculum exude "narcissism" aimed at "making people study about us" amounts to derision and misunderstands Catholic teaching on the value of diversity.[161] Perhaps Professor Esolen's experience varies, but I have encountered thoughtful students at Villanova who do not wish to supplant Augustine or Aquinas with Snoop Dogg (derided by Esolen).[162] For the record, scholars have rigorously applied the methods of their discipline to the academic study of the rich tradition of rap and hip hop music.[163] Nonetheless, students at Villanova (and elsewhere, I surmise) simply ask that Catholicism be treated as a global religion, which recognizes the contributions of scholars from Asia, Africa, and Latin America and addresses the situations and perspectives of Catholics in those regions. They also want to encounter the contributions of minoritized scholars more regularly in their studies.[164] In my judgment, students and faculty calling for diversity in curricula legitimately desire greater parity among voices historically marginalized from the canon and those exalted (rightly or wrongly) by it, not banishment of the latter. Yet, they rightly do not accept what Christian ethicist Ki Joo Choi deems a false unity based on minoritized cultures assimilating to the dominant, White culture.[165]

For certain, Cervantes and other voices historically in the canon should still be studied at a Catholic university. However, we must admit and change the fact that the voices of Chicana authors, people of color, and LGBTQ persons have been systematically ignored for over eight hundred years![166] The refusal to give more than an afterthought to intellectuals and creative people from marginalized groups has helped perpetuate the lie that White people are intellectually superior. As Katie Geneva Cannon, Miguel De La Torre, Bryan Massingale, Ada María Isasi-Díaz, and many other scholars of color have contended, the nefarious omission of voices from the margins helps sustain White supremacy.[167] In this vein, Ismael García has urged rejecting a "cultural imperialism" that sees the "values, culture and ways of life" of non-White groups "not only being different but also being deviant."[168] Cultural imperialism, the henchman of White supremacy, has given rise to what Cornel West calls "nihilism" in Black America.[169] Being told for centuries by White oppressors that your culture is devoid of anything meaningful often generates this sense of despair among some Black people. In the wake of myriad police shootings of young Black and Brown people in recent years, Michael Eric Dyson, Distinguished Professor of Sociology at Georgetown University, opines "black despair piles up with each body that gets snuffed on video and streamed on social media."[170] This is the larger milieu within which discussions about diversity occur in universities today, and these realities must be taken into consideration. For White people like me, it is all too easy to forget about this painful and perilous context when we consider whether we should read Rudyard Kipling or Alice Walker at the university.

Thus, in the charged environment of US society and higher education today, the first step toward the equality and participation of all at the university requires that Whites educate themselves and, most importantly, become willing to be educated by people of color on their campuses about their situation and needs. Studies by social psychologists demonstrate that Whites invariably have "unconscious racial biases." Thus, they need to hear the perspectives of those in the best position to accurately diagnose the prevalence of racism and to understand oppressive realities, i.e., those aggrieved by them.[171] As I contended in Chapter 2, Catholic social teaching calls upon the privileged to recognize the "epistemological advantage" of the marginalized. It is worth recalling Pope Francis's words regarding the preferential option for the poor from *Evangelii Gaudium* here: "Each individual Christian and every community is called to be an instrument of God for the liberation and promotion of the poor, and for enabling them to be fully a part of society. This demands that we be docile and attentive to the cry of the poor and to come to their aid." The pontiff also states that we must "appreciate the poor in their goodness, in their experience of life, in their culture, and in their ways of living the faith."[172] St. John Paul lifts up another aspect of this discussion in the very title of his 1989 World Day of Peace message that remains relevant here: "To Build Peace, Respect Minorities."[173] In this message apropos for our times, St. John Paul argues:

Another right which must be safeguarded is the right of minorities to preserve and develop their own culture. It is not unheard of that minority groups are threatened with cultural extinction. In some places, in fact, laws have been enacted which do not recognize their right to use their own language. At times people are forced to change their family and place names. Some minorities see their artistic and literary expressions ignored, with their festivals and celebrations given no place in public life. All this can lead to the loss of a notable cultural heritage.[174]

John Paul also stresses the duty to accept and defend the diversity of every individual, group, and the state. In a passage that speaks directly to the Esolen controversy, the pontiff stated: "A mind that is open and desirous of knowing better the cultural heritage of the minority groups with which it comes into contact will help to eliminate attitudes of prejudice that hinder healthy social relations. This is a process which has to be continuously fostered, since such attitudes tend to reappear time and again under new forms."

Given St. John Paul's and Pope Francis's repeated calls to practice solidarity with the marginalized, the poor, and the oppressed, I read Francis's words to students about diversity differently than Esolen's defenders. I see it as an exhortation to lift up those voices that have been marginalized by a homogenizing global order.[175] I do not think he has Dante or Kipling in mind, two thinkers purportedly marginalized in the academy today according to Anthony Esolen, though I imagine Pope Francis would not have anything against the study of them per se. In short, three things are missing from the musings of Esolen and his apologists' letter: (1) that the church itself has acknowledged that Catholics and their institutions too often have perpetuated rather than dismantled racism, (2) that there should be a respect for the rights of marginalized peoples to retain and proudly cherish their cultural heritage, and (3) that marginalized, oppressed voices have something crucial to teach those whose perspectives have been privileged in the academy.[176]

This last point warrants more explanation. As Vincent Lloyd has argued, the "epistemic privilege of the oppressed" arises from "the way that suffering attunes us to justice." Conversely, the "wealthy and powerful" perceive reality in a distorted way, as they "are much invested in advancing their own interests at the expense of reverence for the image of God in humanity." Therefore, we should heed the voices of Blacks who have confronted the oppression of their people by advancing a particular understanding of what it means to be a human being.[177] Miguel de La

Torre likewise contends that Euroamericans resist losing the power and privilege conferred to them as members of the dominant culture. They remain either blinded to or supportive of the oppressive social structures fortifying their power. As a result, only marginalized persons can fully comprehend those structures and "propose with any integrity liberative ethical precepts."[178]

Who are the marginalized and the oppressed in the contemporary US higher educational context? I argue here that people of color encounter significant disadvantages in the academy, as well as women and LGBTQ community members (whose situations I will consider in the next chapter). No one argues for relegating Cervantes, Beowulf, Shakespeare, Augustine, or Aquinas to the dustbins of history. Yet, the voices of the marginalized must be able to take their rightful place in the canon. Their insights are crucial to the search for truth.

Succinctly stated, the process of "conscientization" (Paulo Freire) will not be easy.[179] In addition to resistance among some faculty and administrators, many students also reluctantly engage in dialogue around racial issues. As James Keenan points out, research indicates that college students become more resistant to promoting racial understanding as they progress through their college years. Although African American and Hispanic students start off and finish with the highest level of interest in this issue, even among them it wanes over the course of undergraduate study. Creating diversity courses does not suffice. Rather, universities must "commit themselves to 'promoting racial understanding as a good . . . and ensure that good is visible across the campus in a variety of ways.'"[180] Diversity and "minority concerns" cannot be seen as the sole provenance of one department or one diversity officer. Some observers even caution that a "diversity office" can function as a way of sequestering the problems that White administrators and faculty members want to avoid handling.[181]

Brenda G. Juárez and Cleveland Hayes insightfully apply the pedagogical notion of scaffolding to promoting racial understanding on campus.[182] Reflecting on their own experiences of ostracization after challenging White supremacy, confronting racism on campus through dialogue "must happen on terms that take into account the different places along the recognition continuum at which we each sit." This requires listening by all parties involved. It also requires the recognition that people can and do move along the continuum. Though they do not explicitly use biblical language, Juárez and Hayes advocate "seeing the log in one's own eye" (Matt 7:3–5) and devoting the time necessary to "sincere dialogue with colleagues." Rather than delegitimizing one's colleagues' life experiences as "ones of privilege imbued by racism," they advocate starting by asking colleagues "dialogic questions about their experiences of race." This approach might be conducive to "building the relationship foundation necessary" to move toward racial equity and solidarity.[183] In the powerful conclusion to their essay, they proclaim that rather than disengage the oppressor, which sustains his/her "power to exclude," they

> choose to engage the oppressor by asking: *How do we work together for the 'good' against 'goodness?'* Through Brenda's story, in particular, we have come to recognize that what is most crucial about this question is that it does not frame White people as good or bad. Rather it seeks ways to "speak truth to power," particularly when those in power imagine themselves to be committed to goodwill and the democratic ideals of social justice, but act in ways that continue to undermine the good.[184]

The Right to Participation of All: More than Mere Presence

This approach to dialogue represents a promising first step toward the participation in the good of our educational communities. As I mentioned earlier in this book, every member of a community has the right and duty of participation according to Catholic thought.[185] According to CST, authorities should respect and protect the right and duty of participation of all to contribute to and benefit from the common good because "every person, family, and intermediate group has something original to offer to the community."[186] The very nature and dignity of the human person mandates that persons share in the decisions that affect their lives and the good of the community.[187] A community that negates the right and obligation of participation is a deformed community and "totalistic," in the words of John Paul II. It negates the person herself and her good.[188] More recently, Pope Francis maintained that "the future also demands a humanistic vision of the economy and a politics capable of ensuring greater and more effective participation on the part of the people, eliminating forms of elitism and eradicating poverty."[189]

In the context of the university, respecting this right requires dialogue and collaboration that fully recognizes the contributions of all, including people of color. It also requires sharing of power as much as possible. Faculty of color should have the ability to shape important policies relevant to their situation and the university community as a whole through shared governance. In order for this mechanism to be effective, the participatory structures of shared governance must be more than a façade. In recent years the AAUP has called attention to university administrations ignoring or contravening the voices of faculty in matters within their domain (e.g., curriculum).[190] The sidelining of people of color (and women and LGBTQ persons) can happen when decisions about their place at the university are made by mostly White, male administrators either without their consultation or against their recommendations.[191] However, the right to participation as construed in CST mandates that the persons most affected by decisions have a place at the table so that these decisions are not made over their heads.[192] As *Justice in the World* states, all people "as active and responsible members of human society, should be able to cooperate for the attainment of the common good on an equal footing with other peoples."[193] In CST, fostering the participation of all, particularly the marginalized, is the goal of solidarity. The principle of subsidiarity protects the right to participation by insisting that decisions must be made on the closest level to the problem as possible.[194] This mandate does not imply the ability to dictate decisions. The principle of solidarity and the right to participation require the willingness to cooperate and take seriously the expertise and wisdom of others. Making compromises when necessary is demanded.[195] However, these ideals of CST insist that voices of minoritized people are heard and given as much priority as possible, unless some other countervailing good calls for deciding against them. In such cases, the decision-makers must provide transparency by explaining why the voices of the marginalized could not carry the day. Honoring the right to substantively participate in decision-making far exceeds the feigned shared governance that pervades corporatized universities. Presence on committees at what Benjamin Ginsberg has deemed the "All-Administrative University" simply to ensure minority representation, without having a real ability to effect important institutional policies, is especially burdensome.[196] Faculty, staff, and students of color can also be disenfranchised by a lack of representation on boards, which have taken a more active role in the daily operations of many universities.[197] The dominance of White males on corporate boards of trustees also signals that people of color lack power at their colleges and universities. University presidents also remain overwhelmingly White (about 83%).[198] To reiterate, the goal is to move from tokenism to participation.

Practical Suggestions for Promoting the Equality and Participation of People of Color

Participation in the good of our educational communities requires more than mere presence (i.e., making diversity statistics looks better). However, presence is a precondition for participation. Increasing the prevalence of minority faculty and students needs more and *different* effort. A great deal of evidence suggests that more faculty of color are crucially needed to provide mentorship for new faculty and students of color. Achieving this goal requires addressing the "pipeline problem": Not enough people of color undertake doctoral studies to promote proportional representation at our universities. As recently as 2014 only 14 percent of all doctoral degree recipients were Black, Latino/a or Native American.[199] Many choose careers outside the academy.[200]

Thus, Catholic universities with graduate programs should emphasize graduating doctoral students of color as a contribution to the common good. However, they also need to challenge the core structures of the neoliberal, corporatized university. They cannot in good faith encourage young Black, Latina/o, or Native American students to pursue a career in the academy when (1) the majority of jobs available to them are contingent positions; and (2) minoritized people are already overrepresented among adjuncts. It is morally suspect to encourage people of color to take jobs that may consign them to destitution. Increasing racial and ethnic diversity among faculty must therefore include creating more tenure-track positions in general and specifically in fields like African, African American, and Latina/o studies. Until Catholic universities eschew the adjunctification of their faculties, they will not be able to fulfill their responsibility to help diversify the academic labor force with integrity. Clearly the current, well-intentioned efforts to bring more graduate students of color into the "pipeline" have not achieved enough. The success of Loyola Marymount University's efforts to hire for diversity is instructive: Not only did the university implement wide-ranging trainings for faculty on how to hire for diversity, the university put its money where its mouth is and dedicated one hundred new full-time lines, with a goal of significantly increasing faculty diversity. To my mind, this is precisely where the road toward racial inclusion, justice, and participation for people of color begins at our universities.[201]

The neoliberal corporatized university turns people into producers and consumers, whose value must be measured and commodified. This explains the obsessions with rankings and SAT scores and the putative prestige associated with them. Yet abandoning the required SAT exam will likely entice more low-income and students of color to attend our universities, as I mentioned in Chapter 3. Research has indicated that using more "holistic admissions procedures" rather than emphasizing GRE scores can attract more highly talented graduate students of color.[202] It is worth recalling Espenshade's study predicting a 30 percent increase in Black, Latino/a, and low-income students by making the SAT optional.[203] It is time for Catholic universities to consider ways of getting out of the "nuclear arms race" that is the U.S. News and World Report's college ranking system, or at least go SAT-optional (as my former employer Saint Joseph's University did several years ago). As I will discuss in the next chapter, Trinity University Washington has done the former, with terrific mission-driven results. Former Holy Cross president Michael McFarland reported that his institution saw a large increase in applications "from very gifted and highly motivated students." Moreover, it is hard to justify accepting standardized tests in admissions as the case that they have racial and class bias continues to grow.[204]

In addition to going test optional, or better yet, test blind (not considering test scores for anyone), admissions officers need to devote as much time to recruiting talented Black males as their schools' sports coaches do, and universities should provide Black male athletes and nonathletes with the same learning resources, as Shaun Harper rightly contends. Harper's report, which argues that "college sports persistently disadvantage Black male student athletes" is necessary reading for every Catholic college or university that recruits student athletes.[205] While Catholic colleges and universities are working to reach more African American students, much remains to be done. Essence and Money Magazines jointly publish a list of top fifty schools for African Americans. The rankings are based on graduation rates, representation, early career earnings, and affordability. Only three Catholic institutions make their list: Georgetown, Xavier University of Louisiana, and Trinity University Washington.[206]

As I mentioned in Chapter 3, there are numerous ways that Catholic institutions can do a better job of seeking out students often overlooked, such as bright inner-city minoritized youth and low-income students who cannot afford prestigious prep schools. In Chapter 3 I argued that low-income students should receive admissions preferences. In addition, race-based affirmative action policies can and should be employed by Catholic institutions to the extent that is legally permissible, as the bishops stated in *Brothers and Sisters to Us* in 1979. In the current context, the Catholic principles of solidarity, human rights, participation, and the common good can be marshalled in support of admissions policies that seek to admit more numbers of minoritized students.[207] This is especially true given that the courts are narrowing the scope of permissible policies and still today implicit bias makes affirmative action a pair of "corrective lenses" needed to ensure that students of color are given a fair chance in the admissions process, which favors Whites in the first place.[208] In particular, Catholic colleges and universities should increase the prevalence of minoritized students who hail from low-income families. Numerous Catholic institutions, such as Saint Joseph's and Villanova, designate scholarships for minoritized students, but given the numbers presented above and the data from Chapter 3 of this book, more resources need to be devoted to it. Moreover, some institutions tout diversity among their student bodies, but rather than achieving this goal in accordance with the option for the poor, they often recruit more students from abroad who come from affluent families. For example, rather than seeking such students from among wealthy Latin Americans or Chinese, Catholic institutions should place more emphasis on helping undocumented students achieve their dreams of attending college. For starters, institutions should not categorize undocumented students as "foreigners," thereby disqualifying them for aid.[209] In addition to Santa Clara University's Hurtado Scholarship program, which I mentioned in Chapter 3, some Catholic colleges and universities have undertaken strong initiatives to assist undocumented students. Among them are Loyola Marymount, Mount St. Mary's University, Southern Catholic College, and University of Detroit Mercy, all of which grant generous financial aid to undocumented students.[210] Saint Peter's

College in New Jersey exemplified the kind of commitment all Catholic schools should make to undocumented students by opening its Center for Undocumented Students in 2014. The center provides access to myriad resources, including legal aid and donor-funded Dreamers' Scholarships.[211] The presidents of many Catholic colleges and universities have laudably issued statements of support for undocumented students in the wake of the Trump administration's crackdown on undocumented immigrants.[212] Each of their institutions must make the necessary resources available to truly protect and serve the students, whose presence on their campuses enhances diversity by operationalizing the option for the poor.

Acknowledging where people are on the continuum, as Juárez and Hayes recommend, may indicate against policies such as mandatory (as opposed to voluntary) diversity training. Their reflections reveal that a sustained period of dialogue and relationship-building must first take place. Indeed, a recent article in the *Journal of Blacks in Higher Education* cites a major study of 830 companies that reveals that mandatory diversity training fails because it breeds resentment. These companies experienced a decrease in employees from underrepresented groups after five years of such trainings. The researchers concluded that forcing people to undertake such training will not effectively motivate them to create a culture of inclusivity. Instead they recommend strategies such as "active recruiting and mentoring programs aimed at underrepresented groups, voluntary training, and the hiring of a diversity manager," and rewarding such managers for meeting clearly articulated and concrete diversity benchmarks. Even if such mandatory trainings may not be a fruitful avenue, Catholic institutions can undertake equity audits, bringing in outside experts to help identify problems and meaningful pathways forward.[213]

There are many things faculty can do individually as teachers to promote a more racially inclusive learning environment. Educators first need to recognize their own implicit biases and the ways in which they perpetuate racism in their pedagogy and in the classroom.[214] Villanova's Intergroup Relations (IGR) courses and programs and others like them go a long way toward creating the kind of honest and often painful dialogue our campuses desperately need around issues of race (as well as class, gender, sexual orientation, etc.). Formed in 2020 in response to the Black Lives Matter protests, Boston College's promising Forum on Race seeks to encourage its students to engage in meaningful anti-racism and engage them in the conversation about racial justice before even applying to the university. It is notably highlighted on the main admissions page and asks prospective students to reflect on the question "How will you respond?"

We need to make the time and space to have these conversations. As Maggie Berg and Barbara Seeber keenly articulate in their book *The Slow Professor*, the neoliberal corporatized university militates against finding this time, as faculty, staff, and students alike are met by a constant barrage of "productivity metrics" and "outcomes assessments" that have little to do with such conversations.[215] Yet we must find this time, and slowly dismantle the structures of the neoliberal corporatized university that often force us to choose between values such as building racial solidarity on campus, productivity narrowly construed, and our own health and well-being. As a growing body of research indicates, many faculty are beginning to suffer negative health consequences such as anxiety, depression, and even suicidal tendencies due to the "culture of perfection" demanded by our universities.[216] If this is the case for those of us who are White, it is even more deleterious for our colleagues and students of color who face discrimination, racial battle fatigue, cultural taxation, attempts to suppress their identities, and other woes not faced by White inhabitants of the corporatized university.[217]

6 Gender and LGBTQ Equality in the University

A Challenge for CST in the Age of Corporatized Higher Education

We were excited that we had finally surmounted the travails of doctoral studies. Some among our cohort were even beginning to get job interviews. It was time for us to finally take our place among our faculty peers in the academy. Little did we know (or at least little did I know) that factors beyond merit would influence whether or not we got the job. However, when one friend told me she was asked whether or not she planned on getting pregnant in the near future during a job interview, I was dumbfounded. Isn't asking this question illegal? Furthermore, why would a search committee ask such a question? Especially at a Catholic institution, the desire to have a family and balance the rigors of the academy should not only be accepted but lauded and facilitated, right?

Unfortunately, women are asked this question often enough when applying for academic jobs, even though it is legally problematic.[1] It turns out that my friend's experience is not anomalous. Although women comprise a majority of students and almost half of faculty members at institutions of US higher education, they routinely face subtle obstacles and overt discrimination before gaining entrance to the academy and once they enter it. In fact, women face so many injustices at our universities that I cannot treat them all here. I am choosing to focus mainly on those in the arena of worker justice, work/life balance, and student well-being. The chapter concludes with attention to the horrific problem of sexual assault and rape on college campuses.

Although Catholic social teaching has not always attempted to ameliorate the plight of women in the modern world, its principles and values can be marshaled to promote greater parity and justice for women in the academy and elsewhere. Pioneering Catholic theologians such as M. Shawn Copeland, Maria Clara Bingemer, Margaret Farley, Ada María-Isasi Díaz, Agnes Brazal, Christine Firer Hinze, Lisa Sowle Cahill, and many others have creatively brought to bear the resources of the Christian tradition to promote women's rights and liberation.[2] As I hope to demonstrate here, the Catholic social tradition, including the work of feminist theologians and ethicists, can point toward greater equity for women in the academy. I will also discuss the continuing need to create more inclusive university communities for LGBTQ persons. The issues that women face because of their gender and the LGBTQ community's ongoing struggle for equality are not the same, and both deserve more treatment than I can offer in this book due to space limitations. Nonetheless, I hope I can offer some initial insights about how CST can promote the dignity, equality, and full participation of women and LGBTQ persons in Catholic higher education. Together with the previous chapters related to race and class, my intention is to demonstrate that CST demands confronting all forms of discrimination and injustice that persist in the academy, which would also include ableism.

Women at Home or/in the Academy?

Obviously things have changed since the days when women were excluded from higher education. Today women outnumber men among undergraduate (57 percent), graduate (59 percent), and professional school (51 percent) populations.[3] Women have increasingly joined the ranks of the professoriate. In my own guild, women were formally or informally excluded from teaching and writing about theology, especially Catholic theology, well into the second half of the twentieth century. Today many women are among the leading theologians in the world.[4]

In spite of real gains for women in the academy, gender parity remains far from reach. As in the case of students of color, women students have a disproportionately small pool of women faculty mentors, as the proportion of women full-time faculty members is only 42 percent. On the other hand, women comprise 55 percent of the exploited adjunct faculty labor pool.[5] Although the pay differential between male and female adjuncts may be marginal in many fields, women disproportionately bear the brunt of the casualization of the academic workforce. Women earn approximately 40 percent of all doctorates, yet they constitute "about 58 percent of the full-time temporary instructors."[6] The AAUP reports that in 2009 "44 percent of women in full-time faculty positions were off the tenure track, compared with 33 percent of men."[7] Women hold 52.5 percent of all adjunct positions, while men hold 47.5 percent.[8] Bousquet argues that women recognize the "casualization" of the academic workforce as a feminist issue because "the sectors in which women outnumber men in the academy are uniformly the worst paid, frequently involving lessened autonomy—as in writing instruction, where the largely female staff is generally not rewarded for research, usually excluded from governance and even union representation, and frequently barred even from such basic expressions of academic discretion as choosing course texts, syllabus, requirements, and pedagogy."[9] According to New Faculty Majority Executive Director Maria Maisto, the notion of self-sacrificial service and "the fallacy of teaching for love" are often used to justify exploitation of contingent faculty, particularly in disciplines most heavily represented by women.[10] Even the most dedicated adjuncts have less time to mentor, as they shuttle from institution to institution to make a living. This situation adversely affects female students, whose success correlates with the prevalence of women faculty mentors.[11]

Gender-based injustices do not only affect part-time faculty. The average pay of full-time male professors at four-year private institutions is almost $18,000 more than what full-time women earn. As women ascend each rung of the ladder in the academy, their number wanes. As recently as 2014, women only represented 31 percent of all full professors. Women also occupy only 27 percent of all university presidencies. Men outnumber women 2 to 1 on university boards.[12] Given the obstacles women face in the academy, attaining parity and leadership positions among the faculty and administration continues to look like a Sisyphean task, especially for women raising children as they negotiate the rigors of university life. The ratcheting up of demands in the neoliberal corporatized university makes having children a significant liability for a woman's academic career.

Before discussing in more detail what has been dubbed a "chilly climate" for women in the academy, I want to underscore that the Catholic social tradition adds something important to this discussion.[13] It may seem odd to claim that Catholicism can help attenuate injustices for women in the academy. The church itself continues to exclude women from most leadership roles, as contemporary Catholic feminist theologians point out.[14] While Catholic theologians do not officially represent the church, they do hold the responsibility of explaining the church's theology in new and changing contexts.[15] Even though more women teach theology at

Catholic institutions today than ever, Mary Ann Hinsdale, IHM, of Boston College's Theology Department, noted that in 2015 only 33 percent of the Catholic Theological Society of America's members were women. Her survey of Catholic doctoral theology departments revealed a lopsided ratio of 271 male faculty members to 103 female faculty members, or a 72.5 percent male faculty versus a 27.5 percent female faculty. Some of these departments, such as Fordham University, have a ratio closer to 2 to 1. Others, such as St. Louis University and the Catholic University of America, have drastically smaller proportions of women faculty in theology.[16] Thus, one may ask, how can a tradition crafted in an institution marked by patriarchy and sexism in so many ways help overcome patriarchy and sexism in the academy?

Historically CST hardly helped women trying to make their way in the world of work. CST's teaching on a living wage long presumed the male "bread winner" model. According to this model, a male wage earner should earn enough to support himself, his wife, and children. The husband's wages should enable his wife to remain home and raise the children.[17] John Paul II developed this tradition by insisting that women can and should occupy important vocational roles outside the home. In his 1995 *Letter to Women*, he expressed gratitude to women for the work they do "in every area of life-social, economic, cultural, artistic and political."[18] St. John Paul also acknowledged that women still face discrimination in the workplace. He therefore advocated, among other things, "equal pay for equal work, protection for working mothers, fairness in career advancements, and equality of spouses with regard to family rights."[19] Thus, John Paul provided some clear benchmarks for measuring whether or not women are justly treated in the workplace. Pope Francis recently echoed St. John Paul, telling a group of Italian business executives that women's "right to work and the right to motherhood" must be protected by, among other things, safeguarding the right to maternity leave.[20]

In his encyclical on work *Laborem Exercens*, John Paul forcefully asserts that women's career advancement should not be jeopardized for choosing to fulfill their responsibilities as mothers. Rather, the workplace, and society in general, must be structured in a way that recognizes the crucial role of motherhood in the family and for the common good while enabling mothers to successfully undertake work outside the home without being penalized. He also reiterates the tradition's earlier insistence on a family wage.[21] According to Christine Firer Hinze, the pope's discussion of the "family wage" in *Laborem Exercens* does not explicitly recommend that the wage earner working outside the home must be the male spouse. This is a plausible and welcomed interpretation of the encyclical, which signals development of the tradition on the family wage.[22] Nonetheless, Firer Hinze correctly posits that John Paul's stress on the primacy of motherhood for women, in "accordance with their own nature" and their "feminine genius" spells trouble.[23] John Paul contended that in accordance with their "feminine genius," women are better equipped to fulfill the role of primary caregiver in the home.[24] A woman's "nature" demands that she undertake the role of mother at home (without financially jeopardizing the well-being of her family or her own well-being). From this ontological claim follows John Paul's policy recommendation for "grants to mothers devoting themselves exclusively to their families." He does not similarly posit grants for fathers who choose to stay home to raise their children. John Paul insists that economic necessity should not force a mother to work outside the home. He sees this as detrimental to both "the good of society and of the family." Thus, he avers that "women as mothers have an irreplaceable role."[25]

As Hinze contends, the Pope's lack of similar emphasis on fatherhood and the domestic care responsibilities of males subvert his insistence that women can dedicate themselves fully to parenting and a career.[26] After all, if men do not begin to recognize the equal status of their vocation as parents and caregivers, women will continue to face an incredibly burdensome "second shift." This term, coined by Arlie Hochschild in the 1980s, denoted the increasing time spent by women in work outside the home while simultaneously "continuing to pick up the slack at home by working extra hours."[27] This phenomenon creates significant disadvantages for women trying to fulfill their vocation in the academy. In other words, the concern Hinze raises about CST's need to reenvision the roles of males and females in the household clearly applies to the academic workforce.

The "Baby Penalty" in the Academy

The Catholic tradition sees the family as the "first and vital cell of society."[28] Yet, many industries in late capitalism are hostile to workers with families. Capitalism demands that "the 'ideal worker' behaves as if he or she has no responsibilities outside the workplace."[29] In their book, *Do Babies Matter? Gender and Family in the Ivory Tower,* Mary Ann Mason, Nicholas H. Wolfinger, and Mark Goulden argue that the academy is hostile to workers who have families. In fact, they point out that "the academy is less family-friendly for both men and women" than other demanding professions such as law and medicine.[30] Their research found that both male and female faculty members have fewer children than doctors or lawyers. The problem affects women on the tenure track most acutely. These women are 41 percent less likely than female doctors to give birth to a child. They are also 35 percent less likely to have children than men on the tenure track. Only a third of women who begin the tenure track without having a child will ever have one. The authors note that "45 percent of tenured women faculty are childless, compared with 26 percent of their male colleagues."[31] Could it be that academics are simply less interested in having children than physicians and lawyers, or is the academy truly antithetical to raising a family?

Research has shown that many childless faculty members would like to have children, according to Mason, Wolfinger, and Goulden. This is particularly true of women. One study done at The University of California revealed that more than a third of childless women academics between forty and sixty years old would like to have children, with 22 percent of males in the same age cohort expressing a desire to have children.[32] The authors contend that the academy "has many unique job requirements" that hinder taking on the responsibilities of parenthood. They enumerate among them the need to relocate geographically for a university job, "the publish or perish imperative," and the pressure-packed period leading up to the all or nothing tenure decision in the academy. In their view, failing to get tenure represents a "traumatic" and often career-ending fate unknown to almost any other profession.[33] Furthermore, the American Council on Education (ACE) notes that "in the promotion and tenure processes, tenure-track and tenured faculty frequently encounter ambiguous and contradictory criteria, conflicting messages between institutional rhetoric and the reward structure, murky and secretive review procedures, and unmitigated stress."[34] According to an ACE report on work-life balance, women and faculty of color are affected most negatively by this phenomenon.[35] The American Association of University Professors (AAUP) also draws attention to the fact that a "lack of a clear boundary in academic lives between work and family" uniquely impinges on professors.[36] Professors increasingly suffer from what has been called "time poverty," with the accompanying feeling that one constantly has pressure to produce. A growing body of evidence indicates that professors increasingly suffer deleterious physical and emotional consequences from the stress caused by working in corporatized universities.[37] Having children may in some cases just be one too many stressors. Whether or not a career in the academy is more hostile to having children than other professions, compelling evidence exists that women in the academy are penalized for having children.[38] The problem is not confined to the professoriate. According to a new report by the American Council on Education, women university presidents also "less frequently marry, less frequently have children and are more likely to have altered their career for family" than male university presidents.[39]

Graduate students appear to be aware of the problem, as the vast majority of women and most men in graduate studies view careers in the academy, especially at research universities, as inimical to family life.[40] Women especially worry that their future employers will perceive them as inferior academics if they are pregnant or have young children.[41] Women in graduate studies also notice that male professors are much more likely to have children and spouses than their female counterparts. The lack of female mentors with families seems to convince women graduate students that they face a choice between having children or a successful academic career.[42] Add to this the time constraints, financial insecurity, and lack of good health insurance that many graduate students face, and it is no wonder many of them cannot fathom becoming parents. Meanwhile, research shows that graduate students want a balanced life, not absorption in their careers.[43] In my judgment, they are right to reject the strain of the corporatized university.

Graduate students with children sometimes report being denied support from their advisors while seeking a job or having to forgo seeking a university post. *Do Babies Matter?* relates infuriating stories about women being discriminated against or shut out on the job market. One woman noted that when she interviewed for jobs, she was afraid to wear a wedding band or mention her family, while another recalled that her advisor refused to write her a job recommendation because she chose to start a family. As a result, she failed to receive even one job interview.[44] Members of hiring committees may unfortunately remain unaware of such discriminatory behavior faced by women on the job market.[45] For example, two studies of almost one thousand letters of recommendation revealed that women's acumen and accomplishments are often downplayed in favor of descriptors such as "caring, refreshing and diligent."[46]

It is true that single women without children get tenure-track jobs at rates 16 percent better than childless men after graduate school. However, women with young children (under six) are "21 percent less likely to land a tenure-track position" than a female without a child and "16 percent less likely" than "a comparable father."[47] Having children does not appear to create an obstacle for men to getting a tenure-track job. Yet, women on the academic job market with young children often encounter a "baby penalty." These women face "prejudice against mothers and (future mothers)."[48] The neoliberal corporatized university will employ women and use their skills as much as men, so long as they are "unencumbered by husbands and young children."[49]

If a woman is fortunate enough to obtain a tenure-track position, her troubles surrounding parenthood more than likely have only begun. Women on the tenure track are often advised by colleagues or supervisors not to have children before getting tenure. This puts women and their children at greater risk for infertility, pregnancy-related complications, and/or miscarriage, as women on average earn tenure "well past prime childbearing years," i.e., over forty.[50] The authors of *Do Babies Matter?* relate how one woman interviewed for the University of California study was told by her chairperson that she should get an abortion upon learning of her pregnancy.[51] At *The Chronicle of Higher Education* blog "Vitae," Elizabeth Keenan has told her heartbreaking story of infertility due to waiting for the "nothing" of academia, lamenting that she heard many times in graduate school that she needed to wait in order to be "taken seriously."[52]

Regardless of whether or not they have children, women have a 21 percent less chance of earning tenure than men. Women on the tenure track correctly perceive disadvantages in being parents, feel pressured to sacrifice time for family, and sometimes see the tenure system as "designed for males."[53] Young children especially hurt women's chances for tenure, while older children actually slightly increase their chances. According to Mason and her colleagues, this may be because women (and men) with older children may have "best figured out how to negotiate both parenthood and academia"[54] In contrast to mothers, fathers of children of any age generally do not suffer discrimination either on the academic job market or the tenure-track. In fact, hiring committees may actually view them more positively, as marriage and fatherhood connote stability.[55]

Women who do have children during their doctoral studies or early in their careers very often join the ranks of the academic precariat. As I noted in Chapter 2, women are disproportionately represented among contingent faculty members. Women with doctorates who have young children are 26 percent more likely than childless women and 132 percent more likely than men with a young child to belong to the contingent faculty. They are also four times more likely not to get a job at all than women without children.[56] Some women choose this path, but many mothers are often consigned by academic peers to "the mommy track."[57] If a woman does not land a tenure-track job out of graduate school, she has a one in four chance of jumping into tenure-track later, with her chances waning as years go by.[58] While ironically there is a "positive correlation" between being an adjunct and having children for women, adjunct status makes raising a child all but financially impossible for women who do not have a partner earning a decent salary. Adjunct professor Nicole Beth Wallenbrock's story, related on the PBS Newshour in 2014, typifies this precarious situation.[59]

Academic careers also hurt a woman's chances of having a fulfilling, lasting marriage. Mason and her coauthors refer to a persistent "marriage penalty" for women with PhDs employed in full-time jobs (inside or outside the academy). At the outset of her career a female academic on tenure track is "half as likely to be married" as male counterparts (and much less likely than women in contingent faculty positions). This may be the case, at least in part, because women know that marriage severely impacts their ability to get a tenure-track job.[60] Getting a tenure-track job also does not portend well for new marriages, unless the academic is a male. At the outset of their career on the tenure track, women's marriages are almost two and a half times more likely to end in divorce than their male counterparts.[61] Over their entire careers female tenure-track professors are 35 percent more likely to get divorced than males on the tenure track.

Moreover, a tenure-track job seems to increase the chances of a male academic's marriage lasting. According to *Do Babies Matter?* "men are more likely to have spouses that deferred to the requirements of their careers." Succinctly stated, female faculty have a strong likelihood of being "alone in the ivory tower" (unless they accept adjunct status).[62] The reasons are clear: "Like the corporate establishment, academia shows little interest in changing its modus operandi to better support family life."[63] As Lisa Gabbert, PhD, trenchantly put it: "Academia is hostile toward any interest outside of itself, but particularly . . . towards relationships and towards having children."[64]

Fathers in the academy undeniably do not face many of the hurdles tenure-track female professors raising children must overcome. Although many male academics do much more domestic/care work than previously, women academics on average devote fifteen more hours per week to it.[65] However, men who attempt to balance fatherhood and university life swim against the tide of a culture that sees childrearing and domestic work as the sole provenance of women. As Mason and her coauthors state, the academy presumes that males will have stay at home spouses or partners to care for the children. The male professor completely engulfed in his research and unencumbered by other demands is still envisioned as the "ideal worker" in the academy.[66] Hence, my colleague was astonished when I told him I was heading home immediately after office hours to attend to my toddler. He baldly asked, "Isn't that what why you have a wife?" In his judgment, my childcare duties were cutting into my productivity. This attitude typifies the culture that Hinze contends must change if women will be able to balance caregiving and professional responsibilities outside the home in a more equitable way.[67] Of course, men need to change their mentalities themselves about their responsibilities in the home, shedding the "ideal worker" persona that they have embodied. If they take paternity leave, men should primarily *parent*, not turn it into a sabbatical while women academics endure the hard labor of childbirth and infant care, as some evidence shows.[68] Nonetheless, penalties such as lower raises and the stigma attached to males and females who want to take parental leave while on the tenure-track must be also eradicated.[69] As Margaret W. Sallee states, some campuses are neither "family-friendly" nor "father-friendly" and "work/life issues affect both men and women."[70]

In short, children are seen as a burden, not a gift from God by many denizens of our universities. In the neoliberal corporate university, nothing must impede the academic production machine! Nor should the expenses associated with children require university employees without children to express solidarity with those that do. I recall in this vein a professor bemoaning in an email to the entire faculty that a Catholic university was paying her childbearing colleagues more than her via subsidies for family health plans. Apparently such hostility toward "children and breeders" and their "special privileges" wafts through many of our hallways.[71]

Given the teachings of the church about the family and the primacy of motherhood, and Hinze's helpful corrective concerning the reconceptualization of domestic care, one would hope that Catholic colleges and universities do not exhibit this animus toward faculty and their children. But are they any different? Do they reflect St. John Paul II's and Pope Francis's dictum that women should be able to be mothers and successful in demanding professions like the academy? Do Catholic institutions of higher learning valorize the vocation of fatherhood in a way that eases the domestic care burden on women? I cannot provide a full-blown analysis of these questions here. However, it is safe to say that Catholic universities vary, with some approximating the normative ideals of the Catholic tradition better than others. Generally speaking, work still needs to be done toward gender parity and a family-friendly ethos at Catholic institutions.

Catholic ethicists Bridget Burke Ravizza and Karen Peterson-Iyer have considered this question. Their conclusions can be summarized as follows: "Women are not adequately supported in academia, even at Catholic universities, in spite of that tradition's professed commitment to the health and well-being of families." They contend that Catholic universities are not in the vanguard among family-friendly institutions.[72] They point to a 1996 study that highlighted the top twenty-nine family-friendly US colleges and universities. Although this study is dated, the authors chose to examine it because it is the most comprehensive of its kind, in their view. The only Catholic institutions to appear in the list are Fairfield University and University of San Diego. None of the profiled "model initiatives" were located at a Catholic institution.[73] The study also deemed almost one hundred institutions "leadership schools" for having an average of roughly thirty institutional family-friendly policies. Such policies include flextime and part-time work; benefits for part-time workers; job sharing; family leave; on-campus childcare; and "sensitivity training about work-family issues." According to Burke Ravizza and Peterson-Iyer, "there is nothing in the study to indicate that Catholic schools are progressive and pushing family-friendly agendas on their campuses." The authors of the original 1996 study maintained that "family-friendly institutions are significantly more likely to be public institutions" than religiously-based institutions.[74]

While the results of this study raise concerns about Catholic institutions, they do not warrant a conclusively negative judgment, especially given that the data is from the 1990s. More recent data is available. The 2015 *Chronicle of Higher Education* report "Great Colleges to Work For" surveyed 43,500 people at 278 institutions. The *Chronicle* invites all accredited colleges and universities with more than five hundred students to participate free of charge. This survey is likely the most comprehensive of its kind given that it was sent to more than 100,000 potential participants at US institutions of higher learning. The survey does have one glaring weakness: It was not sent to part-time faculty.[75]

Among the categories of evaluation are "collaborative governance; compensation and benefits; confidence in senior leadership; diversity; facilities, workspace and security; job satisfaction; professional/career development programs; respect and appreciation; supervisor or department-chair relationship; teaching environment; tenure clarity and process; and work/life balance." Of the forty-two institutions of higher education recognized by their faculty and staff for promoting work/life balance, the category most aligned with family-friendly policies, only two are Catholic: St. Leo University and University of The Incarnate Word. These same institutions appear on the "honor roll," which lists twelve institutions that were consistently highly rated in all of the survey's categories. Only four Catholic colleges or universities appear on the list of eighty-six institutions recognized in total: Gannon University, University of Notre Dame, and the two on the "honor roll."[76]

To reiterate, even if the Chronicle's survey does not reflect favorably on Catholic institutions, evidence shows that some Catholic institutions have adopted forward-thinking policies. For example, Canisius College received an Alfred P. Sloan Award for Faculty Career Flexibility. The Alfred P. Sloan Awards for Faculty Career Flexibility were created by the Alfred P. Sloan Foundation, the American Council on Education, and the Families and Work Institute, to honor those institutions of higher education that undertake changes "to create more flexible career paths and to make academic careers compatible with family care giving responsibilities." Toward that end, Canisius College was recognized among 325 Carnegie classification masters institutions eligible for the award for "instituting a second extension of the probationary period; establishing a half-time or part-time appointment with proportional salary; allowing faculty to count summer teaching as part of their annual course load; providing employment assistance to faculty spouses as well as use of the employee assistance program; and creating an emergency family travel loan in the event of a distant family emergency such as a death, accident, or sickness."[77] Santa Clara University and Benedictine University have also received this award. At Santa Clara, all faculty are automatically eligible for extension of the tenure clock for up to two years following the birth or adoption of a child. The policy also covers faculty who have experienced the loss of a loved one, including spouses, partners, or children. Discretionary extensions may also be granted in other scenarios such as the serious illness of a child, spouse, partner, or parent. The university also has a flexible course scheduling policy, which enables faculty to distribute their required number of annual courses in a way that suits child or dependent care.[78] Benedictine University undertook a "two-year culture change initiative to educate, expand, and assess faculty flexibility." The process culminated in the 2009 University Faculty Career Flexibility Summit, which enlisted a significant portion of full-time and part-time faculty with the administration in dialogue about how to insert "career flexibility" into the core of the academic environment. The participants considered more than 250 promising practices from selected exemplary institutions. The dialogue resulted in clarification and codification of eleven leave policies, a policy for pausing the tenure clock, and other possibilities.[79] Benedictine University has implemented many policies that were discussed at the summit, as evidenced by their Career Flexibility for Faculty webpage. Among the numerous leaves available, many of which are paid, the family leave policy stands out. Professors with two years of employment can take this leave either to care for a child under the age of one or a family member with a serious health concern. During this time the faculty member will still gain credit toward tenure and be paid full salary minus the cost of paying "replacement personnel." The fact that such a policy depends upon the availability of an unjustly paid adjunct labor pool should disturb the conscience. On the other hand, this policy does enable tenure-track faculty members to manage family responsibilities without major detriment. It is especially commendable in light of the university's small endowment.[80] Villanova University has recently joined the relatively few institutions that grant a full semester of paid maternity or paternity leave for professors if they are parents of newborns (though staff only have six weeks of paid leave). The previous policy granted only six weeks. Tenure clock extensions for up to one year are also possible.[81] Parents also have up to $1,000 available for child care and a $50 per diem for up to five days annually for emergency dependent care as well as planning assistance for it.[82] Such dependent care options are helpful, even if they do not completely satisfy the caregiving needs of faculty and staff.

Academics often cite the availability of affordable childcare on campus as one of the most important ways of making family and work responsibilities manageable.[83] Some Catholic colleges and universities do operate childcare facilities on campus. Others contract with external facilities for subsidized rates for university employees. However, these facilities often financially stretch many faculty, staff, and graduate students. For example, Santa Clara University, which advertises a two-year wait list for its child care facility on campus, charges university employees $1,515 per month, or $18,000 annually per child in its infant/toddler program.[84] Loyola Marymount University charges faculty and staff a monthly tuition fee of $1,716 to enroll infants in its childcare center.[85] The University of Notre Dame's Early Childhood Development Center prorates its weekly tuition according to family income. An assistant professor at Notre Dame who earns the average salary of $104,000 at that rank would be required to pay full tuition, which amounts to $238 per week ($952 per month). An adjunct faculty member would obviously make much less and therefore pay less. Adjuncts making between $30,000 and $58,000 annually would pay $137 weekly.[86] Childcare facilities are generally very expensive in the United States, one of the few highly industrialized countries without universal preschool and/or subsidized daycare.[87] Unfortunately few universities charge less than the average cost of childcare, which is $1,230.[88]

In short, many Catholic colleges and universities understand the need to implement family-friendly policies at their institutions. Nonetheless, I argue that Catholic colleges and universities should continue to consider how they can make their institutions more family-friendly in order to conform to Catholic teaching on the priority of parenthood and the family. This imperative also reflects papal teaching on the requirement of making motherhood and succeeding in a career outside the home more compatible. In the framework of CST, succeeding of course means not only enabling women to find fulfillment in one's work, but also being paid a just wage and receiving benefits necessary to promote integral human development.[89] Many of us can surely point to examples of how Catholic institutions fail to embody this teaching.[90]

On the other hand, researchers have identified the most promising practices for making the university a place where mothers and fathers can thrive.[91] These policies largely reflect CST in this domain. Implemented in 2003, The University of California Berkeley's Faculty Family-Friendly Edge Program, which has many benefits and flexible policies, has generated tremendous results. The chances of a woman assistant professor having a child are now twice as high as they were in 2003. Graduate students often avail themselves of paid maternity leave.[92] The university conveys its commitment to family-friendly programs in its comprehensive brochure *Balancing Work & Life: Faculty Friendly Programs, Policies, and Resources.* Catholic colleges and universities, and all institutions of higher education, should strive to make their faculty feel just like these two UC Berkeley faculty members, who thus reflected on being a mother and father and an academic:

> The various family-oriented programs and resources at UC Berkeley made me feel like I didn't have to choose between being a professor and having a family, and they gave me the time and confidence to truly enjoy time with my son when he was first born. My department chair and colleagues have been thoroughly supportive—some straight out enthusiastic—which has enabled me to integrate work and family life in ways that I had not anticipated.[93]
>
> . . . That I was able to enjoy [my son] as much as I did during his first year without risking my career owes in good measure to the architects of the UC Faculty Family Friendly Edge program. They designed enlightened policies that children of all working parents should receive, as Ezra did and for which I am forever grateful.[94]

Among the policies repeatedly mentioned in the literature on helping parents experience the joy of parenthood while managing academic careers are: paid parental and family leaves (a minimum twelve weeks, but ideally a semester), longer-term unpaid leaves for family care, modified duties for parents of young children, lactation rooms, emergency child care, on-campus or subsidized affordable childcare, tenure clock extensions for up to two years, transparent and equitable tenure and promotion policies, mentoring and support, tenure-track appointments allowing for part-time status when necessitated by family responsibilities, dual hires for academic couples, and tuition remission for dependents.[95] While universities generally have adopted the less costly policies such as tenure clock stoppage and unpaid leaves, few adopt the more expensive ones such as affordable on-campus childcare.[96] A large number of US institutions of higher learning do not offer paid maternity leave independent of vacation and sick leave. A study published about ten years ago based on a survey of five hundred colleges and universities determined that "the average university offers only 1.9 of 7 possible family-friendly policies."[97]

Thus, even though many universities have made progress, a significant number of institutions need to redouble their efforts to make it possible for faculty and graduate students to have families. As Mason, Wolfinger, and Goulden contend, "the future of universities as we know them . . . depends on a serious rethinking of a system that has proved highly successful for scholarship, but often falls short in retaining some of our best and brightest young minds."[98] Given their dire need to become more family-friendly and flexible workplaces, perhaps colleges and universities can appeal to donors to help them make this goal more financially feasible. Perhaps enlightened donors will be willing to fund a day care center rather than an athletics complex or arena.[99]

Enabling women to be mothers while participating in the work of the academy not only pertains to faculty and staff. Women who become mothers during their student years also need to be supported in answering the call to motherhood. A number of years ago Catholic ethicist Angela Senander argued that "Catholic colleges and universities often try to embody Catholic teaching about sexuality in their housing and health services policies, but rarely do they communicate Catholic pro-life teaching through organized institutional support for pregnant students."[100] She rightly contends that assuming Catholic students will not get pregnant before marriage is naïve (see the discussion of the "hookup culture" at Catholic institutions below). Thus, Catholic colleges and universities must assist these pregnant women in choosing life over abortion if they do not want their Catholic pro-life stance to ring hollow. Senander is surely right.

I personally knew women who had abortions in college. On the other hand, I never met a young mother or father among my peers. When she began to speak on college campuses in the 1990s, president of Feminists for Life Serrin Foster also noticed the conspicuous absence of pregnant students and concluded that they generally had abortions if they wanted to stay in school.[101]

Senander states that among the twenty-eight US Jesuit institutions of higher education she analyzed, very few "had anything to say about assisting pregnant students" on their websites. Only a handful identified assistance with pregnancy such as counseling, campus ministry resources, women's centers, or deferral of student loans. According to Senander, only Marquette University and Georgetown University had comprehensive information on their websites designed to address the concerns of pregnant students.[102] Those websites still exist today under the auspices of campus ministry and health services respectively at these institutions.[103] In 1997 Georgetown students who were also Feminists for Life interns founded the annual Pregnancy Resource Forum, which began a successful push for assistance to pregnant students.[104]

Today Georgetown provides resources such as campus housing for student mothers, and financial assistance for on-site childcare is available for students. The information is, importantly, communicated in a non-judgmental and supportive manner.[105] Marquette's Campus Ministry web page indicates that pregnant students can get help with issues such as what rights and resources the student can expect on campus, where to find support, etc.[106] In the 1980s campus ministry housed Life After Pregnancy, Placement, and Parenting (LAP), which provided an array of services to as many as fifteen students per year. However, in 2002 the staff member running the program departed, leaving a lacuna that was ultimately not filled. While there are still supportive campus ministry staff members, some students have complained that the needs of pregnant students exceed the limited resources available, as indicated in the Marquette student newspaper. Moreover, Marquette students are not always aware that they do have help available through campus ministry (even though it is listed on the website).[107] Students need more assistance, such as the Virginia D. Murphy Endowment, which was originated in 2008 by the Saint Louis University Students for Life. The fund provides scholarships so that "no student should ever have to choose between having a child and receiving an education."[108] The College of Saint Mary strongly attested to being pro-life and pro-woman when it began providing housing in 2000 for single mothers. The college, which has over 30 percent Pell-eligible students, later built a new $10 million residence with rooms accommodating forty-eight mothers with up to two children.[109]

Fortunately, in addition to these positive examples, some other institutions seem to have made progress in more recent times. Students for Life, a longstanding organization dedicated to ending abortion, publishes information for pregnant students pertaining to their campus environs at their Pregnant Students on Campus Initiative website.[110] The organization also commends "top schools for pregnant and parenting students." Catholic institutions dominate the list of eleven institutions, with the following seven appearing: The College of Saint Mary (Omaha), Belmont Abbey College, St. Catherine University (St. Paul), Misericordia University, University of Notre Dame, Saint Louis University, and John Carroll University. Each of these institutions has specific programs designed to support pregnant students and students with children. They typically provide counseling services, financial support for parents, lactation rooms on campus, and permission to live in dormitories.[111] These universities obviously deserve to be commended and should be emulated by other Catholic institutions. Notre Dame's semester-long parental-leave provision for graduate students, which permits retaining standing in their program and their funding, represents a benchmark for all Catholic graduate programs.[112] Thus, greater attention is being paid to the needs of students with children, including on some Catholic campuses. Even *U.S. News & World Report* has begun to showcase Child-Friendly College Programs for Parents. Misericordia University and St. Catherine University are mentioned there.[113] Princeton Review lists its top ten family-friendly business schools (only Notre Dame's Mendoza School makes the list among Catholic institutions).[114]

Unfortunately, not all Catholic colleges and universities link orthodoxy and orthopraxis (to recall Dean Brackley's argument) when it comes to this issue. At the time of this writing, a scan of both the Pregnant on Campus Initiative website and a few university websites yielded scant on-campus resources for pregnant students. For example, I found nothing on the University of Dallas website.[115] Franciscan University of Steubenville honored a crisis pregnancy center in its region. Yet, I could not find any support services listed on its health services and campus ministry web pages.[116] Likewise, the Pregnant on Campus Initiative website lists only off-campus assistance for pregnant students at Ave Maria University. However, the Students for Life group at Ave Maria started a pregnant on campus initiative in the spring of 2017. The website lists several university staff members who are available to help pregnant students and to connect students to other resources external to the university.[117]

To summarize, mothers (and fathers) who want to complete their college education while raising children still lack support at many institutions. For example, only a tiny fraction of campuses nationally offer child-care centers for students.[118] Some Catholic institutions are living out the tradition's great stress on the sacredness of human life, the vocation of parenthood, and the centrality of family. It seems that in many cases students catalyzed positive change on these campuses. Others institutions still need to consider how they can improve in this area. Given that hopelessness, depression, and suicidal tendencies already affect college-age young people increasingly, it is even more incumbent upon Catholic universities to demonstrate abiding love to pregnant students, as well as to all students in distress.[119] Catholic colleges and universities must not communicate to their students that they have no one to help them "carry their burdens" (Gal. 6:2) in times of great need such as pregnancy. In this vein, the beautiful video produced by the Loyola University Chicago Students for Life epitomizes the Pauline injunction to solidarity with brothers and sisters.[120]

The "Chilly Climate" and Intersectionality

Although women without children have a greater chance of getting a tenure-track job and succeeding in the academy than mothers, they too face obstacles unknown to their male counterparts. As I already mentioned, all women are underrepresented at every academic rank (except that of adjunct professor) and are less likely to obtain tenure. Search committees often exhibit biases against female candidates. Women face a disproportionate and unfair service burden that hampers their ability to rise up through the ranks and to obtain grants as successfully as males. This phenomenon partly explains why men still hold 75 percent of full professorships and why it takes on average several years longer for women to attain the rank of full professor.[121] Leading scholar Annemarie Vaccaro contends that "while the oppression of women may not look exactly like it did when Hall and Sandler began writing about the chilly climate [in 1984], it is still present in multiple manifestations, including violence against women, everyday sexism (Swim, Mallett, and Stangor 2004), objectification (Fredrickson and Roberts 1997) and benevolent sexism (Glick and Fiske 2001). These manifestations are common on college campuses." She notes that according to one study women face one or two instances of "everyday sexism" weekly on campuses. Such occurrences may include "gender-role stereotypes and prejudice, degrading comments, and objectification."[122] Vaccaro enumerates eight types of "gender macroaggressions" that continue to create "chilly climates" on campuses for women: (1) sexual objectification; (2) second-class citizenship; (3) assumptions of inferiority; (4) assumptions of traditional gender roles; (5) use of sexist language; (6) denial of the reality of sexism; (7) men's denial of individual sexism; and (8) environmental microaggressions.[123] I cannot repeat Vaccaro's descriptions of each of these terms. However, for those that are not self-explanatory, a brief discussion is in order.

Sexual objectification includes a range of behaviors from referring to women as body parts to sexual violence. Some people on campus may send messages to women conveying they are inferior intellectually, physically, or emotionally. This may play out, for example, through dissuading women from participating in sports or from majoring in STEM fields. Women are still sometimes expected to shoulder "feminine" tasks such as cooking or clean-up after events, caring for others, etc. The absence of women in leadership roles and curriculum design constitute examples of environmental microaggressions. Finally, men may either characterize women as being "too sensitive" about sexism and depression and/or deny their own sexist behavior.[124] Elsewhere Vaccaro has described research indicating that men, particularly White male students, exhibit "hostility toward diversity efforts, resentment of liberal bias, and symbolic racism." It appears that far too often men are interested in protecting their White male privilege rather than promoting inclusivity and participation.[125]

Vaccaro and others rightly inject intersectionality into the discussion of sexism on campus. As Vaccaro states, "chilly climates continue to exist, particularly for women with multiple marginal identities."[126] Legal scholar Kimberlé Crenshaw coined the term "intersectionality" in 1989 to conceptualize the "interaction of race and gender" that occurs when Black women are discriminated against based on their race and gender. She argued that feminists and civil rights leaders alike overlooked how the overlapping existential realities of racism and sexism marginalized Black women in ways alien to White women or Black men.[127] Patricia Hill Collins and Sirma Birge maintain that "core ideas of intersectionality" pre-date the coining of the term, locating its roots in the 1960s and 1970s.[128] In more recent times, scholars and activists have since expanded the se-mantic range of the term to refer to interlocking forms of discrimination based on sexual orientation, class, disability, nationality, as well as race and gender.[129] Hill Collins and Birge explicitly note the usefulness of this "analytic tool" for colleges and universities that "face the challenge of building more inclusive and fair campus communities."[130] Utilizing the analytic tool of intersectionality allows us to see that campuses can have even "chillier" climates for "women of color, nontraditionally aged stu-dents," women outnumbered by men in their majors or fields, women with disabilities, or lesbian, bisexual, and transgender students.[131] In ad-dition to all the obstacles and discrimination White women face in the academy, women of color encounter particular challenges rooted in both racism and sexism.[132] For starters, White women far outnumber women of color, as campuses may even have only one or two women of color on the faculty. This leads to an even greater service and mentoring load for women of color than for White women, which may jeopardize their chances at tenure given the premium placed on publishing.[133] Story after story in the anthology *Presumed Incompetent: The Intersections of Race and Class for Women in Academia* conveys the pain and anger borne by women of color in the academy for being mistreated, vilified, disrespected, and discriminated against. For example, Elvia R. Arriola describes the hatred she faced by those who disliked her for being a Latina, lesbian woman. Those who resented her for being an "affirmative action hire" ultimately ensured she did not get tenure. She painfully opines that "women of color are frequent outsiders whose identities have been brightly burned at the stake of academic politics."[134] Sherri L. Wallace, Sharon E. Moore, Linda L. Wilson, and Brenda G. Hart attest to the "unspoken, yet perva-sive racism and sexism," which they encountered and learned to challenge in the classroom and elsewhere. They lament that students, other faculty, administrators, and staff often cast women of color as "incompetent." They also relate that women of color particularly perceive that their research is often "undervalued" and not seen as sufficiently robust for tenure and promotion.[135] Yolanda Flores Niemann insists that women of color should not be expected to forsake "their culture because they have entered the white academic world," yet they face the threat of negative peer or student evaluations rooted in these cultural differences.[136] In short, women whose identities place them "outside" the domain of White, heterosexual, cisgender, abled, and middle- or upper-class women face greater obstacles and harms that institutions must acknowledge and attenuate.[137] The solidarity of the Catholic social tradition requires seeing and listening to minoritized and marginalized women and men in all of their particularities in our institutions. Those of us in positions of privilege (such as White, heterosexual, cisgender males like me) must be attentive to the fullness of their stories, not just fragmented elements. Put another way, solidarity means acknowledging and respecting each individual as a whole person, as the Ignatian notion of *cura personalis* holds. Solidarity requires removing every barrier to each person's participation in the community, whether based on race, gender, class, ability, or sexual orientation.[138] It also requires owning the fact that we have benefited from those barriers if we have enjoyed White, male, heteronormative privilege in the academy.

The "Chilly Climate" at Catholic Colleges and Universities

As in the case of race, Catholic colleges and universities historically trailed secular institutions in promoting full access to and participation of women. Women were long excluded from Catholic colleges and universities. Oberlin College first opened its doors to women in 1833. By the end of the nineteenth century more than half of American institutions of higher learning were coeducational.[139] Catholic higher education was much slower to accept women, preferring to found women's colleges run by religious orders rather than to embrace coeducation. Religious leaders expressed disdain toward coeducation. In 1929 Pope Pius XI warned against it.[140] Only twenty percent of Catholic institutions accepted women by the middle of the century, and even then women's presence on campuses was marginal and largely limited to preprofessional programs. In the 1960s and 1970s financial necessity, the need to retain a growing and talented applicant pool, and cultural shifts compelled Catholic colleges and universities to become coeducational. As Susan Poulson and Loretta Higgins state, Catholic institutions of higher learning finally "dropped their identities as all-male institutions" between 1965 and 1975.[141] Georgetown University finally admitted women into the College of Arts and Sciences in 1968. Undergraduate women could enter any program they desired for the first time at Boston College in 1970. After a failed bid to merge with St. Mary's College, Notre Dame became coeducational in 1972. Women continued to face discrimination in admissions and social stigma even after they were admitted to these institutions.[142]

A full-scale assessment of whether Catholic institutions of higher education still preserve a chilly climate exceeds the scope of this book. Women have undoubtedly made significant progress at Catholic colleges and universities. For example, in 1973 faculty and staff pressured Boston College to found one of the first women's centers on a Catholic campus. Today such centers are commonplace among Catholic institutions. Although their numbers are relatively small, a growing number of women have assumed presidencies at Catholic colleges and universities. By 2013 at least thirty-two lay women held presidencies, with a number of Catholic institutions also led by women in religious orders.[143] Women's leadership at once all-male Catholic institutions is making strides as the schools inch away from their sexist past.

Ever since 1895 when the School Sisters of Notre Dame founded the College of Notre Dame of Maryland, the first Catholic college for women in Baltimore, women's religious orders have sought to empower young women in the face of a good deal of resistance from within the church and elsewhere.[144] At their zenith, Catholic colleges for women numbered more than 190. Today, the seventeen remaining Catholic women's colleges continue the tradition of empowering women students in myriad and remarkable ways.[145] While they vary in this regard, some of these women's colleges, such as Trinity Washington University in DC, have boldly put CST into action in their operations. Although the new direction met with some resistance from alumnae, Trinity has consciously decided to focus on educating underrepresented populations of women and rejected much of the corporatized model of higher education under the leadership of Dr. Patricia McGuire. For example, the university no longer participates in the U.S. News rankings, deeming commitment to its mission of social justice and the right to education for all more important. More than 90 percent of Trinity students are working Black or Latina women, and the university is helping them to realize their ambitions while thriving as an institution.[146] The university also recognized the adjunct union election rather than legally contest it, which can be deemed a victory for women who disproportionately struggle to make ends meet as adjunct faculty nationally.[147]

Given that women were essentially *personae non gratae* until late in the twentieth century at many Catholic colleges and universities, vestiges of the bias against women are bound to remain even if much has changed for the better. Dr. Mary-Antoinette Smith, a professor of English and women's and gender studies at Seattle University and Director of the National Association for Women in Catholic Higher Education (NAWCHE) presents a view that resonates with the thesis of this book. NAWCHE's existence since 1992 testifies to the fact that women at Catholic institutions have come together in solidarity to foster an environment in which they can flourish. However, according to Smith, too often Catholic institutions like hers "were closer to living out the principles of our mission statement two decades ago than we are now." She laments that "nowadays, we're operating more like a corporation than a Jesuit and Catholic institution." The solidarity that she once knew at her institution, which prompted senior faculty to forgo cost-of-living raises for several years to allocate more resources for junior faculty struggling to buy homes, is a relic of a bygone era. Therefore, women who want to live out the social teachings of their faith in their workplace find themselves in difficult terrain even though they work at Catholic institutions of higher learning. Smith also bemoans the waning resources devoted to programs central to the social justice mission of a Catholic university, such as women's and gender studies and ethnic studies.[148]

Reflecting on her decades of experience in Catholic higher education, Dr. Susan Ross provides a balanced and realistic assessment of the situation for women today. Her institution, Loyola University Chicago, was the first Jesuit University to implement a women's studies program in 1979. The program has continued to "thrive" ever since, with robust enrollments and a larger number of women faculty members to support it. On the other hand, the program (now women's and gender studies) lacks its own faculty, thus relying on "volunteers" from other departments. Increasing demands of scholarship placed upon them inhibit their ability to devote time to the program. Ross acknowledges that it is "no longer problematic to focus on feminist or gender-based scholarship" as it was in the past. But the individualistic and traditional means for evaluating scholarship stifle the kind of cross disciplinary and collaborative work required by women's and gender studies. Other Catholic institutions, such as Santa Clara University, have addressed these problems by dedicating faculty lines to women's and gender studies program.[149]

Although Ross celebrates that the provost is a woman, she also states that her university lags far behind peer institutions in the number of women in senior leadership positions. On the other hand, she commends Marquette University because roughly 41 percent of its deans and key administrators are women.[150] She points out that in 2005 her university created a committee on the status of women, akin to a similar committee at Marquette University. While this was necessary and welcomed, she and other female faculty members grew increasingly frustrated by the committee's ineffectiveness. The committee's recommendations, such as a "clear maternity and paternity leave policy" and a more aggressive strategy for hiring women leaders, were rejected. According to Ross, conversations with peers at other Jesuit institutions lead her to conclude that "many schools are stuck in situations where little is done to challenge the present situation."[151] I would add that I heard similar frustrations from women trying to foster change via a committee on the status of women. They felt that their efforts were dismissed or met with resistance. As Ross succinctly stated, in many ways women are better off than they were ten years ago, but many problems "stubbornly" persist.[152] Ross acknowledges that members of religious orders such as the Jesuits have tried to form meaningful relationships with women on their campuses. Nonetheless, a culture rooted in the patriarchy of religious orders that founded institutions such as Jesuit universities and the continual existence of "old boys networks" still prompt questions about who makes the "real decisions" and "who holds the real power" at these institutions.[153]

As Ross, Vaccaro, and others indicate, a comprehensive approach to eliminating the "chilly climate" is required. Pay parity constitutes but one useful lens for evaluating how well Catholic universities have done. Though not a panacea, focusing on it here jibes with CST. To reiterate, CST calls for "equal pay for equal work," as St. John Paul II stated. To see how Catholic colleges and universities are doing in this regard, the AAUP annual salary survey proves useful, as it provides a salary equity index. As mentioned at the outset of this chapter, women still earn less than men at every academic rank. On average, women at all ranks earn on average 87 cents for every dollar a man earns. Male full professors earn on average $104,493, while women earn $98,524. The gaps are slightly smaller at the ranks of associate and assistant professor.[154] However, at some institutions the pay parity ratio has reached or even exceeded 100. In other words, women are outearning men on average, at some institutions.[155] At the rank of professor, some Catholic institutions fall into this category, such as Albertus Magnus College (119), Notre Dame of Maryland (111.9), and The College of Our Lady of the Elms (110.7).[156] Seton Hill University (73.6), St. Mary's University of Texas (83.9), Duquesne University (84.1), and Seattle University (84.5), for example, fall among institutions at the other end of the spectrum, with less pay parity.[157] At the rank of assistant professor, St. Mary's College of Maryland (119), Trinity University of Texas (115.1), Chaminade University of Honolulu (114.3), and University of St. Francis in Illinois (112.9) have higher average salaries for women than men. Avila University (67.1), University of Scranton (79.4), John Carroll University (83.8), Wheeling Jesuit University (84.2), and Santa Clara University (85) are among the institutions listed with the lowest pay parity ratio.[158] To give those figures some concreteness, we can look at average salaries rather than ratios. For example, assistant professors at Santa Clara University earn an average of $102,000 annually whereas the figure for women is $86,700. Some institutions, such as The College of the Holy Cross and Villanova University, pay female assistant professors a slightly higher average salary than their male counterparts, but the pay reverses in favor of males at the higher ranks.

The AAUP attributes the pay gap to differences in male versus female representation in various disciplines. Fields that are heavily dominated by males, such as business management, biological sciences, and engineering, pay higher. Conversely, women tend to predominate in fields in the humanities, such as English, sociology, and women's and gender studies, where the pay scales are lower.[159] I have often heard a justification rooted in market fundamentalism for discrepancies between pay in such disciplines: Purportedly the market would pay professors in the higher-paying fields better if they were to leave the academy for the job market.

However, it is worth reiterating that St. John XXIII made plain that the Catholic tradition rejects the idea that wages should be based solely on the logic of the market.[160] Thus, the Catholic just wage tradition points toward mitigating differences in pay among the disciplines in order to promote greater pay parity between men and women. Of course, this represents one step among many others needed to promote the full and equal participation of women in our academic communities. Catholic institutions must strive toward eradicating all of the microaggressions against women mentioned by Vaccaro and others. A comprehensive list of approaches exceeds the scope of this chapter, but let me briefly enumerate some of the key steps appearing repeatedly in the literature. For starters, Catholic universities and colleges that do not already have a standing commission on women should institute one. While such commissions and their periodic reports are not a panacea, they do "enhance the awareness" of problems facing women in the university and "provide a good platform for all parties to communicate."[161] To amplify the concern expressed by Ross and her colleagues, these commissions must have real leverage and not just serve as a fig leaf hiding the inertia of the males leading the institution. Colleges and universities must "consistently review policies, procedures and protocols" in order to gauge how they are faring in addressing institutional sexism.[162] Institutions must also do a better job of fostering parity and real participation of women's leadership at the highest levels.[163] They must eschew tokenism and avoid seeing strong women leaders as "double deviants" who have rejected "gender norms" to assume roles stereotypically reserved for males.[164]

Hiring processes can be tailored in numerous ways to decrease the chance of bias against women. For example, the AAUP suggests not penalizing for gaps in "productivity" on a résumé during childbearing and childrearing years. In addition, department chairs can ensure that women staff and students from underrepresented groups have a voice in the search process.[165] While increasing the presence of female faculty on campus is important, institutions must also move "beyond their frequent focus on statistical parity so that they can include how different women may experience a campus climate," as Vaccaro contends. In other words, institutions must "support women as they organize around intersectionality." Campus centers, organizations, programs, and departments focusing on women's issues must be maintained to shine a light on women's issues. However, institutions must also ensure safe and welcoming environments for women across all backgrounds.[166] Fortunately, the proportion of Catholic colleges and universities with women's studies programs well exceeds the national average. As Tara M. Tuttle argues, Catholic institutions of higher learning recognize shared values with pedagogical approaches in women's and gender studies, such as the pursuit of "justice" and "truth" in solidarity with others.[167] But the point Vaccaro raises about intersectionality surely represents an area of growth for some of these programs, as the previous chapter of this book indicates. Moreover, Ross's concern about understaffing and underfunding these programs must be addressed. In short, institutions need to devote significant attention and resources to creating a culture and policies that are "women and family friendly," as Ross maintains.[168] This task remains urgent for the well-being and dignity of women.

The Dignity and Participation of LGBTQ Persons on Campus

I will never forget the conversation from my undergraduate days with a friend who questioned God's love for him because he is gay. Perhaps aided by the Spirit, my response was "if I can love you as my friend, so can God love you." I was, for most of my young life, homophobic. That moment was the inbreaking of a new attitude toward my LGBTQ brothers and sisters in Christ.

Adopting the intersectional approach in the higher educational milieu advocated by Vaccaro and others means that Catholic institutions must expand their concerns about diversity and inclusion to include LGBTQ students, faculty, and staff. Higher education generally has been slower in "expanding the circle" of diversity to include sexual orientation and gender identity.[169] As I have stressed repeatedly, one of the hallmarks of Catholic education is care for the whole person, or *cura personalis*, in Ignatian terms. This means attending to the needs of the person in her or his totality; again, this resembles Vaccaro's call to see women, and men, in the fullness of their "intersectional identities."[170] Sexual orientation and gender identity are constitutive elements of personhood. Care for the whole person should not ignore these facets of one's identity.

My own institution, Villanova University, lists *caritas* as one of its core values (*veritas* and *unitas* round out the triad on the university seal). As

St. Augustine proposed, we aspire to "set love as the criterion for all that you say, and whatever you teach, teach in such a way that the person to whom you speak, by hearing may believe, by believing, hope, and by hoping, love."[171] This is a beautiful ideal, but love obviously can and has been interpreted in myriad and conflicting ways. Christians, however, can draw pretty clear implications from the life, death, and resurrection of Jesus Christ that specify the content and demands of love. Jesus's love extends to all, but as the Gospels reveal, he exhibited particular love and solicitude toward the poor and the marginalized. The Gospel call to love enjoins Christians to practice solidarity with those who are on the margins.[172]

The Orlando nightclub shooting on June 12, 2016, painfully revealed that the LGBTQ community still remains vulnerable to discrimination and brutal violence, even if LGBTQ persons have won the right to marry and are more accepted by more Americans today than ever before. The death of forty-nine people at the Pulse nightclub that evening shook the nation. Members of faith communities, including the Catholic Church, rightly began to wonder if their traditions contributed to the homophobia that ended in a horrific tragedy that evening. In the days after the massacre, Bishop Robert Lynch of the Diocese of St. Petersburg trenchantly stated: "Sadly it is religion, including our own, which targets, mostly verbally, and also often breeds contempt for, gays, lesbians and transgender people."[173] As he expressed his sorrow for the victims and their families, Bishop Robert McElroy of San Diego added, "this tragedy is a call for us as Catholics to combat ever more vigorously the antigay prejudice which exists in our Catholic community and in our country."[174] Yet, as James Martin, SJ, points out in his book *Building a Bridge: How the Catholic Church and the LGBT Community Can Enter into a Relationship of Respect, Compassion, and Sensitivity*, far too many Catholic leaders do not express solidarity with the LGBTQ community and explicitly condemn homophobia.[175] Martin's important book, an excellent resource for discussion groups on Catholic campuses, reminds us of the prejudice within the church toward the LGBTQ community. In contrast to Bishop Lynch and Bishop McElroy, some bishops continue to harshly chastise homosexual persons, such as the bishop who recently stated that people in same-sex marriages could not have a funeral in the church.[176] Some critics, including Catholic theologians, believe that the church uses language (such as "objectively disordered") that continues to demean, offend, and harm LGBTQ persons.[177]

A deep chasm exists between what the church teaches about sexual orientation and what most Catholics believe. Citing a plethora of data, Patrick Hornbeck and Michael Norko demonstrate that most Catholics accept homosexual relationships and affirm the rights of gays and lesbians to marry, to be free of discrimination in the workplace, and to serve openly in the military significantly more than other Christians and the general public.[178] As Fr. Martin reminds us, the church itself teaches that gays and lesbians should be treated with "respect, compassion, and sensitivity."[179] Jesus's ministry to Zaccheus and the Roman Centurion and other marginalized people reflects the need for the church to embrace LGBTQ persons.[180] Theologian Elisabeth Vasko argues that Jesus's encounter with the Syro-Phoenician woman in Mark 7: 24–30 calls the church to confront its own complicity in "racism, heterosexism, homophobia, xenophobia and misogyny" and to "hear God's word in our midst" among the marginalized, which includes LGBTQ persons in our contemporary context.[181] Numerous priests, nuns, chaplains, and campus ministers have tried to put this into practice in their ministries in the LGBTQ community. Archbishop Joseph Tobin's remarkable recent welcoming of an LGBTQ pilgrimage exemplifies the loving disposition all Christians should exhibit.[182] Archbishop Wilton Gregory has likewise supported Fortunate and Faithful Families, which promotes "inclusion of all gender and sexually diverse individuals and their families" in the church. He also recently told a transgender Catholic, "you belong to the heart of this church."[183] However, the language and treatment of LGBTQ persons by the church has often done more harm than good, as Bishop Lynch intimated.[184]

In accordance with the Gospel message, Catholic colleges and universities must show love and solidarity toward LGBTQ members of their communities.[185] Although some people perceive higher education as a bastion of liberalism, colleges and universities are not free of homophobia and discrimination against LGBTQ persons.[186] LGBTQ students, faculty, and administrators report harassment (36 percent of undergraduates, 29 percent of all respondents, 92 percent of transgender students), fear (20 percent of respondents), and the need to hide their identities (50 percent) to "avoid intimidation."[187] Suicide rates among LGBTQ young people cause grave concern, as they are two to three times that of heterosexuals. Many LGBTQ

young people experiencing suicidal thoughts or carrying out suicide attempts have encountered verbal and/or physical bullying.[188] While many
members of the LGBTQ community feel secure in their identities and welcomed in their communities, it is clear that not all of them feel safe on our
campuses. Moreover, more than 40 percent of students nationally believe
that their college or university does not adequately handle sexual orientation and gender identity issues.[189] Transgender students especially feel
abandoned and vulnerable on their campuses.[190] According to Vaccaro,
"research suggests that heterosexism, genderism, homophobia, and transphobia are a reality on contemporary college campuses" for undergraduate
students, graduate students, faculty, and staff (although each of these populations experience them differently).[191]

Fortunately, some institutions of higher education, including some
Catholic colleges and universities, have demonstrated a commitment to
the right of LGBTQ members to be respected, full participants in the life of
their campuses. In 2006 *The Advocate College Guide for LGBT Students* listed
the top one hundred LGBTQ-friendly colleges and universities. This initial
assessment did not recommend any Catholic institutions.[192] Campus Pride,
which was founded by nationally recognized LGBTQ researchers, has continued to rate colleges and universities according to how safe and more inclusive their campuses are for LGBTQ students. In order to be evaluated,
institutions must complete a self-assessment index with more than fifty
questions pertaining to: "1. LGBTQ Policy Inclusion, 2. LGBTQ Support &
Institutional Commitment, 3. LGBTQ Academic Life, 4. LGBTQ Student
Life, 5. LGBTQ Housing, 6. LGBTQ Campus Safety, 7. LGBTQ Counseling
& Health and 8. LGBTQ Recruitment and Retention Efforts." All colleges can
participate for free and can elect to share their results publicly on the
Campus Pride website or not.[193] Among those Catholic institutions recognized on the website with very positive ratings (four out of five stars) are
Loyola Marymount University and Georgetown University. Loyola scored
particularly well for the comprehensive programming in the LGBT Student Services Office, LGBTQ studies and academic courses, efforts to ensure the safety of LGBTQ community members, and the inclusion of
sexual orientation and gender identity in its nondiscrimination policy.
The LGBT Student Services Office explicitly seeks to address issues within
the frameworks of interculturalism and Catholic social teaching.[194] A few
other Catholic institutions appear on the Campus Pride Index with

three-star ratings, which indicates an average score but also a willingness to learn about the campus climate for LGBTQ persons. On the other hand, the organization currently lists five Catholic colleges and universities among the least friendly for LGBTQ students.[195]

Thus, Catholic colleges and universities display a familiar pattern to readers of this book: They exhibit a wide range of differences on LGBTQ issues. At least one Catholic university reportedly offers a course that teaches homosexuality as a form of deviance.[196] On the other hand, New Ways Ministry, which was founded in 1977 to minister to gay and lesbian Catholics, lists 118 Catholic Colleges on its website that are "gay-friendly." Although these institutions do not necessarily meet the more robust criteria delineated by Campus Pride, to be listed they must at least have a support group for gay and lesbian students.[197]

Some institutions that once were regarded as hostile to the LGBTQ community have made great strides. For example, Frank D. Golom describes how one Catholic college transformed itself in just a few years from being "pretty homophobic," according to the Princeton Review, to a leader among religiously affiliated higher educational institutions on LGBTQ concerns.[198] Former Dean of Religious Life at Stanford University Rev. Scotty McLennan criticizes the Catholic Church's position, which not only condemns homosexual acts but also precludes supporting groups on Catholic campuses that "seek to undermine the teaching of the Church."[199] However, he applauds Georgetown's approach, which entailed opening an LGBTQ Resource Center staffed by two full-time employees in response to a student assaulting a peer on campus in 2008.[200] That same year 61 percent of surveyed students deemed homophobia an important issue on campus.[201] In his remarks concerning the opening of the center, President DeGioia clarified that while any center on campus cannot "advocate" against church teaching, the university can "advocate for LGBTQ students" (recall my argument about *cura personalis*). The university "can and must advocate for respect, inclusion, understanding, safety, mentoring, dignity, growth and equal opportunity . . . freedom from prejudice, exclusion, discrimination, and homophobia."[202] Teresa Delgado speaks of the "delicate dance" she and others do at her Catholic college in order to be "attentive to and aware of the church's official doctrinal stance regarding sexuality" while affirming the dignity and rights of LGBTIQ persons. This solidarity requires "challenging that doctrine when it is death dealing rather than life affirming." She also commends how her colleague "found the most welcoming and affirming space" after undergoing genital reassignment surgery and lauds the activities of the student-run Gay/Straight Alliance on her campus.[203] DePaul University offered courses in LGBTQ studies already in the 1990s and later created the first LGBTQ studies minor at a Catholic institution.[204] Villanova University has a VU Pride Group for LGBTQ persons and allies, an LGBTQ outreach group in campus ministry, a Safe Zone program, and explicitly prohibits discrimination on the basis of sexual orientation and gender identity. The university grounds all of these in the Gospel mandate to love the neighbor.[205] Other Catholic institutions have similar programs and nondiscrimination policies.[206] In short, many Catholic colleges and universities are striving, with varying degrees of success, to affirm the dignity and participation of their LGBTQ members in an ecclesial context that creates challenges. Some institutions, however, appear to circumscribe the love commands of the Gospel, excluding members of the LGBTQ community.

An exhaustive discussion of the most successful ways to promote the rights and dignity of LGBTQ persons on campus surpasses possibilities here. Fortunately, other scholars have done pioneering work in this area, and I refer the reader to them.[207] I will outline here just a few of the policies and practices that experts repeat most often. Prior to the 2015 *Obergefell vs. Hodges* decision, some Catholic institutions already extended benefits to domestic partners.[208] Scholars have deemed extending family-friendly policies to domestic partners as an important means of becoming more inclusive.[209] Some Catholic scholars, and the USCCB, have expressed disagreement over extending benefits to same-sex spouses.[210] However, their argument that doing so equates with a rejection of a "traditional view" of marriage falls flat. As Rev. John Jenkins, CSC, and Fr. Timothy Lannon, SJ, presidents of University of Notre Dame and Creighton University respectively stated, providing a benefit such as health care to same-sex spouses does not necessarily constitute an endorsement of same-sex marriage.[211] Rather, it is a logical consequence of the church's teaching on the right to health care for all and the right of LGBTQ persons to be treated with "respect, compassion and sensitivity."[212]

Likewise, Catholic colleges and universities must ensure that nondiscrimination against LGBTQ persons is embedded in all recruitment, hiring, promotion, and retention policies. The recent firings of teachers at

Catholic secondary schools because of their sexual orientation are unjust and unacceptable from the standpoint of Catholic ethics.[213] In addition to being discriminatory against those individuals, these firings arguably harm those school communities, as it deprives LGBTQ students of people they can confide in as they discern their own identities and learn to love themselves. Those institutions that have not already done so should follow the lead of others that explicitly inscribe sexual orientation and gender identity into their nondiscrimination policies. These policies must include zero tolerance for bullying and harassment. Experts note that robust nondiscrimination policies represent one of the most needed protections for LGBTQ members of our communities.[214] As Vasko maintains, "gay bashing" affirms "heteropatriarchy" and is a form of "social control" that seeks to limit or deny the full participation of LGBTQ persons in the community.[215] CST calls for unambiguous policies that protect their right to participation.

LGBTQ studies provide an intellectual space to explore issues related to sexual orientation and gender identity. This exploration can and should entail "religious, philosophical, or ethical" perspectives at a Catholic university, as DePaul's administration maintained.[216] One can also see LGBTQ studies as part of the quest for truth, an intrinsic element of Catholic higher education. As *Ex Corde Ecclesiae* states: "'academic freedom' is the guarantee given to those involved in teaching and research that, within their specific specialized branch of knowledge, and according to the methods proper to that specific area, they may search for the truth wherever analysis and evidence leads them, and may teach and publish the results of this search, keeping in mind the cited criteria, that is, safeguarding the rights of the individual and of society within the confines of the truth and the common good."[217] LGBTQ student services offices with full-time staff and LGBTQ student groups are essential to serving the needs of students. These offices and programs must not be "siloed," but rather located together with other diversity and multicultural offices. As Pauline Park maintains, "'intersectionality' must not simply be a slogan; it must be a principle on which the work of student service professionals at colleges and universities operate."[218] In this vein, the faith lives of LGBTQ students should not be ignored. Programming should be developed that integrates their spiritual identities with their sexual orientation and gender identities, as these students may feel shunned by their religious traditions and experience a spiritual void.[219] For the message of LGBTQ inclusion to gain traction, it is also important to couch it in the framework of Catholic mission and Catholic social teaching, as some institutions have already done.[220] Thus, stress should be put on the core CST values of dignity, rights, and participation of LGBTQ members of our academic communities, in addition to the Gospel call to love the neighbor. The right to participation excludes no one.

Sexual Violence on Campus: An Egregious Affront to Human Dignity and Participation

In my judgment, deeming sexual violence an element of a "chilly climate" fails to capture its gravity. Sexual assault and rape constitute a severe negation of a person's right to participate in a community. As Christian ethicist Margaret Farley has written, "in the sexual sphere . . . each person is vulnerable in ways that go deep within." The perpetrator attempts to dominate another human being, usurping the victim's "capacity for self-determination."[221] Sexual violence (sexual assault and rape) on college campuses remains an egregious affront to the dignity and rights of human persons, even if some progress has been made combatting these crimes. Space limitations preclude a complete discussion of this issue here. Others have done excellent work on this issue, and I will refer the reader to these studies.[222] Nonetheless, any discussion of justice on campus cannot ignore sexual violence.

As the father of a teenage daughter, I am acutely aware that university campuses can be dangerous places in the United States: One in five women and one in fourteen men are sexually assaulted while in college, with even higher rates among female bisexual and transgender students.[223] The acclaimed documentary The Hunting Ground reveals not only the extent of the problem, but the lengths that colleges and universities go to cover up sexual assault cases.[224] Even though the federal government's crackdown on colleges has led to results, colleges still do not always treat sexual assault cases, and the victims, appropriately.[225] As James Keenan, SJ, contends: "The universities' inability to address the sexual assault issue without federal oversight is a combination of 'old boy' resistance and the university's general disinterest in ethics that together leaves the university incompetent in adjudicating fairly the reports it receives. . . . Universities are still leaving the woman victim out in the cold."[226]

Those who naively believe that the church's teaching on chastity obviates the problem of sexual assault on Catholic campuses might read Jason E. King's *Faith with Benefits: Hookup Culture on Catholic Campuses*.[227] Engaging in casual sexual activity ("hooking up") is much less prevalent at what King calls "Very Catholic" colleges or universities (based on the perception of students surveyed at these institutions). However, even at these institutions he found that roughly one-quarter of the students hook up.[228] Moreover, his survey of over a thousand students at twenty-six different Catholic institutions found that 47 percent of students hooked up once or more during the course of the year. Over half of these sexual encounters involved intercourse. In addition, King's research indicates that many students at Catholic colleges and universities do not talk about sexual assault candidly. They fail to see, as King does, that "sexual assault is an extension of stereotypical hookup culture, which exerts a subtle social coercion on everyone."[229]

Although based upon a small sampling of Catholic institutions, Nicole Sotelo has shown that sexual assaults are indeed reported on Catholic campuses. In 2009 eleven cases were reported at Boston College. Even Ave Maria University, which does not allow visitation between sexes in dormitories, had two reported cases. Sotelo's survey also included the Catholic University of America (2 cases), Dominican University in Illinois (1 case), and Franciscan University of Steubenville (0).[230] According to the most recent data available in the US Department of Education campus safety and security database, twenty-seven cases of sexual assault (rape or nonconsensual fondling) were reported at Boston College in 2015. Ave Maria University had no reported cases. The remaining universities mentioned in Sotelo's original 2011 article reported sexual assault cases as follows in 2015: University of Notre Dame (21), the Catholic University of America (8), Franciscan University of Steubenville (3), and Dominican University in Illinois (0).[231]

This limited dataset obviously shows a large degree of variance between Catholic institutions. In fact, Catholic institutions appear on self-described lists of the nation's safest campuses and most dangerous campuses.[232] However, some experts caution that comparisons of campus safety based on reported cases are unreliable given large gaps in data, as the vast majority of sexual assaults and rapes go unreported.[233] According to a 2017 White House Task Force on Sexual Assault report, only 7 percent of students who had been raped reported the incident to school authorities. Less than one quarter of reported cases are reflected in the Department of Education's data.[234] In other words, only a tiny fraction of campus sexual assaults and rapes are reflected in official statistics. Many more people suffer this terrible violence on our campuses, including Catholic campuses.

To bring sexual violence into the light, the federal government has urged colleges and universities to undertake campus climate surveys, which are believed to more accurately reflect the prevalence of sexual violence on campus.[235] Institutions can obtain a free survey instrument at the Department of Justice website.[236] Although many institutions choose not to reveal the survey results to the public, some Catholic institutions have done so. Just as with the number of reported offenses, the most recent survey responses at Catholic institutions exhibit variance. For example, at the University of St. Joseph in Connecticut, 0 percent of respondents reported having experienced sexual assault. However, the response rate among undergraduate students for this section of the survey was only 7 percent.[237] At Regis College in Weston, Massachusetts, 8 students reported being sexually assaulted, with a survey response rate of 10.5 percent.[238] The survey at Saint Mary's College, Notre Dame, Indiana, had a 33 percent response rate and indicated that 9.5 percent of respondents reported being sexually assaulted. The results at Saint Mary's were contextualized to compare with rates at the other forty-nine institutions participating in the same Higher Education Data Sharing (HEDS) 2015–16 campus climate survey. At these institutions, 12 percent of women respondents reported being victims of sexual assault. The rate among women respondents to the American Association of Universities (AAU) survey was even higher, at 23 percent.[239]

In a 2016 report, the Catholic University of America summarized its findings as follows: "Catholic University is similar to other colleges in its rates of sexual assault, types of sexual assault, underreporting of assaults by victims, and the role of alcohol in assaults." The report states that 15 percent of female respondents were sexually assaulted, with 6 percent involving nonconsensual sexual intercourse.[240] In a summary of its most recent survey, Notre Dame acknowledged that "6 percent of women and 2 percent of men report they have personally experienced nonconsensual sexual intercourse, and 19 percent of women and 4 percent of men experienced other forms of nonconsensual sexual contact" even though the university has implemented a number of approaches to eliminate sexual violence on campus.[241] Georgetown University's first sexual assault campus climate survey had a 51 percent response rate and revealed that one out of three female undergraduates experienced "nonconsensual sexual contact," with 14 percent of those involving rape. Georgetown's results exceed the AAU survey averages for sexual assault and response rates, which are 23 percent and 19 percent respectively.[242]

These sexual assault climate survey results should be considered carefully, as they can be interpreted in multiple ways. Some observers maintain that higher numbers of reported cases indicate the weakening of a culture of silence and secrecy around sexual violence on campus.[243] Higher response rates may also yield a higher incidence of sexual assault. Regardless, each instance of sexual assault, reported or unreported, denigrates the dignity of the victim and hinders her or his ability to thrive in the university community. Catholic colleges and universities cannot hide from this issue. *The Catechism of the Catholic Church* deems rape a grave, intrinsic evil that violates the right to "respect, freedom and physical and moral integrity" belonging to every human person.[244] It should be obvious that Catholic institutions of higher learning must do everything in their power to confront sexual assault and to avoid the failures in prevention, reporting, prosecuting, and healing perpetrated by the Catholic Church itself.[245] Catholic institutions should be commended for undertaking the sexual violence campus climate surveys. Those schools that make the results publicly available have gone a helpful step further. Transparency and critical self-examination are preconditions for addressing the problem of sexual violence on campus.[246]

Unfortunately, some Catholic institutions of higher education have come under scrutiny for their mishandling of sexual assault cases in the recent past. For example, after a high-profile case in 2010, the Office for Civil Rights of the Department of Education (OCR) determined the University of Notre Dame needed to do more to ensure that cases were treated properly and with due concern for victims. In 2011, the district attorney of Milwaukee criticized Marquette University for not reporting sexual assault cases quickly enough to the authorities.[247] As of this writing, *The Chronicle of Higher Education* Title IX database lists several Catholic institutions under investigation by the OCR for potentially mishandling sexual assault cases.[248]

The failure of some Catholic institutions to properly report and handle sexual assault cases may be rooted in the desire to disavow sexual promiscuity on their campuses. Donna Freitas contends that religiously affiliated institutions that are "heavily invested in proving . . . that sex does not happen on campus" have great difficulty handling sexual assault cases and prevention.[249] Having visited close to fifty Catholic campuses, she concludes that "too often" discussions about sex and sexual assault remain taboo. Furthermore, faculty and staff who problematize issues like sexual assault on Catholic campuses are sometimes ostracized.[250] Echoing Freitas, Elisabeth Vasko maintains that "on religiously affiliated campuses, in the balance is a shying away from the full spectrum of public discourse regarding sexuality, gender identity, and religion. This becomes especially tricky for schools whose marketing strategy and religious identity is tied to traditional notions of chastity and heteronormativity."[251]

The Obama administration's 2011 "Dear Colleague" letter reminded all colleges and universities of their legal "responsibility to take immediate and effective steps to end sexual harassment and sexual violence."[252] Since then some Catholic institutions have taken up this responsibility with more vigor and greater results. Notre Dame has instituted a number of proven approaches, including a "preponderance of evidence" standard and maximum sixty days for adjudicating sexual assault cases.[253] Other campus-wide initiatives include a Committee on Sexual Assault Prevention, a Gender Relations Center, and the adoption of the Green Dot approach to sexual violence prevention, which emphasizes bystander intervention.[254] Marquette University has also transformed its approach to sexual violence on campus in similar, results-oriented ways. The University of Dayton, Boston College, Georgetown, DePaul University, and the Catholic University of America have also adopted bystander intervention programs similar to Green Dot.[255] Attorney and expert consultant Brett Sokolow lauds the University of San Diego for adopting a holistic approach to sexual assault prevention that employs "the ecological model, social norming, bystander intervention and antioppression work." Victim advocates have praised Holy Cross, which adopted an "affirmative consent" policy already in 1998 after being advised by Sokolow. The student handbook thoroughly explains the policy over six pages of text.[256]

Experts maintain that Green Dot and other similar programs that emphasize bystander intervention programs have demonstrated they can reduce the prevalence of sexual violence on campuses.[257] Joy Galarneau and Shannon O'Neill, both administrators at Siena College, have described the merits of bystander intervention training programs and demonstrated how such programs cohere with Catholic social teaching.[258] I cannot rehearse Galarneau and Shannon's compelling arguments for the synergy between bystander intervention education (BIE) and the mission of Catholic universities here. Their informative article, which also concretely illustrates how Siena has effectively addressed sexual violence on campus, serves as an excellent primer on this issue for Catholic institutions. Let it suffice to say, with Galarneau and O'Neill, that even though CST has not focused enough on sexual violence explicitly, CST's principles of human dignity, participation in the common good, solidarity, and the preferential option for the poor "support and strengthen BIE by deepening the potential active bystander's commitment to engaging in his or her community's sexual violence prevention efforts."[259] Moreover, "with a critical mass of buy-in, the mission-driven model of bystander intervention can empower communities to constructively inform the living tradition of CST."[260]

Aligning CST and the mission of Catholic universities with bystander intervention education is paramount. Bystander intervention flows directly from solidarity, which means that "we all really are responsible for all," as St. John Paul II put it.[261] Yet, Sokolow correctly identifies the need to incorporate additional approaches to the problem of sexual violence on campus. In his words, "to truly transform victim-blaming culture, we need to examine root constructs of masculinity and femininity, objectification of the human body, the continuum of sexual violence, and the deeper issues of what makes our society and our campuses rape-prone cultures. Very few campuses have the will to go that deep."[262] Thus, experts in disciplines such as psychology, sociology, political science, history, gender studies, philosophy, and theology must employ the tools of their disciplines to assist in decoding and dismantling the larger culture that breeds sexual violence. As Vasko argues, faculty must overcome the tendency to see sexual violence prevention as solely the purview of the Title IX coordinator and student affairs personnel.[263] Catholic institutions are blessed with a tradition that places concern for the dignity of the human person and the common good at the center of their mission, as Freitas contends. Yet, Catholic colleges and universities must heed her admonition to give fac-

ulty, students, and staff the freedom and space to rigorously and responsibly confront the problem of sexual violence on campus without fear of
negative repercussions.[264] In addition, the systems of assessment used to
evaluate faculty performance in the numbers-driven corporatized university should be changed to reward faculty who undertake this important
work. Currently, narrow notions of "productivity" compel faculty to undertake such endeavors "on top of" their putatively more primary work of
publishing in their field. I contend that a proper understanding of the mission of Catholic universities should rather recognize work such as confronting sexual violence, homophobia, transphobia, racism, sexism, and
all forms of exploitation and injustice on campus as central to faculty
workload, thereby eschewing narrow notions of scholarship and productivity. In 1990, Ernst Boyer called for embracing a more capacious understanding of scholarship in his book *Scholarship Reconsidered: The Priorities
of the Professoriate*. In his paradigm, confronting social problems like
sexual violence constitutes the "scholarship of application." Unfortunately, today many colleges and universities, including Catholic institutions, pay lip service to this language in rank and tenure standards but
essentially evaluate faculty by the prestige of the venues in which they
publish books and articles, not whether their scholarship serves the good
of humanity and the planet.[265]

Researchers and university administrators alike have questioned the
methodologies used in the numerous campus climate surveys available.[266]
Nonetheless, Catholic institutions must methodically obtain information
about sexual assault on campus and implement the best-known practices
to eliminate it. The neoliberal corporatized university's fixation on data may
be beneficial when it comes to the problem of sexual violence on campus.
Confronting the data that indicates this issue continues to be a problem
can be a first step in addressing it. However, it should always be re-
membered that real human beings and real suffering stand behind this
data. Furthermore, as I discussed earlier in this book, the corporatized
culture of the contemporary university obsesses over branding and marketing. As a result, colleges and universities will face pressure to deny or
downplay the fact that their campuses may not be safe for everyone. However, Catholicism's commitment to truth and the dignity of the human
person should always supersede the concern for tarnishing an institution's
reputation by confronting problems such as sexual violence on campus.
To recall once again the words of Blessed Jerzy Popiełuszko, human

dignity requires pursuing "the truth in every situation, even if it costs dearly."[267] In the university context, Dr. M. Shawn Copeland recalls a poignant conversation in which her students asked her how not to be coopted by the powers that be. Her response to those students rings true for all those who care about Catholic higher education: "You critically discern what is right—and you struggle to do it—no matter what it costs."[268] As I have shown, the problem of sexual violence represents but one of myriad challenging and complex issues facing Catholic higher education in the age of the neoliberal corporatized university. I hope that this book, albeit incomplete and imperfect, can serve as an impetus for those of us who are willing to promote the dignity and rights of all on our campuses and fidelity to the Catholic social tradition in fulfilling the mission of our universities.

Epilogue

A good deal of time has elapsed since I began working on this book. I have spoken in many venues about the issues treated in it, benefiting from conversations with generous colleagues. I have also dealt with some of the issues directly in the workplace. I am exhausted from confronting the issues I have discussed here. Those of us who confront rather than look away from the injustices of the corporatized university face the possibility of burnout, criticism, and even scorn. What I offer here in closing does not constitute a systematic or overarching conclusion. The best I can do, for many reasons, is to offer some final thoughts about where we are today and where we might be in the future of Catholic higher education.

Let me first say that I recognize the shortcomings of this book even more than I did when I undertook the project. I wish that I could have addressed them throughout the writing process. At a certain point I realized that a team of researchers is needed to do a fuller analysis of the problems I tried to tackle. My own vantage point, as I stated in the introduction, is obviously limited. Try as we may to reach some sort of objectivity, each observer of any phenomenon has his or her own biases. I regret if some of my biases confounded my ability to produce a better analysis of the situation in Catholic higher education. I tried to envision the problems from the vantage point of others. My training as a Christian ethicist equips me to subject problems to the scrutiny of the social teachings of the church, but it also limits my capacities in some ways. I am not an economist, sociologist, or statistician. I now recognize the complexity of the issues that challenge the stakeholders in US higher education generally, and Catholic higher education particularly, much better. This leads me to conclude that some of my arguments might be provisional. Encouraged by allies and colleagues, I decided that the need to forge ahead with this project outweighed its shortcomings. Not all readers will agree with my conclusions, in some cases perhaps with good reason. I can only hope that they do not doubt my motivation for writing this book: my sincere love for Catholic higher education and sense of duty to contribute to its enhancement.

While I recognize the limitations of my analysis, my conviction that Catholic higher education stands at a crossroads and must choose between allowing corporatization to run amok or becoming more authentically Catholic has persisted. Thankfully, more and more people both within the academy and beyond its walls are joining the growing chorus of critics of neoliberal, corporatized higher education for a while now. I am grateful for their research, advocacy, and efforts on their campuses to bring about change. Resistance to neoliberal higher education, which aspires solely to "producing producers," is rising from various quarters.[1] For certain, I have noticed some positive developments since I began my writing, many of which I tried to incorporate in this book. For example, more people are paying attention to the failure of many colleges and universities to open their doors to members of marginalized groups. Moreover, some institutions, including Catholic colleges and universities, have made serious efforts to increase the number of Pell-eligible and minoritized students since I first examined the problem. Some Catholic institutions, including my own, now better understand the need to accompany working-class and first-generation students once they arrive, if they are fortunate enough to overcome the significant admissions disadvantages they have in being accepted. The intensifying scrutiny of the abusive, multitiered employment system of academics, combined with the burgeoning unionization movement among adjunct professors and graduate students, has compelled institutions to confront the injustices associated with "adjunctification." In the last few years, the proportion of full-time professors compared to part-time professors has grown, which might be considered a success. However, the altered ratio has been more precipitated by a larger decline in the numbers of adjunct professors than the increase of full-time instructors. In other words, the overall size of the faculty at colleges and universities nationally continues to shrink, while other areas of personnel continue to grow.[2] Nonetheless, some part-time faculty have garnered better contracts with tangible improvements, even if their situation remains far from just in most cases.

Although there are victories to celebrate, many of the problems treated in this book remain. Thus, my concern for the dignity and rights of all members of our campus communities has not waned. Regular readers of outlets like *The Chronicle of Higher Education* and *Inside Higher Ed* have surely stayed abreast of the ongoing issues, but the larger public has also become increasingly aware of serious flaws in higher education in the last few years. The 2019 college admissions scandals prompted a flurry of media attention and calls for reform of a "rigged" system utilized by glitterati to gain unfair advantages over the hoi polloi. While other politicians have augured it before, Bernie Sanders's and Elizabeth Warren's championing of free public higher education during the 2020 presidential campaign has resonated with millions of Americans who are buried under college debt and question why college should be affordable only for the rich (even if a slight majority of Americans oppose tuition-free college).[3] Respected higher education experts like William Deresiewicz have argued that only inexpensive or free college can end the neoliberal onslaught against higher education and restore its "intellectual and moral purposes" over the now ascendant "market purposes."[4]

As many pundits and experts have contended, the current model of higher education cannot survive. Whether or not free higher education represents the best solution exceeds my capacities here. I consciously ignored this question in my book, choosing to focus rather on the current system. What I can say with a fair degree of certitude is that public pressure will continue to push higher education leaders toward new and hopefully better paths to an equitable and sustainable system. In my judgement, Catholic higher education needs to find ways to remain afloat while stemming the "eliting phenomenon" occurring at too many of our institutions (some longer than others).[5] Looking back, this book did not grapple sufficiently with the financial exigency that forces some Catholic colleges to shutter their doors. I stand by my argument that in many cases a reallocation of budgets toward truly mission-oriented goals can help sustain Catholic colleges and institutions. However, I also recognize that claim can seem blithe to administrators who genuinely struggle to save their institutions. Unfortunately, I have little advice to offer them. Perhaps wealthier Catholic institutions should consider embodying solidarity with financially strapped Catholic colleges by sharing economic and other resources. This type of solidarity would appear to be all the more important for Catholic universities that refuse to more fully embrace aspects of their mission (by, for example, bending too much to ranking systems). Catholic institutions that have chosen to become elite (perhaps succumbing to pressure from alumni) should at least help enable smaller Catholic colleges more expansively serving the needs of the marginalized to survive. This idea may seem quixotic to some higher education administrators and experts, but it reflects Catholic social teaching's principle of solidarity, by which "we really are responsible for all."[6]

The December 2019 Democratic presidential debate also shined a national spotlight on the ongoing dispute about pay and benefits of food service workers on a Catholic campus. All seven presidential candidates pledged not to participate in the debate unless a fair resolution was reached between the union representing the workers and the campus food supplier, Sodexo.[7] This imbroglio awakened many Americans to the fact that working on a college campus is sometimes little better than working in a sweatshop. Undoubtedly, this news did not ameliorate the already negative public perception that US higher education suffers from today. Students and their parents increasingly question why student tuition is exorbitant when some of the people who teach them, serve them food, maintain their living quarters, and keep them safe on campus cannot pay their bills or see a doctor.[8] As I said earlier in this book, this situation does an injustice to everyone involved and weakens the credibility of Catholic social teaching and the church more broadly. If Catholic educators want to preserve the integrity of their tradition, they must continue to seek ways to ensure that their institutions practice what they teach.

As I close my reflections on Catholic higher education, I want to return to an issue that I mentioned in passing but did not discuss in any detail in the discussion on worker justice on campus. Over time I have become more greatly attuned to the fact that the neoliberal corporatized university runs people from all levels of the organization into the ground. In addition, minoritized people encounter particular burdens that others evade, but the culture of the neoliberal corporatized university harms all people. It fails to reflect the concern for the dignity of human persons and their well-being and the dignity of work so powerfully expounded in the Catholic social tradition. The grind of working in a corporatized university stifles human flourishing in myriad ways. In recent decades, the mental and spiritual health of students has rightly surfaced as a prominent concern on our campuses. However, much less attention has been paid to the deleterious effects of university life on the well-being of faculty, administrators, and staff. On a personal note, I once told a colleague that the "publish or perish" demands, along with teaching and institutional service responsibilities, forced me to deny my bodiliness in some ways (prior to graduate school, I was an avid rower and runner, which for reasons left unstated here surprises many of my colleagues). The constant need to use a computer or other information and communication technologies to write, prepare lessons, assess student work, answer emails etc. is both unnatural and detrimental to one's health in numerous ways. Almost 50 percent of frequent computer users experience musculoskeletal problems.[9] My body has been no exception. Mental health issues have also become more prevalent among academics.[10] Yet a stigma regarding mental health care persists among academics, who feign imperviousness to the stressors of academe for fear of being deemed an impostor by their colleagues or students.[11] Unfortunately, too many of us have become practitioners of the "religion of workism." As a recent article in *The Atlantic* opined, "work has morphed into a religious identity—promising transcendence and community, but failing to deliver."[12] As we worship at the altar of this new religion, we pretend that it is salubrious and fulfilling for us, while we are suffering from spiritual, mental, and physical decay. In their illuminating book *The Slow Professor*, Berg and Seeber address the notion that many of us feel that we cannot succeed in the academy because we are inferior. However, the research revealed to them that these problems are systemic. Those of us who experience burnout, or close to it at times, are not inferior. We are human, and we are being stretched to the limits by an inhumane system.

As I have argued in this book, Catholic institutions of higher education are not much better, if at all, at shedding the ethos of neoliberalism that confers status and meaning based on economic benefit and productivity. The Catholic tradition insists that work is "for us." Human beings are not made "for work." As St. John Paul II contends, the "subjective dimension of work" confers its meaning; it is valuable insofar as it helps us and our communities to grow as human beings and flourish.[13] Work must help us to grow spiritually and emotionally so that we can serve God's purposes, which are vastly different than the purposes of the neoliberal market economy. Christian ethicist and writer Jonathan Malesic has helpfully shared his own experience with burnout at a Catholic university. I imagine that many readers will empathize with his account, whether they are administrators, students, faculty, or staff. Malesic cautions us against the "mythos, the noble lie" bandied by neoliberalism's adherents to hoodwink dedicated workers: If we are truly passionate about our work, it cannot possibly lead to exhaustion and we should experience it as a source of unadulterated joy. Malesic also encourages us to see in St. Thomas Aquinas a "companion" to those who encounter burnout. Following the Dominican scholar Joseph Weisheipl, Malesic writes that Aquinas "worked himself to the point of collapse" by engaging in deep, caring work for the good of the church and humanity. The Angelic Doctor's work was, in many ways, not unlike our own in today's Catholic colleges and universities.[14]

Succinctly put, the success of our colleges and universities should not primarily be measured by what we do (i.e., what we produce or achieve), but by the *quality of our relationships*. Above all, Catholic educators should prioritize our relationships with our students and one another. This is, I believe, what St. John Paul II meant in *Ex Corde Ecclesiae* by referring to a university "animated by the spirit of Christ." The neoliberal, corporatized university threatens this vision, and those of us who wish to foster it in our communities, by prioritizing metrics and prestige over people. May we learn how to avail ourselves of the wisdom of the Catholic social tradition to overcome this problem. If this book has made some contribution to this endeavor, it will have been worth the toil.

Will the corporatized model expand its reach throughout our campus life, or will we be able to stem corporatization? Will we be able to hearken to CST effectively, among other means, to resist it? On a practical level, building relationships founded on trust on our campuses is crucial. We need first to overcome our isolation in our "university silos" and our suspicion of one another, as James Keenan, SJ, has argued.[15] We also should first seek areas of agreement and possible compromise, as social psychology reveals that beginning difficult conversations with hostile conflicts usually leads to retrenchment.[16] The task is daunting for a number of reasons, including the ignorance of or antipathy toward Catholicism generally among a fair number of students, faculty, and administrators at Catholic colleges and universities. I initially learned about the distorted view of Catholicism as inimical to rigorous thinking as a graduate student at Boston College. Since then I have heard about or witnessed this prejudice firsthand more than once. Unfortunately, I cannot propose a panacea. It seems to me that sustained, patient, and collegial conversation about the Catholic intellectual tradition and the mission and identity of Catholic universities remains as important as ever. Moreover, hiring committees will need to take hiring for mission even more seriously than they have in the past. To reiterate, this does not require hiring only Catholics. Rather, hiring committees should seek candidates that share values with the Catholic social tradition. Feminist and womanist thinkers, for example, can be strong allies in the struggle against neoliberal corporatized education.[17] On a related note, I have learned that good will exists among many administrators, trustees, faculty and staff, while some members of each category present obstacles. Early in my career, I thought the situation was mainly a conflict between faculty and administrators. However, I now believe that some faculty embrace neoliberal education, while some administrators reject it in favor of mission-oriented education and vice-versa. Once again, social psychology can point toward solutions. Innovating institutional accountability structures to more prominently reward service to the mission, as I have argued in various places throughout this book, can encourage us to hold each other accountable to the mission rather than benchmarks rooted in neoliberalism.[18]

Although compromise is necessary, there are times when "prophetic obedience" to the values of the Catholic social tradition requires organizing effective resistance to the commodification and corporatization of Catholic higher education. Theologian Brad Hinze correctly maintains that many religious believers, particularly Catholics, are often "conflict averse." His ruminations about the need for "prophetic obedience" to promote a more "dialogical church" pertain, in my judgment, equally to Catholic higher education in the age of the corporatized university, which, like the church, often lacks transparency. Practicing prophetic obedience "requires cultivating practices that favor talking through difficult matters when they arise with patience, generosity of spirit, tact and honesty. To enact these skills requires avoiding polarizing postures. At times it may necessitate taking a stand against authoritarian or paternalistic personalities. . . . It may demand vigilant resistance to mob mentalities or groupthink bred by cliques with special interests or elites with special knowledge, without denying the quest for collective wisdom, oriented toward honest consensus."[19] Thus "prophetic obedience" to the Catholic social tradition resembles in some ways what the American Association of University Professors describes as shared governance. In short, all stakeholders at Catholic colleges and universities must overcome their lethargy, fear, paternalism, or autocratic tendencies to cooperate in promoting the common good in higher education. When the common good in higher education is pursued, the dignity and rights of all members of our university communities will be genuinely respected.[20]

Appendix

*Embodying Catholic Social Teaching on
Campus Sample Questionnaire*

PREPARED BY GERALD J. BEYER

*Please circle the response that best describes your view for each question. Any
further insights or explanations you wish to offer can be written in the comments section under each question. Please read each question carefully, as
they may at first glance appear to repeat the previous question.*

*Depending on your role at your institution, you may not feel that you are suited
to answer a particular section of the questionnaire. Please circle "don't know" to
each of those questions rather than simply moving on to the next section.*

Section A. The Right to a Just Wage (at a Minimum, a Living Wage)

1. My college/university has regulations requiring the payment of wages
above minimum wage, such as a living wage policy.

Strongly Agree   Agree   Disagree   Strongly Disagree
Don't Know   Not Applicable

Comment (if available, please also provide a web link to the policy here):

2. A living wage policy exists at my institution, which covers all university
employees, including subcontracted workers.

Strongly Agree   Agree   Disagree   Strongly Disagree
Don't Know   Not Applicable

Comment:

3. A living wage policy exists at my institution, which covers all university
employees, including adjunct faculty.

Strongly Agree   Agree   Disagree   Strongly Disagree
Don't Know   Not Applicable

Comment:

4. If your institution has a living wage policy (or similar policy), how is the wage floor calculated and set? Who calculates it?

5. There have been efforts among students, staff, administrators and/or faculty to promote discussions about fair/just wages at my institution.

Strongly Agree   Agree   Disagree   Strongly Disagree
Don't Know   Not Applicable

Comment:

6. Conversations about living wages have led to positive changes in the way workers are compensated.

Strongly Agree   Agree   Disagree   Strongly Disagree
Don't Know   Not Applicable

Comment:

7. These conversations have led my institution to move toward paying living wages for all employees.

Strongly Agree   Agree   Disagree   Strongly Disagree
Don't Know   Not Applicable

Comment:

8. All workers employed or subcontracted by my institution are able to provide for their basic necessities (and those of their dependents, if they have any) with the wages they make at this one job.

Strongly Agree   Agree   Disagree   Strongly Disagree
Don't Know   Not Applicable

Comment:

9. All workers employed or subcontracted by my institution earn enough money to live a life with dignity.

Strongly Agree   Agree   Disagree   Strongly Disagree
Don't Know   Not Applicable

Comment:

Section B. The Rights to Unionize, Collective Bargaining and Participation in Decision-Making

1. Workers at my institution are free to join a union, without punishment or negative treatment by the employer.

Strongly Agree   Agree   Disagree   Strongly Disagree
Don't Know   Not Applicable

Comment:

2. Some staff members at my institution have joined a union.

Strongly Agree   Agree   Disagree   Strongly Disagree
Don't Know   Not Applicable

Comment:

3. Some staff members at my institution tried to form a union but were blocked by the administration.

Strongly Agree   Agree   Disagree   Strongly Disagree
Don't Know   Not Applicable

Comment:

4. Adjunct faculty at my institution are unionized.

Strongly Agree   Agree   Disagree   Strongly Disagree
Don't Know   Not Applicable

Comment:

5. Adjunct faculty at my institution have tried to form a union but were blocked by the administration.

Strongly Agree   Agree   Disagree   Strongly Disagree
Don't Know   Not Applicable

Comment:

6. Administrators at my institution discourage unionization.

Strongly Agree   Agree   Disagree   Strongly Disagree
Don't Know   Not Applicable

Comment:

7. When employees (staff or faculty) act collectively, management penalizes them in some way.

Strongly Agree   Agree   Disagree   Strongly Disagree
Don't Know   Not Applicable

Comment:

8. My institution respects the right of all employees to bargain collectively for their wages and benefits.

Strongly Agree   Agree   Disagree   Strongly Disagree
Don't Know   Not Applicable

Comment:

9. If I had the choice, I would join a union.

Strongly Agree   Agree   Disagree   Strongly Disagree
Don't Know   Not Applicable

Comment:

10. If given the choice, I believe many staff at my institution would join a union.

Strongly Agree   Agree   Disagree   Strongly Disagree
Don't Know   Not Applicable

Comment:

11. Unionizing at my workplace is important to ensuring the dignity and fair treatment of workers.

Strongly Agree   Agree   Disagree   Strongly Disagree
Don't Know   Not Applicable

Comment:

12. The administration encourages employees to voice their opinions about workplace issues and listens to them.

Strongly Agree   Agree   Disagree   Strongly Disagree
Don't Know   Not Applicable

Comment:

Section C. The Right to Health Care and Other Benefits

1. My institution offers an affordable health care plan for me (and my dependents).

Strongly Agree   Agree   Disagree   Strongly Disagree
Don't Know   Not Applicable

Comment:

2. My institution offers an affordable health care plan for all employees (and their dependents).

Strongly Agree   Agree   Disagree   Strongly Disagree
Don't Know   Not Applicable

Comment:

3. My institution offers an affordable health care plan for adjunct faculty (and their dependents).

Strongly Agree   Agree   Disagree   Strongly Disagree
Don't Know   Not Applicable

Comment:

4. My institution extends tuition benefits to all employees and their dependents.

Strongly Agree   Agree   Disagree   Strongly Disagree
Don't Know   Not Applicable

Comment:

5. My institution provides free instruction designed to help its employees gain admission to the university.

Strongly Agree   Agree   Disagree   Strongly Disagree
Don't Know   Not Applicable

Comment:

6. My institution grants free access to other resources, such as use of the library, exercise, and recreational facilities, etc.

Strongly Agree   Agree   Disagree   Strongly Disagree
Don't Know   Not Applicable

Comment:

7. My institution guarantees paid maternity/paternity leave to all employees.

Strongly Agree   Agree   Disagree   Strongly Disagree
Don't Know   Not Applicable

Comment:

8. My institution pays into a retirement fund for all employees.

Strongly Agree   Agree   Disagree   Strongly Disagree
Don't Know   Not Applicable

Comment:

Section D. Racial and Gender Equity and Diversity on Campus

1. My institution has created policies to hire more administrators from minority racial groups.

Strongly Agree   Agree   Disagree   Strongly Disagree
Don't Know   Not Applicable

Comment:

2. My institution has succeeded in hiring more administrators from minority racial groups.

Strongly Agree   Agree   Disagree   Strongly Disagree
Don't Know   Not Applicable

Comment:

3. My institution has created policies to hire more female administrators.

Strongly Agree   Agree   Disagree   Strongly Disagree
Don't Know   Not Applicable

Comment:

4. My institution has succeeded in hiring more female administrators.

Strongly Agree   Agree   Disagree   Strongly Disagree
Don't Know   Not Applicable

Comment:

5. My institution has made good-faith efforts to higher more full-time faculty from minority racial groups.

Strongly Agree   Agree   Disagree   Strongly Disagree
Don't Know Not Applicable

Comment:

6. My institution has succeeded in hiring more full-time faculty from minority racial groups.

Strongly Agree   Agree   Disagree   Strongly Disagree
Don't Know   Not Applicable

Comment:

7. My institution has made good-faith efforts to higher more female full-time faculty.

Strongly Agree   Agree   Disagree   Strongly Disagree
Don't Know   Not Applicable

Comment:

8. My institution has succeeded in hiring more female, full-time faculty.

Strongly Agree   Agree   Disagree   Strongly Disagree
Don't Know   Not Applicable

Comment:

9. My institution has taken steps to increase racial diversity among the student body.

Strongly Agree   Agree   Disagree   Strongly Disagree
Don't Know   Not Applicable

Comment:

10. My institution has succeeded in increasing racial diversity among the student body.

Strongly Agree   Agree   Disagree   Strongly Disagree
Don't Know   Not Applicable

Comment:

11. My institution has taken steps to increase the number of students from economically disadvantaged backgrounds.

Strongly Agree   Agree   Disagree   Strongly Disagree
Don't Know   Not Applicable

Comment:

12. My institution has succeeded in increasing the number of students from economically disadvantaged backgrounds.

Strongly Agree   Agree   Disagree   Strongly Disagree
Don't Know   Not Applicable

Comment:

13. My institution requires administrators to attend training in hiring for diversity.

Strongly Agree   Agree   Disagree   Strongly Disagree
Don't Know   Not Applicable

Comment:

14. My institution requires department chairs to attend training and hiring for diversity.

Strongly Agree   Agree   Disagree   Strongly Disagree
Don't Know   Not Applicable

Comment:

15. My institution requires all employees to complete sexual harassment training.

Strongly Agree   Agree   Disagree   Strongly Disagree
Don't Know   Not Applicable

Comment:

Section E. Investment and Allocation of University Resources

1. My institution has a committee that attempts to ensure the university's financial resources are invested in a socially responsible manner.

Strongly Agree   Agree   Disagree   Strongly Disagree
Don't Know   Not Applicable

Comment (if available, please also provide a web link to the committee here):

2. My institution has a committee that attempts to ensure the university's financial resources are invested in a manner consistent with Catholic social teaching/moral principles.

Strongly Agree   Agree   Disagree   Strongly Disagree
Don't Know   Not Applicable

Comment (if available, please also provide a web link to the policy here):

3. Students and faculty have input (via a committee or other mechanism) in ensuring that the university's resources are invested in a manner consistent with Catholic social teaching/moral principles.

Strongly Agree   Agree   Disagree   Strongly Disagree
Don't Know Not Applicable

Comment:

4. There have been active divestment campaigns and/or sustained discussions on my campus to encourage the university to invest its financial resources in a socially responsible manner.

Strongly Agree   Agree   Disagree   Strongly Disagree
Don't Know   Not Applicable

Comment:

5. My institution allocates budget resources in a way that reflects the Catholic identity and mission of the university.

Strongly Agree   Agree   Disagree   Strongly Disagree
Don't Know   Not Applicable

Comment:

6. My institution spends financial resources disproportionately on unnecessary building projects/ infrastructure (e.g., luxury dorm suites for students, state-of-the-art athletic facilities)

Strongly Agree   Agree   Disagree   Strongly Disagree
Don't Know   Not Applicable

Comment:

7. My institution spends a disproportionate amount of money on athletic programs.

Strongly Agree   Agree   Disagree   Strongly Disagree
Don't Know   Not Applicable

Comment:

Acknowledgments

There are so many people who have helped me with this project that I will invariably forget some of them. I apologize that I cannot name all of them, but I hope all of you know that I am grateful to you. At various points, the project seemed an insurmountable hurdle. I could not have completed it without abundant assistance and encouragement.

Let me start by expressing my gratitude to the myriad educators who taught me over the years. I was fortunate enough to attend a grammar school run by the Sisters of St. Joseph and a Jesuit high school. Without the dedication of the teachers at these schools, I would not have been able to reach my potential as a student. As an undergraduate at Georgetown searching for meaning and purpose, several professors and priests took me under their wing and gently guided me along my arduous journey. I am grateful especially to Fr. Otto Hentz, SJ, Fr. William Watson, SJ, Alan Mitchell, James Donahue, and Frank Ambrosio, who taught me that Catholicism is compatible with a vibrant life of the mind, that God's love for us is limitless, and that I belonged. In graduate studies, my professors challenged me to avoid oversimplifications, seek the truth, and pursue justice. First among them is Fr. David Hollenbach, SJ, whose life and work continues to inspire me. Other professors who helped sharpen my thinking include Lisa Sowle Cahill; Fr. Thomas Massaro, SJ; Margaret Farley; Fr. James Keenan, SJ; Francine Cardman; Fr. Kevin Burke, SJ; Stephen Pope; Tom Ogletree; and the late Fr. Michael Buckley, SJ. These educators have done much to enhance Christian theology, the Catholic intellectual tradition, and Catholic education in the United States. I have also benefited from formal study and conversation over the last twenty-five years with the following teachers and scholars in Poland: Władysław Miodunka, Jan Lencznarowicz, Danuta Gałyga, Stanisław Mędak, Marta Kijewska-Trembecka, Janina Filek, Wojciech Bonowicz, Jarek Makowski,

Michał Łuczewski, Agnieszka Lekka Kowalik, Fr. Alfred Wierzbicki, and the late Fr. Józef Tischner.

My own education would not have been possible without the generosity of numerous donors and foundations. I have benefited from numerous scholarships, fellowships, and grants that enabled me to pursue further studies and research. I am especially grateful to the McShain family, the Flatley family, the Kosciuszko Foundation, and The Polish-US Fulbright Commission. Saint Joseph's University, Villanova University, and the Program for Research on Religion and Civil Society at the University of Pennsylvania all provided grants or research sabbaticals that facilitated bringing this project to fruition. The Villanova University Subvention of Publication Program covered the indexing cost.

During my career I have been fortunate to have a number of wonderful colleagues who have shared their expertise and/or friendship with me. At Saint Joseph's University, I count among them Paul Aspan, Bruce Wells, Gerard Jacobitz, Rob Moore, Melissa Logue, Jim Caccamo, Millie Feske, Joni Porreca, Beth Ford, Allen Kerkeslager, Peter Norberg, and Amy Lipton. Susan Clampet Lundquist, who admirably works for justice in the academy and beyond, has particularly tried to help me think through issues. Villanova Colleagues Stefanie Knauss and Katie Grimes read parts of the manuscript and shared helpful feedback, as did Mary Beth Yount from Neumann University. Tim Hanchin and I have had countless conversations about issues in higher education, and I am grateful for his wisdom. I have enjoyed collaborating with Tim Brunk and Kathryn GetekSoltis to promote just policies on our campus. We benefit from and build on the tremendous work of our former colleagues Barbara Wall, Sue Toton, and many other Villanova faculty, staff, and administrators. Tony Godzieba has been a friend who understands what it is like to come from the working-class Philly neighborhood of Port Richmond. Other colleagues to whom I am indebted include Massimo Faggioli, Peter Spitaler, Rick Eckstein, Christie Lang Hearlson, Fr. Alan Fitzgerald, OSA, Barbara Wall, Michael Levitan, Roger Van Allen, Beth Hassel, Bob Jantzen, Mark Doorley, Bernie Prusak, and Elizabeth Teleha. Students in my doctoral seminar "Ethics of Higher Education" have proven to be fruitful dialogue partners. Several graduate assistants helped with editing the manuscript citations: Aaron Thomassen, Eric Kindler, and Alexander Hurtsellers.

My former undergraduate student Yvonne Nguyen and her peers in the Villanova Student Labor Action Movement impress me and give me hope that young people are willing to utilize their formidable skills for the cause of justice. Recent Georgetown graduates and GU Kalmanovitz Initiative for Labor and the Working Poor (KI) staff members Nick Wertsch and Alex Taliadoros have taught me a great deal about working toward just employment policies in university settings. Joe McCartin, director of KI and esteemed labor historian, has also been a tremendous help. Kathleen Maas Weigert, a Georgetown faculty member during the just employment campaign and a professor at several other Catholic institutions, supported my work as well. My friends in Catholic Scholars for Worker Justice have encouraged me and modelled what it means to struggle for justice in the workplace. They include Joe Fahey, Sr. Mary Priniski, Joe Holland, Les Schmidt, Kerry Danner, Jack Trumpbour, and Don Carroll. A plethora of colleagues at various colleges and universities have also inspired me and lifted me up when I needed it, far too many to mention here. M. T. Davila, Bryan Massingale, Christine Firer Hinze, John Sheveland, Ki Joo Choi, Vince Miller, and Kristin Heyer deserve special mention and gratitude. After my youngest brother lost his battle with cancer in February 2018, I suffered a crisis of meaning. The Catholic Theological Ethics in the World Church conference in Sarajevo that summer was the blessing I needed to move forward in my work. I am grateful to Jim Keenan for creating the CTEWC network and allowing me to share in the incredible experience. At the conference itself, the words of the Sarajevo-based Youth for Peace, especially Elma Bešlić's reflections about being a child of war lucky enough to survive and undertake the difficult task of peacebuilding, rekindled my desire to work for justice.

The staff at Fordham University Press has been invaluable. Director Fred Nachbaur supported my project from the beginning and patiently waited for me to finish. He showed kind understanding when life events slowed me down. Catholic Practice in North America series editor John Seitz expeditiously provided constructive criticism and encouragement when needed. Will Cerbone always answered my queries quickly and in a friendly manner. David O'Brien, a distinguished historian and expert on Catholic higher education, read the entire manuscript and provided copious suggestions about how to improve it.

Finally, my family has exhibited saintly patience as I have labored to complete this book over what seems like an eternity. My in-laws Prof. Edward Feliksik and Dr. Krystyna Feliksik have provided me a wonderful place to regenerate in Poland and taught me much about education and their beloved homeland. My mother, Mary Beyer, continues to be my biggest cheerleader and to show unwavering faith in me. My daughter Julia, who was a grade schooler when this project started, has grown into an amazing teenager. I now rely on her to help me understand young people today, their vernacular, and how they understand social and political issues. I know that it is not easy to be the child of an academic, and I am grateful for Julia's love. My wife, Ania Feliksik, has sacrificed so much for our family. Though at times she let me know that this book stood between us and the great outdoors and a vacation, she continued to help and encourage me through the countless trials and tribulations. I would not have made it this far without her and remain forever indebted to her.

Notes

Preface

1. I elaborate on these issues in Gerald J. Beyer, "COVID-19 and Higher Education," *Catholic Theological Ethics in the World Church Forum*, June 1, 2020, https://catholicethics.com/forum/covid-19-and-higher-education/.

2. Maureen Groppe and Kristine Phillips, "From Coastal Cities to Rural Towns, Breadth of George Floyd Protests—Most Peaceful—Captured by Data," *USA Today*, June 10, 2020, https://www.usatoday.com/story/news/politics/2020/06/10/george-floyd-black-lives-matter-police-protests-widespread-peaceful/5325737002/.

Introduction

1. The McShain family has generously supported numerous Catholic institutions of higher learning and their students.

2. James L. Marsh, "The North American Jesuit University, Capitalism, and Empire as a Way of Life," in *Jesuit Education 21: Conference Proceedings on the Future of Jesuit Higher Education, 25 to 29 June 1999*, ed. Martin R. Tripole (Philadelphia: Saint Joseph's University Press, 2002), 45.

3. For examples of this critique, see Henry A. Giroux, *Neoliberalism's War on Higher Education* (Chicago: Haymarket Books, 2014); Willem Halffman and Hans Radder, "The Academic Manifesto: From an Occupied to a Public University," *Minerva* 53, no. 2 (2015), 165–87; Lawrence D. Berg, Edward H. Huijbens, and Henrik Gutzon Larsen, "Producing Anxiety in the Neoliberal University," *The Canadian Geographer / Le Géographe canadien* 60, no. 2 (2016): 168–80; Rakesh Khurana, *From Higher Aims to Hired Hands: The Social Transformation of American Business Schools and the Unfulfilled Promise of Management as a Profession* (Princeton: Princeton University Press, 2007), 363.

4. Jesuit Provincials of Latin America, "A Letter on Neoliberalism in Latin America," *Promotio Justitiae* 67 (1997): 48.

5. On the period between 1789 and 1960, see Philip Gleason, *Contending with Modernity: Catholic Higher Education in the 20th Century* (New York: Oxford University Press, 1995). From 1960 onward, see Alice Gallin, *Negotiating*

Identity: Catholic Higher Education since 1960 (Notre Dame, Ind.: University of Notre Dame Press, 2000).

6. Viktor Emil Frankl, *Man's Search for Meaning: An Introduction to Logotherapy* (Boston: Beacon Press, 1963), 104. I am not implying that the situation at Catholic higher education is as dire as what Frankl faced. Conversely, I am arguing that if people can choose to be good in such extreme circumstances, it is possible in less severe, albeit challenging, ones.

7. See Gerald J. Beyer, *Recovering Solidarity: Lessons from Poland's Unfinished Revolution* (Notre Dame, Ind.: University of Notre Dame Press, 2010), 106–12.

8. On the rise of lay boards and the reasons for it, see Gallin, *Negotiating Identity*, 42–47. Gallin reports that by 1992 almost 71 percent of all trustees at Catholic institutions were lay people, with 80 percent lay-leader held board chairs. Alice Gallin, "A Brief History of Trusteeship in Catholic Colleges and Universities. Unpublished Typescript," (Washington, D.C.: Association of Catholic Colleges and Universities). William Byron, SJ, states that 80 percent of board members are lay people at the nation's Jesuit colleges and universities. William Byron, "Essential Ingredients for Trusteeship at Today's Catholic Colleges," *Trusteeship*, September/October 2011, https://www.agb.org /trusteeship/2011/septemberoctober/essential-ingredients-for-trusteeship-at -todays-catholic-colleges.

9. See David J. O'Brien, *From the Heart of the American Church: Catholic Higher Education and American Culture* (Maryknoll, N.Y.: Orbis Books, 1994), 51–68. I personally heard Cardinal Peter Turkson state that the Vatican has no control over US Catholic universities at a conference in Rome on May 3, 2015.

10. See Gallin, *Negotiating Identity*, 18–20, 28–29, 42–47, 84, 89, 118–19, 24–26, 82. I am grateful to Professor David O'Brien for conveying to me the significance of this fact for my analysis in this book.

11. Ibid., 185.

12. Gleason, *Contending with Modernity*, 320.

13. O'Brien, *From the Heart of the American Church*, 68.

14. See Gallin, *Negotiating Identity*; Gleason, *Contending with Modernity*; Melanie M. Morey and John J. Piderit, *Catholic Higher Education: A Culture in Crisis* (New York: Oxford University Press, 2006). On the influence of ranking systems, see Patricia M. McDonough, "College Rankings: Democratized College Knowledge for Whom?," *Research in Higher Education* 39, no. 5 (1998), 513–37; and Goldie Blumenstyck, "The Ever-Growing World of College Rankings," *The Chronicle of Higher Education*, February 27, 2015, https://www .chronicle.com/article/the-ever-growing-world-of-college-rankings/.

15. See Chapter 2 of this book.

16. See Parker J. Palmer, *The Courage to Teach: Exploring the Inner Landscape of a Teacher's Life* (San Francisco, Calif.: Jossey-Bass, 1998), 17–25.

17. Feminist philosophers and theologians have debunked the arguments against experience. In appealing to my own experience, this book adopts a method similar Letty Russell's "spiral method" of theological inquiry, which she described in Letty M. Russell, *Church in the Round: Feminist Interpretation of the Church* (Louisville, Ky.: Westminster John Knox Press, 1993). M. Shawn Copeland has nicely summarized Russell's method as a "spiral-reflection on experience, an analysis of social reality, the questioning of biblical and church traditions, the pursuit of clues for transformation, and action on behalf of justice." M. Shawn Copeland, "Journeying to the Household of God: The Eschatological Implications of Method in the Theology of Letty Mandeville Russell," in *Liberating Eschatology: Essays in Honor of Letty M. Russell*, ed. Margaret A. Farley and Serene Jones (Louisville, Ky.: Westminster John Knox Press, 1999), 31. In this same vein, I have also been influenced by Margaret A. Farley, "The Role of Experience in Moral Discernment," in *Christian Ethics: Problems and Prospects*, ed. Lisa Sowle Cahill and James F. Childress (Cleveland, Ohio: Pilgrim Press, 1996).

18. For helpful discussions of this concept, see Suzanne C. Toton, *Justice Education: From Service to Solidarity* (Milwaukee, Wisc.: Marquette University Press, 2006), 22–26, 45–51; Daniel J. Daly, "Structures of Virtue and Vice," *New Blackfriars* 92, no. 1039 (2011), 341–57. Toton explains the relationship between structures and individuals, and the understanding of "structural and systemic evil" in the Bible. Daly traces the development of this concept in official Catholic teaching.

19. I make this claim based on my own experience, but others have echoed it. For example, Donna Freitas writes: "University higher-ups fear research that may directly challenge their own communities and the behavior of those communities, and actively work against faculty who take up such research." Donna Freitas, "Review of *University Ethics: How Colleges Can Build and Benefit from a Culture of Ethics*, by James F. Keenan," *Horizons* 44, no. 1 (2017): 177.

20. Agbonkhianmeghe E. Orobator, "*Caritas in Veritate* and Africa's Burden of (under)Development," *Theological Studies* 71, no. 2 (2010): 329–31.

21. This book in some ways resembles the work of the National Association of Church Personnel Administrators, which heeded the call of *Justitia in Mundo* by issuing the document "Just Treatment for Those Who Work in the Church" and examined the working conditions of church employees. Unlike this book, the analysis did not treat Catholic higher education. See National Association of Church Personnel Administrators, *Working in the Catholic Church* (Kansas City, Mo.: Sheed & Ward, 1993).

22. See the Catholic Scholars for Worker Justice website, http://www .catholicscholarsforworkerjustice.org/

23. See the Just Employment Policy website, http://www.justemployment policy.org/

24. I am indebted to Dr. Kathleen Maas Weigert for this term and for the support that she has given to this project.

25. See for example United States Conference of Catholic Bishops, "Socially Responsible Investment Guidelines" (November 12, 2003), http://www.usccb .org/about/financial-reporting/socially-responsible-investment-guidelines.cfm. On worker justice, see for example John Paul II, *Laborem Exercens* (September 14, 1992), http://www.vatican.va/content/john-paul-ii/en/encyclicals /documents/hf_jp-ii_enc_14091981_laborem-exercens.html. All papal encyclicals herein are cited from the Vatican website http://www.vatican.va /content/vatican/en.html unless otherwise noted.

26. I decided that the potential risk to interviewees outweighed the benefit of reporting their views in this book.

27. I hoped to disseminate a questionnaire to employees at Catholic colleges and universities. I ultimately decided that a major undertaking of this sort requires a team of interdisciplinary scholars and must await a future project. I include the questionnaire that I developed as an appendix to this book in order to demonstrate the kind of research I think needs to be done in the future.

28. See John XXIII, *Mater et Magistra*, in *Catholic Social Thought: The Documentary Heritage*, ed. David J. O'Brien and Thomas A. Shannon (Maryknoll, N.Y.: Orbis Books, 1992), 122, section 236. This method was originally proposed by Cardinal Joseph Cardijn, who founded the Young Christian Workers movement. See Marvin L. Krier Mich, *Catholic Social Teaching and Movements* (Mystic, Conn.: Twenty-Third Publications, 1998), 74.

29. See Hans-Georg Gadamer, *Truth and Method*, trans. Joel Weinsheimer and Donald G. Marshall, 2nd, rev. ed., Continuum Impacts (London: Continuum, 2004). Gadamer maintains that all people bring "prejudices" to their interpretation of texts, and to all of reality, in the act of understanding. However, dialogue can enhance understanding and produce a "fusion of horizons" (305).

30. Józef Tischner, *The Spirit of Solidarity*, trans. Marek B. Zaleski and Benjamin Fiore (San Francisco: Harper & Row, 1984), 11.

1. The Mission of Catholic Higher Education in the Age of the Corporatized University

1. Unless noted otherwise, I have changed the names of students, faculty, and staff to preserve their anonymity.

2. See United States Conference of Catholic Bishops, *Economic Justice for All: A Catholic Framework for Economic Life* in *Catholic Social Thought: The Documentary Heritage*, ed. David J. O'Brien and Thomas A. Shannon (Maryknoll, N.Y.: Orbis Books, 1992), no. 104: 603. The next chapter will discuss this issue in detail.

3. Johann-Baptist Metz and Jürgen Moltmann, *Faith and the Future: Essays on Theology, Solidarity, and Modernity* (Maryknoll, N.Y.: Orbis Book, 1995), 23. See also Thomas P. Rausch, *Educating for Faith and Justice: Catholic Higher Education Today* (Collegeville, Minn.: Liturgical Press, 2010), 64; and Glen Harold Stassen, *A Thicker Jesus: Incarnational Discipleship in a Secular Age*, 1st ed. (Louisville, Ky.: Westminster John Knox Press, 2012), 6–7.

4. Peter Steinfels, "Further Adrift: The American Church's Crisis of Attrition," *Commonweal*, October 22, 2010, https://www.commonwealmagazine.org /further-adrift. Steinfels discusses the data from the 2008 Pew Forum on Religion and Public Life's U.S. Religious Landscape Survey.

5. See Rausch, *Educating for Faith and Justice*, 58–75. Rausch reviews numerous recent studies of young adult Catholics.

6. Dean R. Hoge, *Young Adult Catholics: Religion in the Culture of Choice* (Notre Dame, Ind.: University of Notre Dame Press, 2001), 224. Cited in Rausch, *Educating for Faith and Justice*, 74.

7. An important study maintains that conservative politics and hypocrisy are two of the main factors that have driven many young people away from Christianity, especially from Evangelical Protestantism. See Robert D. Putnam and David E. Campbell, *American Grace: How Religion Divides and Unites Us* (New York: Simon & Schuster, 2010). See also David E. Campbell and Robert Putnam, "God and Caesar in America: Why Mixing Religion and Politics Is Bad for Both," *Foreign Affairs*, March/April, 2012, https://www.foreignaffairs .com/articles/united-states/2012-02-12/god-and-caesar-america.

8. See John Paul II, *Ex Corde Ecclesiae* (August 15, 1990), part II, art. 4, §5, http://www.vatican.va/holy_father/john_paul_ii/apost_constitutions /documents/hf_jp-ii_apc_15081990_ex-corde-ecclesiae_en.html.; John Paul II, *Centesimus Annus* (May 1, 1991), no. 5, http://www.vatican.va/content/john-paul -ii/en/encyclicals/documents/hf_jp-ii_enc_01051991_centesimus-annus.html; Benedict XVI, *Caritas in Veritate* (June 29, 2009), nos. 5, 9, 30, 31, 45, http:// www.vatican.va/content/benedict-xvi/en/encyclicals/documents/hf_ben-xvi _enc_20090629_caritas-in-veritate.html; United States Catholic Conference of Bishops, *Sharing Catholic Social Teaching: Challenges and Directions*, 1998, http://www.usccb.org/beliefs-and-teachings/what-we-believe/catholic-social -teaching/sharing-catholic-social-teaching-challenges-and-directions.cfm.

9. See United States Catholic Conference of Bishops, *Sharing Catholic Social Teaching*. This document states, "if Catholic education and formation fail to communicate our social tradition, they are not fully Catholic."

10. See John Paul II, *Ex Corde Ecclesiae*, nos. 31–37.

11. See William C. Spohn, "Developing a Moral Conscience in Jesuit Higher Education," in *Jesuit Education 21: Conference Proceedings of the Future of Jesuit*

Higher Education, ed. Martin R. Tripole (Philadelphia: Saint Joseph's University, 2000), 393. On this point, see also Stassen, *A Thicker Jesus: Incarnational Discipleship in a Secular Age*, 8.

12. Rick Malloy, "Why Not Us? Making Our Jesuit Universities and Colleges Moral Institutions," in *Jesuit Education 21*, 213.

13. Ibid., 214.

14. David L. Kirp, *Shakespeare, Einstein, and the Bottom Line: The Marketing of Higher Education* (Cambridge, Mass.: Harvard University Press, 2003), 2.

15. James F. Keenan, *University Ethics: How Colleges Can Build and Benefit from a Culture of Ethics* (Lanham, Md.: Rowman & Littlefield, 2015), 85.

16. Benedict XVI, "Meeting with Catholic Educators: Conference Hall of the Catholic University of America in Washington, D.C." (April 17, 2008), http://w2.vatican.va/content/benedict-xvi/en/speeches/2008/april/documents/hf_ben-xvi_spe_20080417_cath-univ-washington.html.

17. See ibid.

18. Rick Malloy, "The Truly Catholic University," *America*, October 11, 2004, https://www.americamagazine.org/issue/499/article/truly-catholic-university. Malloy aptly states, "Capitalism makes demands on their lives. Students tremble at the thought of never getting a high-paying job, yet salvation in Christ is a vague notion at best. The gospel of Donald too often trumps the call of the good news of Jesus."

19. Andrew Delbanco argues that most students expect college to be a "playground of unregulated freedom." See Andrew Delbanco, *College: What It Was, Is, and Should Be* (Princeton, N.J.: Princeton University Press, 2012), 17–24, 138–49. For a more comprehensive discussion of this culture, see the chapter "Undergraduates Acting Badly" in Keenan, *University Ethics*, 97–124.

20. Rick Malloy, "Liberating Students—from Paris Hilton, Howard Stern, and Jim Beam," in *A Jesuit Education Reader*, ed. George W. Traub (Chicago, Ill.: Loyola Press, 2008), 301.

21. Keenan, *University Ethics*, 121.

22. Murray A. Sperber, *Beer and Circus: How Big-Time College Sports Is Crippling Undergraduate Education*, 1st ed. (New York: Henry Holt, 2000). Sperber also rightly maintains that there are other subcultures, such as the academic one, but they coexist with the often dominant culture at many universities: the "Beer and Circus" culture. On Catholic universities in particular, see Joseph A. Califano, "Wasting the Best and the Brightest," *America*, May 28, 2007. Another resource is Jason E. King, *Faith with Benefits: Hookup Culture on Catholic Campuses* (New York: Oxford University Press, 2016).

23. See Delbanco, *College*, 135–49. See also Cary Nelson and Stephen Watt, *Office Hours: Activism and Change in the Academy* (New York: Routledge, 2004),

117–37; Kirp, *Shakespeare, Einstein, and the Bottom Line*, 23–24. Nelson and Watt's chapter, which deals with expenditures on nonacademic building projects such as golf courses, is fittingly titled "Is It a University or Is It a Country Club?"

24. Henry Steck, "The Corporatization of the University: Seeking Conceptual Clarity," *Annals of the American Association of Political Science* 585 (2003): 74.

25. I draw here on Steck, "The Corporatization of the University," 75–76, and Delbanco, *College*, 140–43. See also Joe Berry, *Reclaiming the Ivory Tower: Organizing Adjuncts to Change Higher Education* (New York: Monthly Review Press, 2005), 3–4; Keenan, *University Ethics*, 173–200; "How The American University was Killed, in Five Easy Steps," The Homeless Adjunct Blog, August 12, 2012, http://junctrebellion.wordpress.com/2012/08/12/how-the -american-university-was-killed-in-five-easy-steps/.

26. Marc Bousquet, *How the University Works: Higher Education and the Low-Wage Nation* (New York: New York University Press, 2008), 25. Bousquet discusses other studies that describe "academic capitalism."

27. For a more extensive treatment of the commodification of higher education, see Kirp, *Shakespeare, Einstein, and the Bottom Line*; Delbanco, *College*, 140–44; Keenan, *University Ethics*, 173–200; E. Wayne Ross and Rich Gibson, ed., *Neoliberalism and Education Reform* (Cresskill, N.J.: Hampton Press, 2007).

28. David M. Perry, "Faculty Members Are Not Cashiers," *The Chronicle of Higher Education*, March 17, 2014, https://www.chronicle.com/article/Faculty -Members-Are-Not/145363.

29. Douglas Belkin, "Using Salary Prospects to Choose a College Major," *Wall Street Journal*, March 17, 2014, https://www.wsj.com/articles/should-salary -prospects-guide-the-choice-of-a-college-major-1394808081; Melissa Korn, "Colleges Are Tested by Push to Prove Graduates' Career Success," *Wall Street Journal*, March 17, 2014, https://www.wsj.com/articles/colleges-are-tested-by -push-to-prove-graduates-career-success-1395013628.

30. See Delbanco, *College*, 148–49. Respondents to A New America Foundation 2015 study stated that the top three reasons for going to college are: "1) To improve my employment opportunities; 2) To make more money; and 3) To get a good job." However, it is also noteworthy that 85 percent and 81 percent of respondents said that "to learn more about a favorite topic or area of interest" and "to become a better person" were very important or important reasons. Rachel Fishman, "Deciding to Go to College: 2015 College Decisions Survey: Part I," New America Foundation (2015), 4, https://www.newamerica .org/education-policy/policy-papers/deciding-to-go-to-college/.

31. Kirp, *Shakespeare, Einstein, and the Bottom Line*, 24.

32. Keenan, *University Ethics*, 173.

33. Henry A. Giroux, *Neoliberalism's War on Higher Education* (Chicago: Haymarket Books, 2014), 20.

34. Jeffrey R. Brown, "How Endowment Hoarding Hurts Universities," *The Chronicle of Higher Education*, March 17, 2014, https://www.chronicle.com/article /How-Endowment-Hoarding-Hurts/145343/.

35. Kirp, *Shakespeare, Einstein, and the Bottom Line*, 3. See also Keenan, *University Ethics*, 175.

36. Bousquet, *How the University Works*, 20–22.

37. Ibid., 21. See also Berry, *Reclaiming the Ivory Tower*, 3. Berry argues that education has been largely transformed to provide a trained workforce to private businesses.

38. Kirp, *Shakespeare, Einstein, and the Bottom Line*, 4.

39. David Hill, "Educational Perversion and Global Neoliberalism," in *Neoliberalism and Education Reform*, ed. E. Wayne Ross and Rich Gibson (Cresskill, N.J.: Hampton Press, 2007), 119–20. See also Rakesh Khurana, *From Higher Aims to Hired Hands: The Social Transformation of American Business Schools and the Unfulfilled Promise of Management as a Profession* (Princeton: Princeton University Press, 2007). I discuss the problem of business schools and corporatized universities more extensively in Gerald J. Beyer, "Curing the 'Disease' in Corporatized Higher Education: Prescriptions from Catholic Social Thought," in *Working Alternatives: American and Catholic Experiments in Work and Economy*, ed. John Seitz and Christine Firer Hinze (New York: Fordham University Press, 2020), 148–88.

40. Bousquet, *How the University Works*, 23. See also Benjamin Ginsberg, *The Fall of the Faculty: The Rise of the All-Administrative University and Why It Matters* (Oxford: Oxford University Press, 2011), 20–27.

41. John Curtis and Saranna Thornton, "Losing Focus: The Annual Report on the Economic Status of the Profession, 2013–14," American Association of University Professors (2014), 7–8, http://www.aaup.org/reports-publications /2013-14salarysurvey.

42. Bousquet, *How the University Works*, 23.

43. Ibid., 26–28.

44. Ginsberg, *The Fall of the Faculty*, 15; Giroux, *Neoliberalism's War on Higher Education*, 110–11. For a more detailed description of shared governance than I can provide here, see American Association of University Professors, American Council on Education, and Association of Governing Boards of Universities and Colleges, "Statement on Government of Colleges and Universities," (1966), https://www.aaup.org/report/statement-government-colleges-and-universities. I argue that shared governance correlates with Catholic social teaching's affirmation of the right to participation in Beyer, "Curing the 'Disease' in Corporatized Higher Education."

45. See American Association of University Professors, "Ralph S. Brown Award for Shared Governance," https://www.aaup.org/about/awards/ralph-s -brown-award-shared-governance.

46. Jack Stripling, "The Mount St. Mary's Presidency Was a Corporate Test Case. It Failed Miserably," *The Chronicle of Higher Education*, March 2, 2016, https://www.chronicle.com/article/The-Mount-St-Mary-s/235558. The president allegedly told faculty they should "drown the bunnies . . . put a Glock to their heads" when dealing with struggling students.

47. See Rudy Fichtenbaum, "From the President: After the Corporate University . . . Now What?," *Academe* (November/December 2012), https:// www.aaup.org/article/president-after-corporate-university-%E2%80%A6-now -what#.XffegGRKjcs; David Schultz, "The Rise and Demise of the Neo-Liberal University: The Collapsing Business Plan of American Higher Education," *Logos: A Journal of Modern Society and Culture* (September, 2012), http://logosjournal .com/2012/spring-summer_schultz/; Tarak Barkawi, "The Neoliberal Assault on Academia," *Al Jazeera*, April 25, 2013, https://www.aljazeera.com/indepth /opinion/2013/04/20134238284530760.html; Bousquet, *How the University Works*, 34–35, 193; Berry, *Reclaiming the Ivory Tower: Organizing Adjuncts to Change Higher Education*, 5; Jan Clausen and Eva Maria Swidler, "Academic Freedom from Below: Toward an Adjunct-Centered Struggle," *Journal of Academic Freedom* 4 (2013): 6–8. This last article discusses the role of international institutions such as the World Bank, IMF, and WTO in bringing the neoliberal revolution to universities.

48. Barkawi, "The Neoliberal Assault on Academia." Although not mentioned, the parallels to Naomi Klein's theory of "shock doctrine" are striking. See Naomi Klein, *The Shock Doctrine: The Rise of Disaster Capitalism* (New York: Picador, 2008).

49. Giroux, *Neoliberalism's War on Higher Education*, 21.

50. John Paul II, *Ecclesia in America* (January 22, 1999), no. 56, http://www .vatican.va/content/john-paul-ii/en/apost_exhortations/documents/hf_jp-ii_exh _22011999_ecclesia-in-america.html. I have written more extensively about neoliberalism and its history in Gerald J. Beyer, *Recovering Solidarity: Lessons from Poland's Unfinished Revolution* (Notre Dame, Ind.: University of Notre Dame Press, 2010).

51. See George Monbiot, "Neoliberalism—the Ideology at the Root of All Our Problems," *The Guardian*, April 15, 2016, https://www.theguardian.com /books/2016/apr/15/neoliberalism-ideology-problem-george-monbiot and George Monbiot, *How Did We Get into This Mess?: Politics, Equality, Nature* (London: Verso, 2017).

52. Keri Day, *Religious Resistance to Neoliberalism: Womanist and Black Feminist Perspectives* (New York: Palgrave Macmillan US, 2016), 4, 8–9. See also Jeremy

Gilbert, "Neoliberal Culture," *New Formations: a Journal of Culture/Theory/Politics* 80, no. 80 (2013).

53. Day, *Religious Resistance to Neoliberalism*, 4, 8–9; Monbiot, "Neoliberalism—the Ideology at the Root of All Our Problems."

54. Giroux, *Neoliberalism's War on Higher Education*, 2.

55. On the pervasive influence of neoliberalism, see the variegated essays introduced by Gilbert in this special journal issue on neoliberal culture: Jeremy Gilbert, "What Kind of Thing Is Neoliberalism?," *New Formations: a Journal of Culture/Theory/Politics* 80, no. 80 (2013): 7–22. For more on its effects on higher education, see Giroux, *Neoliberalism's War on Higher Education*; Ross and Gibson, *Neoliberalism and Education Reform*.

56. On the business community, see Hill, "Educational Perversion and Global Neoliberalism"; Khurana, *From Higher Aims to Hired Hands*; Jane Mayer, *Dark Money: The Hidden History of the Billionaires Behind the Rise of the Radical Right* (New York: Doubleday, 2016), 93–119; Jane Mayer, "How Right-Wing Billionaires Infiltrated Higher Education," *The Chronicle of Higher Education*, February 12, 2016, https://www.chronicle.com/article/how-right-wing-billionaires-infiltrated -higher-education/. On the IMF and World Bank, see Clausen and Swidler, "Academic Freedom from Below,"; Les Levidow, "Marketizing Higher Education: Neoliberal Strategies and Counter-Strategies," in *Neoliberalism and Education Reform*, ed. E. Wayne Ross and Rich Gibson (Cresskill, N.J.: Hampton Press, 2007).

57. For a more detailed account of the relationship between neoliberalism and corporatization than I can offer here, see Beyer, "Curing the 'Disease' in Corporatized Higher Education."

58. Michael J. Sandel, *What Money Can't Buy: The Moral Limits of Markets* (New York: Farrar, Straus and Giroux, 2012), 10; see also 48–51.

59. Ibid., 37–39.

60. John Paul II, *Centesimus Annus*, no. 40. See also nos. 34–35, 41–42.

61. Ibid., no. 41. Fr. Andrzej Szostek traces the pope's use the concept of alienation from his prepapal work *The Acting Person* through *Centesimus Annus*. He argues that John Paul appealed to alienation to criticize both socialism and the individualism that lies at the very foundation of capitalism. See Andrzej Szostek, "Alienacja—Wciaz Aktualny Problem," in *Jan Paweł II: Centesimus Annus, Tekst i Komentarze*, ed. Franciszek Kampka and Cezary Ritter (Lublin: Redakcja Wydawnictw KUL, 1998).

62. See Benedict XVI, *Caritas in Veritate*, nos. 35–36, 69; and Francis, "Address of Pope Francis to the New Nonresident-Ambassadors to the Holy See: Kyrgyzstan, Antigua and Barbuda, Luxembourg and Botswana" (May 16, 2013), http://www.vatican.va/holy_father/francesco/speeches/2013/may /documents/papafrancesco_20130516_nuovi-ambasciatori_en.html.

63. Francis, *Evangelii Gaudium* (November 24, 2013), no. 55, http://w2.vatican .va/content/francesco/en/apost_exhortations/documents/papa-francesco _esortazione-ap_20131124_evangelii-gaudium.html. Vincent Miller discusses how consumerism has pervaded religious identities, practices, and communities in Vincent Jude Miller, *Consuming Religion: Christian Faith and Practice in a Consumer Culture* (New York: Continuum, 2004).

64. The popes refer to the idolatry of the market, which is tantamount to what others have called "market fundamentalism." Stan Duncan defines market fundamentalism as "the slavish adherence to the principles of free markets as if they were unassailable dogma." In other words, it is a kind of "new religious faith." Stan G. Duncan, *The Greatest Story Oversold: Understanding Economic Globalization* (Maryknoll, N.Y.: Orbis Books, 2010), 44. See also Joerg Rieger, *No Rising Tide: Theology, Economics, and the Future* (Minneapolis: Fortress Press, 2009), 14–24.

65. See Rausch, *Educating for Faith and Justice*, 19.

66. David Hollenbach, "The Catholic University under the Sign of the Cross: Christian Humanism in a Broken World," in *Finding God in All Things*, ed. Stephen J. Pope (New York: Crossroad, 1996), 287.

67. See Hollenbach, who mentions his experience on multiple boards of trustees. On the ignorance of most Catholics of CST, see Paul Sullins, "Catholic Social Teaching: What Do Catholics Know, and What Do They Believe?," *Catholic Social Science Review* 7 (2003): 243–64.

68. Association of Jesuit Colleges and Universities, "Some Characteristics of Jesuit Colleges and Universities: A Self-Evaluation Instrument" (2012), http://www .ajcunet.edu/mission-documents/.

69. William Byron, "Essential Ingredients for Trusteeship at Today's Catholic Colleges," *Trusteeship*, September/October 2011, 4–5.

70. Alice Gallin, *Negotiating Identity: Catholic Higher Education since 1960* (Notre Dame, Ind.: University of Notre Dame Press, 2000), 119–20, 26.

71. See Kevin Kiley, "What's up with Boards These Days?," *Inside Higher Ed*, July 2, 2012, https://www.insidehighered.com/news/2012/07/02/trustees-are -different-they-used-be-and-uva-clashes-will-be-more-common.

72. See Laura McKenna, "Why Are Fewer College Presidents Academics?," *The Atlantic*, December 3, 2015, https://www.theatlantic.com/education/archive /2015/12/college-president-mizzou-tim-wolfe/418599/; Sonny Cheng, Jeffrey Selingo, Cole Clark, "Pathways to the University Presidency: The Future of Higher Education Leadership" (2017), https://www2.deloitte.com/insights/us /en/industry/public-sector/college-presidency-higher-education-leadership .html.

73. I spell this argument out more fully in Beyer, "Curing the 'Disease' in Corporatized Higher Education." While it may not be true about all board

members, there is a tendency to elitism among some that contradicts CST. See Jack Stripling and Benjamin Mueller, "College Trustees in Wall Street Club Clash with Campus Culture," *The Chronicle of Higher Education*, March 31, 2014, https://www.chronicle.com/article/College-Trustees-in-Wall/145621.

74. On this point, see Karol Wojtyła, *The Acting Person*, ed. Anna-Teresa Tymieniecka, trans. Andrzej Potocki, Analecta Husserliana, vol. 10 (Dordrecht/Boston: D. Reidel, 1979); Jacques Maritain, *The Person and the Common Good*, trans. John J. Fitzgerald (New York: C. Scribner's Sons, 1947); Catherine Mowry LaCugna, *God for Us: The Trinity and Christian Life*, 1st ed. (San Francisco, Calif.: HarperSanFrancisco, 1991); Michael J. Himes and Kenneth R. Himes, *Fullness of Faith: The Public Significance of Theology* (New York: Paulist Press, 1993), 56–61.

75. Khurana, *From Higher Aims to Hired Hands*, 19, 291, 343, 63, 70. For similar critiques, see Claus Dierksmeier, *Reframing Economic Ethics: The Philosophical Foundations of Humanistic Management*, Humanism in Business Series (Switzerland: Palgrave MacMillan, 2016), 2–3; Luigi Zingales, *A Capitalism for the People: Recapturing the Lost Genius of American Prosperity* (New York: Basic Books, 2012), 174–81.

76. See Amartya Sen, *On Ethics and Economics* (Oxford: Blackwell, 1987), 19; F. B. M. de Waal, *The Age of Empathy: Nature's Lessons for a Kinder Society* (New York: Harmony Books, 2009), 162–63. I discuss these anthropologies in more detail in Gerald J. Beyer, "Solidarity by Grace, Nature or Both? The Possibility of Human Solidarity in the Light of Evolutionary Biology and Catholic Moral Theology," *Heythrop Journal* 55, no. 5 (2013): 732–55.

77. Michael A. Pirson and Paul R. Lawrence, "Humanism in Business—Towards a Paradigm Shift?," *Journal of Business Ethics* 93, no. 4 (2010): 554.

78. On the anthropology of neoliberalism, see Day, *Religious Resistance to Neoliberalism*, 4–10; Gilbert, "Neoliberal Culture," 8. On management and business, see Pirson and Lawrence, "Humanism in Business," 554.

79. Pirson and Lawrence, "Humanism in Business," 557–58. Tarak Barkawi, who has been on the faculty at US and British institutions, characterizes higher education in this manner. See Barkawi, "The Neoliberal Assault on Academia."

80. Keenan, *University Ethics*, 65.

81. F. B. M. de Waal, *Our Inner Ape: A Leading Primatologist Explains Why We Are Who We Are* (New York: Riverhead Books, 2005), 243; Stephen J. Pope, *Human Evolution and Christian Ethics* (Cambridge, UK: Cambridge University Press, 2007), 214. At least one study argues against what it describes as the dominant hypothesis among academics, stated bluntly by American economist Robert Frank: "[There is] a heavy burden of proof on those who insist that economics training does not inhibit cooperation." The authors of the study maintained that business students exhibit less prosocial tendencies because

students who opt for business studies tend to be less prosocial prior to their economics training. See Stephan Meier and Bruno S. Frey, "Do Business Students Make Good Citizens?," *International Journal of the Economics of Business* 11, no. 2 (2004): 141–63. It should be noted, however, that their dataset relates only to students at the University of Zürich, and therefore says little about students from US institutions.

82. Pirson and Lawrence, "Humanism in Business," 554–55. This challenge to *homo economicus* resembles recent work by evolutionary biologists Frans de Waal and D.S. Wilson. I review their work in Beyer, "Solidarity by Grace, Nature or Both? The Possibility of Human Solidarity in the Light of Evolutionary Biology and Catholic Moral Theology."

83. Pirson and Lawrence, "Humanism in Business—Towards a Paradigm Shift?," 563. On this problem in business schools and suggested solutions, see Wolfgang Amann et al., eds., *Business Schools Under Fire: Humanistic Management Education as the Way Forward* (Houndmills, Basingstoke, Hampshire: Palgrave Macmillan, 2011). The assumption here, not unfounded, is that the financial crisis of 2008 was largely rooted in greed that generated destructive behaviors. On this, see Simon Johnson and James Kwak, *13 Bankers: The Wall Street Takeover and the Next Financial Meltdown*, 1st ed. (New York: Pantheon Books, 2010), 113. The authors cite Wall Street executives who stated that Gordon Gecko's famous "greed is good" speech in Oliver Stone's movie *Wall Street* inspired them.

84. Gallin, *Negotiating Identity: Catholic Higher Education since 1960*, 125. See also Association of Jesuit Colleges and Universities, "Some Characteristics of Jesuit Colleges and Universities," 7.

85. See Giroux, *Neoliberalism's War on Higher Education*.

86. Keenan, *University Ethics*, 57–64.

87. Frank Donoghue, *The Last Professors: The Corporate University and the Fate of the Humanities*, 1st ed. (New York: Fordham University Press, 2008), 26. See also Maggie Berg and Barbara K. Seeber, *The Slow Professor: Challenging the Culture of Speed in the Academy* (Toronto: University of Toronto Press, 2015).

88. Giroux, *Neoliberalism's War on Higher Education*, 89, see also 77–102. See also Mayer, "How Right-Wing Billionaires Infiltrated Higher Education"; and Delbanco, *College*, 141–42.

89. See Berg and Seeber, *The Slow Professor*, 13. See also Lawrence D. Berg, Edward H. Huijbens, and Henrik Gutzon Larsen, "Producing Anxiety in the Neoliberal University," *The Canadian Geographer / Le Géographe canadien* 60, no. 2 (2016).

90. For discussion of the concrete manifestations of the economistic paradigm in business and corporate governance, see Pirson and Lawrence, "Humanism in Business" and Michael Pirson and Shann Turnbull, "Toward a

More Humanistic Governance Model: Network Governance Structures," *Journal of Business Ethics* 99, no. 1 (2011): 101–14.

91. See also Donna Freitas, "Review of *University Ethics*," 177; Gallin, *Negotiating Identity: Catholic Higher Education since 1960*, 124, 72–73, 83.

92. John Paul II, *Ex Corde Ecclesiae*, part I, no. 21; italics added. See also part II, art. 2, §2: "A Catholic University, as Catholic, informs and carries out its research, teaching, and all other activities with Catholic ideals, principles and attitudes."

93. See John Paul II, *Laborem Exercens*, no. 19. See also Pontifical Council for Justice and Peace, *Compendium of Social Doctrine of the Church*, no. 301, http://www.vatican.va/roman_curia/pontifical_councils/justpeace/documents /rc_pc_justpeace_doc_20060526_compendio-dott-soc_en.html; John Paul II, *Centesimus Annus*, no. 15; United States Conference of Catholic Bishops, *Economic Justice for All*, no. 80.

94. See Sinclair Oubre, "Labor Law for 1.1 Billion People: How Canon Law, and Catholic Social Justice Principles Can Give a Third Way," speech given at the Social Science Division of the Special Libraries Association Annual Convention in New Orleans, La., June 14, 2010. Unfortunately, the text was available but is no longer at the Catholic Labor Network website, http://www.catholiclabor.org /gen-art/CanonLaw_CatholicLabor_Principles_6014010.pdf. See also Francis G. Morrisey, "Just Wages: It's in Church Law," *Health Progress* 92, no. 4 (2011).

95. United States Conference of Catholic Bishops, *Economic Justice for All*, no. 347: 10.

96. John Paul II, *Ex Corde Ecclesiae*, Part I.A.1.13, §17.

97. See John Paul II *Centesimus Annus*, no. 40. See also Benedict XVI, *Caritas in Veritate*, nos. 35–36, 69; and Francis, "Address of Pope Francis to the New Nonresident-Ambassadors to the Holy See: Kyrgyzstan, Antigua and Barbuda, Luxembourg and Botswana."

98. I discuss education as a right in CST in Chapter 3.

99. See John Paul II, *Ex Corde Ecclesiae*; Paul VI, *Declaration on Christian Education: Gravissimum Educationis*, (October 28, 1965), http://www.vatican.va /archive/hist_councils/ii_vatican_council/documents/vat-ii_decl_19651028 _gravissimum-educationis_en.html.

100. As Spohn states, "The aimlessness and cynicism of some young people may say less about them than it does about their parents and the other adults in their world." Spohn, "Developing a Moral Conscience in Jesuit Higher Education," 393.

101. Dean Brackley, "Higher Standards," in *A Jesuit Education Reader*, ed. George W. Traub (Chicago, Ill.: Loyola Press, 2008), 193.

102. On promoting CST as a means of evangelization, see John Paul II, *Centesimus Annus*, nos. 5, 54; and Pontifical Council for Justice and Peace, *Compendium*, nos. 62–67.

103. John Paul II, *Ex Corde Ecclesiae*, part I, no. 48.

104. Ibid.

105. John Paul II, *Ex Corde Ecclesiae*, part I, no. 49.

106. Francis, *Evangelii Gaudium*, no. 134.

107. John Paul II *Centesimus Annus*, no. 58.

108. William Spohn discusses the meaning of this passage for discipleship in William C. Spohn, *Go and Do Likewise: Jesus and Ethics* (New York: Continuum, 1999), 110. Spohn states that "we cannot expect good actions from a twisted character."

109. Benedict XVI, *Message of His Holiness Benedict XVI for the World Mission Sunday* (Vatican City, January 6, 2011), http://www.vatican.va/holy_father/benedict_xvi/messages/missions/documents/hf_ben-xvi_mes_20110106_world-mission-day-2011_en.html. See also Paul VI, *Evangelii Nuntiandi* (December 8, 1975), nos. 13, 14, 27, 29, 31, 41, http://www.vatican.va/content/paul-vi/en/apost_exhortations/documents/hf_p-vi_exh_19751208_evangelii-nuntiandi.html and Pope Francis's discussion of the "social dimension of evangelization" in *Evangelii Gaudium*, nos. 176–207. I discuss the relationship between solidarity, social justice, and evangelization in Catholic doctrine more fully in Gerald J. Beyer, "The Continuing Relevance of *Brothers and Sisters to Us* to Confronting Racism and White Privilege," *Josephinum Journal of Theology* 19, no. 2 (2012).

110. Some examples are: O'Brien, *From the Heart of the American Church*; Gleason, *Contending with Modernity*; Michael J. Buckley, *The Catholic University as Promise and Project: Reflections in a Jesuit Idiom* (Washington, D.C.: Georgetown University Press, 1998); Gallin, *Negotiating Identity*; John R. Wilcox and Irene King, *Enhancing Religious Identity: Best Practices from Catholic Campuses* (Washington, D.C.: Georgetown University Press, 2000); Melanie M. Morey and John J. Piderit, *Catholic Higher Education: A Culture in Crisis* (New York: Oxford University Press, 2006) and Cyril Orji, *The Catholic University and the Search for Truth* (Winona, Minn.: Anselm Academic, 2013).

111. For example, Morey and Piderit mention in passing the issue of access for economically disadvantaged students in a paragraph that contains no analysis of how Catholic institutions are faring in this regard. See Morey and Piderit, *Catholic Higher Education*, 58. Their book also fails to consider issues such as how worker compensation and endowment investing should be influenced by CST. Michael Buckley's *The Catholic University as Promise and Project* helpfully discusses the role of the humanities and cultivation of concern for justice at Catholic universities, but does not consider the importance of justice in institutional arrangements themselves. Alice Gallin's *Negotiating Identity* does draw attention to justice issues on campus, but only in the final pages of the book. Discussions of *Ex Corde Ecclesiae* also reflect this tendency, even though

its status as papal teaching requires Catholic universities to heed it, and it treats issues such as access for disadvantaged students. See for example, John Langan, *Catholic Universities in Church and Society: A Dialogue on Ex Corde Ecclesiae* (Washington, D.C.: Georgetown University Press, 1993).

112. O'Brien, *From the Heart of the American Church*, 188–91.

113. Another helpful book is Roger Bergman, *Catholic Social Learning: Educating the Faith That Does Justice*, (New York: Fordham University Press, 2011).

114. Rausch, *Educating for Faith and Justice*; Suzanne C. Toton, *Justice Education: From Service to Solidarity* (Milwaukee, Wisc.: Marquette University Press, 2006).

115. See Rausch, *Educating for Faith and Justice*, 55, 57, 69. In addition to Rausch's reflections, see the contributions by Kristin Heyer, Stephen Pope and Mark Ravizza, SJ.

116. See Toton, *Justice Education*, 12, 100–102, 110–13.

117. Matt Bernacki and Frank Bernt, "Service-Learning as a Transformative Experience: An Analysis of the Impact of Service-Learning on Student Attitudes and Behaviors after Two Years of College," in *From Passion to Objectivity: International and Cross Disciplinary Perspectives on Service Learning Research*, ed. Sherril B. Gelmon and Shelley Billig (Charlotte, N.C.: Information Age Publishing, 2007), 111–34.

118. The meaning of solidarity will be discussed below in an overview of CST. For a more in-depth treatment, see Gerald J. Beyer, "The Meaning of Solidarity in Catholic Social Teaching," *Political Theology* 15, no. 1 (2014), 7–25, and Beyer, *Recovering Solidarity: Lessons from Poland's Unfinished Revolution*.

119. Toton, *Justice Education*, 113, see also 12, 100–102, 110–113.

120. Ibid., 173.

121. See especially Chapters 4–9 in Susan Crawford Sullivan, *A Vision of Justice: Engaging Catholic Social Teaching on the College Campus* (Collegeville, Minn.: Liturgical Press).

122. For a discussion of service-learning, global outreach programs and community-based pedagogy and research as components of the *proyecto social*, see Bradford. E. Hinze, "The Tasks of Theology in the Proyecto Social of the University's Mission," *Horizons* 39, no. 2 (2012): 282–309.

123. John Paul II, *Ex Corde Ecclesiae*, no. 31.

124. Ibid., part I, no. 33.

125. On the demonization of the poor, see Pew Research Center, "Most See Inequality Growing, but Partisans Differ over Solutions," January 23, 2014, https://www.people-press.org/2014/01/23/most-see-inequality-growing-but -partisans-differ-over-solutions/

126. See for example Peter-Hans Kolvenbach, SJ, "The Service of Faith and the Promotion of Justice in American Jesuit Higher Education" (Santa Clara

University, Calif., October 6, 2003), http://www.sjweb.info/documents/phk /2000santa_clara_en.doc.

127. See Association of Catholic Colleges and Universities, "Catholic Higher Education and Catholic Social Teaching: A Vision Statement," https://www .accunet.org/CST.

128. See Karol Wojtyla, *Sign of Contradiction* (New York: Seabury Press, 1979), 108. St. John Paul argued that "Jesus is the symbol of liberation from unjust structures, both social and economic. . . . He is in every way a reproach to affluent, acquisitive consumer societies." Like Jesus, the church must also be a sign of contradiction to the ways of the world.

129. I am indebted to my colleague Dr. Timothy Hanchin on the need to build community and relationships to pursue our mission successfully. On the need to deepen knowledge of the Catholic tradition among faculty, see for example Christian Smith and John C. Cavadini, *Building Catholic Higher Education: Unofficial Reflections from the University of Notre Dame* (Eugene, Ore.: Cascade Books, 2014), 49–50, 56–58.

130. Parker J. Palmer, Arthur Zajonc, and Megan Scribner, *The Heart of Higher Education: A Call to Renewal: Transforming the Academy through Collegial Conversations* (San Francisco: Jossey-Bass, 2010), 125–49.

131. See for example Berg and Seeber, *The Slow Professor*, 7–8, 18, and passim; Donoghue, *The Last Professors*, 24–54.

132. bell hooks, *Teaching Community: A Pedagogy of Hope* (New York: Routledge, 2003), xv. See also Berg and Seeber, *The Slow Professor*, 71–90.

133. On the obsession with publication for tenure, see Donoghue, *The Last Professors*, 39–50; Berg and Seeber, *The Slow Professor*, 52–70.

134. See Regis University, "Traditions: The Jesuit University of the Rocky Mountain West: Our Intellectual, Ethical, and Religious Foundations," (2011), https://www.regis.edu/About-Regis-University/JesuitEducated/Office-of -Mission/Traditions-Booklet.aspx.

135. Ibid.

136. Monica Clark, "Schools Entrust Religious Mission to Lay Boards, Trustees," *National Catholic Reporter*, July 20, 2012, https://www.ncronline.org /news/parish/schools-entrust-religious-mission-lay-boards-trustees.

137. See "The Annual Curriculum Development Workshop: Catholic Social Teaching and Issues of Justice" at https://www1.villanova.edu/villanova /mission/office/programs/workshops.html. On the need for learning CST at Catholic universities, see Barbara E. Wall, "Mission and Ministry of American Catholic Colleges and Universities for the Next Century," *Journal for Peace and Justice Studies* 11, no. 2 (2000): 53–56.

138. I borrow this phrase from Delbanco, *College*, 17–24, 138–49. At a conference in Rome, Cardinal Peter Turkson, prefect of the Holy See Dicastery

for Promoting Integral Human Development, expressed concern that Catholic universities in the United States were reluctant to adopt mandatory units on Catholic social teaching for all students.

139. John Paul II, *Centesimus Annus*, nos. 5, 56–57; USCCB, *Economic Justice for All*, nos. 61–68; and Pontifical Council for Justice and Peace, *Compendium*, nos. 62–67.

140. See for example Thomas Massaro, *Living Justice: Catholic Social Teaching in Action*, 2nd classroom ed. (Lanham, Md.: Rowman & Littlefield Publishers, 2012); Marvin L. Krier Mich, *Catholic Social Teaching and Movements* (Mystic, Conn.: Twenty-Third Publications, 1998); Judith A. Merkle, *From the Heart of the Church: The Catholic Social Tradition* (Collegeville, Minn.: Liturgical Press, 2004); Judith A. Dwyer and Elizabeth L. Montgomery, *The New Dictionary of Catholic Social Thought* (Collegeville, Minn.: Liturgical Press, 1994); Elias O. Opongo and A. E. Orobator, *Faith Doing Justice: A Manual for Social Analysis, Catholic Social Teachings and Social Justice* (Kenya: Paulines Publications Africa, 2008); Kenneth R. Himes and Lisa Sowle Cahill, *Modern Catholic Social Teaching: Commentaries and Interpretations* (Washington, D.C.: Georgetown University Press, 2005); Daniel McDonald, *Catholic Social Teaching in Global Perspective* (Maryknoll, N.Y.: Orbis Books, 2010); David Matzko McCarthy, *The Heart of Catholic Social Teaching: Its Origins and Contemporary Significance* (Grand Rapids, Mich.: Brazos Press, 2009). Most of the major official documents can be found on the Vatican website or in David J. O'Brien and Thomas A. Shannon, *Catholic Social Thought: Encyclicals and Documents from Pope Leo XIII to Pope Francis*, 3rd revised ed. (Maryknoll, N.Y.: Orbis Books, 2016). In addition, *The Compendium of the Social Doctrine of the Church* is an indispensable resource. See Pontifical Council for Justice and Peace, "Compendium of the Social Doctrine of the Church," (Washington, D.C.: United States Conference of Catholic Bishops, 2005), also available at http://www.vatican.va/roman_curia/pontifical_councils/justpeace /documents/rc_pc_justpeace_doc_20060526_compendio-dott-soc_en.html.

141. See Pontifical Council for Justice and Peace, *Compendium*, nos. 108–111; 192; John Paul II, *Sollicitudo Rei Socialis* (December 30, 1987), no. 40, http://w2 .vatican.va/content/john-paul-ii/en/encyclicals/documents/hf_jp-ii_enc_30121987 _sollicitudo-rei-socialis.html. See also the discussion of human dignity as the "linchpin" of CST's social anthropology in *Gaudium et Spes* in Christine Firer Hinze, "Straining toward Solidarity in a Suffering World: *Gaudium et Spes* after Forty Years," in *Vatican II: 40 Years Later*, ed. William Madges (Maryknoll, N.Y.: Orbis Books, 2006), 170.

142. See Second Vatican Council, *Gaudium et Spes* (December 7, 1965), nos. 2, 13, 22, 32, 38, 39, http://www.vatican.va/archive/hist_councils/ii_vatican _council/documents/vat-ii_const_19651207_gaudium-et-spes_en.html, and John Paul II, *Redemptor Hominis* (March 4, 1979), no. 8, no. 16, http://w2.vatican

.va/content/john-paul-ii/en/encyclicals/documents/hf_jp-ii_enc_04031979
_redemptor-hominis.html.

143. For a discussion of this point, see Gerald J. Beyer, "Beyond 'Nonsense on Stilts': Towards Conceptual Clarity and Resolution of Conflicting Economic Rights," *Human Rights Review* 6, no. 4 (2005), 5–32.

144. See Mary Ann Glendon, "Knowing the Universal Declaration of Human Rights," *Notre Dame Law Review* 73, no. 5 (1998): 1172. She points out that "human dignity" appears five times in the declaration in key places.

145. David Hollenbach, *Claims in Conflict: Retrieving and Renewing the Catholic Human Rights Tradition*, Woodstock Studies (New York: Paulist Press, 1979), 68. For examples in official Catholic teaching, see John XXIII, *Pacem in Terris* (April 11, 1963), no. 9–27, http://w2.vatican.va/content/john-xxiii/en/encyclicals/documents /hf_j-xxiii_enc_11041963_pacem.html; John Paul II, *Centesimus Annus*, nos. 28, 34, 47; and US Catholic Bishops, *Economic Justice For All*, no. 79–84.

146. Mich, *Catholic Social Teaching and Movements*, 27.

147. See Francis, *Laudato Si* (May 24, 2015), no. 115, http://w2.vatican.va /content/francesco/en/encyclicals/documents/papa-francesco_20150524 _enciclica-laudato-si.html.

148. The exact beginning of this endorsement is debated. See Drew Christiansen, "Pacem in Terris," in *Modern Catholic Social Teaching: Commentaries and Interpretations*, ed. Kenneth R. Himes (Washington, D.C.: Georgetown University Press, 2005), 217–43; Gerald J. Beyer, "Economic Rights: Past, Present, and Future," in *Handbook of Human Rights*, ed. Thomas Cushman (London; New York: Routledge, 2012), 291–310.

149. The failure of the Catholic Church to do more to stop the genocide in Rwanda in 1994 and the failure of church leaders to adequately protect young people from sexual abuse serve as obvious examples. On the former, see Elisee Rutagambwa, "The Rwandan Church: The Challenge of Reconciliation," in *The Catholic Church and the Nation-State: Comparative Perspectives*, ed. Paul Christopher Manuel, Lawrence C. Reardon, and Clyde Wilcox (Washington, D.C.: Georgetown University Press, 2006), 173–90; Carol Rittner, John K. Roth, and Wendy Whitworth, eds., *Genocide in Rwanda: Complicity of the Churches?* (St. Paul, Minn.: Paragon House, 2004). On sexual abuse, see for example the interview with Archbishop Diarmuid Martin, "The Archbishop of Dublin Challenges the Church," *60 Minutes*, http://www.cbsnews.com/8301-18560_162-57390125/the -archbishop-of-dublin-challenges-the-church/ and John N. Sheveland, "Redeeming Trauma: An Agenda for Theology Fifteen Years On," in *American Catholicism in the 21st Century: Crossroads, Crisis, or Renewal?*, ed. Benjamin Peters and Nicholas Rademacher (Maryknoll, N.Y.: Orbis, 2018), 137–51.

150. David Hollenbach, "Pacem in Terris and Human Rights," *Journal of Catholic Social Thought* 10, no. 1 (2013): 8.

151. See Beyer, "Economic Rights: Past, Present, and Future."

152. Hollenbach, *Claims in Conflict: Retrieving and Renewing the Catholic Human Rights Tradition*, 98.

153. See John XXIII, *Pacem in Terris*, nos. 1, 130, 163, 167; See Christiansen, "Pacem in Terris," 223.

154. United States Conference of Catholic Bishops, *Economic Justice for All*, no. 17.

155. Ibid. This paragraph is drawn from Beyer, "Economic Rights: Past, Present, and Future," 298.

156. John XXIII, *Pacem in Terris*, no. 28, in O'Brien and Shannon, 135.

157. John XXIII, *Pacem in Terris*, no. 5, http://www.vatican.va/content /john-xxiii/en/encyclicals/documents/hf_j-xxiii_enc11041963_pacem.html.

158. Todd Whitmore, "Pacem in Terris," in *The Harpercollins Encyclopedia of Catholicism*, ed. Richard P. McBrien and Harold W. Attridge (New York: HarperCollins, 1995), 950. See also John XXIII, *Pacem in Terris*, no. 6.

159. See Avery Dulles, *Church and Society: The Laurence J Mcginley Lectures, 1988–2007* (New York: Fordham University Press, 2008), 278–79.

160. See John Paul II, *Redemptor Hominis*, nos. 1, 8, 10, 13. I draw here on Gerald J. Beyer, "John XXIII and John Paul II: The Human Rights Popes," *Ethos: Quarterly of the John Paul II Institute at the Catholic University of Lublin* 2, no. 106 (2014): 51–91.

161. Himes and Himes, *Fullness of Faith: The Public Significance of Theology* (Mahwah, N.J.: Paulist Press), 55–73. See also Pontifical Council for Justice and Peace, *Compendium*, nos. 34–37.

162. See Beyer, "Economic Rights: Past, Present, and Future," 297–99.

163. E. J. Dionne, *Our Divided Political Heart: The Battle for the American Idea in an Age of Discontent*, 1st US ed. (New York: Bloomsbury USA, 2012). On neoliberalism and hyperindividualism, see also Angus Sibley, *The "Poisoned Spring" of Economic Libertarianism* (Washington, D.C.: Pax Romana, 2011); Monbiot, *How Did We Get into This Mess?: Politics, Equality, Nature*, 9–18.

164. Himes and Himes, *Fullness of Faith*, 55–73; LaCugna, *God for Us: The Trinity and Christian Life*. See also Pontifical Council for Justice and Peace, *Compendium*, nos. 34–37. On Thatcher's words, see Samuel Brittan, "Thatcher Was Right—There Is No 'Society,'" *The Financial Times*, April 18, 2013, https:// www.ft.com/content/d1387b70-a5d5-11e2-9b77-00144feabdco

165. I am indebted to Hollenbach here. For a more detailed account of the common good in Catholic thought, see David Hollenbach, *The Common Good and Christian Ethics* (New York: Cambridge University Press, 2002). See also Todd Whitmore, "Catholic Social Teaching: Starting with the Common Good," in *Living the Catholic Social Tradition*, ed. Kathleen Maas Weigert and Alexia Kelley (Lanham, Md.: Rowman & Littlefield 2005), 59–86.

166. See Pontifical Council for Justice and Peace, *Compendium*, nos. 164–70.

167. Second Vatican Council, *Gaudium et Spes*, no. 26.

168. Hollenbach, *The Common Good and Christian Ethics*, 24–61.

169. For example, CST holds that paying taxes is required for the common good and a "duty of solidarity," not an infringement of individual freedom. See Pontifical Council for Justice and Peace, *Compendium*, no. 355.

170. See Maritain, *The Person and the Common Good*.

171. Pontifical Council for Justice and Peace, *Compendium*, nos. 165–67.

172. See John Courtney Murray, "The Problem of Religious Freedom," *Theological Studies* 25 (1964): 520–21.

173. Second Vatican Council, *Dignitatis Humanae* (December 7, 1965), no. 7, http://www.vatican.va/archive/hist_councils/ii_vatican_council/documents /vat-ii_decl_19651207_dignitatis-humanae_en.html. For a more detailed account of public order, see Gerald J. Beyer, "Freedom, Truth, and Law in the Mind and Homeland of John Paul II," *Notre Dame Journal of Law, Ethics and Public Policy* 21, no. 1 (2007): 17–49.

174. See Gerald J. Beyer, "What Ryan Missed: What Catholic Social Teaching Says About Solidarity and Subsidiarity," *America*, June 4, 2012, http://www .americamagazine.org/content/article.cfm?article_id=13455.

175. The following paragraph is derived from Beyer, "What Ryan Missed." For discussions of recent controversy surrounding the principle of subsidiarity, see this article and Vincent J. Miller, "Saving Subsidiarity," *America*, July 30, 2012, http://americamagazine.org/issue/5147/article/saving-subsidiarity. On subsidiarity in official CST, see Pontifical Council for Justice and Peace, *Compendium*, nos. 185–88; See John XXIII, *Mater et Magistra*, nos. 53–61, 116–17.

176. See Beyer, *Recovering Solidarity*, 93.

177. See John XXIII, *Mater et Magistra*, nos. 59–61.

178. See for example, Joseph S. Nye Jr., "Globalization's Democratic Deficit: How to Make International Institutions More Accountable," *Foreign Affairs*, July/August 2001, https://www.foreignaffairs.com/articles/2001-07-01 /globalizations-democratic-deficit-how-make-international-institutions-more.

179. See Michael J. Naughton et al., *Respect in Action: Applying Subsidiarity in Business* (St. Paul, Minn.: UNAIPAC and University of St. Thomas, 2015).

180. See Beyer, "What Ryan Missed." The following is excerpted from Beyer, "Solidarity by Grace, Nature or Both? The Possibility of Human Solidarity in the Light of Evolutionary Biology and Catholic Moral Theology." I am grateful to *Heythrop Journal* editor Dr. Patrick Madigan for permission to reprint.

181. I use here parts of my more thorough discussion of solidarity and its biblical and theological foundations in Beyer, "The Meaning of Solidarity in Catholic Social Teaching," and Beyer, *Recovering Solidarity*.

182. Franciszek Kampka, "Solidarność w Nauczaniu Jana Pawła II," in *Idea Solidarności Dzisiaj*, ed. Władysław Zuziak (Kraków: Wydawnictwo Naukowe PAT, 2001), 8–9. Heinrich Pesch, SJ, spoke of 'factual solidarity.' See Anton Rauscher, "Źródła Idei Solidarności," in *Idea Solidarności Dzisiaj*, ed. Władysław Zuziak (Kraków: Wydawnictwo Naukowe PAT, 2001), 25. John Paul II discusses the recognition of interdependence as an aspect of solidarity in *Sollicitudo Rei Socialis*, nos. 38–39.

183. Józef Tischner, *The Spirit of Solidarity*, trans. Marek B. Zaleski and Benjamin Fiore (San Francisco: Harper & Row, 1984), 9.

184. Kampka, "Solidarność w Nauczaniu Jana Pawła II," 8–9. See also Paul VI, *Populorum Progressio*, no. 17.

185. John Paul II, *Sollicitudo Rei Socialis*, no. 38.

186. For a more thorough discussion of solidarity's relationship to the option for the poor, see Beyer, *Recovering Solidarity*, 21–24.

187. Francis, *Evangelii Gaudium*, no. 189.

188. Hollenbach, *The Common Good and Christian Ethics*, 159–65, 90–93; See also Kampka, "Solidarność w Nauczaniu Jana Pawła II," 9; Rauscher, "Zrodła Idei Solidarności," 26.

189. Karol Wojtyła, *Osoba i Czyn oraz Inne Studia Antropologiczne*, 3rd ed. (Lublin: Towarzystwo Naukowe KUL, 2000), 307.

190. Tischner, *The Spirit of Solidarity*, 18. I discuss this difference in Beyer, *Recovering Solidarity*, 88–96.

191. See the various understandings of solidarity in Steinar Stjernø, *Solidarity in Europe: The History of an Idea* (Cambridge: Cambridge University Press, 2005), 74, 85–88.

192. See for example John XXIII, *Mater et Magistra*, nos. 23, 92; John XXIII, *Pacem in Terris*, no. 80; Paul VI, *Populorum Progressio*, no. 62. I am indebted here to the analysis of solidarity as a regulatory principle in economic life in Franciszek Kampka, *Antropologiczne i Społeczne Podstawy Ładu Gospodarczego w Świetle Nauczania Kościoła* (Lublin: Red. Wydawnictw Katolickiego Uniwersytetu Lubelskiego, 1995), 60–61.

193. On the need for conflict to promote solidarity sometimes, see Wojtyła, *Osoba i Czyn*, 325; and John Paul II, *Centesimus Annus*, no. 14.

194. Second Vatican Council, *Gaudium et Spes*, no. 32.

195. See John Paul II, *Sollicitudo Rei Socialis*, no. 42. For a concise history of the term, see Charles E. Curran, *Catholic Social Teaching, 1891–Present: A Historical, Theological, and Ethical Analysis* (Washington, D.C.: Georgetown University Press, 2002), 183–88, and Maria Clara Bingemer, *Latin American Theology: Roots and Branches* (Maryknoll, N.Y.: Orbis Books, 2016).

196. See Jon Sobrino and Juan Hernández Pico, *Theology of Christian Solidarity*, trans. Philip Berryman (Maryknoll, N.Y.: Orbis Books, 1985), 12, 25, 30,

37–40, 60–61, 66, 71, 86, 89; and Oscar Romero, *Voice of the Voiceless: The Four Pastoral Letters and Other Statements* (Maryknoll, N.Y.: Orbis, 1985), 125, 77–87.

197. See Roberto Suro, "The Writing of an Encyclical," in *Aspiring to Freedom: Commentaries on John Paul II's Encyclical "The Social Concerns of the Church*," ed. Ken Myers (Grand Rapids, Mich.: W.B. Eerdmans Pub. Co., 1988), 167; Elizabeth A. Johnson, *Quest for the Living God: Mapping Frontiers in the Theology of God*, (New York: Continuum, 2011), 87; Curran, *Catholic Social Teaching, 1891–Present: A Historical, Theological, and Ethical Analysis*, 183–86.

198. See his discussion of the biblical basis in Gustavo Gutierrez, "The Option for the Poor," in *Mysterium Liberationis: Fundamental Concepts of Liberation Theology*, ed. Ignacio Ellacuría and Jon Sobrino (Maryknoll, N.Y.: Orbis, 1993), 235–50.

199. Ronald J. Sider, "Justice, Human Rights and Government," in *Toward an Evangelical Public Policy: Political Strategies for the Health of the Nation*, ed. Ronald J. Sider and Diane Knippers (Grand Rapids, Mich.: Baker Books, 2005), 171n5. See also Ronald J. Sider, *Fixing the Moral Deficit: A Balanced Way to Balance the Budget* (Downers Grove, Ill.: IVP Books, 2012), 50. In Sider's view, those who neglect the poor risk permanently severing their relationship with God.

200. See Basil, "I Will Pull Down My Barns," in *The Sunday Sermons of the Great Fathers*, ed. and trans. M. F. Toal (Chicago: Regnery, 1957), 325–32; John Chrysostom, "First Sermon on Lazarus and the Rich Man," in *On Wealth and Poverty*, ed. and trans. Catharine P. Roth (Crestwood, N.Y.: St. Vladimir's Seminary Press, 1984), 19–38.

201. See for example, Francis, *Evangelii Gaudium*, nos. 187–89, 192–93, 212; Francis, *Laudato Si*, no. 30, 90, 93.

202. John Paul II, "Message of the Holy Father on the Occasion of the 14th World Youth Day," (1999), http://w2.vatican.va/content/john-paul-ii/en/messages/youth/documents/hf_jp-ii_mes_09011999_xiv-world-youth-day.html.

203. United States Conference of Catholic Bishops, *Economic Justice for All*, no. 86.

204. See Philip S. Land, *Catholic Social Teaching as I Have Lived, Loathed and Loved It* (Chicago, Ill.: Loyola University Press, 1994), 83–84.

205. Mich, *Catholic Social Teaching and Movements*, 11.

206. Benedict XVI, *Caritas in Veritate*, no. 6.

207. See John Paul II, *Centesimus Annus*, no. 59.

208. This paragraph is dependent on United States Conference of Catholic Bishops, *Economic Justice for All*, 72–76.

209. Ibid., no. 71.

210. See Pontifical Council for Justice and Peace, *Compendium*, nos. 171–84.

211. On solidarity promoting participation, see for example John Paul II, *Laborem Exercens*, 1981, no. 14; John Paul II, *Sollicitudo Rei Socialis*, no. 27; John

Paul II, *Centesimus Annus*, 1991, nos. 33, 3. I draw here from my fuller discussion of participation in Beyer, *Recovering Solidarity*, 90–94.

212. Hollenbach, *Claims in Conflict*, 86–87.

213. See Amartya Kumar Sen, *Development as Freedom* (New York: Knopf, 1999).

214. World Synod of Catholic Bishops, *Justitia in Mundo*, 1971, no. 71, https://www.cctwincities.org/wp-content/uploads/2015/10/Justicia-in-Mundo.pdf.

215. John Paul II stressed that "the manner and means for achieving a public life which has true human development as its goal is *solidarity*. This concerns the active and responsible *participation* of all in public life, from individual citizens to various groups, from labor unions to political parties." See John Paul II, *Christifideles Laici* (December 30, 1988), no. 42, http://w2.vatican.va/content/john-paul-ii/en/apost_exhortations/documents/hf_jp-ii_exh_30121988_christifideles-laici.html.

216. See Karol Wojtyła, *Osoba i Czyn*, 307.

217. See Second Vatican Council, *Gaudium et Spes*, nos. 34, 39.

218. See John XXIII, *Pacem in Terris*, 1963, no. 53.

219. John XXIII, *Mater et Magistra*, 1961, no. 73; John XXIII, *Pacem in Terris*, no. 82.

220. See John XXIII, *Mater et Magistra*, no. 77, 97; Paul VI, *Octogesima Adveniens* (May 14, 1971), no. 15, http://w2.vatican.va/content/paul-vi/en/apost_letters/documents/hf_p-vi_apl_19710514_octogesima-adveniens.html; John Paul II, *Laborem Exercens*, no. 14; John Paul II, *Centesimus Annus*, no. 15; Pontifical Council for Justice and Peace, *Compendium*, no. 307; United States Conference of Catholic Bishops, *Economic Justice for All*, nos. 71, 72.

221. I take this up more fully, including applying the right to participation to academic freedom in Beyer, "Curing the 'Disease' in Corporatized Higher Education."

222. See Beyer, "John XXIII and John Paul II: The Human Rights Popes."

223. John Paul II, "Apostolic Journey of His Holiness John Paul II to The United States Of America: Address of His Holiness John Paul II to the Fiftieth General Assembly of the United Nations Organization" (October 5, 1995), http://www.vatican.va/holy_father/john_paul_ii/speeches/1995/october/documents/hf_jp-ii_spe_05101995_address-to-uno_en.html.

224. Ibid., no. 1.

225. This text, along with articles on human rights in world religions, can be found in Joseph Runzo, Nancy M. Martin, and Arvind Sharma, *Human Rights and Responsibilities in the World Religions* (Oxford: Oneworld, 2003). I provide a brief overview of this topic in Beyer, "Economic Rights: Past, Present, and Future."

226. See Joy Heine and Cynthia Brooke, eds., *A Worker Justice Reader: Essential Writings on Religion and Labor* (Maryknoll, N.Y.: Orbis Books, 2010); and The Interfaith Worker Justice Website at http://www.iwj.org/resources#on-faith.

227. For a thoughtful discussion of this issue, see Smith and Cavadini, *Building Catholic Higher Education*, 39–63. On hiring for mission, see also Gallin, *Negotiating Identity*, 85–87, 125–28; Morey and Piderit, *Catholic Higher Education*, 110–12.

228. Smith and Cavadini, *Building Catholic Higher Education*, 48.

229. On the AAUP and CST, see Beyer, "Curing the 'Disease' in Corporatized Higher Education."

230. See the statement at University of Notre Dame, "The Idea of the Catholic University," http://archives.nd.edu/episodes/visitors/lol/idea.htm.

231. This section draws on Beyer, *Recovering Solidarity*, 24–27.

232. Jerzy Popiełuszko, *Myśli Wyszukane* (Kraków: Znak, 2002), 77.

233. Tischner, *The Spirit of Solidarity*, 1–5. See also Havel on conscience in Václav Havel and Paul Wilson, *Open Letters: Selected Writings, 1965–1990* (New York: Vintage Books, 1992), 247–71.

234. Jaroslaw Gowin, "Kościoł a 'Solidarność,'" in *Lekcja Sierpnia: Dziedzictwo 'Solidarnosci' Po Dwudziestu Latach*, ed. Dariusz Gawin (Warsaw: Wydawnictwo IFiS PAN, 2002), 28.

235. Havel and Wilson, *Open Letters*, 248, see also 85.

236. Adam Michnik, "The Moral and Spiritual Origins of Solidarity," in *Without Force or Lies: Voices from the Revolution of Central Europe in 1989–90: Essays, Speeches, and Eyewitness Accounts*, ed. William M. Brinton and Alan Rinzler (San Francisco: Mercury House, 1990), 239–40.

237. Jerzy Popiełuszko, *The Way of My Cross: Masses at Warsaw* (Chicago: Regnery Books, 1986), 227.

238. Ibid., 227–29. On John Paul II on this subject, see Beyer, "Freedom, Truth, and Law in the Mind and Homeland of John Paul II."

239. Martin Luther King Jr., Speech in Selma, Alabama on March 8, 1965. Cited in Frederick Mayer, *Narrative Politics: Stories and Collective Action* (Oxford: Oxford University Press, 2014), 133. See also Martin Luther King Jr., "Letter from a Birmingham Jail," https://www.africa.upenn.edu/Articles_Gen/Letter_Birmingham.html.

240. Malcolm X and Alex Haley, *The Autobiography of Malcolm X* (New York: Ballantine Books, 1992), 366. On the misconceptions of Malcolm X and his relevance for Catholic ethics, see Bryan N. Massingale, "Vox Victimarum Vox Dei: Malcolm X as Neglected 'Classic' for Catholic Theological Reflection." *Catholic Theological Society of America Proceedings* 65 (2010): 63–88. On a personal note, *The Autobiography of Malcolm X* was the first book that made me fully aware of the depths of racism and White supremacy in the United States.

241. Elizabeth Cady Stanton, 1890 Speech to the American Woman Suffrage Association. Cited in Constance H. Buchanan, *Choosing to Lead: Women and the Crisis of American Values* (Boston: Beacon Press, 1996), 169.

242. Charles Taylor, *The Ethics of Authenticity* (Cambridge, Mass.: Harvard University Press, 1992), 40–41. See also Václav Havel, "On Human Rights," *Ethical Perspectives* 6, no. 1 (1999): 7.

243. See the discussion of this problem in Smith and Cavadini, *Building Catholic Higher Education*, 38–63.

244. Havel and Wilson, *Open Letters: Selected Writings, 1965–1990*, 132. I am indebted to the following article on this point: Katy Scrogin, "Toward a Hopeful Politics: Václav Havel's Legacy of Responsible Commitment," *The Other Journal*, January 10, 2012, http://theotherjournal.com/2012/01/10/toward-a-hopeful -politics-vaclav-havels-legacy-of-responsible-commitment/. See also Slawomir Sierakowski, "Vaclav Havel's Fairy Tale," *The New York Times*, December 17, 2013, https://www.nytimes.com/2013/12/18/opinion/sierakowski-vaclav-havels -fairy-tale.html.

245. John Paul II, *Ex Corde Ecclesiae*, part I, no. 20 and 32.

246. Adam Michnik, *Letters from Prison and Other Essays* (Berkeley: University of California Press, 1985), 7.

247. Smith makes an analogous claim in Smith and Cavadini, *Building Catholic Higher Education*, 51–62.

248. Day, *Religious Resistance to Neoliberalism*, 77.

249. Second Vatican Council, *Gaudium et Spes*, no. 43.

250. Popiełuszko, *The Way of My Cross*, 229.

251. I am indebted here to the discussion of how to discern what Jesus's teaching requires of Christian disciples today in Spohn, *Go and Do Likewise: Jesus and Ethics*. Spohn's methodological proposal of analogical imagination is especially helpful.

252. Maureen H. O'Connell, *Compassion: Loving Our Neighbor in an Age of Globalization* (Maryknoll, N.Y.: Orbis Books, 2009), 72.

253. Stassen, *A Thicker Jesus: Incarnational Discipleship in a Secular Age*, 14.

254. Ibid., 20–21. Stassen describes three aspects of incarnational discipleship: "the holistic sovereignty of God and Lordship of Christ through all of life. . . . God revealed incarnationally, embodied historically, realistically, in Jesus of Nazareth, thickly interpreted and [the] Holy Spirit, independent of all powers and authorities, calling us to repentance from ideological entanglement." See ibid., 17; also 29, 40, 45, 47.

255. Carnegie Council on Policy Studies in Higher Education, *Three Thousand Futures: The Next Twenty Years for Higher Education* (San Francisco, Calif.: Jossey-Bass, 1980). Cited in Regis University, "Traditions: The Jesuit University of the Rocky Mountain West: Our Intellectual, Ethical, and Religious Foundations," 1.

2. Embodying Solidarity on Catholic Campuses:
The Case of Worker Justice

1. Pontifical Council for Justice and Peace, "Compendium of the Social Doctrine of the Church," (Washington, D.C.: United States Conference of Catholic Bishops, 2005), no. 211.

2. See Worker Rights Consortium, Affiliate Institutions, https://www.workersrights.org/affiliate-schools/. I will discuss this elsewhere in this book.

3. See Daniel Kovalik, "Death of an Adjunct: Margaret Mary Died Underpaid and Underappreciated," *Pittsburgh Post-Gazette*, September 18, 2013, http://www.post-gazette.com/Op-Ed/2013/09/18/Death-of-an-adjunct/stories/201309180224 and L.V. Anderson, "Death of a Professor," *Slate*, November 17 2013, http://www.slate.com/articles/news_and_politics/education/2013/11/death_of_duquesne_adjunct_margaret_mary_vojtko_what_really_happened_to_her.html. The Slate article states that while her case is more complicated than meets the eye, it "highlights the devil's bargain universities have made by exploiting adjuncts." It also links to Duquesne's rebuttal of the claims that the university shared responsibility for Margaret Mary Vojtko's death.

4. See Stacey Patton, "From Welfare to the Tenure Track," *Chronicle Vitae*, October 25, 2018, https://chroniclevitae.com/news/97-from-welfare-to-the-tenure-track; Stacey Patton, "The PhD Now Comes with Food Stamps," *The Chronicle of Higher Education*, May 6, 2012, http://chronicle.com/article/From-Graduate-School-to/131795/?cid=vem; Arik Greenberg, "How One Professor's American Dream—Teaching—Turned into the American Nightmare," *PBS News Hour* 2014, https://www.pbs.org/newshour/economy/one-professors-american-dream-teaching-turned-american-nightmare; "The Rise of Adjunct Faculty," *Radio Times*, January 7, 2014, http://whyy.org/cms/radiotimes/2014/01/07/the-rise-of-adjunct-faculty/; Elizabeth Segran, "The Adjunct Revolt: How Poor Professors Are Fighting Back," *The Atlantic*, April 28, 2014, http://m.theatlantic.com/business/archive/2014/04/the-adjunct-professor-crisis/361336/

5. Alastair Gee, "Facing Poverty, Academics Turn to Sex Work and Sleeping in Cars," *The Guardian*, September 28, 2017, https://www.theguardian.com/us-news/2017/sep/28/adjunct-professors-homeless-sex-work-academia-poverty?CMP=fb_gu.

6. See their websites: http://www.newfacultymajority.info/; http://www.cocalinternational.org/; and http://www.academicworkforce.org/

7. See, for example, Nathan Schneider, "Faculty and Students Are Walking Out Today for Catholic Identity," *America*, February 25, 2015, https://www.americamagazine.org/content/all-things/faculty-and-students-are-walking-out-today-catholic-identity; Brian Roewe, "Seattle U Teachers, Students Join National Adjunct Walkout Day," *National Catholic Reporter*, February 27, 2015,

https://www.ncronline.org/blogs/ncr-today/seattle-u-teachers-students-join-national-adjunct-walkout-day; Lisa Pemberton, "Saint Martin's Faculty, Students Walk out over Union Representation," *The Olympian* (2017), https://www.theolympian.com/news/local/education/article135857573.html;; Victor Ordonez, "Faculty Deliver Student Petition to McShane," *The Fordham Ram*, March 11 2017, https://fordhamram.com/51670/news/faculty-deliver-student-petition-to-mcshane/.

8. Marc Bousquet, *How the University Works: Higher Education and the Low-Wage Nation* (New York: New York University Press, 2008), 64.

9. Ibid., 64–69. See *Teachers on Wheels* at http://www.youtube.com/watch?v=fpZ3nixDHus.

10. House Committee on Education and the Workforce, "The Just-in-Time Professor" (Washington, D.C.: United States House of Representatives, 2014), https://edlabor.house.gov/imo/media/doc/1.24.14-AdjunctEforumReport.pdf. Another relevant and insightful blog is "The Homeless Adjunct" at http://junctrebellion.wordpress.com/

11. Maria Maisto, "Taking Heart, Taking Part: New Faculty Majority and the Praxis of Contingent Faculty Activism," in *Embracing Nontenure Track Faculty: Changing Campuses for the New Faculty Majority*, ed. Adrianna J. Kezar (New York: Routledge, 2012), 190.

12. On the various terms used to refer to contingent faculty, see John Curtis and Saranna Thornton, "Here's the News: The Annual Report on the Economic Status of the Profession, 2012–13," (Washington, D.C.: American Association of University Professors, 2013), 8, http://www.aaup.org/report/heres-news-annual-report-economic-status-profession-2012-13.

13. According to an interview with a reporter from Slate, the Provost of Duquesne University stated "My response to all of the frenetic email and blogging traffic is that I find it a little puzzling that it is being directed at one institution . . . as if somehow other institutions were not confronting exactly the same or almost exactly the same issues." See Anderson, "Death of a Professor."

14. See Pablo Eisenberg, "Living Wages and College Campuses," *Huffington Post*, January 18, 2013, https://www.huffingtonpost.com/pablo-eisenberg/university-employee-wages_b_2154836.html.

15. Jan Clausen and Eva Maria Swidler, "Academic Freedom from Below: Toward an Adjunct-Centered Struggle," *Journal of Academic Freedom* 4 (2013): 13. On how tenure-track faculty benefit from the adjunct situation, see also Bousquet, *How the University Works*,

16. James F. Keenan, *University Ethics: How Colleges Can Build and Benefit from a Culture of Ethics* (Rowman & Littlefield, 2015), 59.

17. See Mick Forgey, "Catholic University Raises Minimum Wage to $15 an Hour," *National Catholic Reporter* (2014), http://ncronline.org/news/people

/catholic-university-raises-minimum-wage-15-hour and my discussion later in this chapter.

18. See Maisto, "Taking Heart, Taking Part," 195. Maisto cites a study concerning attitudes of tenure-track faculty toward adjuncts. See also Joe Berry, *Reclaiming the Ivory Tower: Organizing Adjuncts to Change Higher Education* (New York: Monthly Review Press, 2005), 137–38.

19. I have encountered this personally in efforts to advocate for adjuncts. See also Maisto, "Taking Heart, Taking Part," 198–99; Clausen and Swidler, "Academic Freedom from Below: Toward an Adjunct-Centered Struggle," 3–12; and Berry, *Reclaiming the Ivory Tower,* 138.

20. Parts of the following are borrowed from Gerald J. Beyer, "Labor Unions, Adjuncts, and the Mission and Identity of Catholic Universities," *Horizons* 42, no. 1 (2015). © 2015 College Theology Society. Reprinted with permission. The letter is available on the Catholic Scholars for Worker Justice web site at http://cswj.us/wp-content/uploads/2017/11/2014-03-10-ADJUNCT-Sign-on -Statement.pdf.

21. In addition to Chapter 1's discussion of the option for the poor, see John Paul II, *Laborem Exercens,* (September 14, 1992), http://www.vatican.va/content /john-paul-ii/en/encyclicals/documents/hf_jp-ii_enc_14091981_laborem -exercens.html, no. 8; John Paul II, *Sollicitudo Rei Socialis,* no. 42; John Paul II, *Centesimus Annus,* no. 11; United States Conference of Catholic Bishops, *Economic Justice for All: A Catholic Framework for Economic Life* (Washington, D.C.: United States Conference of Catholic Bishops Website, 1992), http://www .usccb.org/upload/economic_justice_for_all.pdf., nos. 15, 86–90.

22. John Curtis, "The Employment Status of Instructional Staff Members in Higher Education, Fall 2011" (Washington, D.C.: American Association of University Professors, 2014) and Coalition on the Academic Workforce, "A Portrait of Part-Time Faculty Members," (2012), 9, http://www.academicworkforce .org/survey.html.

23. Coalition on the Academic Workforce, "A Portrait of Part-Time Faculty Members," 9. This report also states that the vast majority of the thirty thousand respondents were in their prime earning years, i.e., between the ages of thirty-five and sixty-five. This challenges the assumption that most contingent faculty members are either at the beginning of their careers or teaching as an avocation after retirement from another profession.

24. Cary Nelson and Stephen Watt, *Office Hours: Activism and Change in the Academy* (New York: Routledge, 2004), 28–29.

25. The American Association of University Professors, for example, uses the term "adjunctification." See American Association of University Professors, "Resisting the Increase in Contingent Appointments," https://www.aaup.org /resisting-increase-contingent-appointments.

26. Berry, *Reclaiming the Ivory Tower*, 4. See also Clausen and Swidler, "Academic Freedom from Below," 9.

27. Kimberley Tolley, ed. *Professors in the Gig Economy: Unionizing Adjunct Faculty in America* (Baltimore, Md.: Johns Hopkins University Press, 2018), viii.

28. American Association of University Professors, "Trends in the Academic Labor Force, 1975–2015," (Washington, D.C.: American Association of University Professors, 2017), https://www.aaup.org/sites/default/files/Academic%20Labor%20Force%20Trends%201975-2015.pdf.

29. John Curtis and Saranna Thornton, "Losing Focus: The Annual Report on the Economic Status of the Profession, 2013–14," (Washington, D.C.: American Association of University Professors, 2014), 8.

30. See Coalition on the Academic Workforce, "A Portrait of Part-Time Faculty Members," 2, 10.

31. Steven Shulman, "The Costs and Benefits of Adjunct Justice: A Critique of Brennan and Magness," *Journal of Business Ethics* (2017): 4.

32. Coalition on the Academic Workforce, "A Portrait of Part-Time Faculty Members,"11, http://www.academicworkforce.org/CAW_portrait_2012.pdf.

33. Kimberley Tolley and Kristen Edwards, "Conclusion: Reflections on the Possibilities and Limitations of Collective Bargaining," in *Professors in the Gig Economy*, 188. See also Kristen Edwards and Kimberley Tolley, "Do Unions Help Adjuncts?," *The Chronicle of Higher Education*, June 3, 2018; Timothy Reese Cain, *Campus Unions: Organized Faculty and Graduate Students in American Higher Education* (Jossey-Bass, 2017), 62–74.

34. Coalition on the Academic Workforce, "A Portrait of Part-Time Faculty Members," 10–12. See also the tables in ibid. at 18–50.

35. House Committee on Education and the Workforce, "The Just-in-Time Professor," 6.

36. American Association of University Professors, "Visualizing Change: The Annual Report on the Economic Status of the Profession, 2016–17," (2017), https://www.aaup.org/report/visualizing-change-annual-report-economic-status-profession-2016-17.

37. Caroline Fredrickson, "There Is No Excuse for How Universities Treat Adjuncts," *The Atlantic*, September 15, 2015, https://www.theatlantic.com/business/archive/2015/09/higher-education-college-adjunct-professor-salary/404461/.

38. Ken Jacobs, Ian Perry, and Jenifer MacGillvary, "The High Public Cost of Low Wages: Poverty-Level Wages Cost U.S. Taxpayers $152.8 Billion Each Year in Public Support for Working Families" (UC Berkeley Center for Labor Research and Education, 2015), http://laborcenter.berkeley.edu/pdf/2015/the-high-public-cost-of-low-wages.pdf.

39. Patton, "The Ph.D. Now Comes with Food Stamps."

40. House Committee on Education and the Workforce, "The Just-in-Time Professor," 16–21; and Adrianna Kezar and Daniel Maxey, "Dispelling the Myths: Locating the Resources Needed to Support Non-Tenure-Track Faculty" (The Delphi Project on the Changing Faculty and Student Success, 2013), 12, https://pullias.usc.edu/wp-content/uploads/2013/10/DelphiProject-Dispelling _the_Myths.pdf. The situation improved with the Affordable Care Act, but the AAUP cautions that the current political leadership in the US has threatened to repeal the ACA, which would adversely affect adjuncts making low wages. American Association of University Professors, "Visualizing Change: The Annual Report on the Economic Status of the Profession, 2016–17," 9.

41. Alissa Quart, *Squeezed: Why Our Families Can't Afford America* (New York: Ecco, 2018), 33–62. Quart narrates stories of penury and despair faced by adjuncts.

42. Data on the composition of the faculty at individual institutions can be obtained at The College Factual database at http://www.collegefactual.com/ and The College Navigator website at http://nces.ed.gov/collegenavigator/. Jacob A. Bennet has provided a summary chart of the data on Catholic institutions here: https://antigloss.wordpress.com/links-to-labor-and-education -articles-and-reports/2013-ipeds-tables/.

43. See for example Mark Oppenheimer, "For Duquesne Professors, a Union Fight That Transcends Religion," *New York Times*, June 22, 2012; Greenberg, "How One Professor's American Dream—Teaching—Turned into the Ameri-can Nightmare"; Peter Schmidt, "Adjuncts Appeal to Higher Power in Debate over Unions at Religious Colleges," *The Chronicle of Higher Education*, Decem-ber 9, 2013; Nikki Dowling, "MC Adjuncts Attempt to Unionize," *The Riverdale Press* (2010), https://riverdalepress.com/stories/MC-adjuncts-attempt-to -unionize-,47324; Dave Zirin, "Loyola Soars in March Madness While a Faculty Strike Looms," *The Nation*, March 19, 2018; Jody Lawrence-Turner, "Gonzaga University Adjuncts Plan First Faculty Union," *The Spokesman Review*, May 22, 2014; Audrey Williams June, "Adjuncts Build Strength in Numbers," *The Chronicle of Higher Education*, November 5, 2012; Kim Tolley, Marianne Delaporte, and Lorenzo Giachetti, "Unionizing Adjunct and Tenure-Track Faculty at Notre Dame de Namur University," in *Professors in the Gig Economy*; Nicholas M. Wertsch and Joseph A. McCartin, "A Just Employment Approach to Adjunct Unionization: The Georgetown Model," in *Professors in the Gig Economy*; Mike Byrne, "Adjunct Faculty Protest Low Wages, Deliver Petition to University President," *The Fordham Ram*, September 13, 2016, https://fordhamram.com/2016/09/adjunct-faculty -protest-low-wages-deliver-petition-to-university-president/.

44. On the connection between student learning outcomes and faculty working conditions, see Adrianna Kezar and Tom Depaola, "Understanding the Need for Unions: Contingent Faculty Working Conditions and the Relationship

to Student Learning," in *Professors in the Gig Economy*, 27–45; and Shulman, "The Costs and Benefits of Adjunct Justice: A Critique of Brennan and Magness," 1–9.

45. American Association of University Professors, "Visualizing Change: The Annual Report on the Economic Status of the Profession, 2016–17," 23.

46. Bousquet, *How the University Works*, 58 and 94; and Kezar and Maxey, "Dispelling the Myths," 3.

47. Kezar and Maxey, "Dispelling the Myths" and House Committee on Education and the Workforce, "The Just-in-Time Professor," 9.

48. See Kezar and Maxey, "Dispelling the Myths," 3; and Kezar and Depaola, "Understanding the Need for Unions: Contingent Faculty Working Conditions and the Relationship to Student Learning," 33–39.

49. Kezar and Maxey, "Dispelling the Myths," 2–3. See also Clausen and Swidler, "Academic Freedom from Below," 1–3, 9. The latter article reports that some institutions have made "tenure-like arrangements for their adjuncts." I argue for the importance of academic freedom in Beyer, "Curing the 'Disease' in Corporatized Higher Education: Prescriptions from Catholic Social Thought," in *Working Alternatives: American Catholic Experiments in Work and Economy*, ed. John Seitz and Christine Firer Hinze (New York: Fordham University Press, 2020), 148–88.

50. Bousquet, *How the University Works*, 30.

51. See ibid.; Berry, *Reclaiming the Ivory Tower*, 123; and the essays in Michael Dubson, *Ghosts in the Classroom: Stories of College Adjunct Faculty—and the Price We All Pay* (Boston: Camel's Back Books, 2001).

52. Michael Dubson, "I Am an Adjunct," in *Ghosts in the Classroom*, 9–10. Cited in Nelson and Watt, *Office Hours: Activism and Change in the Academy*, 28. A recent study has documented the psychological impact of contingency on faculty members. See Gretchen M. Reevy and Grace Deason, "Predictors of Depression, Stress, and Anxiety among Non-Tenure Track Faculty," *Frontiers in Psychology* 5, no. 701 (2014): 1–17.

53. Reevy and Deason, "Predictors of Depression, Stress, and Anxiety,"

54. Kezar and Depaola, "Understanding the Need for Unions," 31.

55. Maria Maisto discusses a study that concluded that contingent faculty often do not advocate for themselves because they have internalized a sense of inferiority and negative attitudes toward them. However, she also contends that "the more complex tropes of the self-hating adjunct and the satisfied or apathetic adjunct can be countered" by highlighting narratives of contingent faculty activism and empowerment. Maisto, "Taking Heart, Taking Part," 195–97. On the disrespect toward adjuncts, see also Paivi Hoikkala, "'Lecturers Anonymous': Moving Contingent Faculty to Visibility at a Masters Institution," in *Embracing Nontenure Track Faculty: Changing Campuses for the New Faculty*

Majority, ed. Adrianna J. Kezar (New York: Routledge, 2012), 130–45. On adjuncts organizing see also Clausen and Swidler, "Academic Freedom from Below."

56. Józef Tischner, *The Spirit of Solidarity*, trans. Marek B. Zaleski and Benjamin Fiore (San Francisco: Harper & Row, 1984), 20–21.

57. See the discussion of justice in Chapter 1.

58. Tischner, *The Spirit of Solidarity*, 23–24.

59. See Keith Hoeller, "The Wal-Mart-ization of Higher Education: How Young Professors Are Getting Screwed," *Salon* (2014), https://www.salon.com/2014/02/16/the_wal_mart_ization_of_higher_education_how_young_professors_are_getting_screwed/.

60. John Paul II, *Laborem Exercens*, no. 8.

61. I borrow the term "lumpen professoriate" from Cary Nelson as cited in Bousquet, *How the University Works*, 18.

62. See Robert B. Archibald and David Henry Feldman, *Why Does College Cost So Much?* (New York: Oxford University Press, 2011), 25.

63. Shulman, "The Costs and Benefits of Adjunct Justice," 5. See also Stephen Mockabee, "Why Full-Time Faculty Don't Teach More Low-Level Courses: Steve Mockabee's Testimony," *Academe Blog: The Blog of Academe Magazine* (October 17, 2017), https://academeblog.org/2017/10/17/why-full-time-faculty-dont-teach-more-low-level-courses-steve-mockabees-testimony/. Mockabee indicates that converting 50 percent of part-time positions to full-time positions would cost public institutions in Ohio between 1.23 percent and 8.99 percent of their overall budget.

64. Bousquet, *How the University Works*, 56.

65. Ibid., 107, 11. As an example he points to the now infamous words of the former NYU dean Ann Marcus who apparently said with regard to adjuncts "we need people we can abuse, exploit and turn loose."

66. John G. Cross and Edie N. Goldenberg, *Off-Track Profs: Nontenured Teachers in Higher Education* (Cambridge, Mass.: MIT Press, 2009), 91–92. I explain RCM and its underlying individualistic anthropology in Beyer, "Curing the 'Disease' in Corporatized Higher Education," 166–72.

67. See Kellie Woodhouse, "Closures to Triple," *Inside Higher Ed*, September 28, 2015, https://www.insidehighered.com/news/2015/09/28/moodys-predicts-college-closures-triple-2017; Rick Seltzer, "Deficits at Small Colleges and Large Universities," *Inside Higher Ed*, June 13, 2017, https://www.insidehighered.com/quicktakes/2017/06/13/deficits-small-colleges-and-large-universities. The AAUP has contended that upon examining the evidence many claims of "financial exigency" or "budget crisis" are exaggerated. See American Association of University Professors, "Financial Exigency, Academic Governance, and Related Matters," https://www.aaup.org/AAUP/comm/rep/finexg.htm#b1and

AAUP, "Voices of the AAUP: Howard Bunsis on How the Budget Crisis at Some Universities is 'Made Up,'" August 6, 2010, YouTube video, https://www.youtube.com/watch?v=ob-d_RfSg2c.

68. Shulman rebuts analysts who have offered what he deems unrealistically high costs of adjunct justice. See Shulman, "The Costs and Benefits of Adjunct Justice," 1–9.

69. Donna M. Desrochers, "Academic Spending Versus Athletic Spending: Who Wins?" (Delta Cost Project at American Institutes for Research, 2013) and Knight Commission on Intercollegiate Athletics, "Knight Commission Launches Groundbreaking, Interactive College Sports Spending Database," December 4, 2013, http://www.knightcommission.org/resources/press-room/845-december-4-2013-knight-commission-launches-groundbreaking-interactive-college-sports-spending-database. The Knight Commission states that "from 2005–2011, academic spending per student at institutions in the FBS grew just 3 percent after adjusting for inflation, while athletic spending per athlete grew 31 percent and football spending per football player grew 52 percent even without considering spending on athletic scholarships." The data from this report pertains only to public universities. See also Knight Commission on Intercollegiate Athletics, "Restoring the Balance: Dollars, Values, and the Future of College Sports" (Miami, Fl: Knight Commission on Intercollegiate Athletics, 2010), https://www.knightcommission.org/wp-content/uploads/2010/05/KCIA_Report_F.pdf, and Rick Eckstein, *How College Athletics Are Hurting Girls' Sports: The Pay-to-Play Pipeline* (Lanham, Md.: Rowman & Littlefield Publishers, 2017), 180.

70. Curtis and Thornton, "Losing Focus: The Annual Report on the Economic Status of the Profession, 2013–14," 13.

71. Eckstein, *How College Athletics Are Hurting Girls' Sports*, 180.

72. Charlotte Gibson, "Who's the Highest-Paid Person in Your State?," *ESPN* (March 20, 2018), http://www.espn.com/espn/feature/story/_/id/22454170/highest-paid-state-employees-include-ncaa-coaches-nick-saban-john-calipari-dabo-swinney-bill-self-bob-huggins; Laura McKenna, "The Madness of College Basketball Coaches' Salaries," *The Atlantic*, March 24, 2016, https://www.theatlantic.com/education/archive/2016/03/the-madness-of-college-basketball-coaches-salaries/475146/; Jonah Newman, "Coaches, Not Presidents, Top Public-College Pay List," *The Chronicle of Higher Education*, May 16, 2014, https://www.chronicle.com/blogs/data/2014/05/16/coaches-not-presidents-top-public-college-pay-list/.

73. Curtis and Thornton, "Losing Focus: The Annual Report on the Economic Status of the Profession, 2013–14," 15. On the increase in coaches' salaries, see also the Knight Commission on Intercollegiate Athletics, "Knight Commission Updates Athletic and Academic Spending Database," March 23,

2015, https://www.knightcommission.org/2015/03/knight-commission-updates
-athletic-and-academic-spending-database/.

74. Lauren Camera, "Survey: Coach's Salary Shouldn't Best President's,"
U.S. News and World Report, March 15, 2016, https://www.usnews.com/news
/articles/2016-03-15/new-survey-college-coaches-shouldnt-make-more-than
-college-presidents.

75. See the Athletics expenditures of individual institutions at the US
Department of Education's Equity in Athletics Database at https://ope.ed.gov
/athletics/#/.

76. The median travel expenditure alone among FBS (football subdivision
schools) public universities was $2.5 million annually. See Center for College
Affordability and Productivity, "25 Ways to Reduce the Cost of College," (Center
for College Affordability and Productivity, 2010), 72, https://files.eric.ed.gov
/fulltext/ED536144.pdf.

77. Ibid., 66. See also Desrochers, "Academic Spending Versus Athletic
Spending: Who Wins?," 10; Suzanne E. Estler and Laurie Jan Nelson, *Who Calls
the Shots?: Sports and University Leadership, Culture, and Decision Making* (San
Francisco, Calif.: Wiley Subscription Services, 2005), 73–87; Murray A. Sperber,
*Beer and Circus: How Big-Time College Sports Is Crippling Undergraduate Educa-
tion* (New York: Henry Holt, 2000); Peter A. French, *Ethics and College Sports:
Ethics, Sports, and the University*, Issues in Academic Ethics (Lanham, Md.:
Rowman & Littlefield Publishers, 2004), 79–101; Eckstein, *How College
Athletics Are Hurting Girls' Sports*, 58. Rick Eckstein, "Men's Basketball Does
Not Pay for Other Villanova Athletic Teams," *The Villanovan* (2017), http://
www.villanovan.com/sports/men-s-basketball-does-not-pay-for-other-villanova
-athletic/article_7ee1994a-f18e-5a4c-825d-8d4bae35712b.html; and Jonathan
Berr, "How Villanova Gets Its Money's Worth from Basketball," *CBS News*
(2017), https://www.cbsnews.com/news/how-villanova-gets-its-moneys-worth
-from-basketball/.

78. Curtis and Thornton, "Losing Focus: The Annual Report on the
Economic Status of the Profession, 2013–14," 14. See also Victor A Matheson,
"The Bottom Line: Accounting for Revenues and Expenditures in Intercolle-
giate Athletics," *International Journal of Sport Finance* 7, no. 1 (2012): 30–45; and
Dashiell Bennett, "Only 22 of 120 Division I Athletic Programs Made Money
Last Year," *Business Insider* (2011), https://www.businessinsider.com/ncaa
-revenue-expense-report-2011-6.

79. Brad Wolverton et al., "The $10-Billion Sports Tab: How College Students
Are Funding the Athletics Arms Race," *The Chronicle of Higher Education*,
November 15, 2015, https://www.chronicle.com/article/the-10-billion-sports-tab
/#id=table_2014. See also Eckstein, *How College Athletics Are Hurting Girls'
Sports*, 179.

80. See ibid.

81. Rachel Fishman, "Deciding to Go to College: 2015 College Decisions Survey: Part I" (New America Foundation, 2015), 6–7.

82. Desrochers, "Academic Spending Versus Athletic Spending: Who Wins?," 2. See also Matheson, "The Bottom Line: Accounting for Revenues and Expenditures in Intercollegiate Athletics," 35. Sperber places some stock in the "Flutie factor," citing polls that seem to validate it. However, he sees it as contributing to the declining interest in academics and states that it does not preclude deficit spending on athletics on many campuses. He maintains that many university administrators justify this by embracing the notion of "mission-driven athletics," which sees athletics as a central part of the institution's raison d'être. See Sperber, *Beer and Circus*, 60–68, 211–12. For recent data-driven challenges to the "Flutie factor," see Elka Peterson-Horner and Rick Eckstein, "Challenging the 'Flutie Factor': Intercollegiate Sports, Undergraduate Enrollments, and the Neoliberal University," *Humanity & Society* 39, no. 1 (2015): 64–85; and Eckstein, *How College Athletics Are Hurting Girls' Sports*, 63–66.

83. Curtis and Thornton, "Losing Focus: The Annual Report on the Economic Status of the Profession, 2013–14," 14.

84. Sperber, *Beer and Circus*. See also Estler and Nelson, *Who Calls the Shots?: Sports and University Leadership, Culture, and Decision Making*, 68–70; and French, *Ethics and College Sports: Ethics, Sports, and the University*, 1–9, 31–62. The scandal involving four Notre Dame athletes who committed academic fraud is just one example of cases involving athletes at Catholic universities. See Chris Hine, "Notre Dame Should Not Allow or Take Shortcuts," *Chicago Tribune*, August 17, 2014; Melinda Hennenberger, "Why I Won't Be Cheering for Good Old Notre Dame," *Washington Post*, December 4, 2012; and Malcom Moran, "Boston College Bans 13 Football Players over Bets," *The New York Times*, Nov. 7, 1996, https://www.nytimes.com/1996/11/07/sports/boston-college-bans-13-football-players-over-bets.html. For an alternative view, see Marcia W. Mount Shoop, *Touchdowns for Jesus and Other Signs of Apocalypse: Lifting the Veil on Big-Time Sports* (Eugene, Ore.: Cascade Books, 2014), 79. Mount Shoop argues that sports "add to the mix" when it comes to the "crisis of integrity" in higher education, "but perhaps not even remarkably so."

85. Peterson-Horner and Eckstein, "Challenging the 'Flutie Factor,'" 64–65.

86. Eckstein, *How College Athletics Are Hurting Girls' Sports*, 66, 175.

87. See Kezar and Maxey, "Dispelling the Myths," 15.

88. See for example Mount Shoop, *Touchdowns for Jesus and Other Signs of Apocalypse*, 61–84; Shaun R. Harper, "Black Male Student-Athletes and Racial Inequities in NCAA Division I College Sports: 2016 Edition" (Center for the Study of Race and Equity in Education: University of Pennsylvania Graduate School of Education 2016), http://www.gse.upenn.edu/equity/sites/gse.upenn

.edu.equity/files/publications/Harper_Sports_2016.pdf; Jake New, "Lobbying for Athletics," *Inside Higher Ed*, March 8, 2017, https://www.insidehighered .com/news/2017/03/08/facing-scrutiny-college-sports-organizations-ramp -lobbying-efforts.

89. My brother Jamie Beyer (1973–2018) rowed at Temple University from 1990–1994 and was a two-time US Junior National Team member. I would add that at least some sports were quite different then. Our rowing teams had no corporate sponsorships. We were expected to raise money to pay for our own uniforms. Team members drove rented vans long distances, etc. For a positive appraisal of sport generally, with which I agree, see for example John White, "John Paul II's Interpretation of 1 Corinthians 9:24–27: A Paradigm for a Christian Ethic of Sport," *Studies in Christian Ethics* 25, no. 1 (2012): 73–88.

90. In this regard, I agree with Eckstein's proposal to give greater priority to intramural and club sports. See Eckstein, *How College Athletics Are Hurting Girls' Sports*, 176.

91. Bill Miscamble, C.S.C., "Notre Dame at a Crossroads: Misplaced Priorities and a Flawed Vision," *The Irish Rover*, February 23, 2017, https:// irishrover.net/2014/02/notre-dame-at-a-crossroads-misplaced-priorities-and-a -flawed-vision/. For a more descriptive account of the extravagances, see Margaret Fosmoe, "Curtain Rises on Notre Dame Stadium Renovations," *South Bend Tribune*, August 12, 2017, https://www.southbendtribune.com/news/local /curtain-rises-on-notre-dame-stadium-renovations/article_54a39c0a-ea65-5b4c -baf6-b99b7a6ffa28.html.

92. See "New Athletics Center to Be Named for Legendary Basketball Coach," https://www.georgetown.edu/news/georgetown-names-new -intercollegiate-athletic-center-for-thompson.html and "Video of the Month: The John R. Thompson Jr. Intercollegiate Athletic Center at Georgetown," https://alumni.georgetown.edu/video-month-john-r-thompson-jr-intercollegiate -athletic-center-georgetown-0.

93. John Marks, "Villanova's $65 Million Renovated Finneran Pavilion Incorporates Hoops with History," *Forbes*, October 6, 2018, https://www.forbes .com/sites/jonmarks/2018/10/06/villanovas-65-million-renovated-finneran -pavilion-incorporates-hoops-with-history/#6a2048133af1.

94. Jerry DiPaola, "Duquesne Unveils Plans for $45 Million Renovation of Palumbo Center," *Trib Live*, October 23, 2018, https://archive.triblive.com /sports/college/duquesne/duquesne-unveils-plans-for-45-million-renovation-of -palumbo-center/. For a fuller discussion of Duquesne's recent investments in athletics, see Eckstein, *How College Athletics Are Hurting Girls' Sports*, 178–80.

95. Dave Zirin, "Loyola Basketball's March Madness Success Shaded by Student Unrest," *The Nation*, March 16, 2018, https://www.thenation.com /article/loyola-basketballs-march-madness-success-shaded-by-student-unrest/

96. See for example Eckstein, *How College Athletics Are Hurting Girls' Sports*, 176, and *The Chronicle of Higher Education*, "Interactive Table: Who Foots the Bill in College Sports?," https://www.chronicle.com/interactives/ncaa-subsidies -main#id=table_2014.

97. John Paul II, *Jan Paweł II Polska 1999: Przemówienia i Homilie* (Marki: Michalineum, 1999), 75–76.

98. I elaborate this argument on the priority of basic rights in Gerald J. Beyer, "Beyond 'Nonsense on Stilts': Towards Conceptual Clarity and Resolution of Conflicting Economic Rights," *Human Rights Review* 6, no. 4 (2005).

99. Curtis and Thornton, "Losing Focus: The Annual Report on the Economic Status of the Profession, 2013–14," 10.

100. American Association of University Professors, "Visualizing Change: The Annual Report on the Economic Status of the Profession, 2016–17," 21.

101. Dan Bauman, "Private Colleges Had 58 Millionaire Presidents in 2015," *The Chronicle of Higher Education*, December 10, 2017.

102. Calculations are based on publicly available IRS 990 forms and *The Chronicle of Higher Education Executive Compensation* database.

103. See "NCAA Salaries: NCAAF Coaches," http://sports.usatoday.com /ncaa/salaries/football/coach and "NCAA Salaries: NCAAB Coaches," http:// sports.usatoday.com/ncaa/salaries/mens-basketball/coach.

104. See "NCAA Salaries: NCAAB Coaches," http://sports.usatoday.com /ncaa/salaries/mens-basketball/coach. See also Dan Bauman, Tyler Davis, and Brian O'Leary, "Executive Compensation at Private Colleges," (2016), *The Chronicle of Higher Education*, July 14, 2019, https://www.chronicle.com /interactives/executive-compensation#id=table_private_2016 ("Updated January 14, 2020, with 2017 private-college data").

105. See "NCAA Salaries: NCAAF Coaches," http://sports.usatoday.com /ncaa/salaries/football/coach and "NCAA Salaries: NCAAB Coaches," http:// sports.usatoday.com/ncaa/salaries/mens-basketball/coach. According to the USA Today database the basketball coach's total compensation, including from an outside source, reached $2,377,910.

106. See the 2014 and 2013 data at Bauman, Davis, and O'Leary, "Executive Compensation at Private Colleges."

107. See the 2011 data at Bauman, Davis, and O'Leary, "Executive Compensation at Private Colleges."

108. See ibid.

109. See ibid.

110. See the 2011 men's basketball coaches' salaries according to the Chronicle executive compensation database at Bauman, Davis, and O'Leary, "Executive Compensation at Private Colleges": DePaul ($2,274,592); Dayton ($328,296); Duquesne ($468,444); Univ. of San Diego ($579,334); Loyola

Marymount ($378,772); Univ. of Portland ($377,391); Lasalle Univ. ($406,630); St. Louis Univ. ($756,920); Univ. of San Francisco ($378,620); Xavier Univ. ($838,757).

111. On pressure coaches face, see Mount Shoop, *Touchdowns for Jesus and Other Signs of Apocalypse*, 67–68.

112. See Frank Fear, "Coaching Endowments: Good for College Sports?" *The Sports Column*, April 20, 2015, http://www.thesportscol.com/2015/04/endowed -coaches-good-for-college-sports/; Ted Miller, "Endowed Titles New Trend in Coaching," *ESPN*, February 18, 2014, http://www.espn.com/college-football /story/_/id/10473550/endowments-exchange-namesakes-new-trend-coaching.

113. See McKenna, "The Madness of College Basketball Coaches' Salaries," *The Atlantic*, March 24, 2016, https://www.theatlantic.com/education/archive /2016/03/the-madness-of-college-basketball-coaches-salaries/475146/. The author points out that fans and state legislatures demand coaches be paid handsomely.

114. Parts of the following discussion of just wages in CST are borrowed from Gerald J. Beyer, "Workers' Rights and Socially Responsible Investment in the Catholic Tradition: A Case Study," *Journal of Catholic Social Thought* 10, no. 1 (2013): 123–26. Reprinted here with permission.

115. Frank D. Almade, "Just Wage," in *The New Dictionary of Catholic Social Thought*, ed. Judith A. Dwyer (Collegeville, Minn.: Liturgical Press, 1994), 492.

116. John Ryan points to the defense of the just wage by the Catholic bishops "Ketteler in Germany, Vogelsang in Austria, de Pascal in France, Pottier in Belgium and Manning in England" as precursors to Leo XIII. John A. Ryan, *A Living Wage*, Rev. and abridged ed. (New York: Macmillan, 1920), 49. See also Marvin L. Krier Mich, *Catholic Social Teaching and Movements* (Mystic, Conn.: Twenty-Third Publications, 1998), 8–11.

117. Leo XIII, *Rerum Novarum*, no. 2, 44.

118. Ibid., no. 34.

119. Ibid.

120. See John Paul II, *Laborem Exercens*, no. 19. In this sense, John Paul II harkens to the idea of the "universal destination of all goods," which can be found in the writings of early Christian writers like Basil the Great, John Chrysostom, and Augustine. See also John Paul II, *Laborem Exercens*, no. 14; John Paul II, *Sollicitudo Rei Socialis*, no. 42; John Paul II, *Centesimus Annus*, no. 30; and Paul VI, *Populorum Progressio*, (March 26, 1967), http://www .vatican.va/content/paul-vi/en/encyclicals/documents/hf_p-vi_enc_26031967 _populorum.html. no. 22–23.

121. John Paul II, *Laborem Exercens*, no. 8.

122. CST considers just wages a requirement of commutative, distributive, and social justice. See Almade, "Just Wage," 491–95; Robert G. Kennedy, "The

Practice of Just Compensation," *Journal of Religion and Business Ethics* 1, no. 1 (2009): 1–17; Michael J. Naughton and Robert L. Wahlstedt, "Implementing Just Wages and Ownership: A Dialogue," in *Rediscovering Abundance: Interdisciplinary Essays on Wealth, Income, and Their Distribution in the Catholic Social Tradition*, ed. Helen J. Alford (Notre Dame, Ind.: University of Notre Dame Press, 2006).

123. Second Vatican Council, *Gaudium et Spes*, no. 67.

124. Paul VI, *Populorum Progressio*, 14–21. See also Almade, "Just Wage," 493.

125. The following paragraph appears in my book Gerald J. Beyer, *Recovering Solidarity: Lessons from Poland's Unfinished Revolution* (Notre Dame, Ind.: University of Notre Dame Press, 2010). Reprinted here with permission.

126. For a description of the similarities and differences between a just and living wage, see Patricia Ann Lamoureaux, "Is a Living Wage a Just Wage?," *America*, February 19, 2001. https://www.americamagazine.org/issue/340/article/living-wage-just-wage.

127. See John Paul II, *Laborem Exercens*, no. 8. See also Christine Firer Hinze, "Bridging Discourse on Wage Justice: Roman Catholic and Feminist Perspectives on the Family Living Wage," in *Feminist Ethics and the Catholic Moral Tradition*, ed. Charles E. Curran, Farley, Margaret A., McCormick, Richard A. (New York: Paulist Press, 1996), 511–40; Almade, "Just Wage," 491–95.

128. Michael J. Naughton, "Distributors of Justice: A Case for Just Wage," in *A Worker Justice Reader: Essential Writings on Religion and Labor*, ed. Joy Heine (Maryknoll, N.Y.: Orbis Books, 2010). For relevant passages in CST, see Pius XI, *Quadragesimo Anno*, (May 15, 1931), http://www.vatican.va/content/pius-xi/en/encyclicals/documents/hf_p-xi_enc_19310515_quadragesimo-anno.html., nos. 70–74; John XXIII, *Mater et Magistra*, 70–72; Second Vatican Council, *Gaudium et Spes*, no. 67.

129. Pope John XXIII, *Mater et Magistra*, no. 70.

130. Robert G. Kennedy, "The Practice of Just Compensation," 12. See also David L. Gregory, "Reflections on Current Labor Applications of Catholic Social Thought," *Journal of Catholic Social Thought* 1, no. 2 (2004): 675–78. Edward Welch, "Justice in Executive Compensation," *America* (2003), http://americamagazine.org/node/146521.

131. Michael J. Naughton, "Distributors of Justice: A Case for Just Wage," 166; Robert G. Kennedy, "The Practice of Just Compensation," 14–15.

132. See Leo XIII, *Rerum Novarum*, (May 15, 1891), http://www.vatican.va/content/leo-xiii/en/encyclicals/documents/hf_l-xiii_enc_15051891_rerum-novarum.html, no. 35; Pius XI, *Quadragesimo Anno*, no. 71; John XXIII, *Mater et Magistra*; no. 71; John XXIII, *Pacem in Terris*, no. 20; John Paul II, *Laborem Exercens*, no. 19; John Paul II, *Centesimus Annus*, no. 15; and Benedict XVI,

Caritas in Veritate, no. 63. See also Ryan, *A Living Wage*; and Firer Hinze, "Bridging Discourse on Wage Justice."

133. John XXIII, *Mater et Magistra*, no. 72. See also Almade, "Just Wage," 494.

134. John Paul II, *Centesimus Annus*, no. 15.

135. John XXIII, *Mater et Magistra*, no. 71.

136. See United States Conference of Catholic Bishops, *Economic Justice for All*, nos. 351, 353.

137. Sinclair Oubre, "Labor Law for 1.1 Billion People: How Canon Law, and Catholic Social Justice Principles Can Give a Third Way," (Catholic Labor Network, 2010). This paper is no longer on the Catholic Labor Network website but is on file with the present author. Fr. Oubre, a canon lawyer, points to the canons that obligate church institutions to pay their employees a living wage and to recognize the freedom of association, which includes the right to unionize. He cites Canon 231§2: "Lay persons have the right to decent remuneration appropriate to their condition so that they are able to provide decently for their own needs and those of their family. They also have a right for their social provision, social security, and health benefits to be duly provided." In addition, Canon 215: "The Christian faithful are at liberty freely to found and direct associations for purposes of charity or piety or for the promotion of the Christian vocation in the world and to hold meetings for the common pursuit of these purposes." Quotations here of the relevant canons are from the Code of Canon Law at the Vatican website, http://www.vatican.va/archive/ENG1104/__PU.HTM. See also Francis G. Morrisey, "Just Wages: It's in Church Law," *Health Progress* 92, no. 4 (2011): 102–3.

138. See "Tenured/Tenure-Track Faculty Salaries," *HigherEdJobs*, http://www.higheredjobs.com/salary/salaryDisplay.cfm?SurveyID=28. According to the survey, the average starting salary for a new assistant professor in business is $107,000. The average starting salary for a new assistant professor in education and philosophy is $58,000 and $56,000 respectively.

139. Welch argues that CEO pay should be capped at 100 times that of the average worker. Welch, "Justice in Executive Compensation." I contend that Catholic universities must do better than this, especially given the situation of adjuncts and the limited resources of these institutions compared to many other private industries.

140. See Audrey Williams June, "IRS Suggests 'Reasonable' Ways of Calculating Adjuncts' Hours," *The Chronicle of Higher Education*, February 11, 2014, http://chronicle.com/article/Reasonable-Ways-of/144701/ and Shulman, "The Costs and Benefits of Adjunct Justice," 3.

141. See New Faculty Majority, "NFM's 7 Goals," http://www.newfacultymajority.info/nfms-7-goals/.

142. I argue this more fully in Beyer, "Curing the 'Disease' in Corporatized Higher Education."

143. John Paul II, *Laborem Exercens*, no. 19. See also Pontifical Council for Justice and Peace, "Compendium of the Social Doctrine of the Church," no. 301; John Paul II, *Centesimus Annus*, no. 15; United States Conference of Catholic Bishops, *Economic Justice for All*, no. 80.

144. United States Conference of Catholic Bishops, *Economic Justice for All*, no. 80.

145. John Paul II, *Laborem Exercens*, no. 6. See also Gustavo Gutiérrez, *The Density of the Present: Selected Writings* (Maryknoll, N.Y.: Orbis Books, 1999), 17–19.

146. The following is an abbreviated version of the argument in Beyer, "Labor Unions, Adjuncts, and the Mission and Identity of Catholic Universities," © 2015 College Theology Society. Reprinted with permission.

147. See Maisto, "Taking Heart, Taking Part," 198–99; Berry, *Reclaiming the Ivory Tower*; Tolley, *Professors in the Gig Economy*; and the Adjunct Action website at http://adjunctaction.org/.

148. See Susan Stabile, "Blame It on Catholic Bishop: The Question of NLRB Jurisdiction over Religious Colleges and Universities," *Pepperdine Law Review* 39, no. 5 (2013): 1318–19, notes 7 and 39. The amicus brief (filed April 25, 2011) can be read on the National Labor Relations Board web site at nlrb.gov/case/02-rc-023543. See also the Catholic Scholars for Worker Justice amicus brief, arguing conversely at http://cswj.us/wp-content/uploads/2017/10 /2014-03-26-Amicus-Curiae-Brief-by-CSWJ-to-NLRB.pdf.

149. "Gaudium et Spes Labor Report," *The Catholic Labor Network*, http:// catholiclabor.org/catholic-employer-project/gaudium-et-spes-catholic -institutions-with-union-representation/.

150. See "Catholic Higher Education," *The Catholic Labor Network*, http:// catholiclabor.org/catholic-employer-project/catholic-higher-education/.

151. See Michael Lehmann, "A Short History of the USFFA," *USFFA*, http://www.usffa.net/about/history-2/; "Brief History of FAC," Faculty Affairs Council, http://www.scrantonfac.org/brief-history-of-fac/; Le Moyne Adjunct Faculty, https://echo.lemoyne.edu/Faculty-Staff-Resources/Campus-Resources /Human-Resources/Unions/Adjunct-Union.

152. See "Just Employment Policy for Georgetown University," Georgetown University Office of Public Affairs, http://publicaffairs.georgetown .edu/acbp/just-employment-policy.html. I will discuss this in more detail below.

153. Peter Schmidt, "Union Efforts on Behalf of Adjuncts Meet Resistance within Faculties' Ranks," *The Chronicle of Higher Education*, April 9, 2014, http://chronicle.com/article/Union-Efforts-on-Behalf-of/145833/.

154. Peter Schmidt, "Georgetown U. Adjuncts Vote to Unionize," *The Chronicle of Higher Education*, May 3, 2014, http://chronicle.com/article/Georgetown-U-Adjuncts-Vote-to/139069/.

155. Wertsch and McCartin, "A Just Employment Approach to Adjunct Unionization," 97–99.

156. See for example Sydni Dunn, "Anatomy of a Letter: What Universities Tell Adjuncts about Unions," *Chronicle Vitae*, February 21, 2014, https://chroniclevitae.com/news/348-anatomy-of-a-letter-what-universities-tell-adjuncts-about-unions. Joe Holland rebuts this argument in Joe Holland, *100 Years of Catholic Social Teaching Defending Workers & Their Unions: Summaries & Commentaries for Five Landmark Papal Encyclicals* (Washington, D.C.: Pacem in Terris Press, 2012), 2. Michele Lynn Nelson has noted in her study of the attitudes of senior-level administrators at Catholic institutions toward collective bargaining that they perceive unions as "outsiders" who hinder their ability to work collaboratively with their employees. Michele Lynn Nelson, "Senior-Level Administrator Perceptions of Collective Bargaining at Catholic Colleges and Universities" (PhD diss., Fordham University, 2017), 102–3.

157. James A. Donahue, "Message from November 12, 2014," https://www.stmarys-ca.edu/president/message-from-november-12-2014. Dr. Donahue was my first professor of Christian ethics at Georgetown University.

158. See Collective Bargaining Agreement between St. Mary's College of California and The Service Employees International Union Local 1021, May 20, 2016 through June 30, 2019, https://www.stmarys-ca.edu/sites/default/files/attachments/files/SMC%20—%20Collective%20Bargaining%20Agreement%20—%20FINAL02.09.18.pdf.

159. Jacqueline Thomsen, "Summer Unemployment Reality," *Inside Higher Ed*, July 15, 2015, https://www.insidehighered.com/news/2015/07/15/contingent-faculty-earn-big-win-unemployment-benefits-national-battle-continues.

160. See Saint Mary's College of California, Human Resources, "Salary Scales," https://www.stmarys-ca.edu/human-resources/salary-scales.

161. See Tolley, Delaporte, and Giachetti, "Unionizing Adjunct and Tenure-Track Faculty at Notre Dame De Namur University," and Colleen Flaherty, "Leap of Faith," *Inside Higher Ed*, June 30, 2015, https://www.insidehighered.com/news/2017/06/30/how-tenure-track-and-adjunct-faculty-joined-forces-unionize-notre-dame-de-namur.

162. Emily Deruy, "NDNU Cuts Programs, Lays Off Faculty," May 21, 2018, https://www.mercurynews.com/2018/05/21/ndnu-cuts-programs-lays-off-faculty/.

163. Dave Jamieson, "Catholic Teaching Says Support Unions. Catholic Colleges Are Fighting Them," *Huffington Post*, January 13, 2016, https://www.huffpost.com/entry/catholic-colleges-adjuncts-unions_n_56942dc0e4b09dbb4bac4f84;

Zirin, "Loyola Soars in March Madness While a Faculty Strike Looms," https://www.thenation.com/article/loyola-soars-in-march-madness-while -faculty-strike-looms/; Michelle Chen, "Adjuncts at Loyola University Chicago Want a Union. Will the Jesuit University Respect Their Demands?," *The Nation*, December 28, 2015, https://www.thenation.com/article/adjuncts-at-loyola -university-chicago-want-a-union-will-the-jesuit-university-respect-their -demands/; Gerald J. Beyer and Donald C. Carroll, "Battling Adjunct Unions Fails Legal and Moral Tests," *National Catholic Reporter*, April 5, 2016, https:// www.ncronline.org/news/people/battling-adjunct-unions-fails-legal-and-moral -tests. At the time I coauthored this piece, the university had a publicly accessible letter on its website making this argument. The letter has since been removed.

164. Danielle Douglas-Gabriel, "Adjunct Faculty at Loyola University Chicago Ratify First Contract," April 27, 2018, https://www.washingtonpost .com/news/grade-point/wp/2018/04/27/adjunct-faculty-at-loyola-university -chicago-ratify-first-contract/?utm_term=.07c6c7c5ddc7. See also Christopher Hacker, "Non-Tenured Faculty Threaten April 4 Strike If No Agreement Reached," *Loyola Phoenix*, March 16, 2018, http://loyolaphoenix.com/2018/03/non-tenured -faculty-threaten-april-4-strike-if-no-agreement-reached/.

165. Victor Ordonez, "SEIU Withdraws Adjunct Petition: Admin Claim No Unionization Roadblocks," *The Fordham Ram*, April 14, 2017, https:// fordhamram.com/2017/04/seiu-withdraws-adjunct-petition-admin-claim-no -unionization-roadblocks/.

166. Cecile Neidig, "Adjunct Faculty Protest Low Wages," *The Observer*, September 14, 2016, http://www.fordhamobserver.com/adjunct-faculty-protest -low-wages/.

167. Katherine Smith, "Fordham Responds to Unionization of Adjunct Faculty," *The Observer*, May 19, 2017, http://www.fordhamobserver.com /fordham-responds-to-unionization-of-adjunct-faculty/; Editorial, "Keep Fordham Faculty in Focus," *The Fordham Ram*, April 12, 2017, https:// fordhamram.com/2017/04/keep-fordham-faculty-in-focus/.

168. Editorial, "Keep Fordham Faculty in Focus."

169. "Fordham Cites Catholic Teaching in Accepting Faculty Unionization," *Just Employment Policy* (2017), http://www.justemploymentpolicy.org/fordham- cites-catholic-teaching-in-accepting-faculty-unionization/; and Smith, "Fordham Responds to Unionization of Adjunct Faculty."

170. The Catholic Labor Network, "Luctus et Angor: Labor Disputes at Catholic Institutions," http://catholiclabor.org/catholic-employer-project/luctus -et-angor-labor-disputes-at-catholic-institutions/.

171. See Stabile, "Blame It on Catholic Bishop," 1326–28; Joseph J. Fahey, "Adjunct Unions at Catholic Affiliated Colleges and Universities," (2013),

http://cswj.us/wp-content/uploads/2017/11/2013-11-1-Adjunct-Background-Paper
-FAHEY.pdf; Clayton Sinyai, "Which Side Are We On? Catholic Teachers and
the Right to Unionize," *America*, January 7, 2015, https://www.americamagazine
.org/issue/which-side-are-we; Paul Moses, "Which Side Are They On?,"
Commonweal 138, no. 10 (2011). Moshe Z. Marvit, "The Continuing Struggle for
College Adjunct Unions," (2012), http://tcf.org/blog/detail/the-continuing
-struggle-for-college-adjunct-unions; Peter Schmidt, "Seattle U. Tells Adjuncts
It Opposes Their Unionization," *The Chronicle of Higher Education*, December 9,
2013., http://chronicle.com/blogs/ticker/seattle-u-tells-adjuncts-it-opposes-their
-unionization/70201; Pemberton, "Saint Martin's Faculty, Students Walk out
over Union Representation"; Karen Kelsky, "An Adjunct's Letter to Her
Union-Busting College President," *The Professor Is In*, June 16, 2017, http://
theprofessorisin.com/2017/06/16/an-adjunct-letter-to-her-union-busting-college
-president/.

172. James A. Gross, *A Shameful Business: The Case for Human Rights in the
American Workplace* (Ithaca, N.Y.: ILR Press/Cornell University Press, 2010),
78–80.

173. See Stabile, "Blame It on Catholic Bishop," 1326–28.; Fahey, "Adjunct
Unions at Catholic Affiliated Colleges and Universities"; Moses, "Which Side
Are They On?"; Subcommittee on Health, Employment, Labor and Pensions
jointly with the Subcommittee on Higher Education and Workforce Training,
Testimony of Michael P. Moreland, Expanding the Power of Big Labor: the NLRB's
Growing Intrusion into Higher Education, September 12, 2012, http://edworkforce
.house.gov/uploadedfiles/09.12.12_moreland.pdf; Marvit, "The Continuing
Struggle for College Adjunct Unions." Documentation of all cases involving
Catholic universities can be viewed by using the search function at the NLRB
website, https://www.nlrb.gov/.

174. Dennis H. Holtschneider, "Refereeing Religion?," *Inside Higher Ed*,
January 28, 2016, https://www.insidehighered.com/views/2016/01/28/new-nlrb
-standard-could-have-major-consequences-catholic-colleges-essay.

175. I have paraphrased the 2000 Supreme Court decision in Mitchell vs.
Helms, as cited in *Testimony of Michael P. Moreland*, 4. See also Stabile, "Blame
It on Catholic Bishop," 1317.

176. See, for example, Michael J. O'Loughlin, "Labor Board Rules in Favor
of Workers at Catholic Universities," *America*, April 13, 2017, https://www.america
magazine.org/faith/2017/04/13/labor-board-rules-favor-workers-catholic
-universities.

177. I am summarizing here from Beyer, "Labor Unions, Adjuncts, and the
Mission and Identity of Catholic Universities," and Beyer and Carroll, "Battling
Adjunct Unions Fails Legal and Moral Tests."

178. Stabile, "Blame It on Catholic Bishop," 1333.

179. *Testimony of Michael P. Moreland*, 7–9. See also the discussion of preferential hiring of Catholics and the concern over losing federal funding due to "legal sectarianism" in Alice Gallin, *Negotiating Identity: Catholic Higher Education since 1960* (Notre Dame, Ind.: University of Notre Dame Press, 2000), 86–87, 128.

180. See Gregory, "Reflections on Current Labor Applications of Catholic Social Thought"; David L. Gregory and Charles J. Russo, "Overcoming NLRB V. Yeshiva University by the Implementation of Catholic Labor Theory," *Labor Law Journal* 41 (1990).

181. See Leo XIII, *Rerum Novarum*, nos. 36, 37. For discussion of this point, see Beyer, "Workers' Rights and Socially Responsible Investment in the Catholic Tradition," 135–37.

182. Second Vatican Council, *Gaudium et Spes*, no. 68.

183. John Paul II, *Laborem Exercens*, no. 20.

184. Francis, "Audience with Delegates from the Confederation of Trade Unions in Italy (Confederazione Italiana Sindacati Lavoratori, CISL)," June 28, 2017, http://press.vatican.va/content/salastampa/en/bollettino/pubblico/2017/06/28/170628a.html.

185. United States Conference of Catholic Bishops, *Economic Justice for All*, no. 353. See also United States Catholic Conference of Bishops, "Respecting the Just Rights of Workers: Guidance and Options for Catholic Health Care and Unions," (2009), http://www.usccb.org/issues-and-action/human-life-and-dignity/labor-employment/upload/respecting_the_just_rights_of_workers.pdf.

186. Oubre, "Labor Law for 1.1 Billion People," 10–11. Oubre points to Canon 215, which codifies the freedom of association posited by Leo XIII in *Rerum Novarum*. This canon can be found in The Code of Canon Law at the Vatican website, http://www.vatican.va/archive/ENG1104/__PU.HTM.

187. Canon 22, cited in ibid., 10.

188. Ibid.

189. This is my translation from the Polish text of Jan Paweł II, "Homilia Jana Pawła II Wygłoszona Podczas Mszy Św. w Ogrodzie Klasztornym w Sanktuarium Krzyża Świętego w Krakowie-Mogile (9 Czerwca 1979 R.)," June 9, 1979, http://www.mogila.cystersi.pl/index.php?option=com_content&view=article&id=133:homilia-jana-pawla-ii&Itemid=150. The official Vatican English translation can be found at http://www.vatican.va/holy_father/john_paul_ii/homilies/1979/documents/hf_jp-ii_hom_19790609_polonia-mogila-nowa-huta_en.html.

190. See Joseph Fahey's statement in Schmidt, "Adjuncts Appeal to Higher Power."

191. David L. Gregory, "The Demise of Workers' Rights," *America* 195, no. 5 (2006). See also Adam D. Reich, *With God on Our Side: The Struggle for Workers' Rights in a Catholic Hospital* (Ithaca: Cornell University Press, 2012), 159.

192. On Catholic schools bargaining outside of the NLRB, see David L. Gregory and Charles J. Russo, "The First Amendment and the Labor Relations of Religiously-Affiliated Employers," *Boston University Public Interest Law Journal* 8 (1999); and Sinyai, "Which Side Are We On?"

193. See Maria Mazzenga, "One-Hundred Years of American Catholics and Organized Labor, 1870s–1970s," *Journal Catholic Social Thought* 9, no. 1 (2012).

194. Kathleen Brady, "Religious Organizations and Mandatory Collective Bargaining under Federal and State Labor Laws: Freedom from and Freedom For," *Villanova Law Review* 49 (2004): 80–81, 121–22, 57–58. Michael Moreland repeated this argument in his testimony before the US Congress in a session titled "Expanding the Power of Big Labor: The NLRB's Growing Intrusion into Higher Education." See *Testimony of Michael P. Moreland*, http://edworkforce .house.gov/uploadedfiles/09.12.12_moreland.pdf.

195. On hospitals, see Reich, *With God on Our Side*, 105. On universities, see the letters from several Catholic institutions at https://chroniclevitae.com /news/348-anatomy-of-a-letter-what-universities-tell-adjuncts-about-unions and Nelson, "Senior-Level Administrator Perceptions of Collective Bargaining at Catholic Colleges and Universities," 102–5.

196. Gross, *A Shameful Business*, 63. See also 62–67, 71–73, 196, 204–5 and Reich, *With God on Our Side*, 163.

197. On strict limits to the right to accumulate private property in CST, see Paul VI, *Populorum Progressio*, nos. 23–24; John Paul II, *Sollicitudo Rei Socialis*, no. 42; John Paul II, *Laborem Exercens*, no. 14, John Paul II, *Centesimus Annus*, nos. 15, 30–31, 42; Francis, *Evangelii Gaudium*, nos. 189–90.

198. See John Paul II, *Veritatis Splendor*, no. 13.

199. For more details, see Wertsch and McCartin, "A Just Employment Approach to Adjunct Unionization."

200. Sinyai, "Which Side Are We On?" Sinyai quotes the superintendent of schools in the archdiocese of Pittsburgh. See also Gregory, "Reflections on Current Labor Applications of Catholic Social Thought." Gregory discusses the high regard labor leaders in the Archdiocese of New York had for Cardinal O'Connor, who maintained good relations with them.

201. Reich, *With God on Our Side*, 89.

202. Stabile, "Blame It on Catholic Bishop," 1342–43. The document is United States Conference of Catholic Bishops, "Respecting the Just Rights of Workers."

203. See Thomas Kochan, "4 Ideas Labor Unions Should Consider If They Want to Survive," *Cognoscenti*, February 4, 2013, https://www.wbur.org /cognoscenti/2013/02/04/union-innovation-thomas-kochan.

204. Thomas Kochan, "Editor's Introduction: Introduction to a Symposium on the Kaiser Permanente Labor Management Partnership," *Industrial*

Relations 47 (1998): 1–2. See also Thomas A. Kochan et al., "The Potential and Precariousness of Partnership: The Case of the Kaiser Permanente Labor Management Partnership," *Industrial Relations* 47, no. 1 (2008).

205. Brady, "Religious Organizations and Mandatory Collective Bargaining under Federal and State Labor Laws," 106, 18, 31–38.

206. Ibid., 114.

207. For this perspective in CST, see for example John Paul II, *Laborem Exercens,* and Pontifical Council for Justice and Peace, *Compendium of the Social Doctrine of the Church*, nos. 305–6. An excellent analysis of the points of contact and differences between CST and class struggle is Gregory Baum, "Class Struggle and the Magisterium: A New Note," *Theological Studies* 45 (1984).

208. On the notion that CST sees unions as a remedy to an imbalance of power, I am indebted to Reich, *With God on Our Side: The Struggle for Workers' Rights in a Catholic Hospital*. For sources in CST that state or imply that unions are needed to correct an imbalance of power, see Leo XIII, *Rerum Novarum*, nos. 47–49; John Paul II, *Laborem Exercens*, nos. 11, 14, 20; John Paul II, *Centesimus Annus*, no. 15; Benedict XVI, *Caritas in Veritate*, no. 25.

209. See John Paul II, *Laborem Exercens*, no. 8.

210. John Paul II, *Laborem Exercens*, no. 20.

211. Pontifical Council for Justice and Peace, *Compendium of the Social Doctrine of the Church*, no. 301.

212. Ibid., no. 305. Charles Curran correctly argues that John Paul accepts that "struggle and conflict" will take place between labor and management. See Charles E. Curran, *Catholic Social Teaching, 1891 Present: A Historical, Theological, and Ethical Analysis* (Washington, D.C.: Georgetown University Press, 2002), 210.

213. Benedict XVI, *Caritas in Veritate*, no. 25.

214. On the plight of workers in the neoliberal economy, see for example Gross, *A Shameful Business*; Vincent A. Gallagher, *The True Cost of Low Prices: The Violence of Globalization* (Maryknoll, N.Y.: Orbis Books, 2006); Robert A. Senser, *Justice at Work: Globalization and the Human Rights of Workers* (Bloomington, Ind.: Xlibris, 2009); Jody Heymann and Alison Earle, *Raising the Global Floor: Dismantling the Myth That We Can't Afford Good Working Conditions for Everyone* (Stanford, Calif.: Stanford Politics and Policy, 2010); Stephanie Luce, *Labor Movements: Global Perspectives* (Chichester, Great Britian: Polity, 2011); Sarah Adler-Milstein and John M. Kline, *Sewing Hope: How One Factory Challenges the Apparel Industry's Sweatshops* (Berkeley: University of California Press, 2017).

215. Francis, "Audience with Delegates from the Confederation of Trade Unions in Italy." On the present situation of workers, see also Francis, "Partici-

pation at the Second World Meeting of Popular Movements: Address of the Holy Father," July 9, 2015, http://w2.vatican.va/content/francesco/en/speeches/2015/july/documents/papa-francesco_20150709_bolivia-movimenti-popolari.html and Francis, "Address to World Meeting of Popular Movements," October 29, 2014, https://zenit.org/articles/pope-s-address-to-popular-movements/.

216. I discuss "cheap solidarity" in Gerald J. Beyer, "Advocating Worker Justice: A Catholic Ethicist's 'Toolkit,'" *Journal of Religious Ethics* 45, no. 2 (2017).

217. Tischner, *The Spirit of Solidarity*, 80–81.

218. This is my own translation from Polish. See John Paul II, "Viaggio Apostolico in Polonia Celebrazione Della Parola Con La Gente Del Mare: Omelia Di Giovanni Paolo II," July 11, 1987, http://www.vatican.va/holy_father/john_paul_ii/homilies/1987/documents/hf_jp-ii_hom_19870611_gente-mare_pl.html. For a similar view of solidarity and conflict, see Jon Sobrino and Juan Hernández Pico, *Theology of Christian Solidarity*, trans. Philip Berryman (Maryknoll, N.Y.: Orbis Books, 1985), 61–62, 90, 94, 96; Oscar A. Romero, *Voice of the Voiceless: The Four Pastoral Letters and Other Statements* (Maryknoll, N.Y.: Orbis Books, 1985), 181–88, 86.

219. Cited in Kevin Doran, *Solidarity: A Synthesis of Personalism and Communalism in the Thought of Karol Wojtyla/John Paul II* (New York: P. Lang, 1996), 213; see also 157–58, 213–17.

220. John Paul II, *Centesimus Annus*, no. 14. See also John Paul II, *Laborem Exercens*, no. 20.

221. See Tischner, *The Spirit of Solidarity*, 10–12, 71–74, 79–82; John Paul II, *Laborem Exercens*, no. 20; Francis, *Evangelii Gaudium*, no. 227–28. I borrow the terms "peacemakers" from Pope Francis in *Evangelii Gaudium*.

222. John Paul II, *Laborem Exercens*, no. 19.

223. Second Vatican Council, *Gaudium et Spes*, no. 68.

224. Beyer, "Advocating Worker Justice," 239.

225. Stabile, "Blame It on Catholic Bishop." See also Gee, "Facing Poverty, Academics Turn to Sex Work and Sleeping in Cars."

226. See also Thomas P. Rausch, *Educating for Faith and Justice: Catholic Higher Education Today* (Collegeville, Minn.: Liturgical Press, 2010), 19; David Hollenbach, "The Catholic University under the Sign of the Cross: Christian Humanism in a Broken World," in *Finding God in All Things*, ed. Stephen J. Pope (New York: Crossroads, 1996).

227. Evidence has shown that the majority of Catholics do not understand CST. See Paul Sullins, "Catholic Social Teaching: What Do Catholics Know, and What Do They Believe?," *Catholic Social Science Review* 7 (2003). On the ignorance or rejection of CST on workers' rights by many Catholics, see also

Holland, *100 Years of Catholic Social Teaching Defending Workers & Their Unions*, 1–13, 153–67.

228. Kristen Hannum, "Labor Pains: What Wisconsin Tells Us About Catholics and Unions," *U.S. Catholic* 76, no. 8 (2011), http://www.uscatholic.org /church/2011/07/labor-pains-what-wisconsin-tells-us-about-catholics-and-unions. See also Holland, *100 Years of Catholic Social Teaching Defending Workers & Their Unions*, 1–2.

229. See John Paul II, "Apostolic Journey to Poland Eucharistic Celebration Homily of His Holiness John Paul II (Elk)," June 8, 1999, http://w2.vatican.va /content/john-paul-ii/en/homilies/1999/documents/hf_jp-ii_hom_19990608 _elk.html, and John Paul II, "Apostolic Journey to the Dominican Republic, Mexico and the Bahamas: Meeting with Mexican Indios (Cuilapan, Mexico)," January 29, 1979, http://www.vatican.va/content/john-paul-ii/en/speeches/1979 /january/documents/hf_jp-ii_spe_19790129_messico-cuilapan-indios.html. In this address to Mexican Indians, John Paul quoted *Populorum Progressio* (no. 32), in which Paul VI stated bold changes must be made immediately to promote the integral development of all people.

230. See Nelson, "Senior-Level Administrator Perceptions of Collective Bargaining at Catholic Colleges and Universities," 102–8. The author notes that while administrators understand employees have the right to unionize legally and according to CST, they do not want more unions on their campuses.

231. Stephen E. Blaire, "Placing Work and Workers at the Center of Economic Life," September 3, 2012, United States Conference of Catholic Bishops website, http://www.usccb.org/issues-and-action/human-life-and-dignity/labor -employment/labor-day-statement-2012.cfm.

232. The following section is borrowed from Beyer, "Labor Unions, Adjuncts, and the Mission and Identity of Catholic Universities." © 2015 College Theology Society. Reprinted with permission.

233. For an example of a Catholic university hiring an expensive "union avoidance" firm, see Sinyai, "Which Side Are We On?"

234. New Testament scholar Alan Mitchell has argued that Paul found it particularly egregious for those Corinthians who had power and wealth to file lawsuits against poor Corinthians who had no chance to win in the courts. See Alan C. Mitchell, "Rich and Poor in the Courts of Corinth: Litigiousness and Status in 1 Corinthians 6.1–11," *New Testament Studies* 39, no. 4 (1993): 562–86.

235. William Spohn argues that discerning how a biblical passage relates to Christian discipleship today entails thinking analogically or "spotting the rhyme." William C. Spohn, *What Are They Saying About Scripture and Ethics?* (New York: Paulist Press, 1984), 100.

236. United States Conference of Catholic Bishops, "Respecting the Just Rights of Workers," 10.

237. See Luce, *Labor Movements*, 61–62, and the Human Rights Watch website at https://www.hrw.org/sitesearch/unionbusting.

238. See Gregory and Russo, "The First Amendment and the Labor Relations of Religiously-Affiliated Employers," 466.

239. M. Cathleen Kaveny, "Appropriation of Evil: Cooperation's Mirror Image," *Theological Studies* 61 (2000): 285–86.

240. James F. Keenan and Thomas R. Kopfensteiner, "The Principle of Cooperation," *Health Progress*, (April 1995): 23–27.

241. Angela Senander, *Scandal: The Catholic Church and Public Life* (Collegeville, Minn.: Liturgical Press, 2012), 97.

242. John Paul II, *Centesimus Annus*, no. 5.

243. See Pope Francis, *Evangelii Gaudium*, no. 187. For more theoretically robust discussions of this issue, see Gustavo Gutierrez, "The Option for the Poor," in *Mysterium Liberationis: Fundamental Concepts of Liberation Theology*, ed. Ignacio Ellacuría and Jon Sobrino (Maryknoll, N.Y.: Orbis, 1993), and Margaret Pfeil, "Power and the Preferential Option for the Poor," in *Hope and Solidarity: Jon Sobrino's Challenge to Christian Theology*, ed. Stephen J. Pope (Maryknoll, N.Y.: Orbis Books, 2008).

244. United States Conference of Catholic Bishops, "Respecting the Just Rights of Workers," 3.

245. John Paul deems the belief that the market alone can satisfy all human needs as "idolatry of the market." John Paul II, *Centesimus Annus*, no. 40. See also no. 48, and *Laborem Exercens*, no. 18. For further discussion of the role of the state and other duty bearers in fulfilling human rights, see J. Bryan Hehir, "The Modern Catholic Church and Human Rights: The Impact of the Second Vatican Council," in *Christianity and Human Rights: An Introduction*, ed. John Witte and Frank S. Alexander (Cambridge, UK: Cambridge University Press, 2010), 155–58; and Gerald J. Beyer, *Recovering Solidarity*, 93–94, 100–105, 38–43.

246. See Catholic Scholars for Worker Justice, "Union Busting Is a Mortal Sin," (2010), http://cswj.us/wp-content/uploads/2017/10/2010-01-05-UNION -BUSTING-IS-A-MORTAL-SIN.pdf.

247. Kaveny, "Appropriation of Evil: Cooperation's Mirror Image."

248. I spell this argument out more fully in Beyer, "Advocating Worker Justice." I will also discuss this concept in greater detail in Chapter 4 regarding socially responsible investment.

249. Francis, "Misericordiae Vultus: Bull of Indiction of the Extraodinary Jubilee of Mercy," April 11, 2015, https://w2.vatican.va/content/francesco/en /apost_letters/documents/papa-francesco_bolla_20150411_misericordiae -vultus.html.

250. See Michael Kazin, "Labor Needs More Than Labor," *The New Republic*, April 1, 2011, https://newrepublic.com/article/86091/labor-wisconsin

-georgetown-protests; and Gavin Bade, "Workers Unite: GSC Organizes around Labor Rights," *The Georgetown Voice*, January 19, 2012, http://georgetownvoice .com/2012/01/19/workers-unite-gsc-organizes-around-labor-rights/. I personally heard his story and others at a meeting at Georgetown University in December 2012 of the Jesuit Just Employment Project and the Annual Conference of Catholic Scholars for Worker Justice at Georgetown University in June 2012. This discussion of the Georgetown case is informed by conversations with students, food service workers, and faculty there as well as the accounts cited herein and Clayton Sinai, "Georgetown Models Catholic Social Teaching during Food Service Workers' Union Campaign," *America*, April 10, 2011, https://www .americamagazine.org/content/all-things/georgetown-models-catholic-social -teaching-during-food-service-workers-union; and Clayton Sinai, "Georgetown Students, Workers, Administrators Explain the University's 'Just Employment Policy,'" *America*, February 13, 2014, https://www.americamagazine.org/content /all-things/georgetown-students-workers-administrators-explain-universitys -just-employment.

251. Letter of Margie A. Bryant and Lamar Q. Billips to Aramark CEO Joseph Neubauer, February 3, 2011, http://www.scribd.com/doc/49007133 /Georgetown-s-Letter-to-Aramark-CEO-Joseph-Neubauer. Cited in Sinai, "Georgetown Models Catholic Social Teaching during Food Service Workers' Union Campaign."

252. The policy and information regarding its implementation are available at Georgetown University, Office of Public Affairs, Advisory Committee on Business Practices, http://publicaffairs.georgetown.edu/acbp/.

253. See Christopher Zawora and Annie Chen, "Activists March on Epicurean," November 12, 2013, *The Hoya*, http://www.thehoya.com/activists -march-on-epicurean/.

254. Molly Simio, "Labor Network Honors GU for Fair Labor Practices," *The Hoya*, February 28, 2014, http://www.thehoya.com/labor-network-honors-gu -for-fair-labor-practices/.

255. Joseph A. McCartin, "Georgetown's Game-Changing Agreement," *Commonweal*, April 30, 2018., https://www.commonwealmagazine.org /georgetown%E2%80%99s-game-changing-agreement.

256. These figures are reported in Wertsch and McCartin, "A Just Employ- ment Approach to Adjunct Unionization," 98.

257. See Living Wage Calculator, "Living Wage Calculation for District of Columbia, District of Columbia," http://livingwage.mit.edu/counties/11001. On the term "minimum subsistence wage," see Ibid., "About the Living Wage Calculator," http://livingwage.mit.edu/pages/about. Dr. Amy K. Glasmeier of the Department of Urban Studies and Planning, Massachusetts Institute of Technology, developed this living wage calculator. Dr. Glasmeier states that

her tool provides conservative estimates of the cost of essential needs; it does not allow for a "middle class" lifestyle. She also states that in urban areas it likely underestimates the cost of those needs.

258. Georgetown University, Office of the Provost, "Collective Bargaining Agreement," https://provost.georgetown.edu/CollectiveBargainingAgreement.

259. See Doug Lederman, "Going Hungry at Georgetown," *Inside Higher Ed*, March 22, 2005, http://www.insidehighered.com/news/2005/03/25 /hunger#sthash.EWXOdQca.dpbs; Bade, "Workers Unite: GSC Organizes around Labor Rights"; and Wertsch and McCartin, "A Just Employment Approach to Adjunct Unionization," 90–91.

260. Bade, "Workers Unite: GSC Organizes around Labor Rights."

261. See the comparison at http://livingwage.mit.edu/places/2207155000.

262. The policy is available on the Loyola University of New Orleans website at http://finance.loyno.edu/sites/finance.loyno.edu/files/loyola -university-new-orleans-vendor-contract-policy_5.pdf. I am grateful to Josh Daily, a former employee of Loyola University of New Orleans and key advocate of this policy, for conversation about it. I am solely responsible for the description of it here.

263. The Campus Labor Action Project (CLAP) at the University of Notre Dame has been pushing for a living wage policy on and off since 2005. See Amanda Michaels, "CLAP Presents Wage Report to Administrators," March 9, 2006, http://ndsmcobserver.com/2006/03/clap-presents-wage-report-to -administrators/; Alicia Quiros, "What About Living Wages?," *The Observer*, October 6, 2009, http://ndsmcobserver.com/2009/10/what-about-living-wages /; John Affleck-Graves, "Notre Dame Statement on the 'Living Wage,'" *Notre Dame News*, April 19, 2006, https://news.nd.edu/news/notre-dame-statement -on-the-ldquoliving-wagerdquo/. At over $10 billion, The University of Notre Dame has by far the largest endowment of any Catholic University in United States. See the NACUBO-TIAA Study of Endowments at https://www.nacubo .org/research/2019/nacubo-tiaa-study-of-endowments.

264. See the discussion of "'Health Insurance Subsidies' and 'Professional Development' in Agreement between Le Moyne College and Le Moyne College Adjuncts Association, NYSUT, AFT/NEA, AFL-CIO (July 1, 2019 to June 30, 2020)," http://lemoyne.edu/AZIndex/HumanResources/FacultyStaff /AdjunctFaculty/tabid/3036/Default.aspx.

265. See USF Part Time Faculty Association, https://sites.google.com/site /usfptfa/beneftis.

266. "Group marched to Le Moyne President's Office to Demand Meeting about Janitorial Workers," February 20, 2013, http://www.seiu200united.org /2013/02/20/group-marched-to-le-moyne-presidents-office-to-demand-meeting -about-janitorial-workers/, and "OSHA Fines Eagle Janitorial for Violations at

Le Moyne College," March 7, 2013, http://www.seiu200united.org/2013/03/07 /osha-fines-eagle-janitorial-for-violations-at-le-moyne-college/.

267. See Forgey, "Catholic University Raises Minimum Wage to $15 an Hour," and Duquesne University, "Duquesne University Implements $15-Per-Hour Minimum Wage," July 1, 2014, https://www.duq.edu/news/duquesne-university -implements-15-per-hour-minimum-wage.

268. See Scott Jaschik, "Liberation (of Adjuncts) Theology," *Inside Higher Ed*, April 24, 2008, https://www.insidehighered.com/news/2008/04/24 /liberation-adjuncts-theology, and Kevin Clarke, "Will Teach for Tenure," *U.S. Catholic* 74, no. 7 (July 2009), http://www.uscatholic.org/culture/social-justice /2009/06/will-teach-tenure.

269. I discuss the case of Nike in Chapter 4.

270. See Editorial, "Keep Fordham Faculty in Focus"; Trisha McCauley, "Students Try to Bring Jesuit Justice to Loyola's Workers," *Loyola Phoenix*, September 29, 2015, http://loyolaphoenix.com/2015/09/students-try-to-bring -jesuit-justice-to-loyolas-workers/; and Zirin, "Loyola Soars in March Madness While a Faculty Strike Looms."

271. I am indebted here to Fred Kammer, "Catholic Social Teaching and Taxes," *Just South Quarterly*, Spring (2011): 3, http://loyno.edu/jsri/sites/loyno .edu.jsri/files/CSTandTaxesSpring11.pdf. On CST's support for progressive taxation, see John XXIII, *Mater et Magistra*, no. 102; United States Conference of Catholic Bishops, *Economic Justice for All*, 202.

272. Heidi Schlumpf, "Theologians Question Catholic Universities' Use of Contingent Faculty," *National Catholic Reporter*, June 18, 2018, https://www .ncronline.org/news/justice/theologians-question-catholic-universities-use -contingent-faculty.

273. See the discussion of Shulman's arguments above.

274. For the purpose of these calculations I have gleaned information on faculty composition at Saint Joseph's during 2013–14 from http://www.collegefactual.com /colleges/saint-josephs-university/academic-life/faculty-composition/. I also used the average salary of a tenured associate professor at Saint Joseph's during 2013–14 as indicated in *The Chronicle of Higher Education* faculty salary database at https://data .chronicle.com/. My methodology is imperfect for several reasons, but these imperfections do not detract from my point, in my judgment.

275. Pay information taken from Jane M. Von Bergen, "Adjunct Faculty at Saint Joseph's University Take Steps toward Organizing," *Philadelphia Inquirer*, November 13, 2012, https://www.inquirer.com/philly/business/20121113 _Adjunct_faculty_at_St__Joseph_s_University_take_steps_toward _organizing.html.

276. See "Mayday Declaration on Contingency in Higher Education," https:// docs.google.com/a/insidehighered.com/forms/d/1kPaUl21SMpBNNWh3mqqkdkt

-FX3hNLWeu5KHLYKXsWY/viewform, and Scott Jaschik, "Adjunct Supporters Call for $5,000 Minimum Per Course," *Inside Higher Ed*, May 1, 2013, https://www.insidehighered.com/quicktakes/2013/05/01/adjunct-supporters-call-5000-minimum-course.

277. See "Just Employment Project," http://lwp.georgetown.edu/jep/; Just Employment Policy, "Model Just Employment Policy," http://www.just employmentpolicy.org/policy/. I was involved in this project in its early stages and was one of the presenters at the 2013 Justice in Jesuit Higher Education conference.

278. See Loyola University Chicago, Office of the President, "Just Employment Task Force," https://www.luc.edu/president/justemployment taskforce/. On John Carroll, see Laura Bednar, "The Fight for a 'Living Wage' Continues: JCU Workers' Rights Committee Organizes for Fair Pay for Workers," *The Carroll News*, October 2, 2014, http://www.jcunews.com/2014/10/02/the-fight-for-a-living-wage-continues-jcu-workers-rights-committee-organizes-for-fair-pay-for-workers/. On Saint Joseph's, see Jillian Buckley, "Ensuring Employee Rights," *The Hawk* (n.d.), https://www.sjuhawknews.com/ensuring-employee-rights/. Dr. Ken Weidner of Saint Joseph's University is currently conducting a study to determine the prevalence of living wage policies on US campuses. See https://justwage.org/.

279. See Loyola University Chicago, Office of the President, "Response to the Just Employment Task Force," September 21, 2017, https://www.luc.edu/president/justemploymenttaskforce/responsetothejustemploymenttaskforce/, and The Catholic Labor Network, "Loyola University Chicago President Responds to Just Employment Task Force," October 30, 2017, http://catholiclabor.org/2017/10/loyola-university-chicago-president-responds-to-just-employment-task-force/.

3. Catholic Universities, the Right to Education, and the Option for the Poor: Recruiting, Admitting, and Retaining Economically Disadvantaged Students

1. An earlier version of this chapter was published as Gerald J. Beyer, "Catholic Universities, Solidarity and the Right to Higher Education in the American Context," *Journal of Catholic Social Thought* 7, no. 1 (2010). Portions are reprinted here with permission. I also draw here from my piece Gerald J. Beyer, "Admission Impossible: Preferential Option for the Poor at Catholic Colleges," *U.S. Catholic* 77, no. 2 (2012). I have updated data and expanded the discussion from these articles in this chapter. I also thank The Program for Research on Religion and Urban Civil Society at The University of Pennsylvania, which funded my earlier work examining access for low-income students

at Saint Joseph's University and LaSalle University in Philadelphia. The report is entitled *Catholic Universities, Solidarity and the Right to Education for All: Two Case Studies in the Archdiocese of Philadelphia* (Philadelphia, Penn.: Program for Research on Religion and Urban Civil Society Report, University of Pennsylvania, 2007). Portions of the report are reprinted here with permission.

2. This young man's incredible journey is described in Mark Orrs, "Left Behind No More," *SJU Magazine* (Summer 2007): 14–15, https://sites.sju.edu /magazine/files/2017/06/sjumag_summer2007.pdf.

3. I am aware that terms such as "economically disadvantaged" and "low-income students" can be perceived as stigmatizing. My family's income was low enough to create an estimated family contribution to tuition of zero. I use these terms here because they are terms used in the relevant literature, and I cannot conceive of better terms. They are in no way meant to judge students as less capable or lacking in agency.

4. United States Conference of Catholic Bishops, *Economic Justice for All*, no. 203.

5. Gregor Aisch et al., "Some Colleges Have More Students from the Top 1 Percent Than the Bottom 60. Find Yours," *The New York Times*, *The Upshot*, January 18, 2017, https://www.nytimes.com/interactive/2017/01/18/upshot /some-colleges-have-more-students-from-the-top-1-percent-than-the-bottom-60 .html.

6. Emily Deruy, "Measuring College (Un)Affordability," *The Atlantic*, March 23, 2017, https://www.theatlantic.com/education/archive/2017/03 /measuring-college-unaffordability/520476/.

7. Jeffrey Selingo and Jeffrey Brainard, "The Rich-Poor Gap Widens for Colleges and Students," *The Chronicle of Higher Education* LII, no. 31 (2006), https://www.chronicle.com/article/The-Rich-Poor-Gap-Widens-for/2052.

8. See for example https://edtrust.org/ and https://www.newamerica.org /education-policy/reports/. On Chetty's research, see Raj Chetty et al., *Mobility Report Cards: The Role of Colleges in Intergenerational Mobility* (Cambridge, Mass.: National Bureau of Economic Research, 2017), https://www.nber.org /papers/w23618. Their data is available at https://opportunityinsights.org /education/ and https://www.nytimes.com/interactive/projects/college-mobility /. I use here the data from *The New York Times* interactive tool in this latter link, unless otherwise noted, because it is easy to access. It should be a resource for all college administrators and academics interested in economic diversity.

9. Stephen Burd, *Undermining Pell Volume III: The News Keeps Getting Worse for Low-Income Students*, (Washington, D.C.: New America Foundation 2016), 2, https://www.newamerica.org/education-policy/policy-papers/undermining -pell-volume-iii/.

10. Michael Dannenberg and Mary Nguyen Barry, *Tough Love: Bottom-Line Quality Standards for Colleges* (Washington, D.C.: The Education Trust 2014), 1, https://edtrust.org/resource/tough-love-bottom-line-quality-standards-for-colleges/.

11. Anthony P. Carnevale and Jeff Strohl, *Separate and Unequal: How Higher Education Reinforces the Intergenerational Reproduction of White Racial Privilege* (Washington, D.C.: Georgetown University Center on Education and the Workforce, 2013), 12, https://cew.georgetown.edu/wp-content/uploads/2014/11/SeparateUnequal.FR_.pdf.

12. Lee Gardner, "To Improve Colleges' Performance, Start with the Worst Ones, Report Urges," *The Chronicle of Higher Education*, June 18, 2014, https://www.chronicle.com/article/to-improve-colleges/147213; Dannenberg and Barry, *Tough Love*, 6.

13. Dannenberg and Barry, *Tough Love*, 6. See also Doug Lederman, "Underrepresented Students, Unintended Consequences," *Inside Higher Ed*, January 28, 2019, https://www.insidehighered.com/admissions/article/2019/01/28/study-pressure-enroll-more-pell-eligible-students-has-skewed-colleges.

14. Jon Marcus and Holly K. Hacker, "Here's the Devastating Way Our College System Fails Poor Kids," *The Huffington Post*, December 17, 2015, https://www.huffingtonpost.com/entry/why-its-harder-than-ever-for-a-poor-kid-to-get-into-a-good-college_us_567066bde4b0e292150f7d40. See also Dannenberg and Barry, *Tough Love*, 6.

15. Stephen Burd, *Undermining Pell Volume II: How Colleges' Pursuit of Prestige and Revenue Is Hurting Low-Income Students* (Washington, D.C.: New America Foundation 2014), 17, https://www.newamerica.org/education-policy/policy-papers/undermining-pell-volume-ii/.

16. Selingo and Brainard, "The Rich-Poor Gap Widens for Colleges and Students."

17. See The Education Trust, *College Results Online database*, http://www.collegeresults.org/search1ba.aspx?institutionid=186131,130794,166027.

18. Gregor Aisch et al., "Some Colleges Have More Students from the Top 1 Percent Than the Bottom 60. Find Yours." See also Burd, *Undermining Pell Volume III*, 4.

19. Raj Chetty et al., *Mobility Report Cards: The Role of Colleges in Intergenerational Mobility* (Cambridge, Mass.: National Bureau of Economic Research, 2017), https://opportunityinsights.org/paper/mobilityreportcards/.

20. Burd, *Undermining Pell Volume II*, 3.

21. Michael Dannenberg and Mamie Voight, *Doing Away with Debt: Using Existing Resources to Ensure College Affordability for Low and Middle-Income Families* (Washington, D.C.: The Education Trust 2013), 6–7, https://edtrust.org/resource/

doing-away-with-debt-using-existing-resources-to-ensure-college-affordability-for-low-and-middle-income-families/.

See also Marcus and Hacker, "Here's the Devastating Way Our College System Fails Poor Kids."

22. Burd, *Undermining Pell Volume II*, 4.

23. Ibid.

24. Burd, *Undermining Pell Volume III*, 2–3.

25. Burd, *Undermining Pell Volume II*, 21, see also 3.

26. Burd, *Undermining Pell Volume III*, 7. For an unpersuasive argument that low-income families are benefiting more from slower growth in tuition in recent years, see James L. Doti, "The Growth in College Costs Is Slowing, Particularly for Poorer Families," *The Conversation: Opinion and Ideas, The Chronicle of Higher Education*, May 13, 2015, https://www.chronicle.com/blogs/conversation/2015/05/13/the-growth-in-college-costs-is-slowing-particularly-for-poorer-families/.

27. Paul Moses, "Catholic Colleges Tell Poor Students: Go Somewhere Else," *The Hechinger Report*, December 22, 2014, https://hechingerreport.org/content/catholic-colleges-tell-poor-students-go-somewhere-else_18525/.

28. Stephen Burd, *Undermining Pell Volume IV: How the Privatization of Public Higher Education Is Hurting Low-Income Students* (Washington, D.C.: New America Foundation, 2018), 5, 27, 29, 32, https://www.newamerica.org/education-policy/reports/undermining-pell-iv/.

29. See http://www.collegeresults.org/collegeprofile.aspx?institutionid=234076. On UVA, see also Karin Fischer, "Well-Heeled U. Of Virginia Tries to Balance Access with Prestige," *The Chronicle of Higher Education* LII, no. 36 (2006) and Burd, *Undermining Pell Volume II*, 33. Burd states UVA has joined the "merit aid arms race."

30. See https://www.nytimes.com/interactive/projects/college-mobility/university-of-virginia.

31. Burd, *Undermining Pell Volume IV*, 25–27.

32. Danette Gerald and Kati Haycock, *Engines of Inequality: Diminishing Equity in the Nation's Premier Public Universities* (Washington, D.C.: The Educational Trust, 2006), http://www2.edtrust.org/EdTrust/Press+Room/Engines+of+Inequality.htm.

33. Dannenberg and Barry, *Tough Love*, 24–25.

34. Patrick Kerkstra, "A Tale of Two Temples: The Transformation from Commuter College Has Brought Acclaim—as Well as Critics," *The Philadelphia Inquirer*, June 5, 2005: A1.

35. Burd, *Undermining Pell Volume IV*, 30.

36. Daniel Golden, *The Price of Admission: How America's Ruling Class Buys Its Way into Elite Colleges—and Who Gets Left Outside the Gates*, 1st ed. (New York: Crown Publishers, 2006).

37. Ibid., 5.

38. Ibid., 9.

39. Ibid., 6–7. Golden points out that some college administrators see these estimates as conservative.

40. Ibid., 122. For example, Harvard admits 40 percent of legacy candidates, while its overall acceptance rate hovers at 11 percent. Ibid., 129. Among Catholic universities, Notre Dame tops the list. Almost one out of four admittances each year is an alumni child. Notre Dame accepts half of all legacy applicants, while only 20 percent overall. Ibid., 117, 31.

41. Ibid., 151.

42. Ibid., 193. For more discussion of these kinds of admissions preferences, see William G. Bowen et al., *Equity and Excellence in American Higher Education* (Charlottesville: University of Virginia Press, 2005).

43. Rick Seltzer, "Do Colleges Need to Be Need Blind?," *Inside Higher Ed*, July 21, 2016, https://www.insidehighered.com/news/2016/07/21/what-happens -when-colleges-drop-need-blind-admissions.

44. Dannenberg and Barry, *Tough Love*, 14, 22. On Franklin and Marshall, see also Franklin and Marshall College, "The Next Generation Initiative," https://www.fandm.edu/president/initiatives/the-next-generation-initiative. On Porterfield, see the recent symposium on college access at Princeton University, "Visions for Change: Sharing Experiences of First-Gen, Low-Income Students," https://www.princeton.edu/news/2019/02/19/visions-change -sharing-experiences-first-gen-low-income-students.

45. Burd, *Undermining Pell Volume II*, 8 and Burd, *Undermining Pell Volume III*, 8. The later report adds one institution to the previous list of 24.

46. Burd, *Undermining Pell Volume III*, 8.

47. Ibid., 10. The report mentions, for example, that Samuel Josiah Grinnell was a "conductor" on the Underground Railroad.

48. Burd, *Undermining Pell Volume IV*, 15–17.

49. Catharine B. Hill and Elizabeth Davidson Pisacreta, *The Economic Benefits and Costs of a Liberal Arts Education* (New York: The Mellon Foundation 2019), 10, https://mellon.org/resources/news/articles/economic-benefits-and -costs-liberal-arts-education/, and David Autor, "Skills, Education, and the Rise of Earnings Inequality among the 'Other 99 Percent,'" *Science* 344, no. 6186 (2014): 843.

50. Philip Trostel, "Beyond the College Earnings Premium. Way Beyond," *The Chronicle of Higher Education*, January 29, 2017, https://www.chronicle.com /article/Beyond-the-College-Earnings/239013. See also Autor, "Skills, Education, and the Rise of Earnings Inequality," 844–45. Autor's estimates are similar, but he notes differences in terms of gender and household.

51. Hill and Pisacreta, *The Economic Benefits and Costs of a Liberal Arts Education*, 12.

52. For a more extensive account, see Kate Halvorsen, "Notes on the Realization of the Human Right to Education," *Human Rights Quarterly* 12, no. 3 (1990). The following section hews closely to Beyer, "Catholic Universities, Solidarity and the Right to Higher Education in the American Context," 150–52. Reprinted sections with permission.

53. United Nations, *UN Universal Declaration of Human Rights* (1948), art. 26.1.

54. Quotations are taken from the *Universal Declaration of Human Rights*, https://www.un.org/en/universal-declaration-human-rights/.

55. Quoted from United Nations Human Rights Office of the High Commissioner, *The International Covenant on Economic, Social and Cultural Rights* (1966), https://www.ohchr.org/en/professionalinterest/pages/cescr.aspx.

56. See United Nations Human Rights Office of the High Commissioner, "General Comment No. 13: The right to education (article 13) (1999)," https://www.ohchr.org/EN/Issues/Education/Training/Compilation/Pages/d)GeneralCommentNo13Therighttoeducation(article13)(1999).aspx.

57. This section draws on Yves Daudet and Kishore Singh, *The Right to Education: An Analysis of UNESCO's Standard Setting Instruments* (Paris: UNESCO, 2001), https://www.right-to-education.org/resource/right-education-analysis-unescos-standard-setting-instruments.

58. Quoted from UNESCO, *Framework for Priority Action and Change and Development of Higher Education* (Paris: UNESCO, 1998), no. I.1.a, https://unesdoc.unesco.org/ark:/48223/pf0000113760; italics added.

59. See UNESCO, *World Declaration on Higher Education for the Twenty-First Century* (Paris: UNESCO, 1998), art. 3 (b), (d), https://unesdoc.unesco.org/ark:/48223/pf0000141952.

60. Golden, *The Price of Admission*, 9. Among others, Golden quotes former Yale president Benno Schmidt, who deplores the "total disconnect" between schools like Yale and the third of all high schools in the United States that serve the poor.

61. Daudet and Singh, *The Right to Education*, 76.

62. See Gerald J. Beyer, "Beyond 'Nonsense on Stilts': Towards Conceptual Clarity and Resolution of Conflicting Economic Rights," *Human Rights Review* VI, no. 4 (2005).

63. See Martha M. McCarthy, "The Right to Education: From Rodriguez to Goss," *Educational Leadership* 33, no. 7 (1976), and Douglas Sturm, "The Opening of the American Mind: On the Constitutional Right to Education," *Journal of Law and Religion* 13, no. 1 (1996).

64. For a detailed discussion of the foundation of human rights in Catholic thought, see Beyer, "Beyond 'Nonsense on Stilts.'"

65. Leo XIII, *Spectata Fides: Encyclical of Pope Leo XIII on Christian Education* (November 27, 1885), http://w2.vatican.va/content/leo-xiii/en/encyclicals /documents/hf_l-xiii_enc_27111885_spectata-fides.html., no. 3.

66. Pius XI, *Divini Illius Magistri: Encyclical of Pope Pius XI on Christian Education* (December 31, 1929), http://w2.vatican.va/content/pius-xi/en/encyclicals /documents/hf_p-xi_enc_31121929_divini-illius-magistri.html., nos. 45–46.

67. Pius XII, *1942 Christmas Message of Pope Pius XII* (1942), https://curate .nd.edu/downloads/2r36tx34995.

68. John XXIII, *Pacem in Terris*, no 13.

69. Second Vatican Council, *Gaudium et Spes*, nos. 25, 29.

70. Ibid., no. 60.

71. Pope Paul VI, *Gravissimum Educationis*, no. 1.

72. Ibid., no. 9.

73. Ibid., no. 10.

74. John Paul II, *Sollicitudo Rei Socialis*, no. 15.

75. John Paul II, "Address of John Paul II for the Opening of the Catholic Education Centre," November 30, 1986, http://w2.vatican.va/content/john-paul -ii/en/speeches/1986/november/documents/hf_jp-ii_spe_19861130_centro -cattolico-perth-australia.pdf.

76. John Paul II, "Respect for Human Rights: The Secret of True Peace," January 1, 1999, no. 8, http://w2.vatican.va/content/john-paul-ii/en/messages /peace/documents/hf_jp-ii_mes_14121998_xxxii-world-day-for-peace.html.

77. John Paul II, "Address to UNESCO: Man's Entire Humanity is Expressed in Culture," June 2, 1980, no. 11, http://inters.org/John-Paul-II-UNESCO -Culture.

78. John Paul II, *Ex Corde Ecclesiae*, no. 34.

79. Benedict XVI, "Meeting with Catholic Educators: Conference Hall of the Catholic University of America in Washington, D.C.," April 17, 2008, http://w2.vatican.va/content/benedict-xvi/en/speeches/2008/april/documents /hf_ben-xvi_spe_20080417_cath-univ-washington.html.

80. Benedict XVI, "Letter of His Holiness Benedict XVI to Cardinal Jean-Louis Tauran on the Occasion of the Colloquium 'Culture, Reason, and Freedom,'" May 24, 2005, http://www.vatican.va/holy_father/benedict_xvi /letters/2005/documents/hf_ben-xvi_let_20050524_card-tauran_en.html.

81. Rebecca Winthrop, "Could Pope Francis Be the World's Most Important Education Advocate?," *The Brookings Institution*, February 10, 2015, https:// www.brookings.edu/blog/education-plus-development/2015/02/10/could-pope -francis-be-the-worlds-most-important-education-advocate/.

82. Zenit Staff, "Pope's Q-and-A on the Challenges of Education," *Zenit*, November 23, 2015, https://zenit.org/articles/pope-s-q-and-a-on-the-challenges -of-education/.

83. Francis, "Apostolic Journey of His Holiness Pope Francis to Cuba, to the United States of America and Visit to the United Nations Headquarters (19–28 September 2015): Meeting with the Members of the General Assembly of the United Nations Organization," September 25, 2015, http://w2.vatican.va /content/francesco/en/speeches/2015/september/documents/papa-francesco _20150925_onu-visita.html.

84. Francis, "Apostolic Journey of His Holiness Pope Francis to Ecuador, Bolivia and Paraguay (5–13 July 2015): Meeting with Educators," July 7, 2015, https://w2.vatican.va/content/francesco/en/speeches/2015/july/documents /papafrancesco_20150707_ecuador-scuola-universita.html.

85. See for example, United States Conference of Catholic Bishops, *Economic Justice for All*, no. 80; United States Conference of Catholic Bishops, Department of Education, "Principles for Educational Reform in the United States," (1995), http://www.usccb.org/education/parentassn/reform.shtml; United States Conference of Catholic Bishops, *A Place at the Table: A Catholic Recommitment to Overcome Poverty and to Respect the Dignity of All Children* (2002), http://www.usccb.org/bishops/table.shtml.

86. United States Conference of Catholic Bishops, *Faithful Citizenship: A Call to Political Responsibility from the Catholic Bishops of the United States* (Washington, D.C.: United States Conference of Catholic Bishops, 2011), http://www .usccb.org/faithfulcitizenship/bishopStatement.html.

87. United States Conference of Catholic Bishops, *Economic Justice for All*, no. 203.

88. Ibid., 204.

89. United States Conference of Catholic Bishops, *A Place at the Table*.

90. United States Conference of Catholic Bishops, *Economic Justice for All*, no. 204.

91. For some substantial evidence, see Joseph M. O'Keefe, "Catholic Schools and Vouchers: How the Empirical Reality Should Ground the Debate," in *School Choice: The Moral Debate*, ed. Alan Wolfe (Princeton, N.J.: Princeton University Press, 2003), 195–210. However, O'Keefe draws attention to the waning numbers of students from the lowest socioeconomic quartile at Catholic high schools. He calls this an "eliting phenomenon."

92. John Paul II, *Laborem Exercens*, no. 8.

93. John Paul II, *Sollicitudo Rei Socialis*, no. 42.

94. Pope John Paul II, "Message of His Holiness Pope John Paul II for the Celebration of the World Day of Peace: 'Dialogue for Peace: A Challenge for Our Time,'" January 1, 1983, http://www.vatican.va/holy_father/john_paul_ii /messages/peace/documents/hf_jp-ii_mes_19821208_xvi-world-day-for-peace _en.html.

95. John Paul II, *Sollicitudo Rei Socialis*, nos. 42, 43.

96. See Pope Francis, *Evangelii Gaudium*, no. 189; Pope Francis, *Laudato Si*, no. 158; John Paul II, *Sollicitudo Rei Socialis*, no. 42; John Paul II, *Laborem Exercens*, no. 14; *Centesimus Annus*, nos. 15, 30–31, 42; and *Compendium of the Social Doctrine of the Church*, III, no. 182.

97. John Paul II, *Jan Paweł II Polska 1999: Przemówienia i Homilie* (Marki: Michalineum, 1999), 75–76.

98. United States Conference of Catholic Bishops, *Economic Justice for All*, nos. 13, 15.

99. World Synod of Bishops, *Justice in the World (Justitia in Mundo)* in *Catholic Social Thought: The Documentary Heritage*, ed. David J. O'Brien and Thomas A. Shannon (Maryknoll, N.Y.: Orbis Books, 1992), 289. See also Paul VI, *Evangelii Nuntiandi*, no. 27, 29–31, 44.

100. Of course, effective and affordable job and vocational training may be more beneficial for some people and should be made accessible. On the debate about whether college is for everyone, see Stephanie Owen and Isabel Sawhill, *Should Everyone Go to College?* (Washington, D.C.: The Brookings Institution, 2013), https://www.brookings.edu/wp-content/uploads/2016/06/08-should -everyone-go-to-college-owen-sawhill.pdf; and Scott Carlson, "Should Every- one Go to College? For Poor Kids, 'College for All' Isn't the Mantra It Was Meant to Be," *The Chronicle of Higher Education*, May 1, 2016, https://www .chronicle.com/article/Should-Everyone-Go-to-College-/236316. I am arguing that all people should be afforded the opportunity to choose higher education and that prohibitive cost should not obviate the possibility.

101. See for example World Synod of Bishops, *Justice in the World (Justitia in Mundo)*, 291.

102. David Hollenbach, *Claims in Conflict: Retrieving and Renewing the Catholic Human Rights Tradition* (New York: Paulist Press, 1979), 86–87. The discussion here of the right to participation is indebted to Hollenbach's analysis.

103. World Synod of Bishops, *Justice in the World (Justitia in Mundo)*, 289.

104. For an extended discussion of the nature of solidarity, see Gerald J. Beyer, *Recovering Solidarity*.

105. Hollenbach, *Claims in Conflict*, 91.

106. See Leo XIII, *Rerum Novarum*, nos. 2, 34. For an excellent historical introduction, see Marvin L. Krier Mich, *Catholic Social Teaching and Movements* (Mystic, Conn.: Twenty-Third Publications, 1998), 5–60.

107. Lester C. Thurow, *The Future of Capitalism: How Today's Economic Forces Shape Tomorrow's World*, 1st ed. (New York: W. Morrow, 1996), 180–81. See also World Bank, *World Development Report 2019: The Changing Nature of Work* (Washington, D.C.: World Bank, 2019), 50–65.

108. World Bank, *World Development Report 2019*, 50–51.

109. S. M. Ravi Kanbur, Nora Lustig, and World Bank, *Attacking Poverty,* World Development Report, 2000/2001 (New York: Oxford University Press, 2000), 34, 77–83.

110. See John Paul II, *Centesimus Annus,* nos. 32–33.

111. Amartya Kumar Sen, *Development as Freedom* (New York: Knopf, 1999), 36–41.

112. Bowen et al., *Equity and Excellence in American Higher Education,* 13–48.

113. Caroline Ratcliffe and Emma Kalish, *Escaping Poverty: Predictors of Persistently Poor Children's Economic Success* (Washington, D.C.: Urban Institute, 2017), 11–12, https://www.urban.org/sites/default/files/publication/90321/escaping-poverty.pdf. As I mentioned above, this still holds true despite the growing numbers of low-wage workers with some college education. See Victoria Smith, Brian Halpin, "Low-Wage Work Uncertainty Often Traps Low-Wage Workers. Policy Brief, vol. 2, no. 9," *Center for Poverty Research, University of California, Davis,* 2014, https://doi.org/10.15141/S5VC7P.

114. Autor, "Skills, Education, and the Rise of Earnings Inequality," 842. See also "The Outlook Is Dim for Americans without College Degrees," *The Economist,* January 10, 2019.

115. Ibid., 845.

116. Anthony Carnevale, Nicole Smith, and Jeff Strohl, *Recovery: Job Growth and Education Requirements through 2020* (Washington, D.C.: Center on Education and the Workforce, Georgetown Public Policy Institute, June 2013), https://files.eric.ed.gov/fulltext/ED584413.pdf, 15.

117. As I mentioned above, this still holds true in spite of the growing numbers of low-wage workers with some college education. See Smith and Halpin, "Low-Wage Work Uncertainty Often Traps Low-Wage Workers," 2. Their data reveals the importance of *finishing* a BA.

118. John Rawls, *A Theory of Justice,* Rev. ed. (Cambridge, Mass.: Belknap Press of Harvard University Press, 1999), 199.

119. Norman Daniels, "Equal Liberty and Unequal Worth of Liberty," in *Reading Rawls: Critical Studies on Rawls' "A Theory of Justice,"* ed. Norman Daniels (Stanford, Calif.: Stanford University Press, 1989), 256–57.

120. For empirical evidence in this vein, see Sen, *Development as Freedom,* 175–76, 191–203.

121. Bowen et al., *Equity and Excellence in American Higher Education,* 3.

122. For a persuasive argument along these lines, see Michael Walzer, *Spheres of Justice: A Defense of Pluralism and Equality* (New York: Basic Books, 1983).

123. Józef Tischner, *The Spirit of Solidarity,* 2–3. For some evidence to this effect, see Philip Trostel, "Beyond the College Earnings Premium. Way Beyond," *The Chronicle of Higher Education,* January 29, 2017, https://www

.chronicle.com/article/Beyond-the-College-Earnings/239013. Trostel points to greater civic and political engagement, tax and philanthropic contributions, and a multiplier effect on increased productivity. See also Martha C. Nussbaum, *Not for Profit: Why Democracy Needs the Humanities*, Updated ed. (Princeton, N.J.: Princeton University Press, 2016).

124. Quoted in The International Council for Lasallian Studies, *The Lasallian Charism* (Brothers of the Christian Schools, 2006), https://www.lasalle.org/wp-content/uploads/2019/09/Lasallian-Studies-13.pdf.

125. For an extended discussion of LaSalle University, see my report "Catholic Universities, Solidarity and the Right to Education for All: Two Case Studies."

126. The International Commission on the Apostolate of Jesuit Education, "The Characteristics of Jesuit Education," (1986), http://www.sjwebinfo/education/doclist.cfm, 17. In a letter introducing the document, Fr. Kolvenbach states that although it primarily addresses Jesuit secondary education, the principles of the document apply to all levels of Jesuit education.

127. Ibid. See also Peter-Hans Kolvenbach, SJ, "The Service of Faith and the Promotion of Justice in American Jesuit Higher Education," Address at Santa Clara University, http://www.sjweb.info/documents/phk/2000santa_clara_en.doc.

128. The International Commission on the Apostolate of Jesuit Education, "The Characteristics of Jesuit Education."

129. Cyprian Davis, *The History of Black Catholics in the United States* (New York: Crossroad, 1990), 135–36, 254.

130. Mary C. Sullivan, RSM, PhD, "Catherine McCauley and the Characteristics of Mercy Higher Education," 19, http://www.mercyhighered.org/resources/ewExternalFiles/characteristics.pdf.

131. Maryanne Stevens, RSM, PhD, "Mercy Higher Education: Culture and Characteristics," 1, 2, 9, http://www.mercyhighered.org/resources/ewExternalFiles/culture_characteristics.pdf. More on the characteristics of Mercy higher education can be found here: http://www.mercyhighered.org/resources/mercy-identity-in-higher-education.html.

132. See http://www.collegeresults.org/aboutthedata.aspx. The Education Trust states that it updated its database in May 2018. It uses the latest available data from the US Department of Education's National Center for Education Statistics (NCES), 2018. College Results Online, The Education Trust. All rights reserved.

133. See the explanation of the engines of inequality designation at http://www.collegeresults.org/aboutthedata.aspx#section-3.

134. See NABUCO-TIAA 2018 Endowment Study, https://www.nacubo.org/-/media/Nacubo/Documents/research/2018-Endowment-Market-Values—Final.ashx?la=en&hash=31CF91E74EAAB91288E53E2BCD629C35710C1C03.

135. See *U.S. News & World Report*, "Economic Diversity Regional Universities North," https://www.usnews.com/best-colleges/rankings/regional-universities -north/economic-diversity.

136. On the ATI, see "Holy Cross Joins Partnership of Top Colleges Working to Add More Lower-Income, First-Generation Students," https://news.holycross .edu/blog/2018/12/17/holy-cross-joins-partnership-of-top-colleges-working-to -add-more-lower-income-first-generation-students/, and American Talent Initiative, https://americantalentinitiative.org/. I am using here the definition of "elite" from Gregor Aisch et al., "Some Colleges Have More Students from the Top 1 Percent Than the Bottom 60."

137. See "Economic Diversity and Student Outcomes at College of the Holy Cross," *The New York Times*, *The Upshot*, https://www.nytimes.com/interactive /projects/college-mobility/college-of-the-holy-cross.

138. See Burd, *Undermining Pell Volume III*. The most recent net price data is available at https://nces.ed.gov/collegenavigator/ and http://www.collegeresults .org/default.aspx.

139. See ibid.

140. Data is from Gregor Aisch et al., "Some Colleges Have More Students from the Top 1 Percent Than the Bottom 60." See note 8 above for more about the data.

141. Burd, *Undermining Pell Volume III*, 14.

142. Paul Moses, "Catholic Colleges Tell Poor Students: Go Somewhere Else."

143. Ibid.

144. The most recent net price data is available at https://nces.ed.gov /collegenavigator/ and http://www.collegeresults.org/default.aspx.

145. Annie Waldman, "As Pope Pushes to Help the Poor, Catholic Universities Leave Them Behind," *ProPublica*, September 22, 2015, https://www.propublica .org/article/as-pope-pushes-to-help-the-poor-catholic-universities-leave-them -behind. See also the research tool at Sisi Wei and Annie Waldman, "Debt by Degrees," *ProPublica*, September 12, 2015, https://projects.propublica.org /colleges/.

146. See Boston College, "Affordability," https://www.bc.edu/bc-web /admission/affordability.html.

147. Dennis Brown, "$20 Million Gift to Fund Initiative to Support Students from Low Socioeconomic Families," *Notre Dame News*, September 4, 2015, https://news.nd.edu/news/fighting-irish-initiative/. See also Waldman, "As Pope Pushes to Help the Poor."

148. Georgetown University, "Georgetown Undergraduate Scholarships," https://finaid.georgetown.edu/financial-resources/undergrad-scholarships.

149. Villanova University Media Room, "As Villanova University Announces Third Cohort of O'Toole Family President Scholars, First Cohort Arrives on Campus as Freshmen," https://www1.villanova.edu/villanova/media/pressreleases/2015/1023-1.html.

150. See also Burd, *Undermining Pell Volume III*, 9.

151. I use the latest available data here from The Education Trust, combined with the metrics for "High Pell, Low Net Cost" from Burd, *Undermining Pell Volume III*.

152. On Franklin and Marshall's success, see note 44 above.

153. David Hollenbach, "The Catholic University under the Sign of the Cross: Christian Humanism in a Broken World," in *Finding God in All Things*, ed. Stephen J. Pope (New York: Crossroads, 1996), 287.

154. Ibid.

155. Peter-Hans Kolvenbach, SJ, "The Jesuit University in the Light of the Ignatian Charism," in *The International Meeting of Jesuit Higher Education* (Rome: 2001), http://www.sjweb.info/education/doclist.cfm.

156. See Scott Jaschik, "Massive Admissions Scandal," *Inside Higher Ed*, March 13, 2019, https://www.insidehighered.com/admissions/article/2019/03/13/dozens-indicted-alleged-massive-case-admissions-fraud.

157. See Scott Jaschik, "Pushing for Radical Change in Admissions," *Inside Higher Ed*, February 25, 2019, https://www.insidehighered.com/admissions/article/2019/02/25/democratic-senators-urged-consider-radical-policies-college-admissions, and Jaschik, "Massive Admissions Scandal."

158. See Fischer, "Well-Heeled U. Of Virginia Tries to Balance Access with Prestige."

159. See Golden, *The Price of Admission*, 122–31, 45–76, 77–94. Golden states that at Notre Dame, for example, legacies average eighty points less than students without admissions preferences. At the University of Virginia, out-of-state applicants need to score thirty to thirty-five points higher on the SATs, unless they are alumni children. Bowen et al. claim that the admissions advantage for legacies is only significant for students with strong credentials in the thirteen schools they examined. However, minorities and athletes of all ability levels are given meaningful preferences and tend to underperform in college. See Bowen et al., *Equity and Excellence in American Higher Education*, 112–17, 65–76.

160. See Eric Hoover, "Bribery Scandal Reveals 'Weak Spots' in the Admissions System. Don't Look So Shocked," *The Chronicle of Higher Education*, March 13, 2019, https://www.chronicle.com/article/Bribery-Scandal-Reveals/245877.

161. Both Golden and Bowen and his coauthors document the admissions preferences given for legacies, athletes, faculty children, and development cases. Both also state that no advantage is given to applicants from low-income

families. See Bowen et al., *Equity and Excellence in American Higher Education*, 175.

162. On the need for greater transparency, see Alan B. Morrison and Richard Kahlenberg, "Admissions Policies Lack Credibility. The Cure: Radical Transparency," *The Chronicle of Higher Education*, March 21, 2019, https://www.chronicle.com/article/Admissions-Policies-Lack/245951.

163. Bowen et al., *Equity and Excellence in American Higher Education*, 161–62. This last argument is complex. Analysis of it exceeds the scope of this book. See also ibid., 111–36.

164. See for example Roy O. Freedle, "Correcting the SAT's Ethnic and Social-Class Bias: A Method for Reestimating SAT Scores," *Harvard Educational Review* 73, no. 1 (2003); Nathan O. Hatch, "A Better Measure than the SAT," *The Washington Post*, June 29, 2008; https://www.insidehighered.com/admissions/article/2018/06/19/university-chicago-drops-satact-requirement.

165. Hatch, "A Better Measure than the SAT." See also the "Views of Authorities on Intelligence and Testing," interviews from the PBS Frontline program "Secrets of the SAT: The SAT and the Prep Business," http://www.pbs.org/wgbh/pages/frontline/shows/sats/test/views.html; Eric Hoover, "The Truth About Test-Optional Policies: 'There's Not Just One Truth,'" *The Chronicle of Higher Education*, April 26, 2018, https://www.chronicle.com/article/The-Truth-about-Test-Optional/243238.

166. Golden, *The Price of Admission*, 5, 193.

167. Gerald and Haycock, "Engines of Inequality," 15–16.

168. Brookings, "Key Findings from the 'Hidden Supply of High-Achieving, Low-Income Students,'" (2013), https://www.brookings.edu/interactives/key-findings-from-the-hidden-supply-of-high-achieving-low-income-students/.

169. Scott Jaschik, "The Impact of Dropping the SAT," *Inside Higher Ed*, March 26, 2009, http://www.insidehighered.com/news/2009/03/26/sat.

170. See Hoover, "The Truth About Test-Optional Policies." The study is Valerie W. Franks, Steven T. Syverson, William C. Hiss, *Defining Access: How Test-Optional Works*, (Arlington, Va.: National Association for College Admission Counseling, 2018), https://www.nacacnet.org/globalassets/documents/publications/research/defining-access-report-2018.pdf.

171. Susan Snyder, "SAT Still a Tough Student Hurdle," *Philadelphia Inquirer*, November 9, 2008.

172. See FairTest National Center for Fair & Open Testing, Test Optional Growth Chronology 2005–2019, http://www.fairtest.org/sites/default/files/Optional-Growth-Chronology.pdf, and the article by the former president of Holy Cross: Michael C. McFarland, "What an SAT Score Doesn't Say," *The Boston Globe*, November 27, 2008.

173. Tamar Lewin, "Two Colleges End Entrance Exam Requirement," *New York Times*, May 27, 2008, https://www.nytimes.com/2008/05/27/education/27sat.html.

174. Scott Jaschik, "New Push for Test Optional," *Inside Higher Ed*, April 1, 2019, https://www.insidehighered.com/admissions/article/2019/04/01/more-colleges-go-test-optional-admissions. See also the comprehensive list and arguments in favor of test optional policies and equity at The National Center for Fair and Open Testing website http://fairtest.org/actsat-testoptional-list-tops-1000-colleges-univer.

175. Eric Hoover, "An Ultra-Selective University Just Dropped the Act/Sat. So What?," *The Chronicle of Higher Education*, June 14, 2018, https://www.chronicle.com/article/An-Ultra-Selective-University/243678?cid=trend_right_a.

176. Hoover, "The Truth About Test-Optional Policies" and Steven T. Syverson et al., *"Defining Access: How Test-Optional Works,"* 62.

177. Sara Hebel, "A Matchmaker for Elite Colleges," *The Chronicle of Higher Education*, May 11, 2006; David Leonhardt, "'A National Admissions Office' for Low-Income Strivers," *The New York Times* September, 16, 2014, https://www.nytimes.com/2014/09/16/upshot/a-national-admissions-office-for-low-income-strivers.html.

178. Questbridge, "College Partners," https://www.questbridge.org/college-partners.

179. Rick Dalton, "The Admission Cheating Scam: What's Next?," *Inside Higher Ed*, March 22, 2019, https://www.insidehighered.com/views/2019/03/22/we-should-focus-less-admissions-cheaters-and-more-helping-less-privileged-students.

180. See Strive for College, "I'm First," https://imfirst.org/colleges/.

181. I draw here from a presentation about the McGuire Scholars program at the Justice in Jesuit Higher Education Conference, Creighton University, August 1–4, 2013. See also Loyola University Maryland, Office of Human Resources, McGuire Scholars Program, https://www.loyola.edu/department/hr/development/mcguire-scholars.

182. Stephen N. Katsouros, *Come to Believe: How the Jesuits Are Reinventing Education (Again): Inside the First Year of the New Arrupe College* (Maryknoll, N.Y.: Orbis Books, 2017), 34.

183. Ibid., 174. and Steve Katsouros, SJ, "Message from the Dean and Executive Director," Arrupe College, Loyola University Chicago, https://www.luc.edu/arrupe/about/messagefromthedeanandexecutivedirector/.

184. Maura Lerner, "St. Thomas' New 2-Year College Lures Low-Income Students," *Star Tribune*, August 5, 2017, http://www.startribune.com/st-thomas-new-2-year-college-lures-low-income-students/438638123/?refresh=true.

185. Arrupe College admitted only 183 students from over 1,000 applicants in 2016. Katsouros, *Come to Believe*, 133.

186. On this phenomenon, see Bowen et al., *Equity and Excellence in American Higher Education*, 186–93; Becky Supiano, "A Passion to Highlight Which Colleges Do Well by Low-Income Students," *The Chronicle of Higher Education*, September 17, 2014; Burd, *Undermining Pell Volume IV*, 5, 27, 29, 32.

187. I draw here from a presentation about the Hurtado Scholars program at the Justice in Jesuit Higher Education Conference, Creighton University, August 1–4, 2013. See also Megan O'Connor, "Undocumented and Unemployed," *The Santa Clara*, April 9, 2007, http://thesantaclara.org/undocumented-and -unemployed/#.XbMQFehKhmo.

188. Chris Quintana, "Can This Man Change How Elite Colleges Treat Low-Income Students?," *The Chronicle of Higher Education*, February 15, 2019, https://www.chronicle.com/article/Can-This-Man-Change-How-Elite/245714. See also Anthony Abraham Jack, *The Privileged Poor: How Elite Colleges Are Failing Disadvantaged Students* (Cambridge, Mass.: Harvard University Press, 2019).

189. These claims rely on my own observations and conversations with students. However, there is a body of empirical evidence that first-generation and African American students experience this kind of alienation and self-doubt. See for example Jack, *The Privileged Poor*; Alberta M. Gloria, "African American Students' Persistence at a Predominantly White University: Influences of Social Support, University Comfort and Self-Belief," *Journal of College Student Development* (1999); Stacey Havlik et al., "Strengths and Struggles: First-Generation College-Goers Persisting at One Predominantly White Institution," *Journal of College Student Retention: Research, Theory & Practice* (2017); and bell hooks, *Teaching to Transgress: Education as the Practice of Freedom* (New York: Routledge, 1994), 177–90.

190. Jack, *The Privileged Poor*, 97, see also 237n1.

191. See for example Francis, *Evangelii Gaudium*. See also John Paul II, *Centesimus Annus*, nos. 41–44.

192. Katherine Mangan and Julia Schmalz, "A Culture of Caring: Amarillo College's 'No Excuses' Program for Low-Income Students Has Made It a National Model," *The Chronicle of Higher Education*, April 3, 2019, https://www.chronicle .com/interactives/20190403-amarillo?cid=trend_right_a.

193. See Beth McMurtie, "Georgetown U. Builds a Student-Support System to Substitute for Privilege," *The Chronicle of Higher Education*, May 27, 2014, https://www.chronicle.com/article/Georgetown-U-Builds-a/146713. The Community Scholars Program (in the Center for Multicultural Equity and Access) aids first-generation students from diverse backgrounds in their quest to succeed in Georgetown. The program provides, among other things,

academic enrichment programs and a support network. See http://cmea
.georgetown.edu/community-scholars.

194. See Villanova University Office of the Provost, Center for Access,
Success and Achievement, https://www1.villanova.edu/villanova/provost/casa
.html.

195. Loyola University Chicago, "Resources for DREAMers: The Dreamer
Committee of Loyola University Chicago: Promoting Dignity through Education," https://www.luc.edu/diversityandinclusion/immigrationresources
/resourcesfordreamers/; The Editors, "Jesuit University Students Vote to
Raise Their Own Tuition to Support Undocumented Peers," *America*,
January 19, 2016, https://www.americamagazine.org/issue/students-hike
-own-fees.

196. See Saint Peter's University, "Saint Peter's College Awarded $2.8
Million Federal Grant," October 12, 2010, http://www.saintpeters.edu/news
/2010/10/12/saint-peters-college-awarded-2-8-million-federal-grant/.

197. See Golden, *The Price of Admission*, 261–84.

198. Ibid., 275.

199. Personal interview with admissions director at a Catholic university,
November 22, 2006.

200. Two enrollment officers at Catholic institutions expressed this concern
about the size of the respective alumni bases in personal conversation.

201. Golden, *The Price of Admission*, 267–69.

202. On hiring for mission at Catholic universities, see for example
Peter-Hans Kolvenbach, SJ, "The Service of Faith and the Promotion of Justice
in American Jesuit Higher Education." Father Kolvenbach calls on all employees at Jesuit institutions to adopt the preferential option for the poor. See also
Chapter 1, note 227.

203. Pennsylvania Higher Education Assistance Agency 2018–19 Act 101
Directory, https://www.pheaa.org/documents/sgsp/ph/act-101-directory.pdf.

204. Andrew Kreighbaum, "Partisan Contrast in Spending on Student Aid,"
Inside Higher Ed, May 9, 2019, https://www.insidehighered.com/news/2019/05
/09/house-democrats-spending-proposals-include-big-boosts-student-aid. See
also Kahlenberg, "Left Behind: Unequal Opportunity in Higher Education";
Bowen et al., *Equity and Excellence in American Higher Education*, 194–223; and
New America Foundation, "Pell Grant Funding and History," https://www
.newamerica.org/education-policy/topics/higher-education-funding-and
-financial-aid/federal-student-aid/federal-pell-grants/pell-grant-funding/.

205. Charlotte Allen, "$400k DeGioia Bonus Goes to GSP," *The Hoya*,
January 13, 2015, https://www.thehoya.com/400k-degioia-bonus-goes-gsp/.

206. Golden, *The Price of Admission*, 194–223.

207. See Michelle Chen, "How Unequal School Funding Punishes Poor Kids," *The Nation*, May 11, 2018, https://www.thenation.com/article/how -unequal-school-funding-punishes-poor-kids/.

208. See Georgetown University Institute for College Preparation, http://icp .georgetown.edu/.

209. See Seattle University, "Seattle University Youth Initiative," http:// www.seattleu.edu/suyi/. This impressive example of faith doing justice was also presented at the Justice in Jesuit Higher Education conference at Creigh- ton University on August 1–4, 2013.

210. Charles Upton Sahm, "A New Kind of Catholic School," *City Journal*, Summer 2017, https://www.city-journal.org/html/new-kind-catholic-school -15326.html. See also Katsouros, *Come to Believe*, 32.

4. Socially Responsible Investment, the Stewardship of University Resources, and Integral Ecology

1. On its origins and place at Notre Dame, see Julie Hail Flory, "'Touchdown Jesus' Turns 40," May 5, 2004, https://news.nd.edu/news/touchdown-jesus -turns-40/.

2. See Brian Roewe, "Students Contest Notre Dame Investment in Hotel Group," *National Catholic Reporter*, January 4, 2013, http://ncronline.org/news /peace-justice/students-contest-notre-dame-investment-hotel-group.

3. See the statement at Advisory Committee on Corporate Responsibility in Investment Policy, Brown University, "Major Actions and Divestments," https://www.brown.edu/about/administration/advisory-committee-corporate -responsibility-investment-policies/major-actions-and-divestments. Discussion of other universities that have divested from HEI can be found at Andrew Mytelka, "Harvard Joins Other Elite Universities in Ending Investment in Controversial Hotelier," *The Chronicle of Higher Education*, April 3, 2012, https://www.chronicle.com/blogs/ticker/harvard-joins-other-elite-universities -in-ending-investment-in-controversial-hotelier/41957.

4. I designed the questionnaire for UNITE HERE as an unpaid consultant. The union contacted me via Catholic Scholars for Worker Justice. I have discussed this case more extensively previously and reprint portions here with permission from: Gerald J. Beyer, "Advocating Worker Justice: A Catholic Ethicist's Toolkit," *Journal of Religious Ethics* 45, no. 2 (2017): 226–50, https:// doi.org/10.1111/jore.12175; © 2017 Journal of Religious Ethics, Inc., Wiley- Blackwell; and Gerald J. Beyer, "Workers' Rights and Socially Responsible Investment in the Catholic Tradition: A Case Study," *Journal of Catholic Social Thought* 10, no. 1 (2013):117–54.

5. For a complete discussion of the report, see Beyer, "Workers' Rights and Socially Responsible Investment in the Catholic Tradition."

6. United States Conference of Catholic Bishops, *Forming Consciences for Faithful Citizenship* (2015), no. 80, http://www.usccb.org/issues-and-action /faithful-citizenship/upload/forming-consciences-for-faithful-citizenship.pdf.

7. See the discussion of "direct" and "indirect" employers in John Paul II, *Laborem Exercens*, no. 17.

8. The report was first published here: *Catholic Scholar Unveils Major Case Study on Workers Rights and Socially Responsible Investment in the Hotel Industry* (Washington, D.C.: Kalmanovitz Initiative for Labor and the Working Poor, 2012), http://lwp.georgetown.edu/2012/07/10/catholic-scholar-unveils-major -case-study-on-workers-rights-and-socially-responsible-investment-in-the-hotel -industry/. The revised version was later published as Beyer, "Workers' Rights and Socially Responsible Investment in the Catholic Tradition."

9. John Paul II, *Centesimus Annus*, no. 36.

10. The event was covered in Lilia Draime, "HEI and CST: Notre Dame's Controversial Investment," *The Irish Rover*, December 20, 2012, https:// irishrover.net/2012/12/hei-and-cst-notre-dames-controversial-investment/.

11. Quoted in Roewe, "Students Contest Notre Dame Investment in Hotel Group." Roewe also presents the administration's side of the story, which differs from the HEI workers.

12. See ibid.

13. See "HEI Hotels and UNITE HERE Reach Agreement," *Hotel Business Review*, December 11, 2013, http://hotelexecutive.com/newswire/47282 /function.array-pop.

14. On Brown University's decision to divest, see Beyer, "Workers' Rights and Socially Responsible Investment in the Catholic Tradition," 142.

15. Many college and university endowments are published annually in the NACUBO-TIAA Study of Endowments. See the publicly accessible tables at National Association of College and University Business Officers, Public NTSE Tables, https://www.nacubo.org/Research/2019/NACUBO-TIAA-Study-of -Endowments.

16. The following discussion of socially responsible investment is excerpted from Beyer, "Workers' Rights and Socially Responsible Investment in the Catholic Tradition." Reprinted with permission.

17. John Paul II, *Centesimus Annus*, no. 36.

18. Benedict XVI, *Caritas in Veritate*, no. 45.

19. United States Conference of Catholic Bishops, *Economic Justice for All*, no. 347. See also nos. 305, 306, 354.

20. Ibid., no. 305.

21. See for example Stephen Gandel, "Nuns Versus Bankers: The Share-holder Proxy Wars," *Time*, April 21, 2010, http://content.time.com/time /business/article/0,8599,1981861,00.html; Kevin Roose, "Nuns Who Won't Stop Nudging," *The New York Times*, November 12, 2011, https://www.nytimes .com/2011/11/13/business/sisters-of-st-francis-the-quiet-shareholder-activists .html.

22. See Jesuit Committee on Investment Responsibility, "Corporate Advocacy: JCIR Mission," http://jesuits.org/whatwedo?PAGE=DTN-20130711015452 &SUBPAGE=DTN-20130520124035.

23. See Interfaith Center on Corporate Responsibility website, http://www .iccr.org/; Investor Advocates for Social Justice website, https://iasj.org/; Jesuit Conference Office of Justice and Ecology website http://jesuits.org/socialjustice ?PAGE=DTN-20150722025945.

24. Catholic Investment Services website, http://www.catholicinvest.org.

25. Gregory R. Beabout and Kevin E. Schmiesing, "Socially Responsible Investing: An Application of Catholic Social Thought," *Logos* 6, no. 1 (2003): 69.

26. Jenny Cosgrave, "Mass Appeal? S&P Launches 'Catholic Values' Index," *CNBC*, August 20, 2015, https://www.cnbc.com/2015/08/20/mass-appeal-sp -launches-catholic-values-index.html.

27. Douglas Demeo, "Prudential Investment," *America*, October 26, 2009, https://www.americamagazine.org/issue/712/article/prudential-investment.

28. United States Conference of Catholic Bishops, "To Be a Christian Steward: A Summary of the U.S. Bishops' Pastoral Letter on Stewardship," *United States Conference of Catholic Bishops Website*, http://www.usccb.org /beliefs-and-teachings/what-we-believe/stewardship/.

29. For a helpful and succinct description of each of these, see Mary Ellen Foley McGuire, "Catholic Social Teaching Meets Wall Street," *America*, November 19, 2007, https://www.americamagazine.org/issue/634/article/catholic-social -teaching-meets-wall-street, and Demeo, "Prudential Investment." For a more detailed discussion of SRI and its history, see Gregory R. Beabout and Kevin E. Schmiesing, "Socially Responsible Investing."

30. Mary Ellen Foley McGuire, "Catholic Social Teaching Meets Wall Street."

31. United States Conference of Catholic Bishops, *Socially Responsible Investment Guidelines*, (November 12, 2003), http://www.usccb.org/about /financial-reporting/socially-responsible-investment-guidelines.cfm.

32. M. Cathleen Kaveny has recently argued that "appropriation" of evil would better describe the kind of involvement in evil that we often share today. She explicitly raises the example of a woman buying inexpensive clothing from a discount store, with the awareness that it was likely produced

in a sweatshop. See M. Cathleen Kaveny, "Appropriation of Evil: Cooperation's Mirror Image," *Theological Studies* 61 (2000): 286. However, I agree with Julie Hanlon Rubio that this case does involve cooperation in evil. See Julie Hanlon Rubio, "Moral Cooperation with Evil and Social Ethics," *Journal of the Society of Christian Ethics* 31, no. 1 (2011) and my argument in Beyer, "Advocating Worker Justice."

33. Tobias L. Winright, "The (Im)Morality of Cluster Munitions," in *Can War Be Just in the 21st Century?: Ethicists Engage the Tradition*, ed. Tobias L. Winright and Laurie Johnston (Maryknoll, N.Y.: Orbis, 2015), 29–49.

34. See United States Conference of Catholic Bishops, *Forming Consciences for Faithful Citizenship*, nos. 34–35.

35. I am indebted to M. Cathleen Kaveny for the terms "temporal, geographic, and causal proximity." For recent treatments of the concept of cooperation in evil and its limitations, see M. Cathleen Kaveny, "Appropriation of Evil: Cooperation's Mirror Image"; M. Cathleen Kaveny, "Catholics as Citizens," *America*, November 1, 2010, https://www.americamagazine.org/issue/753/article/catholics-citizens; Rubio, "Moral Cooperation with Evil and Social Ethics"; and Gerald J. Beyer, "Advocating Worker Justice."

36. James F. Keenan and Thomas R. Kopfensteiner, "The Principle of Cooperation," *Health Progress*, April (1995), https://www.chausa.org/publications/health-progress/article/april-1995/the-principle-of-cooperation. See this article for a brief, yet more nuanced overview of this distinction than I can provide here. For example, the authors discuss licit "immediate material cooperation" in intrinsically evil acts while under duress.

37. The principle of cooperation has been discussed and explicitly applied to financial investments in Gregory R. Beabout and Kevin E. Schmiesing, "Socially Responsible Investing."

38. United States Conference of Catholic Bishops, "Socially Responsible Investment Guidelines," USCCB Investment Policies, no. 4.1.

39. According to *Gaudium et Spes* subjecting workers to "disgraceful working conditions" and treating them "as mere instruments of profit" constitutes an "infamy" and "a supreme dishonor to the Creator" that "poisons human society." See Second Vatican Council, *Gaudium et Spes*, no. 27. I discuss this in more detail in Gerald J. Beyer, "Advocating Worker Justice."

40. See also John Paul II, *Veritatis Splendor* (August 6, 1993), no. 80, http://www.vatican.va/holy_father/john_paul_ii/encyclicals/documents/hf_jp-ii_enc_06081993_veritatis-splendor_en.

41. This would be considered remote, mediate, material cooperation in evil, which is allowable if other criteria are met. See Kaveny, "Appropriation of Evil," and United States Conference of Catholic Bishops, *Faithful Citizenship*.

See also Gregory Kalscheur, "Catholics in Public Life: Judges, Legislators and Voters," *Journal of Catholic Legal Studies* 46, no. 2 (2007). Kalscheur cites Pope Benedict saying this kind of cooperation in evil is justified if there are "proportionate reasons."

42. I originally downloaded the "Statement on Shareholder Advocacy Committee Activities" in 2011, which was available at http://www.luc.edu/sac/pdfs/05 -2010StatementSAC.pdf. It has since been removed. The policy has apparently been changed since I originally encountered it. This is unfortunate because this policy was perhaps the most robust of all Catholic universities that made them publicly available. The most current Loyola University Chicago "Investment Policy and Guidelines," which does not mention divestment, can be found at https:// www.luc.edu/media/lucedu/finance/pdfs/LUC_Investment_Policy.pdf.

43. Ibid., 3.

44. Ibid., 1–2.

45. George P. Schwartz, *Good Returns: Making Money by Morally Responsible Investing* (Geodi Publishing, 2010), xv, 28. At the time of their inception, the Ave Maria funds also excluded investments in companies that provided "nonmarital partner benefits."

46. Schwartz unfortunately seems to disparage screening out investments that violate other important church teachings. He derides screening out companies that "despoil the environment," "exploit oppressed minorities," "discriminate against women," "impede sustainable 'Third World' development," "contribute to international conflict," or "create other situations of injustice." He states: "Overshadowing every other consideration is the sanctity of life." See ibid., 10–12, 28.

47. United States Conference of Catholic Bishops, "Socially Responsible Investment Guidelines," §2.1–6. See also Demeo, "Prudential Investment," 12.

48. John Paul II, *Laborem Exercens*, no. 17.

49. See Second Vatican Council, *Gaudium et Spes*, no. 27, and John Paul II, *Veritatis Splendor*, no. 80.

50. See "Pope in Prato: Combat Cancer of Corruption," *Vatican Radio*, November 10, 2015, http://en.radiovaticana.va/news/2015/11/10/pope_in_prato _combat_cancer_of_corruption/1185610. See also his defense of workers' rights in Pope Francis, *Participation at the Second World Meeting of Popular Movements*, July 9, 2015, http://w2.vatican.va/content/francesco/en/speeches /2015/july/documents/papa-francesco_20150709_bolivia-movimenti-popolari .html; Pope Francis, *Address to World Meeting of Popular Movements*, October 29, 2014, https://zenit.org/articles/pope-s-address-to-popular-movements/.

51. Pope Francis, "The Rich Who Exploit the Poor Are Bloodsuckers," *Vatican Radio*, 2016, http://en.radiovaticana.va/news/2016/05/19/pope_the_rich _who_exploit_the_poor_are_bloodsuckers/1230913.

52. Andrea Tornielli, "The Pope: Who Lays-Off and Relocates Is Not a Businessperson but a Speculator," *Vatican Insider,* May 27, 2017, https://www .lastampa.it/vatican-insider-en/2017/05/27/news/the-pope-who-lays-off-and -relocates-is-not-a-businessperson-but-a-speculator-1.34607232.

53. Ethics and Justice Business Leaders for Excellence, *Not Just a Just Wage: A Conversation with Four Popes About the "Living" or "Family" Wage* (Chicago, Ill.: Acta, 2003), 57.

54. See United States Conference of Catholic Bishops, "Socially Responsible Investment Guidelines," §2.2–2.3.

55. Henry A. Giroux, *Neoliberalism's War on Higher Education* (Chicago: Haymarket Books, 2014), 91.

56. S. Prakash Sethi, "The World of Wal-Mart," *Carnegie Council for Ethics in International Affairs,* May 8, 2013, http://www.carnegiecouncil.org/publications /ethics_online/0081; Asia Floor Wage Alliance, "Precarious Work in the Walmart Global Value Chain," in *Workers Voices from the Global Supply Chain: A Report to the ILO 2016* (Geneva: ILO, 2016), http://asia.floorwage.org/workersvoices /reports/precarious-work-in-the-walmart-global-value-chain/view; "Walmart," *International Labor Rights Forum,* http://www.laborrights.org/search/node /walmart.

57. Philip Mattera, "Wal-Mart Stores," *Corporate Research Project,* February 8, 2016, http://www.corp-research.org/wal-mart.

58. Chris Teare, "College Students Starting to Demand 'Living Wage' Sportswear," *Forbes,* March 31, 2016, http://www.forbes.com/sites/christeare /2016/03/31/college-students-learning-about-living-wage-sportswear /#6bf38e0b7fc5. See also Sarah Adler-Milstein and John M. Kline, *Sewing Hope: How One Factory Challenges the Apparel Industry's Sweatshops* (Berkeley: University of California Press, 2017), 22–23, 168–69.

59. Some of the Catholic institutions are listed in "How Adidas, Nike and Under Armour Have Divvied Up Major College Basketball," *Sports Illustrated, SI Wire,* October 2, 2017, https://www.si.com/college-basketball/2017/10/02 /adidas-nike-under-armour-contracts-schools-conferences. For concerns about Nike's business practices and treatment of workers in its supply chain, in addition to the discussion below, see for example, Joshua Hunt, *University of Nike: How Corporate Cash Bought American Higher Education* (Brooklyn: Melville House, 2018); Gerald J. Beyer, "Nike's Token Equality: New Campaign Masks the Truth about Workers' Rights," *Religion Dispatches* (2017), http:// religiondispatches.org/the-moral-and-religious-case-against-nikes-latest -advertising-moves/; Maria Hengeveld, "Nike Boasts of Empowering Women around the World," *Slate,* August 21, 2016, http://www.slate.com/articles /business/the_grind/2016/08/nike_s_supply_chain_doesn_t_live_up_to_the _ideals_of_its_girl_effect_campaign.html; Oxfam Australia, "Nike," https://

www.oxfam.org.au/what-we-do/workers-rights-2/nike/.,; Caitlyn Cobb and Santul Nerkar, "In Foul Trouble: Unlacing Georgetown's Relationship with Nike," *The Georgetown Voice*, February 29, 2016, http://georgetownvoice.com /2016/02/29/81060/; Bethany Allard, "Students Urge NYU to Reevaluate Ties with Nike Due to Its Labor Practices," *Washington Square News*, April 19, 2019, https://nyunews.com/2019/04/11/news/nike-workers-labor-rights-indonesia -visas/; Corinna Vlahoyiannis, "Jim Keady Speaks out against Nike," *The Villanovan*, April 4, 2017, http://www.villanovan.com/news/jim-keady-speaks -out-against-nike/article_9e6f7512-e353-5b69-a10c-35747d476267.html; Mark Di Ionno, "Who's the Bigger Fraud, Nike or Colin Kaepernick? Let's Call It a Tie," *NJ.Com*, September 12, 2018, https://www.nj.com/news/2018/09/meet _the_jersey_who_exposed_nike_hypocrisy_long_be.html.

60. Teare, "College Students Starting to Demand 'Living Wage' Sports-wear." See also Adler-Milstein and Kline, *Sewing Hope*, 22–23, 168–69.

61. Matthew Kish, "From 'Corporate Villain' to Hero?,'" *Portland Business Journal*, May 23, 2014, http://www.bizjournals.com/portland/print-edition /2014/05/23/cover-story-from-corporate-villain-to-hero.html?ana=sm_ptl _ucp31.

62. Shelly Banjo, "Inside Nike's Struggle to Balance Cost and Worker Safety in Bangladesh: Executives Were Divided Amid Debate over Controlling Costs, Maintaining Safe Working Conditions," *The Wall Street Journal Online*, April 21, 2014, https://www.wsj.com/articles/inside-nikes-struggle-to-balance-cost-and -worker-safety-in-bangladesh-1398133855. For Nike's perspective on how it has improved treatment of supply chain workers, see "Making Product Responsi-bly," Nike Website, https://purpose.nike.com/making-product-responsibly.

63. See Zachary Senn, "Modesto Teen Aims to Shine Light on Indonesian Factory Workers' Lives," *The Modesto Bee*, April 10, 2015, http://www.modbee .com/living/article18157610.html#/tabPane=tabs-b0710947-1-1; Mbiyimoh Ghogomu, "U.S. Factory Workers Make 76 Times More Per Hour Than Workers in Indonesia," *The Higher Learning*, April 9, 2015, http:// thehigherlearning.com/2015/04/09/u-s-factory-workers-make-76-times-more -per-hour-than-workers-in-indonesia/; Kieran Guilbert, "Adidas, Nike Urged to Ensure Fair Wages for Asian Workers Making World Cup Kits," *Reuters*, June 11, 2018, https://www.reuters.com/article/us-asia-workers-worldcup /adidas-nike-urged-to-ensure-fair-wages-for-asian-workers-making-world-cup -kits-idUSKBN1J727J; BASIC, *Foul Play: Sponsors Leave Workers (Still) on the Sidelines* (Paris and Amsterdam: Collectif Éthique sur l'étiquette and Clean Clothes Campaign, 2018), https://cleanclothes.org/resources/national-cccs/foul -play-ii-sponsors-leave-workers-still-on-the-sidelines/view; Jason Lemon, "Nike Called out for Low Wages in Asia Amid Colin Kaepernick Ad Promotion," *Newsweek*, September 6, 2018, https://www.newsweek.com/nike-factory

-workers-still-work-long-days-low-wages-asia-1110129; Hengeveld, "Nike Boasts of Empowering Women around the World."

64. See BASIC, *Foul Play*, esp. 18–24. For a summary, see Lemon, "Nike Called out for Low Wages in Asia Amid Colin Kaepernick Ad Promotion."

65. "Piloting a New Compensation Model," Nike, https://purpose.nike.com /new-compensation-and-benefit-model.

66. Niklas Lollo and Dara O'Rourke, "Productivity, Profits, and Pay: A Field Experiment Analyzing the Impacts of Compensation Systems in an Apparel Factory," *IRLE Working Paper No. 104–18* (2018), http://irle.berkeley.edu/files /2018/12/Productivity-Profits-and-Pay.pdf.

67. Hunt, *University of Nike*, 70, see also 23, 32. Filmmaker Michael Moore also addressed this issue in his 1997 documentary *The Big One* and his book *Downsize This!* (New York: HarperPerennial, 1997), 127–29. I note some other sources in Beyer, "Nike's Token Equality."

68. See Jim Keady, "Behind the Swoosh" (Team Sweat You Tube Channel: Rainlake 2001), https://www.youtube.com/watch?v=M5uYCWVfuPQ. See also Ionno, "Who's the Bigger Fraud, Nike or Colin Kaepernick?"; Hunt, *University of Nike*, 76.

69. Among Catholic institutions, Keady has recently visited Georgetown and Villanova. See Rachel Eschelman, "Activist Questions Relationship between Nike and Georgetown, Discusses Labor Practices of Company," *The Georgetown Voice*, November 11, 2015, http://georgetownvoice.com/2015/11/11 /activist-questions-relationship-between-nike-and-georgetown-discusses-labor -practices-of-company/, and Vlahoyiannis, "Jim Keady Speaks out against Nike."

70. Eschelman, "Activist Questions Relationship between Nike and Georgetown." Hunt similarly states that it would have taken a worker producing Nike shoes in an Indonesian factory 492 years to earn what Michael Jordan made for his endorsement contract. Hunt, *University of Nike*, 71.

71. See for example Madison Ashley, "President DeGioia Addresses Nike Labor Disputes," *The Hoya*, April 19, 2016, http://www.thehoya.com/president -degioia-addresses-nike-labor-disputes/; Cobb and Nerkar, "In Foul Trouble: Unlacing Georgetown's Relationship with Nike"; Corinna Vlahoyiannis, "Student Group and President's Office Discuss Relationship with Nike," *The Villanovan*, February 15, 2017, http://www.villanovan.com/news/student-group -and-president-s-office-discuss-relationship-with-nike/article_26186fc6-c829 -5d18-b64f-ab46283747ac.html; John-Patrick Schultz, "Op-Ed: The Trouble with Our Commencement Speaker," *The Villanovan*, April 19, 2016, http://www .villanovan.com/news/view.php/1019834/Op-Ed-The-trouble-with-our -commencement; Max Wasserman, "United Students against Sweatshops

Pressures Administration on Nike Sponsorship," *The Daily of the University of Washington*, May 15, 2017, http://www.dailyuw.com/news/article_626ffb50 -3915-11e7-8daf-c765109b2c44.html; USAS, "Letter Concerning Nike," https://usas.org/2017/08/31/nikevictory2017/.

72. See Ashley, "President DeGioia Addresses Nike Labor Disputes"; Vlahoyiannis, "Student Group and President's Office Discuss Relationship with Nike"; and Scott Nova, "Nike, the WRC and University Labor Codes," *Worker Rights Consortium*, https://www.workersrights.org/communications-to-affiliates /nike-the-wrc-and-university-labor-codes/.

73. Nova, "Nike, the WRC and University Labor Codes."

74. See "Catholic Higher Education," *The Catholic Labor Network*, http:// catholiclabor.org/catholic-employer-project/catholic-higher-education, and "Affiliate Institutions," *Worker Rights Consortium*, https://www.workersrights .org/affiliate-schools/.

75. Nova, "Nike, the WRC and University Labor Codes." On working conditions and abuse at factories used by Nike, see also note 63 above and Scott Nova, "New WRC Report on Hansae Vietnam (Nike)," https://www .workersrights.org/communications-to-affiliates/new-wrc-report-on-hansae -vietnam-nike/; Worker Rights Consortium, *Made in Vietnam: Labor Rights Violations in Vietnam's Export Manufacturing Sector* (Washington, D.C.: Worker Rights Consortium 2013), https://www.workersrights.org/wp-content/uploads /2016/02/WRC_Vietnam_Briefing_Paper.pdf; Dave Jamieson, "Watchdog Group Kept out of Nike Supplier's Factory after Worker Strike," *Huffington Post*, March 3, 2016, http://www.huffingtonpost.com/entry/nike-labor-rights-vietnam _us_56d893f2e4b0000de403b7d0?rlfpqfr; Jim Keady, "Activist Fighting Nike in Vietnam Beaten and Jailed—Is This What Obama's TPP Deal Will Promote?," *The Daily Kos*, November 14, 2015, http://www.dailykos.com/story/2015/11/25 /1454062/-Activist-fighting-Nike-in-Vietnam-beaten-and-jailed-Is-this-what -Obama-s-TPP-deal-will-promote; Senn, "Modesto Teen Aims to Shine Light on Indonesian Factory Workers' Lives"; Eschelman, "Activist Questions Relation- ship between Nike and Georgetown."; Keady, "Behind the Swoosh." Former US Secretary of Labor Robert Reich has argued that Nike's poor treatment of workers must be seen in the larger context of the Trans-Pacific Partnership, which allows Nike to "play by the rules." Robert Reich, "Nike, Obama and the Fiasco of the Trans-Pacific Partnership," *Moyers Perspectives*, May 11, 2015, http://billmoyers.com/2015/05/11/nike-obama-fiasco-trans-pacific-partnership/. Nike provides data about its global supply chain on its website at http:// manufacturingmap.nikeinc.com/.

76. Teare, "College Students Starting to Demand 'Living Wage' Sportswear."

77. Ryan Miller, "University Allows Nike Contract to Expire While Protest- ers Face Student Conduct Meetings," *The Georgetown Voice*, January 3, 2017,

https://georgetownvoice.com/2017/01/03/university-allows-nike-contract-to
-expire-while-protesters-face-student-conduct-meetings/. See also Ashley,
"President DeGioia Addresses Nike Labor Disputes."

78. Hunt, *University of Nike*, 77, see also 77–94, 137–38.

79. See Katherine Long, "New UW Contract with Nike That Allows
Inspections of Overseas Factories Is First of Its Kind," *The Seattle Times*,
November 8, 2017, https://www.seattletimes.com/seattle-news/education/new
-uw-contract-with-nike-that-allows-inspections-of-overseas-factories-is-first-of
-its-kind/; Elizabeth Segran, "Here's How Georgetown Convinced Nike to
Make a Major Concession on Workers' Rights," *Fast Company*, August 30, 2017,
https://www.fastcompany.com/40460462/heres-how-georgetown-convinced
-nike-to-make-a-major-concession-on-workers-rights. The University of
Washington subsequently made a ten-year, $120 million deal with Adidas in
2019. It is unclear if this new deal means the university will no longer sell Nike
collegiate apparel at all. See Ryan S. Clark, "For UW, the Decision to Leave
Nike for Adidas Was 'Not about Uniforms' but 'Something More,'" *The News
Tribune*, April 12, 2018, https://www.thenewstribune.com/sports/college/pac-12
/university-of-washington/article208757209.html.

80. Scott Nova, "Update Concerning Nike and Factory Access," *Worker
Rights Consortium*, https://www.workersrights.org/communications-to-affiliates
/update-concerning-nike-and-factory-access/; https://www.workersrights.org
/communication-to-affiliates-2/083017-2/. For Villanova's engagement on this
issue, see Chris Deucher, "Student Group Stands up to Nike, Engages Administration," *The Villanovan*, October 3, 2017, http://www.villanovan.com/news
/student-group-stands-up-to-nike-engages-administration/article_2f1b0ada
-a8b2-11e7-b6aa-a7afb68d4a50.html.

81. See Daniel Luis Zager, Angeles Solis, and Sonia Adjroud, "These
Georgetown Students Fought Nike—and Won," *The Nation*, September 15,
2017, https://www.thenation.com/article/these-georgetown-students-fought
-nike-and-won/.

82. John M. Kline, *An Issue Primer: Reassessing Collegiate Anti-Sweatshop
Efforts: Can University Licensing Codes Meet Workers' Basic Needs?* (Washington,
D.C.: Engaged Ethics Initiative on Complex Moral Problems, Georgetown
University, 2012), 3, https://georgetown.app.box.com/s/omaqjgvp2xe6vj03z8it.

83. "IMGCL Labor Code Standards Schedule I," Georgetown University,
https://georgetown.app.box.com/s/vvduirqeartax32tpz1fdfyflskhlp5u.

84. Georgetown University, Office of Public Affairs, "Code of Conduct for
Georgetown University Licensees," https://publicaffairs.georgetown.edu
/committees/licensing-oversight-committee/code-of-conduct/. Georgetown's
Assistant Vice President for Public Affairs and Business Policy J. Callahan
Watson stated on the university website that "As part of the new license

contract, Nike has agreed that its manufacturers will abide by IMG College Licensing's (IMGCL) Labor Code Standards, which are aligned with Georgetown's code and include the labor standards under which the WRC investigates factories." See "Georgetown Advances Workers' Rights through New Agreement with Nike and Worker Rights Consortium," Georgetown University, https://www.georgetown.edu/news/georgetown-advances-workers-rights -through-new-agreement-with-nike-and-worker-rights-consortium/. In my judgment, if this means that Nike must comply with the living wage provision in the university's code of conduct, the university should state this clearly.

85. For example, Notre Dame's licensing code of conduct does not refer to a living wage at all. See "University of Notre Dame Licensing Code of Conduct," University of Notre Dame, https://licensing.nd.edu/assets/12740/codeofconduct _document.pdf. Many of these codes are not publicly available. However, in his study based on almost seventy codes, John Kline maintains that the "minimum standard in the majority of individual university codes . . . simply require the legal minimum wage or the prevailing industry wage, whichever is higher." John M. Kline, *An Issue Primer*, 2.

86. See John Paul II, *Laborem Exercens*, no. 19.

87. Scott Nova, "Information Concerning Nike's Indonesia Production," *Worker Rights Consortium*, https://www.workersrights.org/communications-to -affiliates/nike-the-wrc-and-university-labor-codes/.

88. I am indebted here to the detailed work on Alta Gracia and its model by John Kline and Sara Adler-Milstein. See Adler-Milstein and Kline, *Sewing Hope*, and Georgetown University School Foreign Service Landegger Program in International Business Diplomacy, "Alta Gracia Project," https://ibd.georgetown .edu/research/alta-gracia/. On Alta Gracia, see also Milli Legrain, "'Dignity and Respect': Dominican Factory Vows to Never Be a Sweatshop," *The Guardian*, February 14, 2019, https://www.theguardian.com/world/2019/feb/14/alta -gracia-garment-factory-dominican-republic-living-wage.

89. "Model Code," *Worker Rights Consortium*, https://www.workersrights.org /affiliates/model-code/, III.C.1.

90. Abha Bhattarai, "Congresswomen Press Nike About Its Treatment of Pregnant Athletes," *The Washington Post*, May 21, 2019, https://www .washingtonpost.com/business/2019/05/21/congresswomen-press-nike-about -its-treatment-pregnant-athletes/.

91. John Paul II, *Laborem Exercens*, no. 6; italics added. On Francis's claim, see note 51 above.

92. See for example Georgetown University's Principles and Operating Guidelines for the Committee on Investments in Social Responsibility, https://publicaffairs.georgetown.edu/cisr. Several years ago Loyola University

of Chicago used to have a policy that requires this procedure. It appears, however, that the policy has been changed. See note 42 above.

93. Rubio, "Moral Cooperation with Evil and Social Ethics," 111. See also Beyer, "Advocating Worker Justice."

94. Hunt, *University of Nike*, 101, 108. Hunt cites myriad examples of more or less sinister government and corporate influence on universities. For example, he notes that Gannon University, which is Roman Catholic, received money from a corporation to create "pro-business" courses in economics. Among the most egregious cases, Hunt describes the CIA's notorious MK-Ultra project, which entailed mind-control experiments. Some sources have posited Georgetown University Hospital's alleged and possibly unwitting involvement with some of them. See John Miller, "Stranger Georgetown: Declassified," *The Hoya*, September 2, 2016, https://www.thehoya.com/stranger-georgetown-declassified/; Nicholas M. Horrock, "80 Institutions Used in C.I.A. Mind Studies: Admiral Turner Tells Senators of Behavior Control: Research Bars Drug Testing Now," *The New York Times*, August 4, 1977, https://www.nytimes.com/1977/08/04/archives/80-institutions-used-in-cia-mind-studies-admiral-turner-tells.html; Bill Richards and John Jacob, "Three Area Colleges Used by C.I.A. In Behavior Testing," *The Washington Post*, August 18, 1977, https://www.washingtonpost.com/archive/politics/1977/08/18/3-area-colleges-used-by-cia-in-behavior-testing/b750e921-eda1-4e8d-ac99 de63edf2f6cf/?utm_term=.ce9e5c41c5a2.

95. Hunt, *University of Nike*, 114–23. On corporate influence, see also Giroux, *Neoliberalism's War on Higher Education*, 15–23, 34–36, 103–29; Jane Mayer, *Dark Money: The Hidden History of the Billionaires Behind the Rise of the Radical Right* (New York: Doubleday, 2016); Jane Mayer, "How Right-Wing Billionaires Infiltrated Higher Education," *The Chronicle of Higher Education*, February 12, 2016, https://www.chronicle.com/article/How-Right-Wing-Billionaires/235286.

96. "Pope: 'Church Does Not Need "Blood Money" but Openness to God's Mercy,'" *Vatican Radio*, March 2, 2016, http://www.archivioradiovaticana.va/storico/2016/03/02/pope_church_blood_money_openess_gods_mercy/en-1212378.

97. Sondra Ely Wheeler, *Wealth as Peril and Obligation: The New Testament on Possessions* (Grand Rapids, Mich.: W.B. Eerdmans Pub., 1995), 131–32. See also Daniel K. Finn, *Christian Economic Ethics: History and Implications* (Minneapolis, Minn.: Fortress Press, 2013).

98. Ronald J. Sider, *Fixing the Moral Deficit: A Balanced Way to Balance the Budget* (Downers Grove, Ill.: IVP Books, 2012), 54.

99. Basil, "I Will Pull Down My Barns," in *The Sunday Sermons of the Great Fathers*, ed. M. F. Toal (Chicago: Regnery, 1957), 330.

100. Kaveny, "Appropriation of Evil," 307.

101. Hunt, *University of Nike*, 60–61, see also 146–55, 99. See also Knight Commission on Intercollegiate Athletics, *Restoring the Balance: Dollars, Values, and the Future of College Sports* (Miami, Fla: Knight Commission on Intercollegiate Athletics, 2010), 18; Matthew Kish, "Big Brands on Campus: Money Flows to Some Unlikely Places," *Business Journal-Portland* 30, no. 39 (2013), http://www.bizjournals.com/portland/print-edition/2013/11/29/big-brands-on-campus-money-flows-to.html?ana=sm_ptl_ucp6&b=1385592745%5E13353392; Matthew Kish, "How Nike Funnels Money to College Football Coaches," *Business Journal-Portland*, September 3, 2013, http://www.bizjournals.com/portland/blog/threads_and_laces/2013/09/how-nike-funnels-money-football-coaches.html. One source reported that some coaches receive up to $500,000 from Nike. See Howard P. Chudacoff, *Changing the Playbook: How Power, Profit, and Politics Transformed College Sports*, (Champaign: University of Illinois Press, 2015), 134. The Portland Business Journal tracks collegiate deals with Nike by doing requests for public records. See their database: Matthew Kish, "Nike, Adidas, Under Armour Money Floods Universities as NCAA Apparel Battle Intensifies (2015 Database)," in *Portland Business Journal*, September 3, 2015, http://www.bizjournals.com/portland/blog/threads_and_laces/2015/09/nike-adidas-under-armour-ncaa-apparel-deals-2015.html. Unfortunately, Catholic institutions qua private institutions are not subject to the same reporting requirements.

102. Hunt, *University of Nike*, viii. See also Kish, "Nike, Adidas, Under Armour Money Floods Universities."

103. Mark Tracy, "Notre Dame and Under Armour Seek Win-Win with Apparel Deal," *The New York Times*, September 11, 2014, http://www.nytimes.com/2014/09/12/sports/football/notre-dame-and-under-armour-seek-win-win-with-apparel-deal.html?_r=0.

104. See for example, "How Adidas, Nike and Under Armour Have Divvied Up Major College Basketball," *Sports Illustrated*, October 2, 2017, https://www.si.com/college/2017/10/02/adidas-nike-under-armour-contracts-schools-conferences.

105. Hunt, *University of Nike*, 60.

106. Allan Brettman, "How Much Do Nike Executives (and Others) Make?," *Oregon Live* 2015, https://www.oregonlive.com/playbooks-profits/2015/07/how_much_do_nike_executives_an.html#27.

107. For a sample list, see "How Adidas, Nike and Under Armour Have Divvied Up Major College Basketball." On Georgetown, see Cobb and Nerkar, "In Foul Trouble: Unlacing Georgetown's Relationship with Nike." Nike and other athletics brands have heavily infiltrated universities in the US. See Hunt, *University of Nike*; Kish, "Big Brands on Campus: Money Flows to Some

Unlikely Places"; Matthew Kish, "5 Examples of How Nike, Adidas Own College Athletics," *Portland Business Journal*, August 30, 2013, http://www .bizjournals.com/portland/blog/threads_and_laces/2013/08/five-surprises-ncaa -nike-adidas-contract.html?page=all. On wearing compulsory brands, see also Knight Commission on Intercollegiate Athletics, *Restoring the Balance*, 18. Jim Keady's public row with the St. John's University athletic department reveals the cost of refusing to wear Nike gear as a matter of conscience. Keady, "Behind the Swoosh"; Ionno, "Who's the Bigger Fraud, Nike or Colin Kaepernick?"

108. Patricja Okuniewska, "Student Athletes Launch Sweatshop Awareness Campaign," *The Hoya*, November 13, 2015, https://www.thehoya.com/calls-for -nike-boycott-mount/.

109. *Declaration on Religious Freedom Dignitatis Humanae*, (December 7, 1965), http://www.vatican.va/archive/hist_councils/ii_vatican_council /documents/vat-ii_decl_19651207_dignitatis-humanae_en.html.

110. See Kish, "Nike, Adidas, Under Armour Money Floods Universities."

111. The USCCB socially responsible investment guidelines preclude investment in companies making these products. See United States Conference of Catholic Bishops, "Socially Responsible Investment Guidelines," §1.1. and 3.2. On banks divesting from companies producing these weapons, which some countries ban investing in, see Severin Carrell, "UK Banks and Insurers Blacklist Cluster Bomb Manufacturers," *The Guardian*, April 9, 2012, https:// www.theguardian.com/business/2012/apr/09/uk-banks-blacklist-cluster-bomb -manufacturers, and Lauren Gambino, "JP Morgan and Bank of America in Cluster Bomb Investors 'Hall of Shame,'" *The Guardian*, June 16, 2016, https:// www.theguardian.com/world/2016/jun/16/jp-morgan-bank-of-america-cluster -bomb-investors-hall-of-shame. As the first article indicates, most of the companies that manufacture these weapons are US-based.

112. Vinnie Rontondaro, "The Catholic University of America Accepts More Money from Charles Koch Foundation," *National Catholic Reporter*, January 23, 2015, http://ncronline.org/blogs/ncr-today/catholic-university-america-accepts -more-money-charles-koch-foundation; Anthony Annett, "Should a Catholic University Take Koch Funding?," *Commonweal Blog*, April 25, 2016, https:// www.commonwealmagazine.org/blog/should-catholic-university-take-koch -funding; Steve Jordan, "Of Two Minds on Economics: Does Teaching at Creighton Institute Contradict Catholic Social Thought?," *Omaha World Herald*, December 8, 2014, http://www.omaha.com/money/of-two-minds-on -economics-does-teaching-at-creighton-institute/article_e6a8e72e-130c-5c49 -a257-a32f55530905.html.

113. See Charles Koch Foundation, "List of Supported Colleges," https:// www.charleskochfoundation.org/our-giving-and-support/higher-education/list

-of-supported-colleges/. See also Polluterwatch: A Project of Greenpeace, Charles Koch University Funding, https://polluterwatch.org/charles-koch -university-funding-database.

114. Annett, "Should a Catholic University Take Koch Funding?"

115. See the letter and analysis of it in Joshua J. McElwee, "Republican Donors' Gift to Catholic University Comes under Fire," *National Catholic Reporter*, December 16, 2013, http://ncronline.org/news/politics/republican-donors-gift -catholic-university-comes-under-fire. Discussion of the response to the letter from the administration at the Catholic University of America can be found at Joshua J. McElwee, "University: Koch Grant 'Fully Consonant' with Catholic Teaching," *National Catholic Reporter*, December 16, 2013, http://ncronline.org /news/politics/university-koch-grant-fully-consonant-catholic-teaching.

116. See Aysha Khan, "Boston College Students and Faculty Push to Reject Koch Funding—and Koch Values," *Religion News Service*, November 19, 2019, https://religionnews.com/2019/11/19/boston-college-students-and-faculty-push -to-reject-koch-funding-and-koch-values/ and the "UnKoch My Campus" campaign website, http://www.unkochmycampus.org.

117. See for example the discussion of the Koch Brothers in Mayer, *Dark Money*. Equally disturbing is Mayer's contention that the people close to the Koch Brothers orchestrated a smear campaign against her. See David Corn, "How the Kochtopus Went after a Reporter," *Mother Jones*, January 21, 2016, http://www.motherjones.com/politics/2016/01/koch-brothers-jane-mayer-dark -money; Jim Dwyer, "What Happened to Jane Mayer When She Wrote About the Koch Brothers," *New York Times*, January 26, 2016, http://www.nytimes .com/2016/01/27/nyregion/what-happened-to-jane-mayer-when-she-wrote-about -the-koch-brothers.html; Jim Tankersley, "What Charles Koch Really Thinks About Climate Change," *The Washington Post*, June 6, 2016, https://www .washingtonpost.com/news/energy-environment/wp/2016/06/06/what-charles -koch-really-thinks-about-climate-change/; Nell Gluckman, "Undeterred by Criticism, Koch Foundation Increases Spending in Higher Education," *The Chronicle of Higher Education*, May 29, 2018, https://www.chronicle.com/article /Undeterred-by-Criticism-Koch/243528/; and the "UnKoch My Campus" campaign website, http://www.unkochmycampus.org/, particularly *Donor Intent of the Koch Network: Leveraging Universities for Self Interested Policy Change* (UnKoch My Campus, 2018), https://static1.squarespace.com/static /5400da69e4b0cb1fd47c9077/t/5c181cfd562fa7e5dc228ecf/1545084159707/D onor+Intent+of+the+Koch+Network.pdf.

118. Boston College Office of the Treasurer, "Ethical Investment Guide-lines," http://www.bc.edu/offices/endowment/ethicalguidelines.html.

119. Seattle University Finance and Business Affairs, "Investment Policy Statement," https://www.seattleu.edu/finance-and-business-affairs/sri

/investment-policy-statement/. The statement was approved in 2013 and last amended in 2017.

120. See Georgetown University Investment Office, "Socially Responsible Investment," https://investments.georgetown.edu/socially-responsible-investing. See also Georgetown University, "Board Supports Investment Recommendation, Approves Kehoe Design Study," October 5, 2017, https://www.georgetown.edu/news/board-of-directors-meeting-october-2017.

121. Both the former Loyola University Chicago (see note 42) and the Georgetown University Committee on Investments and Social Responsibility Principles and Operating Guidelines (https://georgetown.app.box.com/s/gn7qk k9bfxx5cckk6rysmv9wzbcox5kr) admirably stipulate that the respective committees will investigate any concern about investments brought forth by any member of the University community.

122. See Responsible Endowments Coalition, http://www.endowmentethics .org/.

123. Many, if not most, SRI policies of Catholic universities are not publicly available.

124. Adrian Dominican Sisters, "Criteria for Corporate Responsibility," http://www.adriandominicans.org/Portals/1/Pdf/pab/CR-Criteria-Approved -Feb-2018.pdf.

125. Adrian Dominican Sisters, "PAB—Community Investments," http:// www.adriandominicans.org/PAB/CommunityInvestments.aspx. The numerical data is from Adrian Dominican Sisters Portfolio Advisory Board, *Celebrating 40 Years of Socially Responsible Investing*, (Adrian, Mich.: Portfolio Advisory Board Adrian Dominican Sisters, n.d.), 5, http://www.adriandominicans.org/Portals /1/Pdf/peacejusticecare/PAB%2040th%20Anniversary%20Commemorative%20 Brochure%20lo%20res.pdf.

126. Ibid., 11.

127. See Christian Brothers Investment Services, "Catholic Responsible Investments," http://cbisonline.com/us/catholic-socially-responsible-esg -investing/.

128. Tom Gallagher, "Catholic Investing in Changing Times," *National Catholic Reporter*, July 14, 2015, http://ncronline.org/news/accountability /catholic-investing-changing-times.

129. See United States Conference of Catholic Bishops, *Forming Consciences for Faithful Citizenship*, nos. 32–33.

130. Francis, *Laudato Si* (May 24, 2015), http://www.vatican.va/content /francesco/en/encyclicals/documents/papa-francesco_20150524_enciclica -laudato-si.html.

131. Christian Brothers Investment Services, "Catholic Responsible Investments."

132. Francis, *Laudato Si*, no. 25.

133. Ibid., no. 211.

134. Demeo, "Prudential Investment," 13–14.

135. Biran Roewe, "University of Dayton Divests from Fossil Fuels," *National Catholic Reporter*, June 24, 2014, https://www.ncronline.org/blogs/earthbeat /eco-catholic/university-dayton-divests-fossil-fuels.

136. University of Dayton, Hanley Sustainability Institute, "Divest/Invest Conference," https://udayton.edu/artssciences/ctr/hsi/events/conferences /divest-invest-conference/index.php.

137. Brain Roewe, "Creighton University President Rejects Student Recommendation to Divest from Fossil Fuels," *National Catholic Reporter*, November 13, 2019, https://www.ncronline.org/news/earthbeat/creighton-university -president-rejects-student-recommendation-divest-fossil-fuels.

138. Brian Roewe, "Georgetown Committee Opts against Endorsing Full Fossil Fuel Divestment," *National Catholic Reporter*, January 29, 2015, http:// ncronline.org/blogs/eco-catholic/georgetown-committee-opts-against-endorsing -full-fossil-fuel-divestment. On the 2020 decision, see Committee on Finance and Administration, Georgetown University Board of Directors, "Recommendation on Sustainable Impact Investments and Fossil Fuel Divestment," January 16, 2020, https://georgetown.app.box.com/s/9fjyr5qj5upd35unzhd2siq 93wptfklm.

139. Stephen V. Sundborg, S.J., "Seattle University Board Votes to Divest from Fossil Fuels," Office of the President, Seattle University, https://www.seattleu .edu/president/update/seattle-university-board-votes-to-divest-from-fossil-fuels .html. See also Seattle University Finance and Business Affairs, "Recommendations on Fossil Fuel Divestment," https://www.seattleu.edu/finance-and -business-affairs/sri/divestment/.

140. Alec Downing and Frances Divinagracia, "Fossil-Free Degrees: Seattle U Makes Steps Towards Divestment," *The Spectator*, October 10, 2018, https:// seattlespectator.com/2018/10/10/fossil-free-degrees-seattle-u-makes-steps -towards-divestment/.

141. Mary Ellen Foley McGuire, "Catholic Social Teaching Meets Wall Street."

142. Schwartz, *Good Returns: Making Money by Morally Responsible Investing*, 7.

143. Demeo, "Prudential Investment."

144. See UNITE HERE, "Harvard Will Not Reinvest in HEI Hospitality as HEI Hemorrhages University Investors," (2012), https://unitehere.org/harvard -will-not-reinvest-in-hei-hospitality-as-hei-hemorrhages-university-investors/. For an introduction to shareholder resolutions and proxy voting, see the Forum for Sustainable and Responsible Investment website, https://www.ussif.org /proxies and https://www.ussif.org/resolutions.

145. UNEP Finance Initiative and United Nations Global Compact, *Responsible Investment in Private Equity: A Guide for Limited Partners* (2011), 2–6, https://www.unpri.org/download?ac=260.

146. Gregory R. Beabout and Kevin E. Schmiesing, "Socially Responsible Investing: An Application of Catholic Social Thought," 92. Endowment figures are taken from 2019 NACUBO-TIAA Study of Endowments, https://www.nacubo.org/research/2019/nacubo-tiaa-study-of-endowments.

147. Douglas Demeo, "Getting out of Oil," *America*, April 9, 2014, https://www.americamagazine.org/issue/getting-out-oil.

148. Bob Brecha, "Fossil-Fuel Divestment: Folly or Inevitability," *The Huffington Post*, November 10, 2015, http://www.huffingtonpost.com/bob-brecha/fossilfuel-divestment-fol_b_8513494.html. Brecha is a climatologist at The University of Dayton.

149. See Elizabeth Douglas, *Exxon's Gamble: 25 Years of Rejecting Shareholder Concerns on Climate Change* (ICN Climate Accountability Project, 2015), http://books.insideclimatenews.org/exxonsclimategamble; Elizabeth Douglas, "Exxon Shareholder Climate Vote Blocked, Chevron's Approved by SEC," March 25, 2015, http://insideclimatenews.org/news/25032015/exxon-shareholder-climate-vote-blocked-chevrons-approved-sec. I am indebted to Erin Lothes Biviano, PhD for these sources.

150. Melissa Cronin, "Meet the Nun Trying to Reform Exxon Mobil," *Grist*, May 16, 2016, http://grist.org/climate-energy/meet-the-nun-wielding-100-billion-to-reform-exxon-mobil/?utm_content=buffer8ae6f&utm_medium=social&utm_source=twitter.com&utm_campaign=buffer.

151. See Erin Lothes Biviano, "By Night in a Pillar of Fire: Theological Analysis of Renewable Energy," in *Just Sustainability: Technology, Ecology, and Resource Extraction*, ed. Christiana Z. Peppard and Andrea Vicini (Maryknoll, N.Y.: Orbis, 2015); and Erin Lothes Biviano et al., "Catholic Moral Traditions and Energy Ethics for the 21st Century," *Journal of Moral Theology* 5, no. 2 (2016).

152. See Second Nature, "History," https://secondnature.org/history/.

153. Ignatian Solidarity Network, "Laudato Si: On Care for Our Common Home: Statement of Leaders in Catholic Higher Education Globally," http://ignatiansolidarity.net/catholic-higher-ed-encyclical-sign-on/.

154. Catholic Climate Covenant, "St. Francis/Laudato Si' Pledge," https://catholicclimatecovenant.worldsecuresystems.com/pledge, and Catholic Coalition on Climate Change and Association of Catholic Colleges and Universities, *Sustainability and Catholic Higher Education: A Toolkit for Mission Integration* (Washington, D.C.: United States Conference of Catholic Bishops, 2011), http://www.usccb.org/issues-and-action/human-life-and-dignity/environment/upload/sustainability-catholic-higher-ed-toolkit.pdf.

155. In addition to the examples I provide here, see ibid.

156. Villanova University Media Room, "Villanova University Named 2014 Green Business of the Year by Main Line Chamber of Commerce," https://www1 .villanova.edu/villanova/media/pressreleases/2014/0703.html.

157. Villanova University Sustainability, "Quick Facts," https://www1 .villanova.edu/villanova/sustainability/about/QuickFacts.html.

158. The Princeton Review, *The Princeton Review's Guide to 353 Green Colleges* (2015), 201. Downloaded from https://www.princetonreview.com/college -rankings/green-guide.

159. Center for Environmental Justice and Sustainability, "Campus Sustainability," https://www.seattleu.edu/cejs/campus-sustainability/. See the many other sustainability efforts of Seattle University on this website.

160. University of San Francisco, "University of San Francisco Achieves Carbon Neutrality More Than 30 Years Ahead of Goal," https://www.usfca.edu /newsroom/media-relations/news-releases/carbon-neutrality.

161. "America's Greenest Colleges: The Top 10," *Sierra: The National Magazine of the Sierra Club*, https://www.sierraclub.org/sierra/slideshow/top-ten -coolest-schools-2014#9.

162. See "The Full Ranking," *Sierra: The National Magazine of the Sierra Club*, http://www.sierraclub.org/sierra/2014-5-september-october/cool-schools -2014/full-ranking.

163. "Scoring Key," *Sierra: The National Magazine of the Sierra Club*, https:// www.sierraclub.org/sierra/2014-5-september-october/cool-schools-2014/scoring -key.

164. The Princeton Review, *The Princeton Review's Guide to 353 Green Colleges*, (2015), http://www.princetonreview.com/college-rankings/green-guide.

165. See The Princeton Review, "The Green College Survey," http://www .princetonreview.com/college-rankings/green-guide/data-partnership.

166. Ibid.

167. Association for the Advancement of Sustainability in Higher Education, *Sustainable Campus Index*, (Philadelphia, Pa.: Association for the Advancement of Sustainability in Higher Education, 2015), 44, https://www.aashe.org/wp -content/uploads/2017/10/aashe_2015_sustainable_campus_index.pdf.

168. See ibid., 49. Each institution must report on its compensation policies, which makes this data useful from the standpoint of CST and the argument of this book.

169. Association for the Advancement of Sustainability in Higher Education, *Stars 2.1 Technical Manual*, (Philadelphia, Pa.: Association for the Advancement of Sustainability in Higher Education, 2015), 292. Only institutions that can verify paying a living wage to all employees receive the maximum amount of credit in this category.

170. The Princeton Review, "The Princeton Review's Guide to 353 Green Colleges," 135.

171. Rick Bacigalupi, "Sustainability at SCU, Produced for 2014 Acterra Business Environmental Awards," in *SustainableSCU* (Youtube 2014), https://www.youtube.com/watch?v=qKl7N9ZHbe0&list=UUItUCvIs1OJgpw-gqSIZWZw. See also Center for Sustainability, Santa Clara University, "Buildings and Operations," https://www.scu.edu/sustainability/operations/buildings/; and Center for Sustainability, Santa Clara University, "Climate Neutrality," https://www.scu.edu/sustainability/commitment/climate/.

172. The Princeton Review, "The Princeton Review's Guide to 353 Green Colleges," 132.

173. Saint Michael's College, "Sustainability at a Glance," https://www.smcvt.edu/pages/center-for-the-environment/sustainability/sustainability-at-a-glance.aspx.

174. Robert Andrew Powell, "How Green Is My Campus?," *New York Times Magazine*, April 28, 2008, http://www.nytimes.com/2008/04/20/magazine/20Learn-btext.html?_r=1&oref=slogin. See also Jack Kadden, "Despite Hard Times, Colleges Are Still Going Green," *The New York Times*, October 7, 2009, http://thechoice.blogs.nytimes.com/2009/10/07/despite-hard-times-colleges-are-still-going-green/.

175. Villanova University Media Room, "Villanova University Featured in the Princeton Review's 2014 Guide to 332 Green Colleges," https://www1.villanova.edu/villanova/media/pressreleases/2014/0422.html.

176. See Paul Moses, "Catholic Colleges Tell Poor Students: Go Somewhere Else," *The Hechinger Report*, December 22, 2014; Annie Waldman, "As Pope Pushes to Help the Poor, Catholic Universities Leave Them Behind," *ProPublica*, September 22, 2015.

177. Efficiency Vermont, "Vermont Is a National Leader in College Energy Efficiency Financing," June 7, 2012, https://www.efficiencyvermont.com/news-blog/news/vermont-is-a-national-leader-in-college-energy-efficiency-financing.

178. See Chapter 2, where I draw on Steven Shulman, "The Costs and Benefits of Adjunct Justice: A Critique of Brennan and Magness," *Journal of Business Ethics* (2017). Shulman convincingly critiques the exaggerated estimates in Jason Brennan and Phillip Magness, "Estimating the Cost of Justice for Adjuncts: A Case Study in University Business Ethics," *Journal of Business Ethics* 148, no. 1 (2018).

179. See Drew Christiansen and Walter Glazer, *And God Saw That It Was Good: Catholic Theology and the Environment* (Washington, D.C.: United States Catholic Conference, 1996); and Tobias L. Winright, ed. *Green Discipleship: Catholic Theological Ethics and the Environment* (Winona, Minn.: Anselm Academic, 2011).

180. United States Conference of Catholic Bishops, "Reflections on the Energy Crisis: A Statement by the Committee on Social Development and World Peace" (April 2, 1981), http://www.usccb.org/issues-and-action/human -life-and-dignity/environment/upload/moral-principles-from-1981-energy -statement.pdf.

181. Pope John Paul II, "A Message for the Celebration of the World Day of Peace" (January 1, 1990), https://w2.vatican.va/content/john-paul-ii/en /messages/peace/documents/hf_jp-ii_mes_19891208_xxiii-world-day-for -peace.html.

182. Ed King, "Pope Benedict XVI: The First Green Pontiff?," *The Guardian*, February 21, 2013, https://www.theguardian.com/environment/blog/2013/feb /12/pope-benedict-xvi-first-green-pontiff.

183. Francis, *Laudato Si*, nos. 66, 68.

184. Ibid., nos. 16, 22–23, 43.

185. Ibid., no. 158.

186. John J. Conley, "An Elusive Integral Ecology," *America*, July 21, 2015, http://americamagazine.org/issue/elusive-integral-ecology; Global Catholic Climate Movement, "Laudato Si' Chapter 4: Integral Ecology as a New Paradigm of Justice" (August 27, 2015), https://catholicclimatemovement.global /laudato-si-ch-4-integral-ecology-as-a-new-paradigm-of-justice/; Thomas Reese, "A Readers' Guide to 'Laudato Si,'" *National Catholic Reporter*, June 26, 2015, http://ncronline.org/blogs/faith-and-justice/readers-guide-laudato-si.

187. Francis, *Laudato Si*, no. 137.

188. Augustine, *The City of God against the Pagans*, ed. and trans. R. W. Dyson (Cambridge: Cambridge University Press, 1998), XIV.15.64.

189. Francis, *Laudato Si*, no. 139.

190. Ibid., no. 70.

191. Ibid., no. 49.

192. John Paul II, *Centesimus Annus*, no. 38.

193. Francis, *Laudato Si*, no. 49.

194. Ibid., no. 142.

195. Ibid., no. 141.

5. Racial Inclusion and Justice at Catholic Colleges and Universities: From Tokenism to Participation

1. Joseph A. Brown, SJ, MacLean Chair Lecture: "Plenty Good Room: Diversity, Integration and the University," Saint Joseph's University, Philadelphia, Pa., November 12, 2009.

2. The lyrics to the spiritual "Plenty Good Room" can be found in Delores Carpenter and Nolan E. Williams, eds., *African American Heritage Hymnal*,

1st ed. (Chicago: Gia Publications, 2001), 506. It is based on John 14:2: "In my Father's house there are many dwelling places." Cheryl Townsend Gilkes writes that the spirituals have long provided a "prophetic-apocalyptic reading of the Bible," underscoring that the God of the Bible stands on the side of the oppressed. See Cheryl Townsend Gilkes, "'Go Tell Mary and Martha': The Spirituals, Biblical Options for Women, and Cultural Tensions in the African American Religious Experience," in *Womanist Theological Ethics: A Reader*, ed. Katie G. Cannon, Emilie Maureen Townes, and Angela D. Sims (Louisville, Ky.: Westminster John Knox Press, 2011).

3. The Association of Catholic Colleges and Universities has highlighted ways that member institutions have promoted diversity and inclusion. See Association of Catholic Colleges and Universities, "Ten Ways Your Campus Can Be More Inclusive," http://www.accunet.org/LinkClick.aspx?fileticket =SePPpSN2J_Y%3d&portalid=70.

4. In using the term "minoritized," I follow scholar of racial equity Shaun R. Harper, who contends that the term connotes that people are "rendered minorities in particular situations and institutional environments that sustain an overrepresentation of Whiteness." Shaun R. Harper, "Race without Racism: How Higher Education Researchers Minimize Racist Institutional Norms," *The Review of Higher Education* 36, no. 1 (2012): 1.

5. I am indebted to David Hollenbach, SJ, who wrote about the insufficiency of tolerance to overcome the problems of poverty and racial discrimination in the United States. See David Hollenbach, *The Common Good and Christian Ethics* (New York: Cambridge University Press, 2002). For systematic treatment of the relationship between solidarity and participation, see Gerald J. Beyer, *Recovering Solidarity*, 90–94.

6. Ada Maria Isasi-Diaz, "Solidarity: Love of Neighbor in the Eighties," in *Lift Every Voice: Constructing Christian Theologies from the Underside*, ed. Susan Brook Thistlethwaite and Mary Potter Engle (San Francisco: Harper San Francisco: 1990).

7. I rely here on Bryan Massingale's definition of White supremacy in Bryan N. Massingale, *Racial Justice and the Catholic Church* (Maryknoll, N.Y.: Orbis Books, 2010), 41. For a more extended argument on solidarity against White supremacy, see Gerald J. Beyer, "The Continuing Relevance of *Brothers and Sisters to Us* to Confronting Racism and White Privilege," *Josephinum Journal of Theology* 19, no. 2 (2012).

8. John Paul II, "Angelus" (August 26, 2001), http://w2.vatican.va/content /john-paul-ii/en/angelus/2001/documents/hf_jp-ii_ang_20010826.html.

9. For an insightful analysis of this horrific event, see Nick Roll, "When Your Students Attend White Supremacist Rallies," *Inside Higher Ed*, August 15, 2017, https://www.insidehighered.com/news/2017/08/15/college-students

-unmasked-unite-right-protesters; Shaun R. Harper, "Stop Sustaining White Supremacy," *Inside Higher Ed*, August 21, 2017, https://www.insidehighered .com/views/2017/08/21/what-charlottesville-says-about-white-supremacy -universities-essay; James F. Keenan, "As UVA's Leaders Equivocate, Professors Shine an Ethical Light," *The Chronicle of Higher Education*, August 16, 2017, http://www.chronicle.com/article/As-UVa-s-Leaders-Equivocate/240944?cid =wsinglestory; Marcia Chatelain, "How Universities Embolden White Nationalists," *The Chronicle of Higher Education*, August 17, 2017, http://www .chronicle.com/article/How-Universities-Embolden/240956?cid=wcontentgrid _hp_2.

10. Marvin L. Krier Mich, *Catholic Social Teaching and Movements* (Mystic, Conn.: Twenty-Third Publications, 1998), 142. See also Derald Wing Sue et al., "Racial Microaggressions in Everyday Life: Implications for Clinical Practice," *American Psychologist* 62, no. 4 (2007): 273.

11. Sue et al., "Racial Microaggressions in Everyday Life," 272.

12. Mich, *Catholic Social Teaching and Movements*, 142.

13. See my discussion in Beyer, "The Continuing Relevance of *Brothers and Sisters to Us*," 244–46. I mention, for example, that as recently as 2010 about 25 percent of Catholics supported laws that allow for discrimination in housing (which is higher than the percentage of religiously unaffiliated). More recently, a PRRI report stated that 62 percent of Catholics believe that discrimination against Whites is as big a problem as discrimination against minorities. Conversely, 67 percent of religiously unaffiliated and 61 percent of Hispanic Catholics believe this is not true. In addition, more than half of White Catholics see immigrants as a burden to society, a view that contradicts Catholic teaching on the dignity and rights of immigrants. By contrast, 71 percent of Hispanic Catholics believe immigrants positively contribute to society. See Betsy Cooper et al., "How Immigration and Concerns about Cultural Change are Shaping the 2016 Election," *PRRI/Brookings Survey*, Executive Summary, June 23, 2016, http://www.prri.org/research/prri -brookings-poll-immigration-economy-trade-terrorism-presidential-race/. On Catholic teaching regarding immigrants, see Thomas Betz, "Catholic Social Teaching on Immigration and the Movement of Peoples," United States Conference of Catholic Bishops, http://www.usccb.org/issues-and-action /human-life-and-dignity/immigration/catholic-teaching-on-immigration-and -the-movement-of-peoples.cfm.

14. Massingale, *Racial Justice and the Catholic Church*, 1–2. Massingale provides an excellent discussion of the meaning, scope, and effects of racism in US society broadly, which goes beyond what I can articulate here given my focus on racism in higher education.

15. Ibid., 15.

16. For a succinct overview of some of these profound racial injustices, see Catholic Charities USA, *Poverty and Racism: Overlapping Threats to the Common Good* (Alexandria, Va: Catholic Charities USA, 2009).

17. Massingale, *Racial Justice and the Catholic Church*, 15.

18. Ibid., 26. For examples of White privilege, both historical and current, see Catholic Charities USA, *Poverty and Racism*; Beyer, "The Continuing Relevance of Brothers and Sisters to Us."

19. See Francis Cardinal George, "Dwell in My Love: A Pastoral Letter on Racism," April 4, 2001, Archdiocese of Chicago Website, http://legacy .archchicago.org/Cardinal/pdf/DwellInMyLove_10thAnniversary.pdf; italics added. See also Bishop Dale Melczek's discussion of various kinds of racism, including institutional racism, in "Created in God's Image: A Pastoral Letter on the Sin of Racism and a Call to Conversion," August 6, 2003, Roman Catholic Diocese of Gary Website, http://www.dcgary.org/pdf/Created-In-Gods -Image.pdf (link no longer active).

20. See "The Origins and Authority of the Public Consensus: A Study of the Growing End" in John Courtney Murray, *We Hold These Truths: Catholic Reflections on the American Proposition* (New York: Sheed and Ward, 1960), 97–124. Cardinal Joseph Bernadin describes Murray's use of the "growing edge" in Alphonse P. Spilly, ed., *Selected Works of Joseph Cardinal Bernadin: Church and Society*, vol. 2 (Collegeville, Minn.: The Liturgical Press, 2000), 373.

21. Richard G. Malloy, *A Faith That Frees: Catholic Matters for the 21st Century* (Maryknoll, N.Y.: Orbis Books, 2007), 132.

22. United States Conference of Catholic Bishops, *Brothers and Sisters to Us*, 2, http://www.usccb.org/issues-and-action/cultural-diversity/african-american /brothers-and-sisters-to-us.cfm. This paragraph is adapted from my analysis of the document in Beyer, "The Continuing Relevance of *Brothers and Sisters to Us*," 241.

23. Ibid., 2.

24. Ibid., 6.

25. Ibid., 6. Many of the sources used to glean data for this chapter elide "Hispanics" and "Latinos/Latinas." I am aware of the distinction, but I have chosen to leave the terminology of the source intact rather than guess what the author/s intend. On this issue as well as use of "Latinx" versus "Latinos/as" (which I have opted for throughout) see Mark Hugo Lopez, Jens Manuel Krogstad, and Jeffrey S. Passel, "Who Is Hispanic?", Pew Research Center, September 15, 2020, https://www.pewresearch.org/fact-tank/2020/09/15 /who-is-hispanic/. Similarly, I use the terms "Asian" or "Asian American" the same way the sources that I cite use them. See note 30 below for problems with these categories.

26. Ibid., 1.

27. See Beyer, "The Continuing Relevance of *Brothers and Sisters to Us.*"

28. United States Conference of Catholic Bishops, *Brothers and Sisters to US*, § "Our Community Church."

29. James C. Cavendish, *A Research Report Commemorating the 25th Anniversary of Brothers & Sisters to Us* (Washington, D.C.: United States Conference of Catholic Bishops: 2004), 1, 10–11, http://www.usccb.org/issues-and-action /cultural-diversity/african-american/upload/25th-Ann-ExecutiveSummary.pdf.

30. The racial and ethnic categories that I use when discussing U.S. Department of Education data are those used in the IPEDS. I have chosen to focus on Blacks/African Americans and Hispanics/Latinas/os because generally these two groups, along with Native Americans, are the most marginalized in our society and in the academy. I realize that there is some evidence that Asian Americans are discriminated against by some institutions. On this, see for example Golden, 195–224. However, according to the US Census Bureau 2015 data, Asian Americans also have the highest rate of attaining bachelor's degrees (53.9) and advanced degrees (21.4). See Camille R. Ryan and Kurt Bauman, "Educational Attainment in the United States: 2015," United States Census Bureau, March 2016, http://www.census.gov/content/dam/Census/ library/publications/2016/demo/p20-578.pdf. According to census data, Asian Americans also have the highest household income of any group in the US. See Valerie Wilson, "New Census Data Show No Progress in Closing Stubborn Racial Income Gaps," Economic Policy Institute, September 16, 2015, http://www.epi. org/blog/new-census-data-show-no-progress-in-closing-stubborn-racial-income-gaps/. I realize that "Asian American" is not a helpful category, as there are differences between Korean, Cambodian, Indonesian, Chinese Americans, etc. Nonetheless, the category is used by the US government, Department of Education, and researchers alike. On the differences in educational attainment and income among different Asian groups in the U.S., see Progress 2050, "Who Are Asian Americans?," Center for American Progress, April 28, 2015, https:// www.americanprogress.org/issues/race/report/2015/04/28/111694/who-are-asian-americans/ and Matt Krupnick, "These Groups of Asian-Americans Rarely Attend College, but California Is Trying to Change That," PBS News Hour, May 21, 2015, http://www.pbs.org/newshour/updates/these-groups-of-asian-ameri-cans-rarely-attend-college-but-california-is-trying-to-change-that/. A fuller analysis than I can undertake would take account of these differences.

31. I have chosen to present data from academic year 2013–14 because as of this writing it is the most recent year available from the Department of Education in which all institutions were required to report data. Many readers know that there are more than 166 Catholic institutions of higher learning. However, I chose to look at the prevalence of African Americans and Latinas/os among tenured and tenure-track professors. The reason I focus on this subgroup

of faculty members shall become obvious in later parts of the chapter. What needs to be stressed here is that the US Department of Education (IPEDS) has data for this subgroup of professors at only 166 institutions because the other Catholic institutions do not have tenure systems in place. I also created a data set from the 2013–14 IPEDS that included the variable "has a tenure system." Thus, it is possible to see a fairly significant number of Catholic institutions do not have tenure systems. All of the data is publicly available at the National Center for Education Statistics IPEDS Data Center at https://nces.ed.gov/ipeds /datacenter/.

32. Just as above, data are taken from 2013–14 IPEDS at https://nces.ed.gov /ipeds/datacenter/. The *Chronicle of Higher Education's* database on Race and Ethnicity of Full-Time Faculty Members provides similar data. However it requires a paid subscription. See "Race, Ethnicity, and Gender of Full-Time Faculty at More Than 3,700 Institutions," *The Chronicle of Higher Education*, https://www.chronicle.com/interactives/faculty-diversity.

33. "Fast Facts," *National Center for Education Statistics*, https://nces.ed.gov /FastFacts/display.asp?id=61.

34. Colleen Flaherty, "Study Finds Gains in Faculty Diversity, but Not on the Tenure Track," *Inside Higher Ed*, August 22, 2016, https://www .insidehighered.com/news/2016/08/22/study-finds-gains-faculty-diversity-not -tenure-track.

35. The proportion of Whites also serving as part-time faculty members also swelled from 39.5 percent to 54 percent. See Martin J. Finkelstein, Valerie Martin Conley, and Jack H. Schuster, *Taking the Measure of Faculty Diversity* (New York: TIAA Institute, 2016), https://www.tiaainstitute.org/publication /taking-measure-faculty-diversity.

36. Flaherty, "Study Finds Gains in Faculty Diversity, but Not on the Tenure Track." I introduced the concept of the precariat in Chapter 2. For more, see Guy Standing, *The Precariat: The New Dangerous Class* (London: Bloomsbury Academic, 2011).

37. See Elizabeth Leigh Farrington, "Strategies for Increasing Faculty Diversity," *Women in Higher Education*, Volume 14 (11): 37–38, http://wihe.com /strategies-for-increasing-faculty-diversity/ (link no longer active).

38. "Population Distribution by Race/Ethnicity," *Henry J. Kaiser Family Foundation*, http://kff.org/other/state-indicator/distribution-by-raceethnicity/.

39. Tracy Badalucco, "Space for Dialogue," *National Catholic Reporter*, March 25–April 7, 2016, 2a.

40. I make this claim based on data from the College Insight Data Base, which relies on data from the US Department of Education IPEDS. See http://college-insight.org/. See also "Fast Facts," National Center for Education Statistics, https://nces.ed.gov/fastfacts/display.asp?id=98.

41. Anthony P. Carnevale and Jeff Strohl, *Separate and Unequal: How Higher Education Reinforces the Intergenerational Reproduction of White Racial Privilege* (Washington, D.C.: Georgetown University Center on Education and the Workforce, 2013), 16–17; Ben Casselman, "Race Gap Narrows in College Enrollment, But Not in Graduation," *FiveThirtyEight*, April 30, 2014, http:// fivethirtyeight.com/features/race-gap-narrows-in-college-enrollment-but-not-in -graduation/; and National Center for Education Statistics, *Digest of Educational Statistics*, "Table 235: Percentage of Recent High School Completers Enrolled in Two- and Four-Year Colleges, by Race/Ethnicity: 1960 through 2011," https:// nces.ed.gov/programs/digest/d12/tables/dt12_235.asp.

42. Mark Hugo Lopez and Richard Fry, "Among Recent High School Grads, Hispanic College Enrollment Rate Surpasses That of Whites," *Pew Research Center*, September 4, 2013, http://www.pewresearch.org/fact-tank/2013/09/04 /hispanic-college-enrollment-rate-surpasses-whites-for-the-first-time/.

43. Casselman, "Race Gap Narrows in College Enrollment."

44. Carnevale and Strohl, "*Separate and Unequal*," 12–13.

45. Ibid., 7. Jonathan Rothwell of The Brookings Institution reaches similar conclusions. See Jonathan Rothwell, "Black Students at Top Colleges: Exceptions, Not the Rule," *Brookings Institute*, February 3, 2015, http://www.brookings.edu /blogs/social-mobility-memos/posts/2015/02/03-black-students-top-colleges -rothwell.

46. Ibid., 7–8.

47. Ibid., 9–11, 50.

48. Ibid., 18.

49. See ibid., 12–13.

50. Ibid., 24. See also Rothwell, "Black Students at Top Colleges."

51. "Colleges That Produced The Most Members of Congress," *The Huffington Post*, February 19, 2014, http://www.huffingtonpost.com/entry/colleges -members-of-congress-alumni_n_4818357. See also, "Best Colleges for Future Politicians," *BestColleges*, http://www.bestcolleges.com/features/best-colleges -for-future-politicians/.

52. David Leonhardt, "Revisiting the Value of Elite Colleges," *The New York Times*, February 21, 2011, http://economix.blogs.nytimes.com/2011/02/21 /revisiting-the-value-of-elite-colleges/. See also Jack, *The Privileged Poor*, 7–8.

53. Catholic Charities USA, *Poverty and Racism*, 3.

54. "Campus Ethnic Diversity," *U.S. News and World Report*, http://colleges .usnews.rankingsandreviews.com/best-colleges/rankings/national-universities /campus-ethnic-diversity. See the explanatory note on methodology, which uses a formula to calculate how likely it is for one student of one race to encounter one from another on campus. While this type of diversity is valuable, it does not redress the historic marginalization of African Americans and Latinas/os

per se. Therefore, I believe it is important to look at proportions of students from those racial/ethnic groups in particular.

55. See "Black First-Year Students at the Nation's Leading Research Universities," *The Journal of Blacks in Higher Education*, January 14, 2016, https://www.jbhe .com/2016/01/black-first-year-students-at-leading-research-universities/. Perhaps tellingly, the journal mentions that of the twenty-seven highest ranked universities surveyed twelve declined to provide this information.

56. Data from IPEDS, 2014 Fall undergraduate all students. https://nces.ed .gov/ipeds/.

57. See Scott Jaschik, "The Non-News of Harvard's Alleged Diversity Breakthrough," *Inside Higher Ed*, August 7, 2017, https://www.insidehighered .com/admissions/article/2017/08/07/attention-incorrect-report-harvard -admitted-its-first-undergraduate.

58. See Ann M. Simmons and Melissa Etehad, "No, This Isn't the First Time the Majority of Students Admitted by Harvard University Are Nonwhite," *The Los Angeles Times*, August 4, 2017, http://www.latimes.com/nation/la-na -harvard-minorities-20170804-story.html.

59. See note 38 above.

60. See Carnevale and Strohl, *"Separate and Unequal."*

61. Alex Mikulich, "Jesuit Institutions Must Do More to Undo Racism," *America*, October 15, 2015, https://www.americamagazine.org/politics-society /2015/10/13/jesuit-institutions-must-do-more-undo-racism.

62. Data taken from College Insight for all undergraduates 2013–14 at http://college-insight.org/.

63. Loyola University New Orleans, University Newsroom, "Loyola Receives Role Model Award from Minority Access, Inc.," October 13, 2008, http://www .loyno.edu/news/story/2008/10/13/1606. See also Minority Access Incorporated, "Institutions Committed to Diversity," http://www.minorityaccess.org/div.html. A few other Catholic institutions are listed, such as Loyola University Chicago and Villanova University. However the website does not identify the criteria used to recognize them.

64. For Barron's list, which was used by Carnevale and Stroh in their study, see "Ranking Colleges by Selectivity," *The New York Times*, April 4, 2013, http://www.nytimes.com/interactive/2013/04/04/business/economy/economix -selectivity-table.html?_r=0.

65. Data taken from College Insight for all undergraduates 2013–14 at http://college-insight.org/.

66. Diane Cárdenas Elliot, "Student Heterogeneity and Diversity at Catholic Colleges," *Journal of Catholic Higher Education* 31, no. 1 (2012): 77–79. This study uses a complex methodology involving voluntary surveys. I have used data required of all institutions (IPEDS). Thus, there is some variation.

67. Frances Contreras, "Latino Students in Catholic Postsecondary Institutions," *Journal of Catholic Education* 19, no. 2 (2016): 92, 99–100, http://dx.doi .org/ 10.15365/joce.1902052016.

68. Ibid.

69. *Hispanic Outlook in Higher Education*, May 2015, 8–9, https://issuu.com /hohost/docs/ho-05-18-2015/44?e=15379375/12943718.

70. For examples, see Badalucco, "Space for Dialogue."

71. Diane Cárdenas Elliot, "Student Heterogeneity and Diversity at Catholic Colleges," 80.

72. See Edwin Rios, "How Campus Racism Just Became the Biggest Story in America," *Mother Jones,* November 9, 2015, http://m.motherjones.com/politics /2015/11/university-of-missouri-president-resigns-racism-football-hunger-strike; Chris Bodenner, "Reporter's Notebook: Debating the Campus Protests at Mizzou, Yale, and Elsewhere," *The Atlantic,* December 9, 2015, http://www .theatlantic.com/notes/all/2015/11/debating-the-protests-at-mizzou/415212/; Sophie Reardon, "A Visual Investigation Of Racial Disparity At BC," *The Heights,* April 29, 2015, http://bcheights.com/news/2015/a-visual-investigation -of-racial-disparity-at-bc/.

73. Emily Deruy, "What College Presidents Think About Racial Conflict on Their Campuses," *The Atlantic,* March 16, 2016, http://www.theatlantic.com /education/archive/2016/03/stepping-up-to-racial-conflict-on-campus/474069/. The survey is available at Lorelle Espinosa, Hollie Chessman, and Lindsay Wayt, "Racial Climate on Campus: A Survey of College Presidents," *Higher Education Today: A Blog by the American Council on Education,* March 8, 2016, https://www.higheredtoday.org/2016/03/08/racial-climate-on-campus-a-survey -of-college-presidents/.

74. See "The Demands: Campus Demands," http://www.thedemands.org/. Cited in Deruy, "What College Presidents Think."

75. See Laura Benshoff, "For Many, Villanova's Push for More Inclusive Campus Moving Too Slowly," *WHYY,* December, 22, 2016, https://whyy.org /articles/for-many-villanovas-push-for-more-inclusive-campus-moving-too -slowly/ and Caroline Foley, "Race on Campus," *The Villanovan,* October 26, 2016, http://www.villanovan.com/news/view.php/1025188/Race-on-Campus.

76. Yamiche Alcindor and Doug Standlin, "Two Suspects Arrested in Social Media Threats at Missouri Campuses," *USA Today,* November 11, 2015, http://www.usatoday.com/story/news/2015/11/11/some-at-u-of-missouri-on -edge-after-social-media-threats-of-violence/75559034.

77. Alan Yuhas, "Noose Found Hanging at Duke University Two Weeks after Racist Incident," *The Guardian,* April 1, 2015, https://www.theguardian .com/us-news/2015/apr/01/noose-found-hanging-duke-university-racism-claims ?CMP=share_btn_link.

78. "Image of President Obama in a Noose Appears on Board Member's Web Page," *The Journal of Blacks in Higher Education*, July 22, 2016, https://www.jbhe.com/2016/07/image-of-president-obama-in-a-noose-appears-on-board-members-web-page/.

79. See the updated database at *Journal of Blacks in Higher Education*, "Campus Racial Incidents," https://www.jbhe.com/incidents/.

80. See "2017 Hate Crime Statistics," *The United States Department of Justice*, https://www.justice.gov/hatecrimes/hate-crime-statistics.

81. "New Data on Hate Crimes on College and University Campuses," *The Journal of Blacks in Higher Education*, May 23, 2016, https://www.jbhe.com/2016/05/new-data-on-hate-crimes-on-college-and-university-campuses/. It appears that hate crimes, regardless of location, may be grossly underreported. See Rachel Glickhouse, "5 Things You Need to Know About Hate Crimes in America," *ProPublica*, March 22, 2019, https://www.propublica.org/article/hate-endures-in-america-and-with-it-our-effort-to-document-the-damage.

82. See "Complaints Skyrocket at the Office for Civil Rights of the US Department of Education," *The Journal for Blacks in Higher Education*, December 12, 2016, https://www.jbhe.com/2016/12/complaints-skyrocket-at-the-office-for-civil-rights-of-the-u-s-department-of-education/, and "White Supremacists on College Campuses Emboldened by Trump Victory," *The Journal for Blacks in Higher Education*, November 18, 2016, https://www.jbhe.com/2016/11/white-supremacists-on-college-campuses-emboldened-by-trump-victory/.

83. Megan Zahneis, "White-Supremacist Propaganda on Campuses Rose 77% Last Year," *The Chronicle of Higher Education*, May 28, 2018, https://www.chronicle.com/article/White-Supremacist-Propaganda/243786.

84. Mensah M. Dean, Susan Snyder, and Rebecca Heilweil, "Univ. of Okla. Student Suspended for 'Lynching' Hate Texts Sent to Penn Black Freshmen," *The Philadelphia Inquirer*, November 11, 2016, http://www.philly.com/philly/news/20161112_Racist_messages_target_black_freshmen_at_UPenn_with__lynching__.html. The sender was not a University of Pennsylvania student, but the incident roiled the campus.

85. "Racial Incidents at Three Local Colleges," 6ABC Action News, November 12, 2008, https://6abc.com/archive/6502733/; "Hate Crimes up on Campuses, Group Says," *Philadelphia Inquirer*, November 15, 2008; *Gale In Context: Opposing Viewpoints*, https://link.gale.com/apps/doc/A189002982/OVIC?u=vill_main&sid=OVIC&xid=40feb6a6.

86. "Racial Incident at Saint Louis University," *The Journal of Blacks in Higher Education*, May 12, 2014, https://www.jbhe.com/2014/05/racial-incident-at-saint-louis-university/.

87. "Fairfield University Students Hold a 'Ghetto-Themed' Party," *The Journal of Blacks in Higher Education*, February 26, 2016, https://www.jbhe.com/2016/02/fairfield-university-students-hold-a-ghetto-themed-party/.

88. See James F. Keenan, *University Ethics*, 112–15. Keenan notes fraternities often sponsor these parties.

89. Justin Moore, "Black Doll Found Hanging at Canisius College," *WKBW*, November 9, 2016, http://www.wkbw.com/news/black-doll-with-noose-found-at-canisius-college.

90. Rebecca Heilweil, Stephan Salisbury, and Caitlin McCabe, "Radnor Police, Villanova Investigating: White Males Yelling 'Trump' Knock Down Black Female Student," *Philly.com*, November 13, 2016, http://www.philly.com/philly/news/20161113_Radnor_police__Villanova_investigating__White_males_yelling__Trump__knock_down_black_female_student.html; Julianna Perez, "Investigation into Race-Related Assault Closed," *The Villanovan*, December 6, 2016, http://www.villanovan.com/news/view.php/1026490/Investigation-into-race-related-assault.

91. Sophie Reardon, "A Visual Investigation of Racial Disparity at BC," *The Heights*, April 29, 2015, http://bcheights.com/news/2015/a-visual-investigation-of-racial-disparity-at-bc/; Sophie Reardon, "Administrators Criticize Tactics of 'Eradicate Boston College Racism,'" *The Heights*, November 5, 2015, http://bcheights.com/news/2015/administrators-criticize-tactics-of-eradicate-boston-college-racism/.

92. "LTE: Letter From Faculty And Staff Members Of Boston College," *The Heights*, November 19, 2015, http://bcheights.com/opinions/2015/lte-letter-from-faculty-and-staff-members-of-boston-college/.

93. Adam Vincent, "The End to 'Vanillanova' Will Come from Campus Culture Changes," *The Villanovan*, November 12, 2015, http://www.villanovan.com/news/view.php/1014323/The-end-to-quotVanillanovaquot-will-come.

94. Clara Ritger, "Why Racial Integration Is Still a Problem on Today's Campus," *USA Today*, March 11, 2013.

95. See Dennis Sadowski, "Theologians Press US Bishops to Declare Racism 'Intrinsic Evil,'" *Crux*, July 17, 2016, https://cruxnow.com/church-in-the-usa/2016/07/17/theologians-press-us-bishops-declare-racism-intrinsic-evil/, and Bryan M. Massingale, "Equality Control," *U.S. Catholic* 68, no. 9 (2003).

96. See for example Badalucco, "Space for Dialogue."

97. Craig Steven Wilder, *Ebony & Ivy: Race, Slavery, and the Troubled History of America's Universities*, (New York: Bloomsbury, 2013), 3, 10, 181–210.

98. Ibid., 18–19.

99. Kathryn Brand, "The Jesuits' Slaves," *The Georgetown Voice*, February 8, 2007, http://georgetownvoice.com/2007/02/08/the-jesuits-slaves

/http://georgetownvoice.com/2007/02/08/the-jesuits-slaves/; Craig Steven Wilder, "War and Priests: Catholic Colleges and Slavery in the Age of Revolution," in *Slavery's Capitalism: A New History of American Economic Development*, ed. Sven Beckert and Seth Rockman (Philadelphia: University of Pennsylvania Press, 2016), 241. See also Matthew Quallen, "Beyond the 272 Sold in 1838, Plotting the National Diaspora of Jesuit-Owned Slaves," *The Hoya*, April 30, 2016, http://features.thehoya.com/beyond-the-272-sold-in-1838-plotting-the-national-diaspora-of-jesuit-owned-slaves.

100. Rachel L. Swarns, "272 Slaves Were Sold to Save Georgetown. What Does It Owe Their Descendants?," *The New York Times*, April 16 2016. See also Georgetown Working Group on Slavery, Memory, and Reconciliation, "What We Know: Georgetown University and Slavery," https://georgetown.app.box.com/s/22uiztgt3wy9mdes3r7xlrwofvrvdunx. A list of resources on the topic can be found at Georgetown University Working Group on Slavery, Memory, and Reconciliation, https://sites.google.com/a/georgetown.edu/slavery-memory-reconciliation/reading-list.

101. There were, however, Christians in the United States who had condemned slavery. By 1768 the Maryland Friends (Quakers) forbid their members, some of whom depended on slave labor on their plantations, from buying or selling slaves. Shortly thereafter, Quakers eschewed slavery altogether. See Thomas E. Drake, *Quakers and Slavery in America*, Yale Historical Publications Miscellany (New Haven: Yale University Press, 1950), 66–67.

102. Swarns, "272 Slaves Were Sold to Save Georgetown," and Quallen, "Beyond the 272 Sold in 1838."

103. "Georgetown Shares Slavery, Memory, and Reconciliation Report, Racial Justice Steps," *Georgetown University*, September 1, 2016, https://www.georgetown.edu/slavery-memory-reconciliation-working-group-sept-2016.

104. Rachel L. Swarns, "Moving to Make Amends, Georgetown President Meets with Descendant of Slaves," *The New York Times*, June 14, 2016, http://www.nytimes.com/2016/06/15/us/moving-to-make-amends-georgetown-president-meets-with-descendant-of-slaves.html.

105. "Georgetown Apologizes for 1838 Sale of 272 Slaves, Dedicates Buildings," *Georgetown University*, April 18, 2017, https://www.georgetown.edu/news/liturgy-remembrance-contrition-hope-slavery.

106. Haley Samsel, "Their Ancestors Were Slaves Sold by Georgetown. Now They're Going to School There," *USA Today*, June 9, 2017, http://college.usatoday.com/2017/06/09/their-ancestors-were-slaves-sold-by-georgetown-now-theyre-going-to-school-there/.

107. Wilder, "War and Priests," 228.

108. Craig Steven Wilder and Corey Menafee, "Craig Steven Wilder on How Georgetown & US Catholic Church Expanded Thanks to Slave Holdings,"

Democracy Now, July 15, 2016, http://www.democracynow.org/2016/7/15/craig
_steven_wilder_on_how_georgetown; see also ibid., 227–42.

109. See Katryna Perera, "St. Joe's, the Jesuits, and Slavery," *Hawk Hill News,*
n.d. 2015, https://www.sjuhawknews.com/st-joes-the-jesuits-and-slavery-2/;
Brand, "The Jesuits' Slaves."

110. Wilder, "War and Priests," 241.

111. Keenan, *University Ethics,* 164–65.

112. Cyprian Davis, *The History of Black Catholics in the United States* (New
York: Crossroad, 1990), 215–19; David W. Southern, *John Lafarge and the Limits
of Catholic Interracialism, 1911–1963* (Baton Rouge: Louisiana State University
Press, 1996), 209.

113. Philip Gleason, *Contending with Modernity: Catholic Higher Education in
the 20th Century* (New York: Oxford University Press, 1995), 155.

114. Thomas A. Mogan, "The Limits to Catholic Racial Liberalism: The
Villanova Encounter with Race, 1940–1985" (Temple University Dissertation,
2013), 9–13.

115. Southern, *John Lafarge and the Limits of Catholic Interracialism, 1911–1963,*
208–9; Dianna L. Hayes and Cecilia A. Moore, "We Have Been Believers:
Black Catholic Studies," in *The Catholic Studies Reader,* ed. James Terence
Fisher and Margaret M. McGuinness (New York: Fordham University Press,
2011), 272. Philip Gleason wrote that while about three quarters of Catholic
universities in United States had no formal admissions barriers for African
Americans, very few institutions enrolled them. See Gleason, *Contending with
Modernity,* 155; Philip Gleason, "The Erosion of Racism in Catholic Colleges in
the 40's," *America* 173 (1995): 13.

116. Elizabeth Garbitelli, "First Black Undergraduate Dies," *The Hoya,*
March 15, 2012, http://www.thehoya.com/first-black-undergraduate-dies-2/.

117. Tribune Staff Reporter, "Notre Dame to Honor Theologian and First
Black Students," *South Bend Tribune,* October 12, 2015, https://www.south
bendtribune.com/news/education/notre-dame-to-honor-theologian-and-first
-black-students/article_04954ebe-7115-11e5-a346-8b819690c9a7.html.

118. Keenan, *University Ethics,* 164, 66. See also "Key Events in Black Higher
Education: JBHE Chronology."

119. Even if some popes denounced slavery earlier, scholars debate when the
Roman Catholic Church officially condemned slavery. See Rodney Stark, *For
the Glory of God: How Monotheism Led to Reformations, Science, Witch-Hunts, and
the End of Slavery* (Princeton, N.J.: Princeton University Press, 2003), 329–37;
Mich, *Catholic Social Teaching and Movements,* 136–38; John Thomas Noonan,
*A Church That Can and Cannot Change: The Development of Catholic Moral
Teaching* (Notre Dame, Ind.: University of Notre Dame Press, 2005), 17–126.
On the Gospel's radical egalitarianism, see for example Walter Wink, *The*

Powers That Be: Theology for a New Millennium, 1st ed. (New York: Doubleday, 1998), and Obery M. Hendricks, *The Universe Bends toward Justice: Radical Reflections on the Bible, the Church, and the Body Politic* (Maryknoll, N.Y.: Orbis Books, 2011), 118–23.

120. Kenneth J. Fasching-Varner et al., eds., *Racial Battle Fatigue in Higher Education: Exposing the Myth of Post-Racial America* (Lanham, Md.: Rowman & Littlefield Education, 2015), xvii. See also Tammie Jenkins, "Black. Woman. Nontraditional Other: Creating Hybrid Spaces in Higher Education," in *Racial Battle Fatigue in Higher Education*, 97.

121. Saundra M. Tomlinson-Clarke, "Establishing Critical Relationships with Students: That's Not What White Prof. X Told Us," in *Black Faculty in the Academy: Narratives for Negotiating Identity and Achieving Career Success*, ed. Fred A. Bonner (New York: Routledge, 2015), 140–41.

122. Eduardo Bonilla-Silva, "The White Racial Innocence Game," *Racial Review*, November 12, 2015, http://www.racismreview.com/blog/author/ebs/; Tomlinson-Clarke, "Establishing Critical Relationships with Students," 142.; Noelle Witherspoon Arnold, "Psychological Heuristics: Mental/Emotional Designs of Racial Battle Fatigue and the Tenure Promotion Terrain for Faculty of Color," in *Racial Battle Fatigue in Higher Education*, 82–83; Brenda G. Juárez and Cleveland Hayes, "On the Battlefield for Social Justice in the Education of Teachers: The Dangers and Dangerousness of Challenging Whiteness in Predominantly White Institutions and Teacher Preparation Programs," in *Occupying the Academy: Just How Important Is Diversity Work in Higher Education?*, ed. Christine Clark, Kenneth J. Fasching-Varner, and Mark Brimhall-Vargas (Lanham, Md.: Rowman & Littlefield Publishers, Inc., 2012), 183–93.

123. Cleveland Hayes, "Assault in the Academy: When It Becomes More Than Racial Battle Fatigue," in *Racial Battle Fatigue in Higher Education*, 70–74.

124. Cheryl E. Matias, "'I Ain't Your Doc Student': The Overwhelming Presence of Whiteness and Pain at the Academic Neoplantation," in *Racial Battle Fatigue in Higher Education*, 65.

125. Ibid., 68.

126. Fred A. Bonner, "The Critical Need for Faculty Mentoring," in *Black Faculty in the Academy: Narratives for Negotiating Identity and Achieving Career Success*, ed. Fred A. Bonner (New York: Routledge, 2015), 132–33. See also Hayes, "Assault in the Academy."

127. Bonner, "The Critical Need for Faculty Mentoring," 130–31.

128. Gail L. Thompson and Angela Louque, *Exposing the "Culture of Arrogance" in the Academy: A Blueprint for Increasing Black Faculty Satisfaction in Higher Education* (Sterling, Va.: Stylus Pub., 2005), 77.

129. Dorinda J. Carter Andrews, "Navigating Race-Gendered Microaggressions: The Experiences of a Tenure-Track Black Female Scholar," in *Black Faculty in the Academy*, 85–86.

130. Holley Locher and Rebecca Ropers-Huilman, "Wearing You Down: The Influence of Racial Battle Fatigue on Academic Freedom for Faculty of Color," in *Racial Battle Fatigue in Higher Education*, 103–14.

131. See Bonilla-Silva, "The White Racial Innocence Game."

132. Thompson and Louque, *Exposing the "Culture of Arrogance" in the Academy*, 78.

133. Tomlinson-Clarke, "Establishing Critical Relationships with Students," 141. Bonner, "The Critical Need for Faculty Mentoring," 125; Arnold, "Psychological Heuristics," 85.

134. Marjorie C. Shavers, J. Yasmine Butler, and James L. Moore III, "Cultural Taxation and the Overcommitment of Service at Predominantly White Institutions," in *Black Faculty in the Academy*, 42.

135. Audrey Williams June, "The Invisible Labor of Minority Professors," *Chronicle of Higher Education* 62, no. 11 (2015).

136. See Roberto Montoya, "The Ubiquitous White Shadow: A Counter Narrative of a Doctoral Student in a 'Liberal' Teacher Education Program," in *Racial Battle Fatigue in Higher Education*; Tomlinson-Clarke, "Establishing Critical Relationships with Students," 139; Tapo Chimbganda, "Traumatic Pedagogy: When Epistemic Privilege and White Privilege Collide," in *Racial Battle Fatigue in Higher Education*; Lemuel W. Watson, Melvin C. Terrell, and Doris J. Wright, eds., *How Minority Students Experience College: The Implications for Planning and Policy* (Sterling, Va.: Stylus, 2002), 53–80.

137. Watson, Terrell, and Wright, *How Minority Students Experience College*, 53–66. This book is based on interviews of multicultural students at seven different institutions.

138. Kristie A. Ford, "Exploiting the Body and Denouncing the Mind: Navigating Black Female Professional Identity within the Academy," in *Racial Battle Fatigue in Higher Education*, 194.

139. Hayes, "Assault in the Academy," 70.

140. Jaime C. Slaughter-Acey et al., "Racism in the Form of Micro Aggressions and the Risk of Preterm Birth among Black Women," *Annals of Epidemiology* 26, no. 1 (2016): 7–13.

141. On this and other health problems associated with racism, see Gerald J. Beyer, "Solidarity Strives to Mend the Broken World," *Health Progress* 96, no. 4 (2015).

142. Arnold, "Psychological Heuristics," 77.

143. Sue et al., "Racial Microaggressions in Everyday Life," 273. Cited in Ford, "Exploiting the Body and Denouncing the Mind," 193. See also Mark

Giles, "Acclimating to the Institutional Climate: There's a 'Chill' in the Air," in *Black Faculty in the Academy*, 15. For a more comprehensive description of microaggressions than I can provide here, see Sue et al., "Racial Microaggressions in Everyday Life."

144. Giles, "Acclimating to the Institutional Climate," 15.

145. Arnold, "Psychological Heuristics," 77.

146. Ibid., 87. In this vein, Bonner describes the "leaky pipeline"; fewer and fewer minoritized faculty advanced to each academic rank. Bonner, "The Critical Need for Faculty Mentoring," 130.

147. Arnold, "Psychological Heuristics," 78.

148. Harper, "Race without Racism: How Higher Education Researchers Minimize Racist Institutional Norms," 22–23.

149. Bonilla-Silva, "The White Racial Innocence Game." See also Eduardo Bonilla-Silva, *Racism without Racists: Color-Blind Racism and the Persistence of Racial Inequality in the United States*, 3rd ed. (Lanham: Rowman & Littlefield Publishers, 2010), 308, and the essays in Fasching-Varner et al., *Racial Battle Fatigue in Higher Education*.

150. bell hooks, *Teaching Community: A Pedagogy of Hope* (New York: Routledge, 2003), 35.

151. Ibid., 25.

152. The row was widely covered by Catholic media outlets. See for example Brian Fraga, "The Esolen Affair: Esteemed Providence College Professor Attacked over 'Diversity,'" *National Catholic Register*, December 15, 2016, http://www.ncregister.com/daily-news/the-esolen-affair-esteemed-providence-college-professor-attacked-over-diver. For a more balanced view, see Charles C. Camosy, "Row at Providence College reflects Catholic Identity Tensions," *Crux*, December 27, 2016, https://cruxnow.com/interviews/2016/12/27/row-providence-college-reflects-catholic-identity-tensions/.

153. Anthony Esolen, "The Narcissism of Campus Diversity Activists," *Crisis*, February 24, 2016, http://www.crisismagazine.com/2016/the-narcissism-of-campus-diversity-activists.

154. The letter was cited in Fraga, "The Esolen Affair," which also provided a link to the letter (now inactive). See also Colleen Flaherty, "Diversity vs. Doctrine," *Inside Higher Ed*, November 9, 2016, https://www.insidehighered.com/news/2016/11/09/providence-college-professor-says-diversity-efforts-are-stifling-colleges-religious.

155. Anthony Esolen, "My College Succumbed to the Totalitarian Diversity Cult," *Crisis*, September 26, 2016, http://www.crisismagazine.com/2016/college-succumbed-totalitarian-diversity-cult. By contrast, see the Pastoral Constitution on the Church in the Modern World *Gaudium et Spes* and my discussion below.

156. See Gerald J. Beyer, "John XXIII and John Paul II: The Human Rights Popes," *Ethos: Quarterly of the John Paul II Institute at the Catholic University of Lublin* 2, no. 106 (2014).

157. See for example Lisa Sowle Cahill, "The Feminist Pope," in *Does Christianity Teach Male Headship?: The Equal Regard Marriage and Its Critics*, ed. David Blankenhorn, Don S. Browning, and Mary Stewart Van Leeuwen (Grand Rapids, Mich.: William B. Eerdmans Pub. Co., 2004).

158. John Paul II, *Ex Corde Ecclesiae* (August 15, 1990), §3.43.

159. Ibid., §3.44.

160. Ibid., §3.47, 3.44.

161. Esolen, "The Narcissism of Campus Diversity Activists."

162. Ibid.

163. Michael Eric Dyson, *Between God and Gangsta Rap: Bearing Witness to Black Culture* (New York: Oxford University Press, 1996); Monica R. Miller and Anthony B. Pinn, *The Hip Hop and Religion Reader* (New York: Routledge, 2014); Katie Grimes, "'But Do the Lord Care?': Tupac Shakur as Theologian of the Crucified People," *Political Theology* 15, no. 4 (2014); Carey Walsh, "Shout-Outs to the Creator: The Use of Biblical Themes in Rap Lyrics," *Journal of Religion and Popular Culture* 25, no. 2 (2013).

164. See Emanuel Perris, "University Responds to Student Protest," *The Villanovan*, October 25, 2016, http://www.villanovan.com/news/view.php /1025158/University-responds-to-student-protest. I have participated in a departmental dialogue with students asking for a more diversified curriculum.

165. Ki Joo Choi, "Should Race Matter? A Constructive Ethical Assessment of the Post-Racial Ideal," *Journal of the Society of Christian Ethics* 31, no. 1 (2011).

166. Cervantes and Chicana here denote the oppositional pairing constructed by Esolen in Esolen, "The Narcissism of Campus Diversity Activists."

167. See Katie G. Cannon, "Hitting a Straight Lick with a Crooked Stick: The Womanist Dilemma in the Development of a Black Liberation Ethic," in *Feminist Theological Ethics: A Reader*, ed. Lois K. Daly (Louisville, Ky.: Westminster John Knox Press, 1994); Miguel A. De La Torre, *Doing Christian Ethics from the Margins*, 2nd revised and expanded ed. (Maryknoll, N.Y.: Orbis Books, 2004); Bryan N. Massingale, "The Systemic Erasure of the Black/Dark Skinned Body in Catholic Ethics," in *Catholic Theological Ethics Past, Present, and Future: The Trento Conference* (Maryknoll, N.Y.: Orbis Books, 2011); Ada María Isasi-Díaz, *En La Lucha = in the Struggle: A Hispanic Women's Liberation Theology* (Minneapolis, Minn.: Fortress Press, 1993).

168. Ismael García, *Dignidad: Ethics through Hispanic Eyes* (Nashville: Abingdon Press, 1997), 20.

169. Cornel West, *Race Matters* (Boston: Beacon Press, 1993), 9–20.

170. Michael Eric Dyson, *Tears We Cannot Stop: A Sermon to White America* (New York: St. Martin's Press, 2017), 3.

171. Sue et al., "Racial Microaggressions in Everyday Life," 277–78.

172. Francis, *Evangelii Gaudium*, no. 199.

173. John Paul II, "Message of His Holiness Pope John Paul II for the Celebration of the World Day of Peace: 'To Build Peace, Respect Minorities'" (January 1, 1989), no. 7, http://w2.vatican.va/content/john-paul-ii/en/messages /peace/documents/hf_jp-ii_mes_19881208_xxii-world-day-for-peace.html.

174. Ibid., no. 3.

175. This speech is quoted by the President of Providence College Fr. Shanley and the defenders of Esolen in starkly divergent ways. Francis, "Celebration of Vespers with the University Students of the Roman Atheneums: Homily of Pope Francis" (2013), http://w2.vatican.va/content/francesco/en/homilies/2013 /documents/papa-francesco_20131130_vespri-universitari-romani.html.

176. On the first point, see Stacia L. Brown, "Does Pope Francis Believe that Black Lives Matter?," *The New Republic*, September 25, 2016, https://newrepublic .com/article/122899/does-pope-francis-believe-black-lives-matter. On the second point, see these overview of John Paul II's teaching on the rights of indigenous and marginalized people's and respect for their cultures: Sandie Cornish, "The Catholic Human Rights Tradition and the Rights of Indigenous Peoples," *ACSJ Occasional Paper No. 21* (1994), https://www.socialjustice.catholic.org.au /files/CSJ-series-papers/CSJS_21_-_The_Catholic_Human_Rights_Tradition _and_the_Rights_of_Indigenous_PeoplesA4.pdf, and Caritas Aotearoa New Zealand, *In the Presence of All Peoples: Celebrating Cultural Diversity* (Thorndon, Wellington, New Zealand: Caritas Aotearoa New Zealand, 1997), http:// www.caritas.org.nz/system/files/2005%20Social%20Justice%20Week%20 booklet.pdf.

177. Vincent W. Lloyd, *Black Natural Law* (Oxford: Oxford University Press, 2016), ix, xi. Lloyd recovers the work of key expositors of the Black natural law tradition: Frederick Douglas, Anna Julia Cooper, W.E.B. Dubois, and Martin Luther King.

178. De La Torre, *Doing Christian Ethics from the Margins*, 10.

179. The Freire Institute defines conscientization as "the process of developing a critical awareness of one's social reality through reflection and action." See Freire Institute, "Concepts Used by Paulo Freire," https://www.freire.org /paulo-freire/concepts-used-by-paulo-freire.

180. Keenan, *University Ethics*, 153.

181. Christine Clark, "Extra, Extra Read All About It! Diversity Souled out (and Sold-out) Here," in *Occupying the Academy*, 35.

182. Juárez and Hayes, "On the Battlefield for Social Justice in the Education of Teachers," 191. For another approach to racism and diversity on campus

advocating a scaffolding approach, see Charles Robinson, "Clashing with the Tradition: The Chief Diversity Officer at White Public Institutions," in *Racial Battle Fatigue in Higher Education*.

183. Juárez and Hayes, "On the Battlefield for Social Justice in the Education of Teachers," 191–93.

184. Ibid., 193.

185. My discussion of participation here draws on Beyer, "Curing the 'Disease' in Corporatized Higher Education."

186. Pontifical Council for Justice and Peace, *Compendium of the Social Doctrine of the Church*, no. 187. See also Beyer, *Recovering Solidarity*, 93.

187. John XXIII, *Mater et Magistra*, 1961, no. 73; John XXIII, *Pacem in Terris*, no. 26; 31–34; John Paul II, "Message of His Holiness Pope John Paul II for the Celebration of the World Day of Peace: 'Respect for Human Rights,'" no. 6.

188. Beyer, *Recovering Solidarity*, 92.

189. Francis, "Meeting with the [sic] Brazil's Leaders of Society: Address of Pope Francis" (July 27, 2013), no. 2, http://w2.vatican.va/content/francesco/en/speeches/2013/july/documents/papa-francesco_20130727_gmg-classe-dirigente-rio.html.

190. See for example "Faculty Communication with Governing Boards: Best Practices," *American Association of University Professors*, https://www.aaup.org/report/faculty-communication-governing-boards-best-practices, and "Resources on Government," *American Association of University Professors*, https://www.aaup.org/our-programs/shared-governance/resources-governance. I discuss this issue in greater detail in Beyer, "Curing the 'Disease' in Corporatized Higher Education."

191. See Mark Brimhall-Vargas, "The Myth of Institutionalizing Diversity: Structures and the Covert Decisions They Make," in *Occupying the Academy*, 88–89.

192. See Beyer, *Recovering Solidarity*, 90–94. John Paul II stressed that "the manner and means for achieving a public life which has true human development as its goal is *solidarity*. This concerns the active and responsible *participation* of all in public life, from individual citizens to various groups, from labor unions to political parties." John Paul II, *Christifideles Laici*, 1988, no. 42. See also John XXIII, *Mater et Magistra*, 1961, no. 73; John XXIII, *Pacem in Terris*, no. 26; 31–34; John Paul II, "Message of His Holiness Pope John Paul II for the Celebration of the World Day of Peace: 'Respect for Human Rights.'"

193. World Synod of Bishops, *Justitia in Mundo*, 1971, no. 71, https://www1.villanova.edu/content/dam/villanova/mission/JusticeIntheWorld1971.pdf.

194. For further explanation see discussion of subsidiarity in Chapter 1.

195. See John XXIII, *Pacem in Terris*, 1963, no. 53.

196. Benjamin Ginsberg, *The Fall of the Faculty: The Rise of the All-Administrative University and Why It Matters* (Oxford: Oxford University Press, 2011).

197. Kevin Kiley, "What's up with Boards These Days?," *Inside Higher Ed*, July 2, 2012, https://www.insidehighered.com/news/2012/07/02/trustees-are-different-they-used-be-and-uva-clashes-will-be-more-common.

198. On the White male dominance of boards, see Ingram Center for Public Trusteeship and Governance and Association of Governing Boards of Universities and Colleges, *2010 Policies, Practices, and Composition of Higher Education Coordinating Boards and Commissions* (Washington, D.C.: Association of Governing Boards of Universities and Colleges, 2010), https://agb.org/reports-and-statements/2010-policies-practices-and-composition-of-higher-education-coordinating-boards-and-commissions/, and James L. Anderson, "It's Time for Term Limits," *Inside Higher Ed*, July 18, 2019, https://www.insidehighered.com/views/2019/07/18/college-boards-trustees-should-be-more-generationally-diverse-and-have-term-limits. On presidents, see Rosa Garcia, "Equity Audits Would Strengthen Colleges and Universities," *CLASP: Center for Law and Social Policy*, June 19, 2019, https://www.clasp.org/blog/equity-audits-would-strengthen-colleges-and-universities.

199. Kimberly A. Griffin, "Reconsidering the Pipeline Problem: Increasing Faculty Diversity" *Higher Education Today*, February 10, 2016, https://higheredtoday.org/2016/02/10/reconsidering-the-pipeline-problem-increasing-faculty-diversity/; Maureen Downey, "Black College Students Demanding More Black Professors Don't Realize 'They Are Demanding the Impossible,'" *Atlanta Journal-Constitution*, December 21, 2015, http://getschooled.blog.myajc.com/2015/12/21/black-college-students-demanding-more-black-professors-dont-realize-they-are-demanding-the-impossible/.

200. Thompson and Louque, *Exposing the "Culture of Arrogance" in the Academy*, 18.

201. Kimberly A. Griffin, "Reconsidering the Pipeline Problem." On Loyola Marymount University, see note 37 above.

202. Ibid.

203. Scott Jaschik, "The Impact of Dropping the SAT," *Inside Higher Ed*, March 26, 2009, http://www.insidehighered.com/news/2009/03/26/sat.

204. Michael C. McFarland, "What an SAT Score Doesn't Say," *The Boston Globe*, November 27, 2008, http://archive.boston.com/bostonglobe/editorial_opinion/oped/articles/2008/11/27/what_an_sat_score_doesnt_say/. On the test's bias, see Joseph A. Soares and Jay Rosner, "The Future of College Admissions Is Test Blind," *Inside Higher Ed*, September 14, 2020, https://www.insidehighered.com/admissions/views/2020/09/14/future-college-admissions-test-blind-opinion.

205. Shaun R. Harper, *Black Male Student-Athletes and Racial Inequities in NCAA Division I College Sports: 2016 Edition* (Philadelphia, Pa.: University of Pennsylvania Graduate School of Education Center for the Study of Race and Equity in Education, 2016), 1, 16.

206. See Kenneth Terrell, "The 50 Best Colleges for African Americans," *Essence*, April 11, 2016, http://www.essence.com/2016/04/11/50-best-colleges -african-americans, and Kim Clark, "The 50 Best Colleges for African Americans— in One Handy Chart," *Time*, April 12, 2016, http://time.com/money/4282172 /best-colleges-african-americans/.

207. See Vincent D. Rougeau, "Justice, Community, and Solidarity: Rethinking Affirmative Action through the Lens of Catholic Social Thought," *Journal of Catholic Social Thought* 1, no. 2 (2004); Massingale, "Equality Control."; Beyer, "The Continuing Relevance of *Brothers and Sisters to Us*," 261–63; Harper, "*Black Male Student-Athletes.*"

208. Tanya Katerí Hernández, "Affirmative Action: A Major Requirement," *U.S. Catholic* 80, no. 2 (2015).

209. See "Scholarships for Hispanic and Latino Students," *Best Colleges*, http://www.bestcolleges.com/financial-aid/hispanic-latino-scholarships/.

210. "Colleges 'Friendly' to AB-450 Students," *University of North Carolina Wilmington Website*, http://uncw.edu/centrohispano/documents/CollegesFriend lyForUndocumentedStudents.pdf.

211. "University Opens The Center for Undocumented Students," *Saint Peters University Website*, https://www.saintpeters.edu/news/2014/11/10 /university-opens-the-center-for-undocumented-students/; Alexander Santora, "Undocumented students find a home at Saint Peter's University," *NJ.Com*, September 7, 2016, http://www.nj.com/hudson/index.ssf/2016/09 /undocumented_students_find_a_home_at_saint_peters.html.

212. Lauren Camera, "Catholic College Presidents Pressure Trump Administration to Protect DACA Students," *U.S. News & World Report*, May 23, 2017, https://www.usnews.com/news/education-news/articles/2017-05-23/catholic -college-presidents-pressure-trump-administration-to-protect-daca-students; "Statement of AJCU Presidents on Undocumented Students," November 30, 2016, *Association of Jesuit Colleges and Universities Website*, http://www .ajcunet.edu/press-releases-blog/2016/11/30/statement-of-ajcu-presidents -november-2016.

213. "Study Finds That Mandatory Diversity Training Is Ineffective," *Journal of Blacks in Higher Education*, July 25, 2016, https://www.jbhe.com/2016/07 /study-finds-that-mandatory-diversity-training-is-ineffective/. Annika Olson, "Equity Audits Should Be Commonplace," *Inside Higher Ed*, March 25, 2020, https://www.insidehighered.com/views/2020/03/25/more-colleges-should-use -equity-audits-address-inequalities-their-institutions.

214. For concrete ways educators can address this problem, see Shaun R. Harper and Charles H.F. Davis III, "Eight Actions to Reduce Racism in College Classrooms," *Academe* (November–December 2016), https://www.aaup.org /article/eight-actions-reduce-racism-college-classrooms#.XgusokdKjcs.

215. Maggie Berg and Barbara K. Seeber, *The Slow Professor: Challenging the Culture of Speed in the Academy* (Toronto: University of Toronto Press, 2015). See also my discussion of this in Beyer, "Curing the 'Disease' in Corporatized Higher Education."

216. See Lawrence D. Berg, Edward H. Huijbens, and Henrik Gutzon Larsen, "Producing Anxiety in the Neoliberal University," *The Canadian Geographer / Le Géographe canadien* 60, no. 2 (2016).

217. In addition to the above sections on RBF and microaggressions, see Thompson and Louque, *Exposing the "Culture of Arrogance" in the Academy*, 76.

6. Gender and LGBTQ Equality in the University: A Challenge for CST in the Age of Corporatized Higher Education

1. See Mary Ann Mason, Nicholas H. Wolfinger, and Marc Goulden, *Do Babies Matter? Gender and Family in the Ivory Tower* (New Brunswick, N.J.: Rutgers University Press, 2013), 32–33, 44. On the legal issue, see the United States Equal Employment Opportunity Commission, "Title VII: Pregnancy Discrimination in Job Interviews," February 2, 2007, https://www.eeoc.gov /eeoc/foia/letters/2007/pregnancy_discrimination.html, and Beth Scott, "7 Things You Need to Know about Pregnancy Discrimination," *The American Association of University Women*, October 31, 2013 https://www.aauw.org/2013 /10/31/know-about-pregnancy-discrimination/.

2. See for example M. Shawn Copeland, *Enfleshing Freedom: Body, Race, and Being* (Minneapolis: Fortress Press, 2010); Maria Clara Lucchetti Bingemer, *Latin American Theology: Roots and Branches* (Maryknoll, N.Y.: Orbis, 2016); Lisa Sowle Cahill, *Sex, Gender, and Christian Ethics* (Cambridge: Cambridge University Press, 1996); Ada María Isasi-Díaz, *En La Lucha = in the Struggle: A Hispanic Women's Liberation Theology* (Minneapolis, Minn.: Fortress Press, 1993); Agnes M. Brazal, *Transformative Theological Ethics: East Asian Contexts* (Quezon City: Ateneo de Manila University Press, 2010); Christine Firer Hinze, *Glass Ceilings and Dirt Floors: Women, Work, and the Global Economy* (New York: Paulist Press, 2015); Margaret A. Farley, *Just Love: A Framework for Christian Sexual Ethics* (New York: Continuum International Pub. Group, 2006).

3. John W. Curtis, "Persistent Inequity: Gender and Academic Employment," in *New Voices in Pay Equity: An Event for Equal Pay Day* (April 11, 2011), available at https://www.aaup.org/NR/rdonlyres/08E023AB-E6D8-4DBD-99A0 -24E5EB73A760/0/persistent_inequity.pdf.

4. See for example Mary Ann Hinsdale, *Women Shaping Theology* (New York: Paulist Press, 2006); Mary Ann Hinsdale, "Who Are the 'Begats'? Or Women Theologians Shaping Women Theologians," *Journal of Feminist Studies in Religion* 33, no. 1 (2017); Katie G. Cannon, Emilie Maureen Townes, and Angela D. Sims, eds., *Womanist Theological Ethics: A Reader* (Louisville, Ky.: Westminster John Knox Press, 2011); Linda Hogan and A. E. Orobator, *Feminist Catholic Theological Ethics: Conversations in the World Church* (Maryknoll, N.Y.: Orbis, 2014).

5. John W. Curtis, "Persistent Inequity: Gender and Academic Employment," 2.

6. Marc Bousquet, *How the University Works*, 63; see also 38.

7. John Curtis and Saranna Thornton, *Here's the News: The Annual Report on the Economic Status of the Profession, 2012–13* (Washington, D.C.: American Association of University Professors, 2013).

8. John Curtis, *The Employment Status of Instructional Staff Members in Higher Education, Fall 2011* (Washington, D.C.: American Association of University Professors, 2014), 18.

9. Bousquet, *How the University Works*, 59–60.

10. Maria Maisto, "Taking Heart, Taking Part," 195. Feminist scholars have long been concerned about the use of self-sacrificial tropes to justify many forms of exploitation of women. See Emily Reimer-Barry, "Suffering or Flourishing? Marriage and the Imitation of Christ," in *Women, Wisdom, and Witness: Engaging Contexts in Conversation*, ed. Rosemary P. Carbine and Kathleen Dolphin (Collegeville, Minn.: Liturgical Press, 2012); Margaret A. Farley, *Personal Commitments: Beginning, Keeping, Changing*, revised ed. (Maryknoll, N.Y.: Orbis Books, 2013); Delores. S. Williams, "Black Women, Surrogacy, Experience and the Christian Notion of Redemption," in *Cross Examinations: Readings on the Meaning of the Cross Today*, ed. Marit Trelstad (Minneapolis, Minn.: Augsburg Fortress, 2006).

11. American Council on Education, *An Agenda for Excellence: Creating Flexibility in Tenure-Track Faculty Careers* (Washington, D.C.: American Council on Education, 2005), 3, https://www.acenet.edu/Documents/Agenda-for-Excellence.pdf.

12. American Council of Education, *Pipelines, Pathways, and Institutional Leadership: An Update on the Status of Women in Higher Education* (Washington, D.C.: American Council of Education, 2016), 5, 9, 21, http://www.acenet.edu/news-room/Documents/Higher-Ed-Spotlight-Pipelines-Pathways-and-Institutional-Leadership-Status-of-Women.pdf. On boards, see also Cristin Toutsi, *2010 Policies, Practices, and Composition of Higher Education Coordinating Boards and Commissions* (Washington, D.C.: Association of Governing Boards of Universities and Colleges, 2010), https://www.agb.org/sites/default/files/legacy/2010CompositionSurvey_Report.pdf.

13. See Annemarie Vaccaro, "Still Chilly in 2010: Campus Climates for Women," *On Campus with Women* 39, no. 2 (2010), http://archive.aacu.org /ocww/volume39_2/feature.cfm?section=1.

14. Lisa Sowle Cahill, "Feminist Theology and a Participatory Church," in *Common Calling: The Laity and Governance of the Catholic Church*, ed. Stephen J. Pope (Washington, D.C.: Georgetown University Press, 2004); Susan A. Ross, "Joys and Hopes, Griefs and Anxieties: Catholic Women since Vatican II," *New Theology Review* 25, no. 2 (2013).

15. See The Congregation for the Doctrine of Faith, *Donum Veritatis: On the Ecclesial Vocation of the Theologian*, May 24, 1990, http://www.vatican.va /roman_curia/congregations/cfaith/documents/rc_con_cfaith_doc_19900524 _theologian-vocation_en.html.

16. Hinsdale, "Who Are the 'Begats'?," 94, 102–6.

17. See Leo XIII, *Rerum Novarum*, no. 35; Pius XI, *Quadragesimo Anno*, no. 71; John XXIII, *Mater et Magistra*, no. 71; John XXIII, *Pacem in Terris*, no. 20; John Paul II, *Laborem Exercens*, no. 19; John Paul II, *Centesimus Annus*, no. 15; Benedict XVI, *Caritas in Veritate*, no. 63. For a more detailed discussion of this tradition than I can provide here, see Christine Firer Hinze, "Bridging Discourse on Wage Justice: Roman Catholic and Feminist Perspectives on the Family Living Wage" in *Feminist Ethics and the Catholic Moral Tradition*, ed. Charles E. Curran, Margaret A. Farley, and Richard A. McCormick (New York: Paulist Press, 1996).

18. John Paul II, *Letter of Pope John Paul II to Women*, June 29, 1995, no. 2, http://www.vatican.va/content/john-paul-ii/en/letters/1995/documents/hf_jp-ii _let_29061995_women.html.

19. Ibid., no. 4.

20. "Women's Right to Maternity Leave Must Be Protected, Pope Says," *Catholic News Service*, November 2, 2015, https://www.catholicnews.com /services/englishnews/2015/womens-right-to-maternity-leave-must-be-protected -pope-says.cfm.

21. John Paul II, *Laborem Exercens*, no. 19.

22. See Christine Firer Hinze, "Women, Families, and the Legacy of *Laborem Exercens*: An Unfinished Agenda," *Journal of Catholic Social Thought* 6, no. 1 (2013): 80. Hinze echoes Donald Dorr, who argued that the Latin text uses *homo* rather than "man" and does not use the gendered pronoun "his," as the English translation does, regarding the work to be sufficiently remuner-ated. See Donald Dorr, *Option for the Poor: 100 Years of Vatican Social Teaching*, Rev. ed. (Maryknoll, N.Y.: Orbis, 1992), 300. I would add that the Polish text, like the Latin and Italian, does not use gendered language either.

23. Hinze, "Women, Families, and the Legacy of *Laborem Exercens*," 64, 75–76, inter alia. Hinze shows how John Paul follows the line of thinking of his

papal predecessors. For example, the phrase "in accordance with their own nature" comes from *Gaudium et Spes*, no. 60.

24. John Paul II, *Letter of Pope John Paul II to Women*.

25. John Paul II, *Laborem Exercens*, 19.

26. Hinze, "Women, Families, and the Legacy of *Laborem Exercens*," 74, 82. Hinze points, for example, to John Paul's discussion of fatherhood in *Mulieris Dignitatem*. While the Pope certainly believes that fathers have an important role, saying that fathers must "learn their role from the mother" is problematic. It implies that fatherhood is somehow "outside" of the nature of men. See ibid., 77n22.

27. Ibid., 74.

28. John Paul II, *Familiaris Consortio*, November 22, 1981, no. 42, http://w2 .vatican.va/content/john-paul-ii/en/apost_exhortations/documents/hf_jp-ii_exh _19811122_familiaris-consortio.html. Pope John Paul borrows this phrase from Vatican II's Decree on the Apostolate of the Laity *Apostolicam Actuositatem*.

29. Hinze, "Women, Families, and the Legacy of *Laborem Exercens*," 72. Hinze draws here on the work of feminist legal scholar Joan Williams. See also Hinze, *Glass Ceilings and Dirt Floors: Women, Work, and the Global Economy*, 82.

30. Mason, Wolfinger, and Goulden, *Do Babies Matter? Gender and Family in the Ivory Tower*, 3. For an excellent summary of this book's matter, read Mary Ann Mason, "In the Ivory Tower, Men Only," *Slate*, June 17, 2013, https://slate.com /human-interest/2013/06/female-academics-pay-a-heavy-baby-penalty.html#return.

31. Ibid., 3, 66–69.

32. Ibid., 69, see also 60.

33. Ibid., 68–69. The tenure success rate varies considerably among institutions. The authors state that one study quoted a success rate of slightly more than 50 percent. At the same time, it is greater at "schools where research is less important." Ibid., 48.

34. American Council on Higher Education, "Past Initiatives in Faculty Career Flexibility," http://www.acenet.edu/news-room/Pages/Past-Initiatives-in -Faculty-Career-Flexibility.aspx (link no longer active).

35. American Council on Higher Education, *An Agenda for Excellence: Creating Flexibility in Tenure-Track Faculty Careers*, 6. Women also report that the fuzzy notion of "collegiality" can be used against them in the tenure process, especially if their childcare responsibilities are perceived to interfere with being a "good citizen." See Bridget Burke Ravizza and Karen Peterson-Iyer, "Motherhood and Tenure: Can Catholic Universities Support Both?," *Catholic Education: A Journal of Inquiry and Practice* 8, no. 3 (2005): 309.

36. American Association of University Professors, "Statement of Principles on Family Responsibilities and Academic Work," (2001), http://www.aaup.org /AAUP/pubsres/policydocs/contents/workfam-stmt.htm.

37. Maggie Berg and Barbara K. Seeber, *The Slow Professor: Challenging the Culture of Speed in the Academy* (Toronto: University of Toronto Press, 2015), 7–8, see also 2–6. See also Lawrence D. Berg, Edward H. Huijbens, and Henrik Gutzon Larsen, "Producing Anxiety in the Neoliberal University," *The Canadian Geographer / Le Géographe canadien* 60, no. 2 (2016), and Claire Shaw and Lucy Ward, "Dark Thoughts: Why Mental Illness Is on the Rise in Academia," *The Guardian*, March 6, 2014, https://www.theguardian.com/higher-education-network/2014/mar/06/mental-health-academics-growing-problem-pressure-university.

38. See Mason, Wolfinger, and Goulden, *Do Babies Matter?*; Ravizza and Peterson-Iyer, "Motherhood and Tenure"; American Association of University Professors, "Statement of Principles on Family Responsibilities and Academic Work"; Annemarie Vaccaro, "The Road to Gender Equality in Higher Education: Sexism, Standpoints, and Success," *Wagadu: A Journal of Transnational Women's & Gender Studies* 9 (2011).

39. American Council of Higher Education, *Pipelines, Pathways, and Institutional Leadership*, 11.

40. Mason, Wolfinger, and Goulden, *Do Babies Matter?*, 10.

41. Ibid., 13.

42. Ibid., 15–16.

43. Ibid., 8–9, 12–14.

44. Ibid. 22.

45. Xuhong Su and Monica Gaughan, "Inclusion of Women Academics into American Universities: Analysis of Women Status Reports," *Higher Education Policy* 27, no. 4 (2014): 531.

46. JoAnn Moody, *Faculty Diversity: Removing the Barriers* (New York: Routledge, 2012), 26. Moody also describes other forms of negative bias toward women on the job market.

47. Mason, Wolfinger, and Goulden, *Do Babies Matter?*, 28–29.

48. Ibid., 32, 35.

49. Ibid., 43.

50. Ibid., and Ravizza and Peterson-Iyer, "Motherhood and Tenure," 308. See also AAUP "Statement of Principles on Academic Freedom and Tenure."

51. Mason, Wolfinger, and Goulden, *Do Babies Matter?*, 74.

52. Elizabeth Keenan, "The No-Baby Penalty," *ChronicleVitae*, June 19, 2014, https://chroniclevitae.com/news/570-the-no-baby-penalty?cid=articlepromo. Keenan quotes another piece by Sarah Kendzior on the same blog, who states that many women find "nothing" after long enduring the sacrifices needed to succeed in academia. See "Should You Have a Baby in Graduate School?," *ChronicleVitae*, June 16, 2014, https://chroniclevitae.com/news/549-should-you-have-a-baby-in-graduate-school.

53. Vaccaro, "The Road to Gender Equality in Higher Education," 35.

54. Mason, Wolfinger, and Goulden, *Do Babies Matter?*, 49–50.

55. Ibid., 35.

56. See ibid., 38–39, see also 36, 42.

57. Ibid., 51.

58. Ibid., 40.

59. "Why Adjunct Professors Are Struggling to Make Ends Meet," *PBS News Hour,* February 6, 2014, https://www.youtube.com/watch?time_continue=136&v =Bz4pK8UP4PM&feature=emb_logo.

60. Mason, Wolfinger, and Goulden, *Do Babies Matter?*, 60, 61.

61. Ibid., 62.

62. Ibid., 60–61.

63. Ravizza and Peterson-Iyer, "Motherhood and Tenure," 308. The authors draw on Hal Cohen, "The Baby Bias," *The New York Times*, August 4, 2002, https://www.nytimes.com/2002/08/04/education/the-baby-bias.html.

64. Cited in Mason, Wolfinger, and Goulden, *Do Babies Matter?*, 60.

65. Margaret W. Sallee, "Gender Norms and Institutional Culture: The Family-Friendly Versus the Father-Friendly University," *Journal of Higher Education* 84, no. 3 (2013): 364. See also Mason, Wolfinger, and Goulden, *Do Babies Matter?*, 70–71.

66. Mason, Wolfinger, and Goulden, *Do Babies Matter?*, 35, 43, 51, 81; Margaret W. Sallee, "The Ideal Worker or the Ideal Father: Organizational Structures and Culture in the Gendered University," *Research in Higher Education* 53, no. 7 (2012).

67. See Hinze, *Glass Ceilings and Dirt Floors*, and Hinze, "Women, Families, and the Legacy of *Laborem Exercens*: An Unfinished Agenda."

68. Justin Wolfers, "A Family-Friendly Policy That's Friendliest to Male Professors," *The New York Times,* June 26, 2016, https://www.nytimes.com/2016 /06/26/business/tenure-extension-policies-that-put-women-at-a-disadvantage .html?_r=0.

69. See Kay Steiger, "Family-Friendly University Policies Don't Work as Well as They Should," *The Atlantic* (May 31, 2013), https://www.theatlantic.com /sexes/archive/2013/05/family-friendly-university-policies-dont-work-as-well-as -they-should/276404/; Mason, Wolfinger, and Goulden, *Do Babies Matter? Gender and Family in the Ivory Tower*, 77–78, 81, 111; Sallee, "Gender Norms and Institutional Culture."

70. Sallee, "Gender Norms and Institutional Culture," 364.

71. Cohen, "The Baby Bias." See the discussion of this mentality in Ravizza and Peterson-Iyer, "Motherhood and Tenure," 308–9.

72. Ravizza and Peterson-Iyer, "Motherhood and Tenure," 305, 22–23.

73. Ibid., 309.

74. Ibid., 309–10. The original report is Dana E. Friedman, Cathy Rimsky, and Arlene A. Johnson, *College and University Reference Guide to Work-Family Programs. Report on a Collaborative Study* (Washington, D.C.: CUPA Foundation, 1996).

75. See the note on Great Colleges Methodology at "Great Colleges Methodology," Great Colleges to Work For, *The Chronicle of Higher Education*, July 21, 2014, http://www.chronicle.com/article/Great-Colleges -Methodology/147821, and http://chroniclegreatcolleges.com/participation /methodology/.

76. *The Chronicle of Higher Education*, "Great Colleges to Work for 2015," http://chroniclegreatcolleges.com/recognized-institutions/. More research on family-friendly workplaces, including institutions of higher learning, can be found at the Work and Family Researchers Network, https://wfrn.org/, and Berkeley, The UC Faculty Family Friendly Edge, "Publications," http:// ucfamilyedge.berkeley.edu/publications.

77. American Council on Higher Education, "Past Initiatives in Faculty Career Flexibility."

78. American Council of Education, The Alfred P. Sloan Awards for Faculty Career Flexibility, "ACE Announces the Alfred P. Sloan Awards for Baccalaureate Colleges–Arts and Sciences," https://www.albright.edu/sloan/pdf/2010%20 Sloan%20Newsletter%20Third.pdf. See also the Santa Clara University Faculty Handbook, https://www.scu.edu/media/offices/provost/policy-procedure/SCU -Faculty-Handbook-October-2017.pdf, and The Santa Clara University Flexible Course Scheduling Policy, https://www.scu.edu/media/offices/provost/policy -procedure/4-Flexible-Course-Scheduling-Guidelines.pdf.

79. Ibid.

80. See all of Benedictine University's faculty career flexibility policies, Benedictine University Faculty, "Career Flexibility Opportunities for Benedictine University Faculty Members," http://www.ben.edu/faculty-staff/handbook /faculty_career_flexibility.cfm. Julie L. Nuter, who helped facilitate the career flexibility initiative at Benedictine University, published a dissertation on work-life balance in universities. Julie L. Nuter, "Work-Life Practitioners: A Force for Change in the Academic Setting," (PhD diss., Benedictine University, 2011), at http://pqdtopen.proquest.com/doc/912851349.html?FMT=AI. On Benedictine University's endowment, see Steven R. Strahler, "Benedictine U Chooses First New Leader in 20 Years," *Chicago Business*, June 9, 2015, http:// www.chicagobusiness.com/article/20150609/NEWS13/150609780/benedictine -u-chooses-first-new-leader-in-20-years.

81. Margaret Keane, "University Transforms Maternity and Paternity Policies," *The Villanovan*, January 26, 2015, http://www.villanovan.com/news /university-transforms-maternity-and-paternity-policies/article_8c2796ed-dfc7 -5c21-a9f5-ef9ea797d6b5.html.

82. Ibid.

83. Mason, Wolfinger, and Goulden, *Do Babies Matter?*, 100–101.

84. See Santa Clara University, "Kids on Campus," https://www.scu.edu /kids-on-campus/. Note that the price has risen since this writing.

85. Quoted from LMU Children's Center, https://admin.lmu.edu/lmucc/.

86. "Early Childhood Development Center at Notre Dame 2019–2020 School Year and 2020 Summer Tuition Schedule," Early Childhood Development Center Inc, http://ecdc.nd.edu/registration/tuition/ecdc-nd-tuition -schedule. Salary information about the University of Notre Dame is taken from the 2016–17 AAUP Faculty Compensation survey at https://www .insidehighered.com/aaup-compensation-survey.

87. See Juliana Herman, Sasha Post, and Scott O'Halloran, "The United States Is Far Behind Countries on Pre-K," *Center for American Progress,* May 2, 2013, https://www.americanprogress.org/issues/education/reports/2013/05/02 /62054/the-united-states-is-far-behind-other-countries-on-pre-k/.

88. Simon Workman and Steven Jessen-Howard, "Understanding the True Cost of Child Care for Infants and Toddlers," *Center for American Progress,* https://www.americanprogress.org/issues/early-childhood/reports/2018/11/15 /460970/understanding-true-cost-child-care-infants-toddlers/.

89. See John Paul II, *Laborem Exercens* and Chapter 2 of this book.

90. For one recent example, see Karen Kelsky, "An Adjunct's Letter to Her Union-Busting College President," *The Professor is In,* June 16, 2017, http:// theprofessorisin.com/2017/06/16/an-adjunct-letter-to-her-union-busting-college -president/.

91. Mason, Wolfinger, and Goulden maintain that not enough research has been done on the efficacy of family-friendly and work life balance policies at universities. However there is some "preliminary evidence" that "faculty perceive their institutions as more child friendly" when such policies are implemented. Mason, Wolfinger, and Goulden, *Do Babies Matter?*, 98.

92. Ibid., 7. See UC Berkeley Office for Faculty Equity & Welfare, "Families," a page for policies and resources students at UC Berkeley, available at http://ofew.berkeley.edu/welfare/families.

93. *Balancing Work & Life: Faculty Friendly Programs, Policies, and Resources,* published in 2015 through the initiative of the Office of the Vice Provost for the Faculty, http://ofew.berkeley.edu/sites/default/files/balancing worklife.pdf, 3.

94. Cited in Mason, Wolfinger, and Goulden, *Do Babies Matter?*, 96.

95. See ibid., 98–114; University of Michigan Center for the Education of Women, *Family-Friendly Policies in Higher Education: A Five-Year Report* (Ann Arbor, Mich.: The Center for the Education of Women at the University of Michigan 2007), 2; American Council on Higher Education, *An Agenda for*

Excellence, 31; American Association of University Professors, "Statement of Principles on Family Responsibilities and Academic Work."

96. Amy Novotney, "A More Family-Friendly Ivory Tower?," *Monitor on Psychology* 41, no. 1 (2010), http://www.apa.org/monitor/2010/01/flexibility.aspx.

97. Ibid. The author cites University of Michigan Center for the Education of Women, *Family-Friendly Policies in Higher Education*. See pages 2 and 6 of the report.

98. Mason, Wolfinger, and Goulden, *Do Babies Matter?*, 114.

99. Ibid., 100–101. The authors stress that earnest effort to do fundraising for the more costly initiatives will be necessary.

100. Angela Senander, "Standing with Pregnant Students," *America*, May 24, 2004, https://www.americamagazine.org/issue/486/article/standing-pregnant-students.

101. Nicole M. Callahan, "Revolution on Campus: The History of Feminists for Life's College Outreach Program, an Interview with Serrin M. Foster," *The American Feminist* 11, no. 2–3 (2004), https://feministsforlife.org/-taf/2004/summer-fall/Summer-Fall04.pdf.

102. Senander, "Standing with Pregnant Students."

103. See "Pregnancy," Student Health Services, on the Georgetown University Student Health Service page, https://studenthealth.georgetown.edu/health-promotion/services/pregnancy, and "Pregnancy Resources," Pastoral Care, on Marquette University's Campus Ministry Resources page, http://www.marquette.edu/cm/pastoral_care/pregnancy.shtml.

104. Nicole M. Callahan, "Seeds of Change at Georgetown," *The American Feminist* 11, no. 2–3 (2004), https://feministsforlife.org/-taf/2004/summer-fall/Summer-Fall04.pdf.

105. See Georgetown University, "Pregnancy," https://studenthealth.georgetown.edu/health-promotion/services/pregnancy; Georgetown University Right to Life, https://gurighttolife.wordpress.com/, and Pregnant on Campus Initiative, "Georgetown University," http://pregnantoncampus.studentsforlife.org/campus/georgetown/.

106. Marquette University, "Pregnancy Resources," http://www.marquette.edu/cm/pastoral_care/pregnancy.shtml#.

107. Maria Tsikalas, "Mothering at Marquette," *Marquette Wire*, September 13, 2011, https://marquettewire.org/3793219/tribune/tribune-featured/pregnancy-cc1-td2-mr3-questions/, and Cohen, "The Baby Bias."

108. "Parenting and Pregnant Students," Parents and Families Resources, St. Louis University page for student resources on pregnancy and parenting, https://www.slu.edu/parents/pregnant-parenting.php.

109. Michael Kelly, "In 20 Years since Maryanne Stevens Took Over College of St. Mary, Her Vision Became a Reality," *College of Saint Mary Website*,

http://www.csm.edu/news/maryanne-stevens-anniversary. Pell data from
http://www.collegeresults.org/collegeprofile.aspx?institutionid=181604.

110. Students for Life of America, "Pregnant and Parenting Rights on
Campus," *Pregnant on Campus Initiative* http://pregnantoncampus.students
forlife.org/.

111. For detailed information see each institution's listing at "Top Schools
for Pregnant and Parenting Students 2015," *Students for Life of America*,
http://studentsforlife.org/topschools/.

112. See Graduate Life at Notre Dame, "Family," http://gradlife.nd.edu/life
-at-nd/family/.

113. Katy Hopkins, "Child-Friendly College Programs for Parents," *U.S. News
and World Report,* March 23, 2011, https://www.usnews.com/education/best
-colleges/articles/2011/03/23/child-friendly-college-programs-for-parents.

114. "Most Family-Friendly Schools," 2020-school Rankings, *The Princeton
Review,* https://www.princetonreview.com/business-school-rankings?rankings
=most-family-friendly.

115. In addition to its website, see Pregnant on Campus Initiative, "University of Dallas," http://pregnantoncampus.studentsforlife.org/campus/udallas/.

116. See Franciscan University of Steubenville, "Health Services," https://
wellness.franciscan.edu/health-services/; Franciscan University of Steubenville, "Chapel Ministries," https://chapel.franciscan.edu/, and Pregnant on
Campus Initiative, "Franciscan University of Steubenville," http://
pregnantoncampus.studentsforlife.org/campus/franciscan/.

117. See Pregnant on Campus Initiative, "Ave Maria University," http://
pregnantoncampus.studentsforlife.org/campus/ave-maria/, and Ave Maria
University, Ave for Life, "Pregnant on Campus," https://sfl.avemaria.edu/poc/.

118. Hopkins, "Child-Friendly College Programs for Parents."

119. See Devi Shastri, "Breaking the Silence," *Marquette Wire,* April 9, 2017,
https://marquettewire.org/3969088/tribune/tribune-news/journal-breaking-the
-silence/, and Suicide Prevention Resource Center, "Colleges and Universities,"
http://www.sprc.org/settings/colleges-universities.

120. Loyola Students for Life, "What Can I Do? A Pro-Life Response,"
YouTube video, November 16, 2014, https://www.youtube.com/watch?v=nru
_FL4tVq4&feature=youtu.be.

121. Joya Misra et al., "The Ivory Ceiling of Service Work," *Academe,*
January–February 2011, https://www.aaup.org/article/ivory-ceiling-service
-work#.WVv-kojyvct.

122. Annemarie Vaccaro, "Still Chilly in 2010: Campus Climates for
Women," *On Campus with Women* 39, no. 2 (2010), http://archive.aacu.org
/ocww/volume39_2/feature.cfm?section=1.

123. Ibid.

124. Ibid.

125. Annemarie Vaccaro, "What Lies beneath Seemingly Positive Campus Climate Results: Institutional Sexism, Racism, and Male Hostility toward Equity Initiatives and Liberal Bias," *Equity & Excellence in Education* 43, no. 2 (2010): 207. See also James F. Keenan, *University Ethics*, 135.

126. Vaccaro, "Still Chilly in 2010: Campus Climates for Women," 1.

127. Kimberlé Crenshaw, "Demarginalizing the Intersection of Race and Sex: A Black Feminist Critique of Antidiscrimination Doctrine, Feminist Theory and Antiracist Politics," *The University Of Chicago Legal Forum* 1989, no. 1 (1989): 140, 50. See also Crenshaw's more recent discussion of the concept in Kimberlé Crenshaw, "Why Intersectionality Can't Wait," *The Washington Post*, September 21, 2015, https://www.washingtonpost.com/news/in-theory/wp/2015/09/24/why-intersectionality-cant-wait/?tid=a_inl&utm_term=.b345e693c6eb.

128. Patricia Hill Collins and Sirma Bilge, *Intersectionality* (Cambridge, UK: Polity Press, 2016), 65. See also their definition of intersectionality on 155.

129. Christine Emba, "Intersectionality," *The Washington Post*, September 21, 2015, https://www.washingtonpost.com/news/in-theory/wp/2015/09/21/intersectionality-a-primer/?utm_term=.be0115b5f057.

130. Hill Collins and Bilge, *Intersectionality*, 2.

131. Vaccaro, "Still Chilly in 2010: Campus Climates for Women," 2.

132. See for example Gabriella Gutiérrez y Muhs et al., *Presumed Incompetent: The Intersections of Race and Class for Women in Academia* (Boulder, Colo: Utah State University Press, 2012).

133. Ibid., 479.

134. Ibid., 374–75.

135. Ibid., 421–28.

136. Ibid., 472.

137. See also Vaccaro's helpful and detailed discussion of this in Vaccaro, "Still Chilly in 2010."

138. See the discussion of solidarity in Chapter 1, upon which I am building here.

139. Susan L. Poulson and Lorretta P. Higgins, "Gender, Coeducation, and the Transformation of Catholic Identity in American Catholic Higher Education," *The Catholic Historical Review* 89, no. 3 (2003): 490. The following paragraph is indebted to Poulson and Higgins's article.

140. Ibid., 492.

141. Ibid., 500.

142. See ibid., 496–500, 502, 505, 507.

143. Jenny Rogers, "Not a Sister among Them, but These New Presidents Still Promote a Catholic Vision," *The Chronicle of Higher Education*, July 1,

2013, https://www.chronicle.com/article/Not-a-Sister-Among-Them-but
/140073.

144. Doing justice to the history of Catholic women's colleges and their
many contributions to the common good exceeds the scope of my analysis. For
some historical accounts, see Kathleen Sprows Cummings, "The 'New Woman'
at the 'University': Gender and American Catholic Identity in the Progressive
Era," in *The Religious History of American Women: Reimagining the Past*, ed.
Catherine A. Brekus (Chapel Hill: University of North Carolina Press, 2007);
Tracy Schier and Cynthia Eagle Russett, *Catholic Women's Colleges in America*
(Baltimore, Md.: Johns Hopkins University Press, 2002).

145. See Denise K. Magner, "Head of Maryland's College of Notre Dame
Seeks to 'Empower' Women and Fight Biases," *Chronicle of Higher Education* 35,
February 1, 1989; Burton Bollag, "True to Their Roots," *Chronicle of Higher
Education* (2005): A26–29; Lynn Hughes, "Catholic Women's Colleges Gradu-
ate Strong Student Leaders Prepared to Make a Significant Difference in
Society," *Momentum* 39, no. 1 (2008); Patricia McGuire, "Then and Now: A
Mission to Educate Women," *National Catholic Reporter* 46, no. 2 (2009);
Julienne Gage, "A Higher Calling for Higher Ed: Trinity University Found the
Future of Education—Hiding in Its Own Neighborhood," *Sojourners Magazine*
39, no. 9 (2010).

146. See McGuire, "Then and Now: A Mission to Educate Women"; Bollag,
"True to Their Roots"; Gage, "A Higher Calling for Higher Ed: Trinity University Found the Future of Education—Hiding in Its Own Neighborhood."

147. See Service Employees International Union, "Trinity Washington
University," https://www.seiu500.org/trinity.

148. "Editors' Interview with Mary-Antoinette Smith, Finding a Work-Faith
Balance," *U.S. Catholic*, January 21, 2016, https://www.uscatholic.org/articles
/201601/balancing-act-30527.

149. Susan A. Ross, "Women in Jesuit Higher Education: Ten Years Later,"
in *Jesuit and Feminist Education: Intersections in Teaching and Learning for the
Twenty-First Century*, ed. Jocelyn M. Boryczka and Elizabeth A. Petrino (New
York: Fordham University Press, 2012), 244–45.

150. Ibid., 247–48.

151. Ibid., 248.

152. Ibid., 243–45.

153. Ibid., 249. For research on the isolation women leaders often feel, see
Su and Gaughan, "Inclusion of Women Academics into American Universities,"
533.

154. Colleen Flaherty, "The More Things Change," *Inside Higher Ed*,
April 11, 2017, https://www.insidehighered.com/news/2017/04/11/aaup-faculty
-salaries-slightly-budgets-are-balanced-backs-adjuncts-and-out-state. See also

the report: American Association of University Professors, *Visualizing Change: The Annual Report on the Economic Status of the Profession, 2016–17*, https://www .aaup.org/report/visualizing-change-annual-report-economic-status-profession -2016-17.

155. Flaherty, "The More Things Change."

156. Figures taken from 2016–17 AAUP Faculty Compensation Survey, *Inside Higher Ed*, https://www.insidehighered.com/aaup-compensation-survey ?institution-name=&professor-category=1591&order=field_salary _equality&sort=desc.

157. Ibid. It should be noted that some institutions, including Catholic colleges and universities, do not provide data for this category.

158. Ibid.

159. American Association of University Professors, *Visualizing Change*, 3.

160. John XXIII, *Mater et Magistra*, no. 71.

161. Su and Gaughan, "Inclusion of Women Academics into American Universities," 539–40.

162. Vaccaro, "Still Chilly in 2010," 3.

163. Ross, "Women in Jesuit Higher Education," 252.

164. Su and Gaughan, "Inclusion of Women Academics into American Universities," 533.

165. American Association of University Professors, *Gender Equity Guidelines for Department Chairs* (2008), https://www.aaup.org/issues/women-higher -education/gender-equity-guidelines-department-chairs. On hiring processes, see also Moody, *Faculty Diversity*.

166. Vaccaro, "Still Chilly in 2010," 3.

167. Tara L. Tuttle, "The Intersection of Dominican Values and Women's and Gender Studies Pedagogy," *Journal of Catholic Higher Education* 35, no. 1 (2016).

168. Ross, "Women in Jesuit Higher Education," 28.

169. See John C. Hawley, ed. *Expanding the Circle: Creating an Inclusive Environment in Higher Education for LGBTQ Students and Studies* (Albany: State University of New York Press, 2014), 1–2.

170. Vaccaro, "Still Chilly in 2010," 3.

171. Quoted from "Heritage, History, and Tradition," Villanova University Mission & Ministry, Villanova's webpage for the mission, history, and values of the university, https://www1.villanova.edu/villanova/mission/heritage/values .html#caritas.

172. See Ada Maria Isasi-Diaz, "Solidarity: Love of Neighbor in the Eighties," in *Lift Every Voice: Constructing Christian Theologies from the Underside*, ed. Susan Brook Thistlethwaite and Mary Potter Engle (San Francisco: Harper, 1990); Jon Sobrino and Juan Hernández Pico, *Theology of Christian Solidarity*, trans. Philip

Berryman (Maryknoll, N.Y.: Orbis Books, 1985); Gerald J. Beyer, "The Meaning of Solidarity in Catholic Social Teaching," *Political Theology* 15, no. 1 (2014).

173. Robert Lynch, "Bishop Robert Lynch: 'It Is Religion, Including Our Own, Which Targets LGBT People," *Tampa Bay Times*, June 14, 2016, http://www.tampabay.com/news/religion/bishop-robert-lynch-it-is-religion-including-our-own-which-targets-lgbt/2281687.

174. Tom Roberts, "San Diego Bishop: Mass Shooting a Call to Catholics to Combat Anti-Gay Prejudice Today," June 14, 2016, *National Catholic Reporter*, https://www.ncronline.org/blogs/ncr-today/san-diego-bishop-mass-shooting-call-catholics-combat-anti-gay-prejudice.

175. James Martin, *Building a Bridge: How the Catholic Church and the LGBT Community Can Enter into a Relationship of Respect, Compassion, and Sensitivity* (San Francisco: Harper One, 2017), 2. Martin mentions a few other bishops that did speak out: Bishop Cupich of Chicago, Bishop Zubik of Pittsburgh, and Bishop Stowe of Lexington, Kentucky.

176. Laurel Wamsley, "Illinois Bishop Decrees No Communion, Funeral Rites For Same-Sex Spouses," *The Two Way, a News Blog of the National Public Radio*, June 23, 2017, http://www.npr.org/sections/thetwo-way/2017/06/23/534127330/illinois-bishop-decrees-no-communion-funeral-rites-for-same-sex-spouses.

177. See for example the essays by Harrison, Jordan, Jacobitz, Jung, Cheng, and Roden in J. Patrick Hornbeck and Michael A. Norko, *More Than a Monologue: Sexual Diversity and the Catholic Church. Volume II, Inquiry, Thought, and Expression*, Catholic Practice in North America (New York: Fordham University Press, 2014).

178. See their introduction to ibid., 15–17.

179. *Catechism of the Catholic Church*, 2nd. Ed., no. 2358, http://www.vatican.va/archive/ccc_css/archive/catechism/p3s2c2a6.htm.

180. Martin explores the practical implications of this Church teaching. See Martin, *Building a Bridge*. On the need for Catholics to stand with transgendered persons, see also Bryan Massingale, "We Cannot Abandon Transgender Catholics," *U.S. Catholic*, August, 2016, http://www.uscatholic.org/articles/201608/we-cannot-abandon-transgender-catholics-30726.

181. Elisabeth T. Vasko, *Beyond Apathy: A Theology for Bystanders* (Minneapolis, Minn.: Augsburg Fortress Publishers, 2015), 180–87, see also 29–68.

182. Bryan Anselm, "As Church Shifts, a Cardinal Welcomes Gays; They Embrace a 'Miracle,'" *The New York Times*, June 13, 2017, https://www.nytimes.com/2017/06/13/nyregion/catholic-church-gays-mass-newark-cathedral.html?smprod=nytcore-iphone&smid=nytcore-iphone-share&_r=0. This article also describes some of the other recent positive initiatives taken in some US archdioceses.

183. James Martin, "What Does a Church Open to L.G.B.T. Catholics Look Like?," *America*, August 30, 2019, https://www.americamagazine.org/faith /2019/08/30/what-does-church-open-lgbt-catholics-look. For other positive examples, see John Gehring, "Can the Catholic Church 'Evolve' on L.G.B.T. Rights?," *New York Times*, July 5, 2018., https://www.nytimes.com/2018/07/05 /opinion/pope-francis-catholic-church-lgbt.html.

184. See especially Jung, Cheng, and Roden in Hornbeck and Norko, *More Than a Monologue,* and Martin, *Building a Bridge.*

185. For an alternative perspective by a Catholic scholar, one that deems homosexuals "deviants" and deplores the "gay assault" on her Catholic university, see Anne Hendershott, "Redefining Deviance: The Gay Assault on Franciscan University," *Crisis Magazine,* November 13, 2012, http://www .crisismagazine.com/2012/redefining-deviance-the-gay-assault-on-franciscan -university. It should be obvious that I strongly reject this view.

186. See Scott Jaschik, "Why Republicans Don't Trust Higher Ed," *Inside Higher Ed*, August 17, 2017, https://www.insidehighered.com/news/2017/08/17 /new-data-explain-republican-loss-confidence-higher-education. The article discusses a recent Gallup poll, which indicated many Americans have little confidence in higher education because they perceive it to be "too liberal."

187. Hawley, *Expanding the Circle*, 4. Hawley describes the 2011 study done by Genny Beemyn and Sue Rankin. For similar study results on college campuses, see also Annemarie Vaccaro, Gerri August, and Megan S. Kennedy, *Safe Spaces: Making Schools and Communities Welcoming to LGBT Youth* (Santa Barbara, Calif.: Praeger, 2012), 102.

188. Hornbeck and Norko, *More Than a Monologue*, 193. See also Vaccaro, August, and Kennedy, *Safe Spaces*, 23, 101. In *Safe Spaces*, the authors mention that 50 percent of LGBTQ youths have experienced cyberbullying. Green states that the suicide rate for LGBT students may be 3–4 times greater in the United States. He also cites the extremely high rates of bullying. Erik Green, "LGBT Bullying in Schools," in *Expanding the Circle: Creating an Inclusive Environment in Higher Education for LGBTQ Students and Studies*, ed. John C. Hawley (Albany: State University of New York Press, 2014), 238–39.

189. Hawley, *Expanding the Circle*, 4.

190. See ibid., 8–9. Pauline Park, "Transgendering the Academy: Transforming the Relation between Theory and Praxis," in John C. Hawley ed., *Expanding the Circle*.

191. Annemarie Vaccaro, "Campus Microclimates for LGBT Faculty, Staff, and Students: An Exploration of the Intersections of Social Identity and Campus Roles," *Journal of Student Affairs Research and Practice* 49, no. 4 (2012): 430, see also 31–44.

192. See Hawley, *Expanding the Circle*, 4, 13.

193. See Campus Pride Index, https://www.campusprideindex.org/faqs/index. Other rankings of this type exist, such as the Princeton Review's twenty most LGBTQ-friendly and -unfriendly schools, but Campus Pride's is the most comprehensive. For a critique of The Princeton Review's approach, see Chelsea Fullerton, "Deeply Flawed Ranking: The Princeton Review 'LGBTQ-Friendly & Unfriendly List' Does a Disservice to Prospective LGBTQ+ Students," *Campus Pride (blog)*, August 8, 2017, https://www.campuspride.org/deeply-flawed-ranking-the-princeton-review-lgbtq-friendly-unfriendly-list-does-a-disservice-to-prospective-lgbtq-students/. For other rankings and resources, see "Choosing an LGBTQ-Friendly College," *Center for Online Education*, http://www.onlinecolleges.net/for-students/lgbtq-college-guide, and "Best Colleges for LGBTQ Students," *BestColleges*, http://www.bestcolleges.com/features/best-colleges-for-lgbt-students/.

194. On Loyola Marymount, see "Loyola Marymount," *Campus Pride Index*, https://www.campusprideindex.org/campuses/details/5499?campus=loyola-marymount-university, and the university LGBTSS website at http://student affairs.lmu.edu/community/ethnicandinterculturalservices/lgbtstudentservices/aboutlgbtss/. On Georgetown see, "Georgetown University," *Campus Pride Index*, https://www.campusprideindex.org/campuses/details/254?campus=georgetown-university.

195. "Shame List: The Absolute Worst Campuses for LGBTQ Youth," *Campus Pride Index*, https://www.campuspride.org/shamelist/.

196. See Zach Ford, "Ohio Catholic University Threatens LGBT Alumni for Exposing Anti-Gay Curriculum," *ThinkProgress*, August 31, 2012, https://thinkprogress.org/ohio-catholic-university-threatens-lgbt-alumni-for-exposing-anti-gay-curriculum-3ab2b7e8bb1b/.

197. See New Ways Ministry, "We Created a Partial List of over 130 Known 'LGBTQ Friendly' Catholic Colleges and Universities," https://www.newways ministry.org/resources/lgbt-friendly-colleges/.

198. Frank D. Golom, "Creating Systemic Change around Lesbian, Gay, Bisexual and Transgender (LGBT) Issues," in ed. John C. Hawley, *Expanding the Circle*.

199. Scotty McLennan, "New Perspectives on Religion and Spirituality for LGBTQ Students," in ed. John C. Hawley, *Expanding the Circle*, 300. The quotation here repeats McLennan's citation of the Vatican document http://www.vatican.va/roman_curia/congregations/cfaith/documents/rc_con_cfaith_doc_19861001_homosexual-persons_en.html, no. 17.

200. Ibid.

201. Kyle Spencer, "A Rainbow Over Catholic Colleges: How Georgetown Became a Gay Friendly Campus," June 30, 2013, *The New York Times*, http://

www.nytimes.com/2013/08/04/education/edlife/how-georgetown-became-a
-gay-friendly-campus.html.

202. "Remarks at Open Meeting on LGBTQ Student Resources," *Speeches &
Addresses 2007, Georgetown University*, https://president.georgetown.edu
/speeches/remarks-at-open-meeting-on-lgbtq-student-resources.html.

203. Teresa Delgado, "A Delicate Dance: Utilizing and Challenging the
Sexual Doctrine of the Catholic Church in Support of LGBTIQ Persons," in
More Than a Monologue, 108–9.

204. Michael O'Loughlin, "Being Gay at a Catholic University," *Religion and
Politics*, June 18, 2013, http://religionandpolitics.org/2013/06/18/being-gay-at-a
-catholic-university/. The author describes St. Anselm College and Santa Clara
University as also being welcoming to LGBTQ students.

205. Villanova University Student Life, "VU Pride," http://www1.villanova
.edu/villanova/studentlife/be_empowered/vupride.html.

206. See https://www.campuspride.org/tpc/nondiscrimination.

207. See for example Hawley, *Expanding the Circle*; Vaccaro, August, and
Kennedy, *Safe Spaces*; Christine Firer Hinze and J. Patrick Hornbeck, *More
Than a Monologue: Sexual Diversity and the Catholic Church. Volume I, Voices of
Our Times*.

208. See for example "Bishops Object As Catholic Universities Offer
Benefits To Same-Sex Spouses," *Huffington Post*, November 2, 2014, http://www
.huffingtonpost.com/2014/11/02/catholic-university-same-sex-benefits_n
_6082778.html.

209. Mason, Wolfinger, and Goulden, *Do Babies Matter?*, 99.

210. See Gerald V. Bradley, John Finnis, and Daniel Philpott, "The Implications of Extending Marriage Benefits to Same-Sex Couples," *Public Discourse:
The Journal of the Witherspoon Institute*, February 25, 2015, http://www
.thepublicdiscourse.com/2015/02/14522/; Daniel Philpott, "Polite Persecution,"
First Things, April 2017, https://www.firstthings.com/article/2017/04/polite
-persecution; United States Conference of Catholic Bishops, "FAQs: Religious
Liberty and Marriage," http://www.usccb.org/issues-and-action/marriage-and
-family/marriage/promotion-and-defense-of-marriage/upload/Handout
-Religious-liberty-FAQs-2.pdf; United States Conference of Catholic Bishops,
"Between Man and Woman: Questions and Answers About Marriage and
Same-Sex Unions," http://www.usccb.org/issues-and-action/marriage-and
-family/marriage/promotion-and-defense-of-marriage/questions-and-answers
-about-marriage-and-same-sex-unions.cfm.

211. "Bishops Object as Catholic Universities Offer Benefits to Same-Sex
Spouses," *The Huffington Post*, November 2, 2014, http://www.huffingtonpost
.com/2014/11/02/catholic-university-same-sex-benefits_n_6082778.html, and
Kayla Mullen, "Same Sex Couples Receive Benefits," *The Observer*, Octo-

ber 16, 2014, http://ndsmcobserver.com/2014/10/same-sex-couples-receive
-benefits/.

212. For Catholic ethicists' argument in favor of marriage equality, see
Patricia Jung, "God Sets the Lonely in Families," in *More Than a Monologue,
Volume II;* Lisa Sowle Cahill, "Same-Sex Marriage and Catholicism: Dialogue,
Learning, and Change," in ibid.; Julie Hanlon Rubio, *Hope for Common Ground:
Mediating the Personal and the Political in a Divided Church* (Washington, D.C.:
Georgetown University Press, 2016), 109–13.

213. For a more nuanced discussion than I can offer here, see Daniel J. Daly,
"The Ethics of Exit: What Happens When a Catholic Teacher Violates Church
Teaching?," *America*, June 9, 2014, https://www.americamagazine.org/issue
/ethics-exit, and this response: Lisa Fullam, "The Role of Conscience," *America*,
July 21, 2014, I also address this issue more fully within the framework of the
assault on workers' rights in Gerald J. Beyer, "Strange Bedfellows: Religious
Liberty and Neoliberalism," *National Catholic Reporter*, February 15, 2012,
https://www.ncronline.org/news/politics/strange-bedfellows-religious-liberty
-and-neoliberalism.

214. See Vaccaro, August, and Kennedy, *Safe Spaces*, 103–9.

215. Vasko, *Beyond Apathy*, 52–54.

216. See O'Loughlin, "Being Gay at a Catholic University."

217. John Paul II, *Ex Corde Ecclesiae*, part I, art. 3.29.

218. Park, "Transgendering the Academy," 94.

219. Beth Bradley and Brian J. Patchcoski, "Navigating the Intersection of
Spiritual and Sexual Identity within Lesbian, Gay, Bisexual, Transgender, and
Queer (LGBTQ) College Students," in ed. John C. Hawley, *Expanding the Circle*,
273–76. See also McLennan, "New Perspectives on Religion and Spirituality
for LGBTQ Students."

220. Golom, "Creating Systemic Change around Lesbian, Gay, Bisexual and
Transgender (LGBT) Issues," 115. Golom provides a very helpful, detailed
"roadmap" for bringing about positive change on LGBTQ issues on campus.

221. Margaret A. Farley, *Just Love: A Framework for Christian Sexual Ethics*
(New York: Continuum International Pub. Group, 2006), 217–18. The "Sexual
Assault Myths" website of Minnesota State University states that "studies show
that the major motive for rape is power, not sex. Sex is used as a weapon to
inflict pain, violence and humiliation." See https://www.mnsu.edu/varp
/assault/myths.html.

222. In addition to what follows, see the discussion of literature in Keenan,
University Ethics, 125–32; Jeff Parrott, "Getting Through? How Catholic
Colleges are Responding to Sexual Assault," *U.S. Catholic*, January, 2012,
http://www.uscatholic.org/life/2011/11/getting-through-how-catholic-colleges
-are-responding-sexual-assault; Judy Roberts, "The Campus Sexual Assault

Crisis: Why Did It Happen?," *National Catholic Register*, March 2, 2016, http://www.ncregister.com/daily-news/the-campus-sexual-assault-crisis-why -did-it-happen; and the posts in the digital forum devoted to sexual assault and higher education: Megan K. McCabe, Christine McCarthy, and Bridget O'Brien, *Sexual Assault and Higher Education: An Octave of Theological Reflection. An Introduction*, September 12, 2015, https://dailytheology.org/2015/09/12 /sahe-octave-introduction/.

223. *The Second Report of the White House Task Force to Protect Students from Sexual Assault*, a report published on January 5, 2017, http://www .changingourcampus.org/resources/not-alone/Second-Report-VAW-Event-TF-Report .PDF, 9; see also *Report on the AAU Campus Climate Survey on Sexual Assault and Sexual Misconduct*, September 21, 2015, available at https://www.aau.edu/key-issues /aau-climate-survey-sexual-assault-and-sexual-misconduct-2015?id=16525. Jason King states that gays and lesbians "typically" eschew the hookup culture on campuses for fear of being assaulted. Jason E. King, *Faith with Benefits: Hookup Culture on Catholic Campuses* (New York: Oxford University Press, 2016), 11.

224. "The Hunting Ground," *CNNFilms*, https://www.cnn.com/shows/the -hunting-ground.

225. Jonah Newman and Libby Sander, "Promise Unfulfilled?," *The Chronicle*, April 30, 2014, http://www.chronicle.com/article/Promise -Unfulfilled-/146299.

226. Keenan, *University Ethics*, 130.

227. King, *Faith with Benefits*. Elsewhere King writes that very little work has been done on sexual assault on Catholic campuses specifically. See Jason E. King, "A Review Essay on Catholic Higher Education after *Ex Corde Ecclesiae*," *Journal of Moral Theology* 4, no. 2 (2015): 184.

228. King, *Faith with Benefits*, 39.

229. Ibid., 11.

230. Nicole Sotelo, "Sexual Assault at Catholic Colleges and Universities," *National Catholic Reporter*, March 20, 2011, https://www.ncronline.org/blogs /sexual-assault-catholic-colleges-and-universities.

231. Data taken from https://ope.ed.gov/campussafety/#/. See also Nick Anderson, "These Colleges Have the Most Reports of Rape," *The Washington Post*, June 6, 2016, https://www.washingtonpost.com/news/grade-point/wp /2016/06/07/these-colleges-have-the-most-reports-of-rape/?utm_term= .253862356a75#rapetable.

232. Niche, "2020 Safest College Campuses in America," https://www .niche.com/colleges/rankings/safest-colleges/ and The Daily Beast; "50 Most Dangerous Colleges," The Daily Beast's rankings of the 50 most dangerous colleges in the United States, http://www.thedailybeast.com/50-most -dangerous-colleges.

233. Robert Morse, "Frequently Asked Questions About Federal Campus Crime Statistics," *Morse Code (blog), U.S. News & World Report,* May 8, 2014, https://www.usnews.com/education/blogs/college-rankings-blog/2014/05/08 /frequently-asked-questions-about-federal-campus-crime-statistics. See also Joy Galarneau and Shannon O'Neill, "Educating for Justice: Creating a Mission-Driven Model of Bystander Intervention to Address Sexual Violence at U.S. Catholic Colleges and Universities," *Journal of Catholic Higher Education* 34, no. 2 (2015): 279.

234. *The Second Report of the White House Task Force.*

235. Galarneau and O'Neill, "Educating for Justice," 279.

236. The United States Department of Justice Archives, "Best Practices: Campus Climate Surveys," https://www.justice.gov/archives/ovw/blog/best -practices-campus-climate-surveys.

237. University of Saint Joseph Connecticut, *Sexual Misconduct 2016 Climate Survey Report,* https://my.usj.edu/ics/icsfs/2016_Climate_Survey_Report.pdf ?target=ce63893a-9354-473f-b79b-94aa09ed2d8f.

238. Regis College, "Regis Title IX Campus Climate Survey," http://www .regiscollege.edu/student-life/title9-climate-survey.cfm.

239. See Saint Mary's College, Notre Dame, Office of Institutional Research, *HEDS Sexual Assault Climate Survey Summary Report* (2016), https:// www.saintmarys.edu/files/2015-16%20HEDS%20Sexual%20Assault%20 Survey%20Summary%20Report.pdf.

240. The Catholic University of America, *Title IX Annual Report: Academic Year 2015–2016* (Washington, D.C.: The Catholic University of America, 2016), 1, https://title9.catholic.edu/_media/docs/title-ix-report-2015-16-final.pdf.

241. Dennis Brown, "Results of Sexual Misconduct Climate Survey Released," *Notre Dame News,* April 17, 2016, http://news.nd.edu/news/climate -survey/.

242. Ian Scoville, "Sexual Assault Survey Results Published," *The Hoya,* June 16, 2016, http://www.thehoya.com/sexual-assault-survey-results-published/; see *Report on the Georgetown University Sexual Assault and Misconduct Climate Survey* (Washington, D.C.: Georgetown University, June 2016), https://georgetown.app .box.com/s/wwe8v637v8or2avtzp0oap2265u4jiye.

243. Anderson, "These Colleges," *Washington Post.*

244. *Catechism of the Catholic Church,* 2nd. Ed., no. 2356, http://www.vatican .va/archive/ccc_css/archive/catechism/p3s2c2a6.htm.

245. See John N. Sheveland, "Redeeming Trauma: An Agenda for Theology Fifteen Years On," in *American Catholicism in the 21st Century: Crossroads, Crisis, or Renewal?,* ed. Benjamin Peters and Nicholas Rademacher (Maryknoll, N.Y.: Orbis, 2018).

246. See Galarneau and O'Neill, "Educating for Justice," 277–78.

247. Jeff Parrott, "Getting Through?" The case at Notre Dame involved a young woman committing suicide after she reported that a football player sexually assaulted her. See Melinda Hennenberger, "Reported Sexual Assault at Notre Dame Campus Leaves More Questions than Answers," *National Catholic Reporter*, March 26, 2012, https://www.ncronline.org/news /accountability/reported-sexual-assault-notre-dame-campus-leaves-more -questions-answers.

248. *The Chronicle of Higher Education*, "Title IX: Tracking Sexual Assault Investigations," https://projects.chronicle.com/titleix/.

249. Donna Freitas, *Sex and the Soul: Juggling Sexuality, Spirituality, Romance, and Religion on America's College Campuses*, Oxford University Press pbk. ed. (Oxford; New York: Oxford University Press, 2015), 256–57. Cited in Elisabeth T. Vasko, "Civic Learning and Teaching as a Resource for Sexual Justice: An Undergraduate Religious Studies Course Module," *Teaching Theology & Religion* 20, no. 2 (2017): 163.

250. Donna Freitas, "A Response to Elisabeth T. Vasko: The Risk and Reward of Teaching About Sexual Assault for the Theologian on a Catholic Campus," *Teaching Theology & Religion* 20, no. 2 (2017): 172–73. See also Donna Freitas, "Review of *University Ethics: How Colleges Can Build and Benefit from a Culture of Ethics*, by James F. Keenan," *Horizons* 44, no. 1 (2017): 177.

251. Vasko, "Civic Learning and Teaching as a Resource for Sexual Justice: An Undergraduate Religious Studies Course Module," 163. See the criticism of Franciscan University of Steubenville and the university's new initiative on confronting sexual assault in Jenn Morson, "Alumnae Question Franciscan University of Steubenville's Commitment to Title IX," *National Catholic Reporter*, April 16, 2018, https://www.ncronline.org/news/accountability /alumnae-question-franciscan-university-steubenvilles-commitment-title-ix; and Jenn Morson, "Franciscan University of Steubenville, Ohio, Takes Steps to Address Sexual Assault, Title IX Issues," *National Catholic Reporter*, September 4, 2018, https://www.ncronline.org/news/accountability/franciscan -university-steubenville-ohio-takes-steps-address-sexual-assault-title.

252. The letter can be found at United States Department of Education, "Office for Civil Rights," https://www2.ed.gov/about/offices/list/ocr/letters /colleague-201104.pdf. For the reference to the letter I am indebted to Parrott, "Getting Through?"

253. Ibid.

254. Brown, "Results of Sexual Misconduct Climate Survey Released." See also "GreenDot," *University of Notre Dame*, https://greendot.nd.edu.

255. Laura Fletcher and McKenna Oxenden, "Consenting to Change," *U.S. Catholic* 80, no. 9 (2015): 21. See also Parrott, "Getting Through?"

256. Parrott, "Getting Through?"

257. Galarneau and O'Neill, "Educating for Justice," 262. See also Fletcher and Oxenden, "Consenting to Change."

258. Galarneau and O'Neill, "Educating for Justice."

259. Ibid., 272.

260. Ibid., 277.

261. John Paul II, *Sollicitudo Rei Socialis*, no. 38.

262. Parrott, "Getting Through?"

263. Vasko, "Civic Learning and Teaching as a Resource for Sexual Justice," 168.

264. Freitas, "A Response to Elisabeth T. Vasko," 172–73; Freitas, "Review of *University Ethics: How Colleges Can Build and Benefit from a Culture of Ethics*, by James F. Keenan," 177–80.

265. See the updated and expanded version by Ernest L. Boyer et al., *Scholarship Reconsidered: Priorities of the Professoriate*, expanded edition (San Francisco, Calif: Jossey Bass, 2016).

266. Jake New, "Creating the Right Climate Survey," *Inside Higher Ed*, July 26, 2016, https://www.insidehighered.com/news/2016/07/29/campus-climate-surveys-abound-does-disagreement-over-what-works-best; Michael Stratford, "Declining the AAU Survey," *Inside Higher Ed*, January 13, 2015, https://www.insidehighered.com/news/2015/01/13/more-dozen-research-universities-opt-out-higher-education-groups-sexual-assault.

267. Jerzy Popiełuszko, *Myśli wyszukane* (Kraków: Znak, 2002), 72. See also Jerzy Popiełuszko, *The Way of My Cross: Masses at Warsaw* (Chicago: Regnery Books, 1986), 227.

268. M. Shawn Copeland, "The Intersection of Race, Class, and Gender in Jesuit and Feminist Education: Finding Transcendent Meaning in the Concrete," in *Jesuit and Feminist Education: Intersections in Teaching and Learning for the Twenty-First Century*, ed. Jocelyn M. Boryczka and Elizabeth A. Petrino (Fordham University Press, 2012), 128.

Epilogue

1. This concise definition of neoliberal higher education is from William Deresiewicz, "The Neoliberal Arts: How College Sold Its Soul to the Market," *Harpers*, September 2015, https://harpers.org/archive/2015/09/the-neoliberal-arts/.

2. Doug Lederman, "The Faculty Shrinks, but Tilts to Full-Time," *Inside Higher Ed*, November 27, 2019, https://www.insidehighered.com/news/2019/11/27/federal-data-show-proportion-instructors-who-work-full-time-rising.

3. Ashley A. Smith, "Poll: Voters Oppose Free College, Loan Forgiveness," *Inside Higher Ed*, May 1, 2019, https://www.insidehighered.com/quicktakes/2019/05/01/poll-voters-oppose-free-college-loan-forgiveness.

4. Deresiewicz, "The Neoliberal Arts: How College Sold Its Soul to the Market."

5. I borrow this term from Joseph M. O'Keefe, "Catholic Schools and Vouchers: How the Empirical Reality Should Ground the Debate," in *School Choice: The Moral Debate*, ed. Alan Wolfe (Princeton, N.J.: Princeton University Press, 2003).

6. John Paul II, *Sollicitudo Rei Socialis*, no. 38.

7. Alexander Tin, "'Solidarity': 2020 Candidates Vow to Boycott December Debate to Support Union Protesters," *CBS News*, December 13, 2019, https://www.cbsnews.com/news/democratic-debate-biden-warren-sanders-yang-vow-to-boycott-december-debate-to-support-union-protesters/.

8. See Anna Brown, "Most Americans Say Higher Ed Is Heading in Wrong Direction, but Partisans Disagree on Why," *Fact Tank: News in the Numbers*, July 26, 2018, https://www.pewresearch.org/fact-tank/2018/07/26/most-americans-say-higher-ed-is-heading-in-wrong-direction-but-partisans-disagree-on-why/.

9. Tasneem Borhany et al., "Musculoskeletal Problems in Frequent Computer and Internet Users," *Journal of Family Medicine and Primary Care* 7, no. 2 (2018), https://www.ncbi.nlm.nih.gov/pmc/articles/PMC6060916.

10. See Berg and Seeber, *The Slow Professor*, 2–3, and Lawrence D. Berg, Edward H. Huijbens, and Henrik Gutzon Larsen, "Producing Anxiety in the Neoliberal University."

11. Colleen Flaherty, "Aftermath of a Professor's Suicide," *Inside Higher Ed*, April 21, 2017, https://www.insidehighered.com/news/2017/04/21/recent-suicide-professor-sparks-renewed-discussions-about-access-mental-health.

12. Derek Thompson, "Workism Is Making Americans Miserable," *The Atlantic*, February 24, 2019, https://www.theatlantic.com/ideas/archive/2019/02/religion-workism-making-americans-miserable/583441/.

13. John Paul II, *Laborem Exercens*, no. 6.

14. Jonathan Malesic, "A Burnt-out Case: Aquinas & the Way We Work Now," *Commonweal*, December 14, 2017, https://www.commonwealmagazine.org/burnt-out-case. See his website for numerous insightful articles about work and burnout: https://jonmalesic.com/writing/.

15. James F. Keenan, *University Ethics*, 62–66.

16. See Jonathan Haidt, *The Righteous Mind: Why Good People Are Divided by Politics and Religion*, 1st ed. (New York: Pantheon Books, 2012), 79–83.

17. See for example Keri Day, *Religious Resistance to Neoliberalism: Womanist and Black Feminist Perspectives* (New York: Palgrave Macmillan US, 2016).

18. On accountability structures, see for example Haidt, *The Righteous Mind*, 86.

19. Bradford E. Hinze, *Prophetic Obedience: Ecclesiology for a Dialogical Church* (Maryknoll, N.Y.: Orbis, 2016), 176, see also 68. 168.

20. I discuss shared governance, the right to participation, and the common good in CST in Gerald J. Beyer, "Curing the 'Disease' in Corporatized Higher Education: Prescriptions from Catholic Social Thought," in *Working Alternatives*, ed. John Seitz and Christine Firer Hinze (New York: Fordham University Press, 2020), 148–88.

Index

Note: Information in tables is indicated by *t*.

GERALD J. BEYER is Associate Professor of Christian Ethics at Villanova University. He is the author of *Recovering Solidarity: Lessons from Poland's Unfinished Revolution*.

CATHOLIC PRACTICE IN NORTH AMERICA

Margaret M. McGuinness and Jeffrey M. Burns (eds.), *Preaching with Their Lives: Dominicans on Mission in the United States after 1850*

Gerald J. Beyer, *Just Universities: Catholic Social Teaching Confronts Corporatized Higher Education*

CPSIA information can be obtained
at www.ICGtesting.com
Printed in the USA
JSHW051557231221
21505JS00002B/134